Carter vs Ford

Carter vs Ford

☆ ☆ ☆ ☆ ☆ ☆ ☆ ☆ ☆ ☆ ☆ ☆ ☆ ☆ ☆ ☆ ☆ ☆

The Counterfeit Debates of 1976

Lloyd Bitzer and Theodore Rueter

The University of Wisconsin Press

Published 1980

The University of Wisconsin Press
114 North Murray Street
Madison, Wisconsin 53715

The University of Wisconsin Press, Ltd.
1 Gower Street
London WC1E 6HA, England

First printing

Printed in the United States of America

For LC CIP information see the colophon

ISBN 0-299-08280-6 cloth; 0-299-08284-9 paper

Dr. C.E. Kelley

Contents

PART 2

Texts of the Debates

Preface

Part 1 of this book on the 1976 debates between Gerald R. Ford and Jimmy Carter is a commentary which answers two basic questions—what was wrong with the Ford-Carter debates, and how can future debates be improved? Part 2 provides accurate and readable transcripts of the debates.

We believe that a study of the debates themselves can reveal much to readers who want to understand their nature and quality, how well the candidates performed, and how debate can be improved. With this in mind, our commentary analyzes the 1976 debates in terms of what they purported to be, identifies the properties and dynamics of the debates as well as the skills of the speakers, assesses the debates as instances of discourse befitting presidential candidates, and suggests changes that could markedly improve future debates. This kind of commentary requires close examination of several components, including the questions posed by the three debate panels, the skills of the candidates, the conditions imposed by the format or design, and the speeches of the candidates—evidence, arguments, strategies, rebuttals, style, and image. We have not tried to determine the influence of the debates on attitudes, beliefs, and behavior of the electorate, a subject given detailed treatment in a number of already published studies.

Recognizing that most readers are generalists, we have minimized the use of technical language. For the same reason, we make few references to concepts and research problems of interest to relatively small numbers of scholars. Our intended public is the general audience of readers interested in American politics; those who participate in various ways in local, state, and national politics and debates—debate sponsors, candidates and their advisers, and journalists; and students of politics and communication, who will find in this book techniques of analysis, conclusions, and proposals useful in the study of political communication.

Our analyses and findings in connection with the debate speeches, panel questions, tactics of argument, aggressiveness, initiative, style, and other matters involved critical examination of the debate texts and videotapes, sensitivity to the context of speeches and to the motives of speakers, and judgments of what was possible and desirable for a speaker to say in a given case. For the most part, our classifications and criteria are commonsensical and natural to the objects of study, although others might usefully be employed. Any reader may assess the soundness of our judgments, because our findings are supported by evidence traceable to the debate texts. Some subjects yield to rather precise description—the number and types of argument offered by each candidate, for example. On the other hand, our critical task is sometimes necessarily closer to art than to science—for instance, assessment of the intrinsic merit of issues and the stylistic flaws and excellence in candidates' speeches. Our recommendations for the design of future debates are grounded in our analysis of what actually happened in the 1976 debates as well as in a conception of what presidential debates should be.

The second part of this volume contains the transcripts of the three Ford-Carter debates and the single Dole-Mondale debate. Because accuracy was our most important consideration, the debate texts were developed with very careful attention to audio and videotape recordings of the debates. We frequently sought the assistance of others to help us decipher and verify almost inaudible words and phrases. This set of texts will be found to vary slightly from others with respect to textual matters that legitimately admit of different interpretation: editors rarely use identical punctuation and paragraphing, and when making transition from sound to print they unavoidably hear some words and phrases differently. The texts will also be found to differ occasionally from others with respect to matters that can be interpreted in only one way—in other words, matters of accuracy. We are confident that our texts record the debates accurately. They do not record everything intended or communicated, of course, because candidates and panelists often "spoke" with tone, gesture, inflection, facial expression—modes of communication which no written account of the debates can capture.

In providing the punctuation and paragraphing that are needed for a readable text, we have adhered to our best understanding of the discourse. Insignificant false-word starts, verbal pauses, and word repetitions are omitted, although the text preserves some false-word starts or word repetitions when a "mistake" is thought to signal something of importance to the debate audience. Notes are supplied for each debate text in order to identify persons, events, and references likely to become obscure with the passage of time.

The debate questions and speeches are occasionally quoted in part or in whole in our commentary, and more often paraphrased or cited. The reader may easily refer to questions and speeches in the debate texts by making use of the symbols: for instance, I, II, and III refer to the first, second, and third debates; A, B, and C refer to the questions in sequence in a given debate. Thus "I:A" denotes the opening question by Reynolds in the first debate; "I:B" refers to the Reynolds follow-up question. The speeches of the candidates are similarly numbered in the texts: for example, "I:1" is Carter's first speech in the first debate; "I:2" identifies his second speech; "I:3" refers to Ford's rejoinder speech; "II:1" refers to the first speech of the second debate. The symbols appear in the outside margins of the debate texts, adjacent to the questions and speeches to which they refer.

At this writing, five books concerned with the Ford-Carter

debates are in print. Collections of essays, discussions, and documents representing the work of many authors, these books treat such matters as background, history, legal problems, and effects on voters but surprisingly say very little about the debates themselves. Several of the essays contain complaints about the debates and calls for change, but neither complaints nor recommendations are grounded in a detailed examination of the internal dynamics of the debates, the candidates' speeches, format deficiencies, and related matters which can be uncovered only by study of the debates. We believe our book is a needed corrective as well as supplement to these earlier volumes because it focuses squarely on the debates themselves, providing information, analyses, and perspectives not otherwise available to the reader. Three of the earlier books contain transcripts of the debates, but in each the transcripts are significantly flawed.

The Twentieth Century Fund commissioned a task force to consider the value of presidential campaign debates and how the candidates could be encouraged to participate in them. The result is a work published by Lexington Books in 1979 entitled *With the Nation Watching: Report of the Twentieth Century Fund Task Force on Televised Presidential Debates*. The ten-page task force report, modest in purpose and scope, is accompanied by an eighty-five-page background paper by Lee M. Mitchell. Neither the report nor the background paper provides an analysis of the Ford-Carter debates, although Mitchell and task force members identify some of the many defects. The task force recommends that debates be held and that "presidential debates should become a regular and customary feature of the presidential election campaign." Other recommendations include nonpartisan sponsorship, four debates between the presidential candidates and one between the vice-presidential candidates, a minimized role in agenda-setting by the panelists or questioners, and more initiative and direct confrontation by the candidates.

The Past and Future of Presidential Debates, edited by Austin Ranney and published in 1979 by the American Enterprise Institute for Public Policy Research, Washington, D.C., is a collection of eight essays and symposium discussions by contributors representing practical politics, journalism, communication, and political science. Valuable information on the setting and preparations for the debates is found in two essays, reports of scientific research in two others, and history and commentary in the remainder. The book contains no extended discussion of debate dynamics, qualities, candidates' skills, or format defects, nor does it contain transcripts of the debates.

The Government Printing Office in 1979 issued *The Presidential Campaign, 1976: The Debates*. Prepared at the direction of a congressional committee, the book consists of documents and previously published articles—press releases and press conferences, rulings by the Federal Communications Commission, transcripts of meetings of the Federal Election Commission, several newspaper and magazine articles, and miscellaneous letters and reports. Nearly half of the book consists of transcripts of the debates, including the Dole-Mondale debate. The transcripts are flawed by errors so numerous and serious that no reader should regard them as authoritative.

The most comprehensive book to date is *The Great Debates: Carter vs. Ford, 1976*, edited by Sidney Kraus and published in 1979 by Indiana University Press. The book, nearly 600 pages long, represents the work of fifty authors. A dozen essays in the first part treat background and perspective, and fourteen essays in the second part provide social scientific studies of the effects of the debates. The third part consists of transcripts of the four debates. As this division suggests, the essays have much to say about events leading up to the debates, as well as much to report about the uses and effects of the debates. They say little about the debates themselves. One essay examines the discourse of the debates: chapter 11, "Grilling the Pols: Q and A at the Debates," is Louis T. Milic's examination of the debate panelists and their questions as well as of the responsiveness of candidates' answers. The debate transcripts in the Kraus volume were meant to be verbatim, in the sense that the editors tried to capture in print the many verbal pauses and false-word starts. Paragraphing was shunned and punctuation was often based on other than logical principles. The cluttered result does not permit easy reading. In addition, the transcripts contain a serious number of obvious word omissions, word insertions, and inaccurate word or phrase renditions.

Finally, *The Presidential Debates: Media, Electoral, and Policy Perspectives*, published in 1978 by Praeger Publishers and edited by George F. Bishop, Robert G. Meadow, and Marilyn Jackson-Beeck, consists of debate transcripts and a dozen essays grouped in three parts: the setting, effects of communications context, and cognitive and behavioral consequences of the debates. Most of the essays report empirical research related to the debates, and none provides analysis and assessment of the debate discourse. The transcripts suffer from the same faults as those in the Kraus volume, although there are considerably fewer obvious inaccuracies.

In the construction of this book, we have been grateful to the many colleagues and friends who have offered valuable advice along the way, to Irv Rockwood, whose comments on an early draft sharpened our sense of direction, and to the University of Wisconsin Press editorial and production departments for their help in bringing the work to a speedy completion. We are especially indebted to Jo Ann Bitzer, whose editorial skill is apparent to us on every page.

Part 1

☆ ☆ ☆ ☆ ☆ ☆ ☆ ☆ ☆ ☆ ☆ ☆ ☆ ☆ ☆ ☆ ☆ ☆ ☆

1.   Introduction

Freedom of speech and unfettered exchange of competing ideas are celebrated by Americans as cardinal virtues. But Walter Lippmann reminded us long ago that communication unchecked by rigorous debate in search of truth often leads to "sophistry, propaganda, special pleading, lobbying, and salesmanship." The free expression of ideas, so cherished by Americans, must be accompanied by the practice of debate—"the confrontation of opinion—as in a Socratic dialogue, in a schoolmen's disputation, in the critiques of scientists and savants, in a court of law, in a representative assembly, in an open forum." If guided by rules of evidence and codes of fairness, debate sifts truth from error and moves us closer to "moral and political truth." When debate is absent, Lippmann warned, "unrestricted utterance leads to the degradation of opinion."[1]

In its most general sense, debate involves claim and argument, reply and counterargument, challenge and rebuttal. Through exercise of intelligence and through trial and error, we have developed methods of debate and inquiry which help assure informed decision on legal, philosophical, scientific, and sometimes political issues. Rigorous debate occurs regularly in our courts, scholarly journals, and other situations where truth, justice, and right action are at issue. Yet we do not provide and insist upon a method of debate suitable for candidates seeking the presidency. In the discourse of candidates competing for the nation's highest office, we tolerate sophistry, salesmanship, and sometimes "degradation of opinion." As a result, the body politic is denied a process of truth-seeking, and the individual citizen suffers loss of opportunity to cast a well-informed vote.

Conventional politicians and some intellectuals view debate simply as campaign strategy, a vehicle of victory. In deciding whether and how to debate, the crucial question is what will lead to success and not what is in the interest of the public and of the individual voter. But the public interest must be counted. As Austin Ranney points out, "the candidates' prospects are not the only stake. There is also the stake of the American people in having presidential campaigns organized and conducted in a manner most likely to provide them with correct information about the candidates' personal qualities and positions on issues."[2] Human ingenuity can surely devise methods and formats of presidential debate calculated to serve the public interest, while at the same time allowing candidates to advance their causes.

The so-called debates of the 1976 campaign fell far short of such a goal. In fact, Ford and Carter hardly debated; nor did they adequately answer the questions put to them. Their argumentation was shallow, often defective in reasoning and evidence, and seldom went beyond the commonplaces uttered from the stump. Their debate speeches frequently amounted to little more than the stuff of which their television commercials were made. The hybrid format—part debate and part press conference—did not permit thoughtful, extended, and well-developed speeches of advocacy and defense. Speeches were short and hurried, compressed into brief slugging rounds, and uttered in many instances without a sense of what was at issue. Moreover, the journalists who comprised the panels behaved as a third party, actually corrupting what might have been genuine debate. Instead of placing debatable propositions on the agenda, they entered the fray with gloves on—arguing, asking hostile and one-sided questions, and wasting valuable time with vague and inappropriate questions. The format and the rules of confrontation invited mundane rhetoric—which is exactly what the public witnessed in 1976. If debates are to occur in 1980 and later, new formats should be tried, such as those described in the last chapter. And certainly if contenders are to engage in "great debates," motives more lofty than personal gain must be generated. In short, the American public must demand that candidates reach for the truth, as well as for victory. Candidates, sponsors, journalists, and the interested public can learn from the lessons of 1976.

Our commentary focuses on the debates themselves, and not on public reaction and voting behavior—matters we leave to social science. Social scientific study of causal links between the debates and voter behavior is valuable, but tells us little about the internal dynamics, properties, and qualities of the actual debates, nor about the design of formats likely to improve future debates. These and similar matters can be discovered only by analyzing the debates in search of answers to numerous questions. How did the panelists influence the debates? Did panelists establish a suitable agenda of issues for discussion? Did their questioning promote or hinder debate? To what extent did Ford and Carter debate and answer questions? How much and how well did they argue? What defects marred their speeches? What can we observe about the dynamics of confrontation in the format they used? Did they succeed in moving their own agenda items to the front or respond only to questions posed by panelists? How did the candidates "score" on each other? Which candidate was the more skillful debater in this format? Answers to such questions as these enable us to assess the 1976 debates, learn from them, and design formats more likely to promote debate appropriate to presidential politics.

IN THE ABSENCE OF TRADITION

A tradition of presidential debate does not exist in the United States. There are various models of American *political* debate—Lincoln and Douglas, Webster and Hayne, and others—but the 1960 Kennedy-Nixon debates provide our only model of *presidential* debate. The Ford-Carter debates were shaped on this model. The choice, as we shall see in the course of this study, was an unfortunate one.

There were three debates in 1976: the first was on the general subject of domestic issues and economic policies, the second on foreign and defense issues, and the third on any relevant subject. Specific topics of discourse were introduced in each debate by a panel composed of journalists, each in turn posing a question to Ford and Carter, and often a follow-up question. Speaking time was limited: in response to the original question, each candidate could provide a three-minute speech in the first and second debates and a two-and-a-half-minute speech in the third; each was limited to a two-minute response to follow-up questions; and rejoinder speeches, made after the opponent had spoken on a question, were limited to two minutes. Unlike the Kennedy-Nixon debates, candidates made no opening statements, but they did have three to four minutes at the end of each debate for closing statements, or perorations. A moderator presided over each debate. Candidates were not permitted to bring notes or other written materials. In the main, the 1976 debate format repeated the central features of the 1960 model: both formats were hybrids which crossed press conference with debate and involved three parties in the contest— two candidates and the press.

In the absence of a presidential debate tradition to provide suitable communication forms and governing principles, and with the Kennedy-Nixon debates taken as a model to be essentially repeated, the 1976 debates were influenced in the direction of mediocrity by several factors. First, the principal concern of candidates and their managers was short-term political advantage—the fundamental goal, after all, was to win the election. When planning the debates, most of the strategic decisions were strongly influenced by this goal, as were many of the candidates' speeches. In the debate-planning sessions, Ford and Carter representatives haggled over such matters as stage lighting, physical arrangement of persons and things, camera angles, debate format rules, and the timing of speeches and topics of debate. It is also obvious in reading the debates that short-term political gain was often a strong factor in what the candidates chose to say. For instance, neither Ford nor Carter would candidly answer Joseph Kraft's first question in the third debate, "What sacrifices are you going to call on the American people to make, what price are you going to ask them to pay to realize your objectives?" A candid and sincere answer which fully recognized the scope of national and international problems and the cost required to solve them might have provided discourse satisfactory to Kraft, but it also could have created a major campaign crisis for the candidate.

Second, the candidates were expected to adapt themselves to television, the principal medium of communication. Television presents opportunities to persuade through delivery, appearance, and other visual qualities, as well as through "the message" more narrowly defined as speech content. Whether by accident or design, a speaker's television manner and style merge with content. The image mixes imperceptibly with the "what is said" to create a message combining personality and thought. Each candidate sought to make his own image appealing and at the same time to create public doubts about the personality of the other. By and large, image-building and image-deflating tactics diminished the quality of discourse.

Third, the candidates had to charm, instruct, and persuade the massive and heterogeneous audience created by television— on the whole, an audience not well prepared to hear and judge reflective, weighty, or rigorous debate. Within the extent of their skills, they adjusted their communication to the level, needs, images, and thought patterns of this audience, or at least to that part believed to be persuadable. It is not surprising that the quality of the presidential debates was affected by audience nature and limitations, for messages tend to bend to the audience as a condition of communication.

Fourth, the speeches by the candidates were severely limited by the format. Debate occurred in short bursts within rounds initiated by panel questions, and candidates were hurried from one round to the next with no time for reflection: question; speech; follow-up question; follow-up speech; rejoinder speech by the other candidate; then on to the next round. Each speaker had to respond immediately with impromptu speech; indeed, the candidate who paused for a few seconds to consider what to say risked being judged uncertain, weak, or timid. There was no opportunity for the give-and-take of dialogue; too little time to develop a solid, well-argued position; no chance for a candidate to put a question to his adversary—whether panelist or candidate. Although both speakers prepared for the debates by examining position papers and rehearsing responses to possible questions, they could not know or even accurately predict what questions would be asked. Under such format conditions, Ford and Carter could not possibly deal with every issue in a substantive and reflective manner, but they could be expected to generate earnest and valuable debate in a few rounds out of many.

Fifth, the press played an inordinately important role in the debates—at times a larger role than that of either candidate. The nature of the journalists' questions, as well as the tone and style of their questioning, colored the debates. As panel members, the journalists became participants and, through their power to establish the debate agenda, strongly controlled what could be said by the candidates. Following the Kennedy-Nixon model and their own journalistic inclinations, they treated the debates as joint press conferences.

Sixth, the debates received hurried analysis by the television, radio, and newspaper reporters and commentators—people who had instant access to the machinery of public communication. Practicing their profession in their normal way in a country without a presidential debate tradition, these critics rushed to judgment. They acted as intermediaries, injecting their own evaluations into the public consciousness before the public had time to make independent judgment. And among the first conclusions rendered by the journalists was an answer to the simplistic question *Who won?* This period of interpretation and judgment following each of the Ford-Carter debates was almost as consequential for the candidates as the debates themselves. Furthermore, anticipating instant judgment, the candidates viewed the debates not as ongoing, connected, and rigorous discussion of issues and positions to be judged when the series was finished, but as opportunities to "score" immediately and to enhance their positions in the public opinion polls.

The debates did not center upon a set of critical issues. This was another factor which influenced them in the direction of the mundane. A casual reading of the texts shows the astonishing ease with which candidates and panelists moved from the important to the trivial, the broad to the narrow, as if there were no critical issues demanding attention and no great decisions to be made. Enormous substantive issues existed in 1976, of course: basic health care for all citizens was an unmet goal; pollution of air, water, and land endangered present and future generations; the problems of urban areas were staggering in scope; crime, crime prevention, and apprehension and detention of criminals had become national industries; racial and social inequities defied solution; nuclear weapons proliferation and the arms race were unabated; and more than half of the people in the world were living in hunger and poverty. Panelists and candidates were well aware of these problems, even mentioning them from time to time in the debates and in campaign speeches and literature. Yet neither candidate chose to elevate such issues to a high level of importance or focus his candidacy on them. Why did not these or similar critical issues serve as focal points in the presidential debates? The reason is that no great crisis pressed upon the American voter during the 1976 campaign. The common perception of the national condition was of relative calmness and stability. Both Ford and Carter apparently thought this to be the wrong atmosphere in which to play up critical issues or advocate comprehensive policies that the public might regard as radical—policies which probably would fail to move through the political system anyway.

Any of the foregoing factors could strikingly reduce the prospects for superior debate. And in fact, the Ford-Carter debates proved to be mediocre, an outcome for which responsibility spreads rather evenly: to the faulty Kennedy-Nixon model; to those who selected and used the model with only minor changes; to the candidates, who might have achieved more had they aimed higher; to the panels, whose journalist members perhaps merit the sharpest criticism because theirs was the easiest opportunity to perform well; and to the public, which might have received better debates had it been more demanding.

THE CONCEPTION OF POLITICAL DEBATE

A debate is by nature a conflict of causes, positions, or claims which are examined, attacked, and defended by means of exposition and argument in the speeches of disputing parties, with the objective of obtaining a judgment or action. Political debate is usually not concerned with those things that are fixed and immutable, or true of necessity; it is concerned with the variable—with what is *probably* true and with what *should* be done in the future. By means of debate, we hope to obtain a more balanced view, a more probable truth, a better course of action than we could obtain without debate.

Such an outcome depends, of course, on the "goodness" of debate: deliberations must be serious, truthful, and logically sound. If parties enter dispute without serious purpose, stray from the truth, or disregard standards of evidence and reasoning, the result will be of little value. We may reasonably expect, however, valuable outcome when debate is conducted soundly by persons of intelligence, knowledge, and high purpose. This is not to say that the result will be truths as secure as laws of nature, but the outcome of such debate will enrich thought and perhaps sensibilities, and will better prepare us to decide and act on matters that admit of alternatives.

What elements are essential in genuine debate? In his analysis of the Kennedy-Nixon debates, aptly entitled "The Counterfeit Debates," J. Jeffery Auer noted that the tradition of American debate yields five basic elements: (1) *a confrontation,* (2) *in equal and adequate time,* (3) *of matched contestants,* (4) *on a stated proposition,* (5) *to gain an audience decision.* Insistence upon these elements is not "mere pedantry," for each is essential for true debate and each "has contributed to the vitality of the debate tradition."

Did Kennedy and Nixon engage in head-to-head debate? Did they sharply *confront each other* on issues? No, said Auer, they did not debate—in fact, they hardly talked to each other.

"Instead they were fitted into a new format, like a double public press conference for simultaneous interviewing. . . ." They had *equal time,* but not *adequate time*—and the inadequacy of the time allowed for answering panel questions and refuting the opponent's statements was not only unreasonable, but dangerous as well: "It created the illusion that public questions of great moment can be dealt with in 180 seconds." The third element, *matched contestants,* was present. The fourth, a *stated proposition,* was not. "Instead of a critical and comprehensive analysis of a single and significant issue, the listeners were exposed to a catechism. . . ." And the candidates were bombarded with questions, not propositions. Contestants Nixon and Kennedy, "fencing with their quizmasters, were compelled to contrive facile answers to queries on an encyclopedic range of topics, with none of the rhetorical elements of unity and coherence to bind them together." Finally, did those debates function to *gain a decision?* On this point Auer judged the debates least adequate, concluding that they involved shallow inquiry, poor organization, and an unexciting style. But most important, the emphasis was "inevitably upon instant reactions, not upon developed arguments." Little in the debates contributed to the audience's thoughtful consideration of issues or to a solid rationale for decision on issues. Personalities, not issues, were emphasized.[3]

Auer's judgment of the Kennedy-Nixon debates could have been written with equal justice of the Ford-Carter debates. They fell far short of the conception of "genuine" debate. On the premise that criticism is appropriately grounded in a conception of what presidential debate should be, we shall assess the Ford-Carter debates against ideal principles of genuine debate: Was the agenda of issues established by the panels an appropriate one? Did panelists place truly debatable propositions before the candidates? Did the speakers enjoy equal and adequate time? Did the candidates actually debate, and if so, how much? Did their speeches exhibit basic and necessary qualities—serious treatment of the issues, command of relevant information, observance of standards of evidence and logical reasoning? Did they reach for the truth?

Criteria based on principles of genuine debate will take us only so far, however. Such criteria alone are not fully appropriate to analysis and assessment of the actual debates. The reason is that Ford and Carter debated in a defective, pseudo-debate format which practically ruled out genuine debate. Thus we must understand what sort of "debate" they engaged in and, given that understanding, apply additional, more realistic criteria.

What criteria may be said to fit the actual encounters? In the first place, the format placed a double and contradictory responsibility on the candidates: they were instructed to *answer* questions posed by the panels, but at the same time were expected to *debate* one another. Thus one basic criterion surely should be the following, how adequately did the speakers answer the questions? Secondly, how ably did they debate each other within their sharply constrained speaking conditions? The burden of simultaneously answering questions and debating suggests a third criterion, how successfully did the candidates convert questions into debatable propositions, and answers into speeches of advocacy? In short, did they deal successfully with their contradictory missions to answer the panels and to debate each other?

The format of the debates featured question after question, each one initiating a short round of "mini-debate." The critical virtues were speed, aggressiveness, versatility, and quick "scoring" through attacks and arguments—rather than elaboration of well-argued position statements relating to issues or propositions. Consequently, we shall assess the abilities of the candidates to initiate lines of thought and argument quickly, strike with charges and countercharges, move swiftly from topic to topic, and maneuver to win the several rounds.

The chosen format included certain built-in advantages and disadvantages. For example, when opening a round of debate, a candidate who gave only a straightforward answer to the question left his opponent free to criticize his answer from the rejoinder position and did not take full advantage of the original speech position. Conversely, a candidate used his original speech position to good advantage when he initiated charges, new agenda issues, criticisms, and arguments to which his opponent had to respond. By attacking or otherwise burdening his opponent (even at the expense of departing from the question), the original speaker acquired advantages for himself and placed disadvantages on the rejoinder speaker. Therefore we can apply the following criterion, how well did the candidates discover and use the strategic possibilities implicit in the debate format?

In the Lincoln-Douglas debates, there were only two parties. The Ford-Carter debates involved a third party—the panel—whose role included elements far more complex than mere statement of questions: the panelists argued to and against the candidates, displayed hostility toward them, and frequently framed defective questions. The nature of their questions often sharply diminished the extent to which Ford and Carter could debate—or even provide adequate answers. Therefore we should ask, how ably did the candidates cope with their inquisitors?

It is arguable that the design of the 1976 debates was not only contrary to genuine debate, but actually solicited speeches displaying attractive personality, voicing slogans, and rehearsing old arguments likely to have broad appeal. If the format invited such speeches, then we should ask, how ably did each candidate fashion a credible and attractive image, employ the commonplaces of his campaign, and dress his ideas with effective language?

We conclude that a thorough assessment of the Ford-Carter debates should employ criteria derived from an understanding of the nature of the actual debates, as well as criteria implicit in the notion of ideal presidential debate. Our commentary seeks to employ both sources of criteria in balance.

The next chapter briefly reviews the campaign context, with attention to numerous events which colored the campaign and in some fashion influenced the debates. It also characterizes each of the Ford-Carter debates and the one Dole-Mondale debate. Our intention is to catch the flavor of the campaign conveyed to the public by the candidates and to a larger degree by the press.

The third chapter examines the third-party participants in the debates, the press panelists. Their questions were meant to provide a critical element—the issues to be debated. If debate is to occur, there must be a point at issue, a matter upon which two sides disagree. The disputed matter is expressed either as a proposition or as a question, and must be debatable for both sides—a matter of contention between them. It must be significant enough to merit debate, be stated with clarity and precision, and have such a scope that speakers can address it within the time limits. A debate question is defective if it is obscure and ambiguous, or so broad in scope or overloaded with subordinate parts that candidates cannot treat it adequately. A question is defective if it contains an incidental or covert challenge which produces a second, perhaps dominant, proposition; if it is so framed that it offers debate opportunity to only one party; if the question itself amounts to a hostile attack upon one party, thus throwing advantage to the other; or if the question is inappropriate because of narrowness, triviality, or redundancy. Examination of the questions and the role played by the panels leads to the conclusion that the panelists did little to promote debate, frequently hindered it, and by and large hurt Ford more than Carter through their participation. We shall consider later the value of dismissing panels from any future debates.

Chapters 4 and 5 assess the discourse of the disputing parties in terms of initiative, aggressiveness, argumentation, charge and countercharge, refutation, debate strategy, preparedness, speed, image. We seek to understand the dynamics of the debates and to account for the fact that so little genuine debate occurred. Candidates obviously can speak in response to questions and yet not engage in debate; their speeches may simply fail to make contact because of a defective question or because of distraction, deliberate evasion, or some other cause. Debate occurs when candidates present speeches which affirm and deny, offering evidence and arguments in support of competing claims and positions. Speeches are defective in a debate to the extent that they fail to address a clearly stated and appropriate question or issue; employ evidence that is erroneous, unreliable, inapplicable, or otherwise deficient; use arguments that are logically fallacious or crippled because of impropriety or misdirection, shallowness of conception, or weak logical force; or introduce irrelevant matters or simply waste time. Chapter 4 analyzes the chief skills of verbal combat appropriate to the chosen format and shows why Carter "outslugged" Ford. Chapter 5 treats the argumentation of the debates—the strategies of argument as well as the quality of evidence and reasoning.

Chapter 6 evaluates the format: that is, the rules to be observed and the organization of the debates according to general topics, specific questions or propositions, order of speaking, length of speeches, opportunity for rebuttal, and similar factors. All debate—whether political, scientific, or philosophical—must have structure, if only to permit the orderly exposition of ideas and arguments and to assure that competing speakers listen to one another, have an opportunity to respond to each other, and at the same time have access to the audience who is to decide. But debates also ought to be so structured that issues can be discussed adequately; thus format must be adjusted to issues, or issues to format. All parties must observe rules to assure fairness and to increase the probability that the discourse will be excellent. By these standards, the format of the Ford-Carter debates would be satisfactory if it allowed adequate treatment of issues that were placed on the debate agenda, if it provided almost equal debate opportunity to the candidates, and if the rules constraining panelists and candidates were well designed to enhance the quality of debate. We shall observe that candidates neither answered questions well nor debated much. The format was contrary to the idea of debate—indeed, it was severely and fundamentally flawed.

Chapter 7 recommends changes for future presidential debates. The basic reasons for these changes are set forth in each chapter: the performance of the panelists in all of the debates greatly reduced the chance that significant debate could occur; the speeches of the candidates contained weaknesses so serious as to call into question the wisdom of repeating the 1976-style debates; major defects in the format practically foreclosed the possibility that issues could be discussed ably. We recommend changes calculated to improve presidential debates which might occur in face-to-face settings, but also suggest alternative modes of deliberation which would minimize certain risks and offer rewards to candidates and to the public far beyond those realized through the 1976 Ford-Carter debates.

2.   The Campaign Context

Several months before the debates, a political analyst could have confidently wagered that incumbent President Ford would prefer not to engage in face-to-face nationally televised debates, and that his challenger would want to debate. Mr. Ford was the president; he had ready access to the public through the perquisites of his office; he was known and liked as an honest and decent man; he had won praise for restoring trust and dignity to the presidency in the aftermath of Watergate; and he was serving during a time of relative calm. Furthermore, he was not known as an effective speaker; for this reason, too, he appeared to have little to gain and much to lose by taking part in debates. In a contest with a skillful opponent, his modest communicative talents might be magnified and highlighted to his detriment by press coverage and public attention.

On the other hand, Carter—a former governor of a southern state—was a Washington outsider who had never been a national political figure. To millions of Americans, he was "Jimmy Who?" He came to public attention with early victories during the primary campaign, but was still relatively undefined compared with Ford. One could assume that Carter would welcome debates as a part of his campaign in order to demonstrate competence and to acquire much-needed national exposure. Thus, an early assessment of prospects for debates would be: Carter will want to debate if he wins the nomination, but Ford will be reluctant.

As the primary campaign progressed, however, the fortunes of the candidates changed, and so did the prospects for presidential debates. Carter won in key states. His principal announced rivals—Henry Jackson, Morris Udall, and George Wallace—dropped out. After months of hesitation, his principal unannounced opponent—Hubert Humphrey—decided not to run. Carter withstood last-minute challenges from California Governor Jerry Brown and Idaho Senator Frank Church, and his nomination by the Democratic National Convention was practically assured weeks in advance. At the close of the convention, some public opinion polls showed him leading Ford by as much as 30 points. While this lead gave comfort to Carter and distress to Republicans, it was short-lived and probably reflected little more than a temporary Carter popularity at a time when Ford's nomination was still in doubt. Ford's path to the Republican nomination became clouded by a challenge from former California Governor Ronald Reagan, who battled Ford in the primaries and won enough states and delegates not only to keep the race lively and close, but also to carry the challenge to the floor of the convention.

The prospects for debate were brighter as the Republican convention neared a close. Ford had survived the divisive battle with Reagan, narrowly winning the nomination. He was trailing badly in the polls, had not yet developed a full-scale campaign plan, and sorely needed something to elevate him and give momentum to his campaign. He chose a prime moment at the convention to announce his intention to debate. In his speech accepting the nomination and with the style of an aggressive and confident campaigner, Ford said, "This year the issues are on our side. I'm ready—I'm eager to go before the American people and debate the real issues face-to-face with Jimmy Carter." The convention audience gave sustained applause.

Ford issued his debate challenge to Carter on August 19. Within two weeks the Federal Election Commission decided that presidential debates between the two major nominees could be held legally as "news events" without compliance with equal time provisions for third-party candidates—a question that had been a major stumbling block to network coverage. The League of Women Voters of the United States, esteemed for its long record of nonpartisan political activity, provided sponsorship and planning. The candidates' managers huddled with League representatives to plan the debates: three ninety-minute debates between Ford and Carter, and one between the vice-presidential candidates, Robert Dole and Walter Mondale. Announcement of agreement on plans came on the first of September and procedural details were worked out during the following days.

STRATEGY AND IMAGE

The debates provided the candidates with access to massive audiences during prime television time—and at no monetary cost. One clear sign of the extraordinary importance given the debates by both candidates is the fact that neither Ford nor Carter budgeted campaign funds for nationally televised "major addresses."[1] They reached the voting public through press coverage of their routine campaign activities, paid advertising, and the debates. The candidates could have reduced the significance of the debates, and perhaps increased the stature of the campaign, by adding several major addresses to the nation.

Ford campaign headquarters saw the debates as their man's chance to catch up—"this is the ball game," said one of his advisers.[2] With Ford trailing Carter 10 to 15 points in public opinion polls and representing a minority party, strategy pointed toward debates, even though Carter was acknowledged to be quick and bright; the challenger "might be too quick, too bright and come off as slick against the slow, simple but straightforward manner of Jerry Ford."[3] Ford would gamble on the debates—a "strategy forced upon an ordinarily rather cautious man by the weakness of his position," as R. W. Apple observed.[4] Two effects of the decision to debate, both benefiting Ford, were accurately noted by David Broder: in the first place, the real beginning of the campaign was postponed until the first debate; and secondly, the debates "absolutely determine that the public perception of the presidential contest will be a battle between two individuals and not between the nominees of opposing political parties."[5] This meant that Ford would have time to get his campaign in order, and that the contest would pit his image against Carter's. Numerous polls indicated that large numbers of voters would do what Ford advisers wanted—hold off making a decision until the debates. Before the debates, Carter would be campaigning vigorously and might make an error, a slip of the tongue, which is exactly what Ford strategists wanted. Ford would be presidential before and during the debates. In the debates, he would rely on his ability to answer panelists' questions, an ability in which many of his advisers had confidence; and he would hope for a Carter gaffe. He would depend heavily on voter perception of contrasting images: his own as steady, trustworthy, presidential, and Carter's as fuzzy, inexperienced, and untrustworthy. According to Ford's strategy, the central issue in the campaign would become Carter himself. This strategy very nearly succeeded—with Carter's *Playboy* interview and other mistakes contributing to it. Ford's own blunder in the second debate was a critical obstacle to the success of his strategy, because his claim that Eastern European countries are not dominated by the Soviet Union undermined his own image. A number of post-election analyses agreed with R. W. Apple: ". . . it seems highly probable that had the President not stumbled over a question about Eastern Europe in the second debate, costing his campaign 10 days of momentum, the outcome would have been reversed."[6]

Carter's pre-debate announcements of strategy indicated that he would aim not to outscore Ford but to show himself equal to the president, experienced, and not fuzzy on issues. Acknowledging that his image needed firming up and that voters regarded him as relatively unknown, he would seek, in his words, to "maintain an image throughout the debates that I am relatively knowledgeable, that I am a good manager and not a spendthrift." Carter said that if he emerged from the debates equal to Ford in his apparent knowledge of the issues, he would consider it the equivalent of victory.[7] Common opinion held that

Ford, trailing Carter, needed victory in the debates, while Carter needed only to hold his own. The first debate changed the prognosis: Ford bested Carter. As a consequence, Carter needed more than a draw in the second debate; he needed a clear victory, and he got it. In the third, Ford needed a victory but did not get it. The debates, then, became the centerpiece in the campaign; and the stakes increased from debate to debate.

The full role of the press in dramatizing and focusing public attention on the debates is a matter beyond the scope of this study. But anyone who examines newspaper, radio, and television news reports during the days before the debates will recognize that press reports and commentaries regularly magnified the significance of the debates—and to a far greater extent than did the candidates. The press recalled the Kennedy-Nixon debates and compared them to the upcoming encounters; and public television carried a condensed version of the 1960 debates on September 14. News reports focused on the methods used by Ford and Carter to prepare; they emphasized the special importance of the first debate; and they portrayed the debates as likely to be decisive in the fortunes of both candidates. The drumbeat of expectations continued from one debate to the next: because Carter did poorly in the first debate, the second one would be critical for him; because Carter whipped Ford in the second and the candidates were now even, the third would be the rubber match. Newspapers and broadcast news shows typically gave the lead in post-debate stories to the latest poll results, to blunders, and to strategies. Ironically, while calling repeatedly for a campaign conducted on issues rather than images, the press did as much as the candidates, if not more, to assure that the public would focus on images.

Carter's campaign speeches pictured Ford as a weak leader—unimaginative, a caretaker, lacking vision, and a typical Republican. In chapter 4, we will discuss the ways in which Carter's debate speeches cultivated this image. The press was tougher than Carter; time and again, it underscored major problems with Ford's image. Richard Reeves, in a September 6 article in *New York* magazine, said, "One of the incumbent's problems has always been to 'appear presidential,' which, in his case, has come down to first proving that he is not a dummy, that he can read and write. He can do both. . . ." In the debates, "if Ford doesn't trip, he's a winner." Reeves continued, "His only problem would seem to be that in three or four debates the comparative quality of the candidates' thinking may come through. . . ."[8] Saul Pett wrote, "Ford needs to be presidential, non-bumbling, and as crisp and combative as he was in his nomination acceptance speech."[9] Joseph Lelyveld wrote that "polls taken for Ford by Robert Teeter of Detroit plainly indicated that the President was widely deemed to be neither forceful nor very intelligent."[10] David Broder, reflecting on causes of Ford's poor image, stated that the fault might trace in part to the White House staff's failure to present Ford "presidentially"; but chiefly "the fault lies in the central figure" who "works very hard, but he often seems to be running in place." Broder's column remarked that Ford's campaign slogan might be "You Could Do Worse."[11] Ford's command of information, his intelligence, rapidity of thought, and clumsiness received press lampooning. Photos and cartoons pictured Ford bumping his head on helicopter doors; and Ford's press secretary, Ron Nessen, remarked after the campaign that his reputation as a "bumbler" played a major role in his defeat.[12]

This unflattering portrait of Ford was emphasized again and again following his blunder in the second debate. A cartoon by Stayskal in the *Chicago Tribune* on October 10 showed Ford being interviewed by a representative of "Girlie Magazine"; on the coffee table near his chair rested a newspaper with glaring headline, "Ford's East European Gaffe." While the "Girlie" reporter wrote, the caption had Ford saying, "I'm only human and I've committed stupidity in my heart many times." A Sandy Huffaker cartoon in the October 10 *New York Times* showed Ford's blunder statement coming out of his mouth and striking him in the head. In an October 10 commentary entitled "Will Ford Really Do?" James Reston wrote, ". . . Tip O'Neill of Massachusetts, the next Speaker of the House of Representatives—who has served with Jerry Ford for almost a generation, respects him, and even has an affectionate regard for him as a friend—had insisted that you had to know Ford

well in order to know how little he knew.''[13] A final example
comes from columnists Rowland Evans and Robert Novak, who
wrote in reaction to the second-debate blunder that Ford seemed
incapable of improving beyond his briefing book: " 'I'm very
much afraid that this was the real Jerry Ford,' one high-ranking
administration official confided to us. That implies a
disorganized White House inadequately supporting a President
so befuddled by criticism that he was unable to probe Carter's
vulnerable points." And later in the same column: "Whatever
its shortcomings, however, the White House staff is not the core
of the problem. It is clearly Gerald Ford, who Wednesday night
resurrected the old image of fumbler and stumbler he had very
nearly shaken off."[14] Other factors which inflicted additional
damage will be discussed shortly. For now, we note this critical
point: Ford's strategy of battling Carter on images was blunted
by his own campaign mistakes, by a critical press, and by events
over which he had little or no control.

The Ford campaign cultivated an image of Carter as vague
on issues, inconsistent, "waffling," an unknown quantity, and
not to be trusted. Part of this image was made credible because
Democratic rivals in the primary campaign had accused Carter
of waffling and failing to treat issues with specificity.[15] Ford
speeches as well as commercials and campaign literature sought
to create distrust of Carter.[16] The press also sounded these
themes. For example, Ed Bradley summed up his report on CBS
TV "Evening News" for September 3 by saying that some
people see Carter "trying to be all things to all people." CBS
reporter Ed Rabel, covering Carter's Labor Day speeches, told
the public that Carter "offered nothing new, rather a parroting
of his campaign creed, of broad promises and ideals which have
made him vulnerable to charges of fuzziness." Taking into
account the day's campaign events, Rabel judged that "Carter
did little on this opening day of the campaign to counter charges
that he sometimes straddles the fence and flip-flops on the
issues." On September 19, Associated Press writer Saul Pett
wrote of image needs, "Carter needs to be positive, clear and
unequivocal." Robert Shogan wrote that Carter's own pollster
found "that many voters, although favorably inclined to Carter,

are waiting for the debates to make up their minds. They apparently want to be convinced that Carter is knowledgeable enough and sound enough to be President."[17] Carter was acknowledged to be bright, in command of information, and quick of mind. Saul Pett said, "Carter's mind seems capable of operating on several levels at once. Ask him a question and, even before you finish the asking, he is answering the direct point, the implications and the possible side effects of the question."[18] Broder compared the computer in Carter's campaign airplane with the computer-like mind of the candidate and commented on Carter's ability "to convey to an extraordinary variety of audiences his desire to share with them the most basic emotions—love, trust, pride, patriotism and compassion." His speeches were finely tuned to his audiences, and hardly anything he did was accidental, according to Broder.[19] Although Carter suffered from numerous unfavorable press accounts, particularly those related to the *Playboy* interview, it must be said that the image the press conveyed of him was more interesting and more favorable than the press image of Ford.

PRATFALLS AND PRESSURES

The campaign was formally opened, in the days preceding the first debate, by Carter on September 6 at Warm Springs, Georgia, and by Ford nine days later at the University of Michigan. Speaking from the front porch of Franklin Roosevelt's "Little White House," Carter sought symbolic linkage with Roosevelt, Truman, and Kennedy. His speech claimed that the nation was divided, out of work, and drifting; and he underscored the theme of weak Republican leadership, saying that "every time the ship runs aground, the captain hides in his stateroom, and the crew argues about who is to blame." Ford's kick-off speech at his alma mater celebrated his record of the last two years, provided his vision of America, and announced new proposals. The theme of trust was clearly sounded. With obvious reference to Carter, Ford said, "A person has to prove his trustworthiness. Trust is leveling with the people before the election. Trust is not being all things to all people, but being the same to all people. Trust is not cleverly shadowing words, to let different people draw different conclusions." The nation demands specifics, not smiles, he said. After the formal start, Carter's campaign moved swiftly to all parts of the country, but Ford chose to linger for several days at the White House, conducting his campaign "from the Rose Garden" as numerous reporters complained.[20] Public opinion polls in early and mid September showed that the Carter lead had dropped sharply from its high at the time of the Republican National Convention and was diminishing. On August 24, CBS News announced a poll by Opinion Research Corporation of Princeton, New Jersey, showing that if the election were held then, 46 percent would vote for Carter and 37 percent for Ford. A Lou Harris poll released September 3 gave Carter the lead by 52 to 39. A few days later Harris revised the figures: Carter 44 and Ford 39 in the ten largest states. A CBS-*New York Times* poll reported on September 20 that Carter led Ford 47 to 40. The race became closer and closer until, during the final week, pollsters said the election was too close to call. Although Carter "won" the second and third debates, his lead steadily withered; and Ford, though losing two debates and injuring himself with his Eastern Europe blunder, came within an eyelash of victory.

The campaign was marred by candidates' mistakes and by historical events, some of which came to light before the first debate and all of which had life in the campaign. The news on September 20, just three days before the first debate, was dominated by two matters affecting Jimmy Carter. One was publication of an Associated Press interview with Carter which seemed to say that Carter would increase taxes for middle-income taxpayers. The interview was erroneous (some critical words had been omitted) but charges against Carter came swiftly from Republicans. Corrections were issued, but damage was nevertheless done; one of Ford's first-debate speeches cited the interview to discredit Carter. The AP mix-up was short-lived, but Carter's *Playboy* interview worked its influence throughout the campaign; it was the kind of serious blunder for which the Ford strategists had hoped.

On the morning of September 20, NBC's "Today Show"

featured a splashy interview with two *Playboy* representatives
who had come to tell the nation about Jimmy Carter and
publicize an interview appearing in *Playboy's* November issue.
The published interview covered many topics—reorganization
of government, tax policy, court appointments, etc. While the
"Today Show" touched some of these topics, the juiciest parts
were spotlighted. Two passages in Carter's interview captured
headlines, forced him to explain himself again and again, and
haunted his campaign until the very end. One passage illustrated
his concept of Christian humility, and the other—related to the
first—made derogatory comments about Lyndon Johnson. The
passages in question came in response to a last-minute query in
the final interview session. Carter was asked, "Do you feel
you've reassured people with this interview, people who are
uneasy about your religious beliefs, who wonder if you're going
to make a rigid, unbending President?" In answer, Carter
pointed out that his Baptist heritage teaches local church
autonomy and separation of church and state, and that he did
not "accept any domination of [his] life by the Baptist Church,
none." He also stressed that Christ taught the virtue of humility
and the sin of pride. Amplifying upon humility and pride, he
sought to assure his interviewers of his own sense of Christian
humility:

The thing that's drummed into us all the time is not to be proud, not to
be better than anyone else, not to look down on people but to make
ourselves acceptable in God's eyes through our own actions and
recognize the simple truth that we're saved by grace. It's just a free gift
through faith in Christ. This gives us a mechanism by which we can
relate permanently to God. I'm not speaking for other people, but it
gives me a sense of peace and equanimity and assurance.

I try not to commit a deliberate sin. I recognize that I'm going to
do it anyhow, because I'm human and I'm tempted. And Christ set
some almost impossible standards for us. Christ said, "I tell you that
anyone who looks on a woman with lust has in his heart already
committed adultery."

I've looked on a lot of women with lust. I've committed adultery
in my heart many times. This is something that God recognizes I will
do—and I have done it—and God forgives me for it. But that doesn't
mean that I condemn someone who not only looks on a woman with

lust but who leaves his wife and shacks up with somebody out of wedlock.

Christ says, Don't consider yourself better than someone else because one guy screws a whole bunch of women while the other guy is loyal to his wife. The guy who's loyal to his wife ought not to be condescending or proud because of the relative degree of sinfulness. One thing Paul Tillich said was that religion is a search for the truth about man's existence and his relationship with God and his fellow man; and that once you stop searching and think you've got it made— at that point, you lose your religion. Constant reassessment, searching in one's heart—it gives me a feeling of confidence.

I don't inject these beliefs in my answers to your secular questions. But I don't think I would ever take on the same frame of mind that Nixon or Johnson did—lying, cheating and distorting the truth. Not taking into consideration my hope for my strength of character, I think that my religious beliefs alone would prevent that from happening to me. I have that confidence. I hope it's justified.[21]

Many Democratic leaders sought to downplay the interview, but others admitted it was imprudent and wished Carter had stayed away from *Playboy* altogether. Republicans jabbed at Carter repeatedly: Nelson Rockefeller said he thought he would never see the day when Christ's teachings would appear in *Playboy*. Numerous church leaders spoke out—some who thought Carter's candid remarks were appropriate, but others who thought his comments poorly stated or distasteful. Immediately after the first debate, Carter began a campaign trip which took him to Texas, where he apologized to Texans and to Mrs. Johnson for his comments about Lyndon Johnson. On September 27, the lead story of ABC Television's evening news featured Sam Donaldson's coverage of Carter, with Donaldson commencing, "It is following him wherever he goes now—the *Playboy* interview," then reporting Carter's attempt to explain his meaning to labor leaders in Portland, Oregon.[22] The *Playboy* interview was discussed in newspaper columns during the remainder of the campaign, ridiculed in Ford campaign speeches and literature, and introduced into the final debate by panelist Robert Maynard. The story played for about six weeks, challenging Carter's prudence and his "Mr. Clean" image.

Ford's problems were no less severe; indeed, they were

more numerous and ominous. Two serious episodes commenced with news reports on September 21. First, the press reported that Ford had accepted weekends of golf and relaxation at the expense of a United States Steel lobbyist. A related charge—that Ford twice went to a country club at the expense of Gulf Oil—appeared in Jack Anderson's column. Second, the public learned that Charles Ruff, Watergate special prosecutor, had subpoenaed Ford's campaign finance records in Grand Rapids, Michigan. These stories came before the first debate and appeared again and again in subsequent days. The special prosecutor investigation stories were the most serious because they continued for weeks and raised spectres of Nixon, Watergate, and scandal.

On September 24, reporters announced that the special prosecutor, with FBI involvement, was investigating whether funds contributed to Ford's campaigns had been laundered.[23] On the morning of September 27 the *Washington Post* reported: "The Watergate Special Prosecutor's office is investigating what an authoritative source said Sunday are 'serious' and 'significant' allegations that Gerald R. Ford, while a Michigan congressman, illegally diverted campaign contributions to personal or political use." The story was written by Bob Woodward and Carl Bernstein, the investigative reporters of Watergate fame; the fact that they were on Ford's trail raised expectations of startling revelations. At a hastily called news conference on September 30, at which cameras and microphones were barred, Ford denied any impropriety and expressed confidence that he would "be free of any allegations." News reports on October 1 indicated that the special prosecutor would clear Ford, but no statement was issued to clear Ford and close the matter until October 14. For nearly a month, the investigation threw a cloud over the Ford campaign—though nothing of substance ever materialized.

In the meantime, a new and ugly problem was facing Ford. Singer Pat Boone and Watergate insider John Dean had heard a vulgar racial joke told them on an airplane just after the Republican National Convention by Ford's Secretary of

Agriculture, Earl Butz. Dean reported it in *Rolling Stone* magazine. The "joke" was so offensive that nearly all newspapers refused to print it. Butz referred to black people as "coloreds"; the punch line, paraphrased, said that blacks want only three things—good sex, loose shoes, and a warm toilet.[24] The reports of the Butz affair commenced on October 1 with word that Ford had forced Butz to make a formal apology and that Senator Edward Brooke of Massachusetts, a Republican and a black, had called for firing Butz. The next day Robert Dole called Butz's statements ill conceived and tasteless. Carter said that Butz must go and that he would never tolerate anyone in his cabinet who expressed such attitudes. Ford indicated that he would wait to assess the seriousness of the problem. Butz resigned on Monday, October 4, after discussion with Ford. "This is the price I pay for gross indiscretion in a private conversation," he said. Carter charged that Ford should have fired Butz immediately instead of waiting to calculate political consequences and plot the expedient course. Some commentators took note that Ford was overly tolerant of a cabinet member whose sense of humor was gutter variety.[25]

The distasteful Butz matter was settled two days before the second debate. However, Ford scarcely had breathing space, because on October 5 another story broke—one day before the debate on foreign policy and defense. The House International Relations Committee issued a report prepared by the General Accounting Office which was highly critical of Ford's handling of the *Mayaguez* incident. Seventeen months earlier the naval ship *Mayaguez* had been captured by Cambodians; at Ford's direction, a rescue was accomplished—but with loss of forty-one American lives. The report suggested that the rescue mission was mismanaged and perhaps unnecessary. The White House immediately rejected these suggestions. On the morning of the second debate, CBS News speculated that Carter might use the *Mayaguez* matter against Ford in the debate; instead, one of the panelists did.

Ford went into the debate worried about *Mayaguez*, but came out burdened with the major problem of his campaign—a self-inflicted blow. In answer to a panelist's question, he declared, "There is no Soviet domination of Eastern Europe and there never will be under a Ford administration." The questioner, Max Frankel, obviously astonished, asked a follow-up question, giving Ford an opportunity to retract or clarify the statement. Ford responded by reasserting it with amplification. "Utterly unbelievable," said Mondale; a ridiculous and shameful statement, said Carter; a critical blunder, said reporters and commentators; a major gaffe, said overseas newspapers. Ford's mistake dominated the news for days, set back his campaign for ten days, reminded voters of his "bumbler" image, called in question his intelligence and command of information, and perhaps cost him the election. The blunder and its consequences receive fuller discussion later in this chapter, as well as in chapters 4 and 5.

Ford was buffeted from problem to problem. On October 12 he finally retracted his statement on Eastern Europe. On the morning of October 13, John Dean—claiming that records and White House tapes would support him—appeared on NBC's "Today Show" to say that Ford had aided an attempt to delay or stop an early Watergate investigation by the House Banking Committee. The White House immediately issued a denial and said that Ford stood behind the testimony he had given during congressional confirmation hearings on his elevation to the vice-presidency. Two days later the Watergate special prosecutor, after being asked to investigate Dean's charges, said he would not initiate an inquiry, but the story persisted in the press.

Two other major problems hurt Ford. One was the performance of his running mate, Robert Dole, in debating Walter Mondale. The second was the hostile panel which damaged Ford in the third debate, probably more than did Carter. (These problems are discussed subsequently in more detail.)

This account of pratfalls and pressures leaves unmentioned many less-important and in many cases trivial matters in the campaign scene. Our purpose is not to construct a history, but to point out some of the hazardous realities which formed the context or setting of the presidential debates. These realities were at various times the work of the candidates, other persons, and the press; some may have been the outcome of sheer accident or unintentional error. Whatever their origin, they entered the public consciousness, influencing the debates and the fortunes of the candidates in complex ways.

THE FIRST DEBATE

The first debate was held on Thursday evening, September 23, at the Walnut Street Theatre in Philadelphia. Visibly nervous and hesitant during the first half of the debate, Carter only occasionally showed the toughness that would come in the second debate. Ford, on the other hand, jabbed at Carter's image, charged him with vagueness and inconsistency, and linked him to costly programs and the high-spending Democratic Congress. Panelists' questions focused on domestic issues, as the rules prescribed, and the topics of taxation, budget balancing, and new federal programs were raised repeatedly. Ford's pardon of Nixon was questioned by panelist Frank Reynolds, but Carter chose not to make it an issue: he had resolved earlier that the pardon would not be in his arsenal of issues.[26]

Whatever other flaws marred the first debate, the best-remembered defect undoubtedly was the technical failure in audio equipment which came just as Carter commenced his final rejoinder speech. Suddenly there was no sound, and for approximately twenty-eight minutes television commentators filled time and the candidates waited—Ford standing at his podium for the entire period and Carter sitting for a short time. The audio failure embarrassed ABC Television, which provided the "feed" for this debate to other broadcasters. The problem traced to a small and inexpensive (25-cent) but not insignificant electronic part. It was a quite "humble" electrolytic capacitor— reported the New York Times—"a tube of foil paper and chemicals" which failed.[27]

Both candidates expressed satisfaction with their performances. Ford thought the debate went well: "We did all right. The momentum is on our side." His advisers were very pleased because Ford had scored exceedingly well in a debate on domestic issues, which was supposed to be Democratic territory. Carter's people knew he had not performed well, although Carter said he felt "good about the debate." He acknowledged that he was shaky at the beginning: "I didn't know exactly how to deal with the fact that Mr. Ford was President. But after the first question, I felt that we were equal," and after the initial nervousness "I relaxed and enjoyed the debate." Convinced that Ford had made charges in rejoinder speeches when Carter was unable to answer, some Carter aides wanted the format changed to allow the candidate to whom a question was addressed to be able to respond to his opponent's rejoinder.[28] After the second debate, Ford aides talked of the need for a rule that would require the speaker to address the question asked by the panelist; they charged that Carter did not stick to the issues. Both complaints were sound, but each candidate was guilty of both failings. The suggested changes in format and rules were not made.

Some commentators called the debate a draw, or nearly so. The next day CBS commentator Roger Mudd said that various score cards gave Ford a slight edge; he judged that the debate generally was "flat and dull," and the speakers overtrained and overprepared. Surveys quickly declared that Ford had won the first debate. One survey was conducted during the last minutes of the debate and its results announced immediately: the Roper poll announced that 39 percent thought Ford did best, 31 percent gave the nod to Carter, while 30 percent called it a draw. A CBS-*New York Times* poll taken twenty-four hours after the debate showed Ford winning by a margin of 37 to 24 percent; and the CBS "Sunday Evening News" television broadcast of September 26 reminded viewers that this margin duplicated Kennedy's debate victory over Nixon.[29] New surveys of voter preference were announced. A Lou Harris poll after the debate found that Carter's lead over Ford had slipped by 2 percentage points: the new reading was Carter 50, Ford 41. A Gallup poll announced on October 1 gave Carter 50 percent and Ford 42, with 8 percent undecided. On October 3, the press announced a poll conducted for Carter by Pat Caddell showing that Ford bested Carter in the first debate 40 to 23 percent, but that Carter's overall lead among voters was 9 points.

THE SECOND DEBATE

The second debate was held on October 6 in San Francisco. *Newsweek* later declared, "Jimmy Carter's camp was ecstatic at the change in the course of political events. His advisers confidently predicted that the polls, which had shown him slipping in a number of key states, would soon reflect a Carter upswing."[30] The reason for elation was clear: Carter had soundly whipped Ford in the second debate. The subject matter, foreign affairs and national defense, was supposed to have been Ford's stronghold—the subject in which, according to James Reston, Ford "should have a clear advantage. . . . For most of his long career in the House of Representatives, he worked diligently, if uncritically, on the Pentagon budget, and knows all the questions if not the answers."[31] Contrary to Reston's and many other such predictions, Ford did not outshine Carter in the second debate; in round after round he was pressured by Carter and on the defensive. Moreover, he blundered by asserting, and then repeating, that Eastern European countries are not dominated by the Soviet Union. This was the sort of gaffe that Ford strategists had hoped Carter would make. But the president made it, and in a subject he was thought to have mastered.

Editorial commentary was immediate, critical, and widespread. The blunder was characterized in an October 8 *Los Angeles Times* editorial as "either a momentary lapse of reason or evidence of a profound misunderstanding of one of the most important world security problems." *Time* magazine wrote, "Ford's grasp of foreign policy and even his mere competence were called into question."[32] Ford thus damaged his own image, giving voters reason to think that he really didn't know the basics of contemporary political history, or that he really was the bumbler depicted by the press. Not only did Ford make the assertions in the debate, but he delayed afterwards and failed to immediately correct his statements, even in the face of advice by his strategists. As a consequence, the story played repeatedly for five days until October 12, when he finally admitted his mistake. Speaking at the White House to persons of Eastern European background, Ford said, "The original mistake was mine. I did not express myself clearly. I admit it. The countries of Eastern Europe are of course dominated by the Soviet Union." This did not lay the matter to rest; broadcast and newspaper commentators referred time and again to the Ford blunder. Ford adviser Stuart Spencer said that the blunder and the delay in correcting it "stopped momentum for 10 important days."[33]

The second debate was Carter's, not just because Ford stumbled, but because Carter drastically altered his debate style: gone was the tension and hesitancy, gone the deferential attitude. He was aggressive from the opening question onward, mounting charge and argument in quick succession. Ford was defensive; and while stern in his visual image, he was timid in speech content. Haynes Johnson judged that Carter was the confident one.[34] Carter "seized the initiative at the outset" and "forced Mr. Ford onto the defensive," wrote R. W. Apple.[35] The post-debate polls favored Carter. The Roper Organization conducted a survey during the last twenty minutes of the debate and found that 40 percent thought Carter was winning, 30 percent gave the verdict to Ford, and the remaining 30 percent called it a draw. A Gallup poll gave Carter a greater margin—50 to 27.

President Ford suffered from attacks from all sides after the second debate. Carter campaigned with new enthusiasm and bore down hard on Ford, so much that his advisers urged him to use restraint. The debate battle between Ford and Carter would resume on October 22. In the meantime, on October 15—the day of the Dole-Mondale contest—the Carter lead remained at about 6 points; Gallup reported Carter leading Ford by 48 to 42, and Harris reported 47 to 42.

THE VICE-PRESIDENTIAL DEBATE

The debate between Robert Dole and Walter Mondale, the first formal debate between vice-presidential candidates, took place in Houston on Friday, October 15—a high school football night, as Dole observed. The president's chances for reelection might have been greater had Dole declined debate in favor of sport that night; his sour humor, biting comments, and charges of "Democrat wars" were in sharp contrast to Mondale's "sincere style." Douglas Bailey, a Ford publicist, suspected that Dole made the difference for a significant number of voters who leaned toward Ford but, upon seeing the name Ford-Dole in the voting booth, pulled the lever for Carter instead. Bailey believed this to have been the most important factor in the campaign's final stage when the race was neck and neck.[36]

This debate differed in some respects from the presidential debates: both speakers made brief opening statements before the rounds of questioning; and the initial speaker had a chance in each round to respond briefly to his opponent's rebuttal speech. One result of this difference was more rebuttal arguments than in the Ford-Carter debates. Several panel questions were obviously constrained by the fact that the speakers, being "seconds," had to avoid comments not in agreement with the positions of their running mates. In other respects, this debate resembled the presidential debates: panelists asked questions, and the candidates responded; they moved speedily from round to round—ten rounds of debate. Each defended and praised his running mate, and both spoke predictably on common campaign topics. Dole often criticized Carter and Mondale, and took aim at costly government programs proposed by the Democratic candidates. Mondale called for reduced unemployment, cure of inflation, government reorganization, conduct of foreign policy on fundamental American values, and support for housing, education, and health programs. The debate's most vehement exchanges concerned Ford's pardon of Richard Nixon, the Watergate affair, Dole's charge that wars in this century were "Democrat wars," and the stands of the candidates regarding "people issues."

The tone of the debate was perhaps more important than the issues. Mondale debated ably and with dignity; he defended Carter, as was his mission; and he spoke with passion about programs that assist the sick, aged, and disadvantaged. Dole joked, often inappropriately; he used ridicule and personal abuse; his attitude toward the debate and his opponent seemed flippant; and he made numerous substantive claims that defied logic and history. A few examples are sufficient:

> I'm glad you mentioned Ford Motor Company not paying taxes. Again, the Democrats control the committee; I'm on the committee; Senator Mondale is on the Finance Committee. Henry Ford happens to be supporting Governor Carter. Maybe that's why. Governor Carter did have a little meeting with him at the 21 Club, met some small businessmen there, said "don't worry about taxes, I won't do anything for at least a year." That's after he said the tax system was a disgrace. . . .

> Well, I think Senator Mondale is a little nervous. . . .

> . . . I've been suggesting that George Meany was probably Senator Mondale's makeup man. He may or may not have been. They did a good job. . . .

> . . . Senator Mondale . . . He's got a 95 percent labor rating, or higher—the most liberal Senator in the United States Senate, and that's his right. He wants to be liberal and spend your money, and tax and tax, and spend and spend—that's his right. First he was appointed as attorney general, and then appointed to the Senate. Some of us had to run for what we have. But when you have things given to you, you like to give something else to someone else. . . .

> . . . The only mystery to me is how do you know what Governor Carter stands for. I've been trying to find out for six weeks. He has three positions on everything. That's why they're having three TV debates. . . .

> . . . the war in Vietnam . . . or World War II, or World War I, or the war in Korea—all Democrat wars, all in this century. I figured up the other day: if we added up the killed and wounded in Democrat wars in this century, it'd be about 1.6 million Americans, enough to fill the city of Detroit.

This final Dole statement brought from the usually calm and restrained Mondale his most vehement speech of the evening:

> I think Senator Dole has richly earned his reputation as a hatchet man tonight, by implying and stating that World War II and the Korean War were Democratic wars. Does he really mean to suggest to the American people that there was a partisan difference over our involvement in the war to fight Nazi Germany? I don't think any reasonable American would accept that. Does he really mean to suggest that it was only partisanship that got us into the war in Korea? Does he

really mean to forget that part of the record where Mr. Nixon and the Republican party wanted us to get involved earlier in the war in Vietnam? And long after Mr. Nixon and the Republican party promised to finish the war in Vietnam, they kept urging us forward, and that in fact it was the Democratic Congress that passed the law ending the war in Vietnam and preventing a new war in Angola.

In all, Mondale played his part well, but Dole let the president down. Shortly after the debate, Democratic National Chairman Robert Strauss made a comment judged correct by impartial observers: "I really think, without being mean, that Senator Dole's performance tonight probably did the president—did the Republican Party—a great disservice." On October 17, a *Chicago Tribune* article by Harry Kelly characterized Dole as "street fighter of the year." William Greider of the *Washington Post* said on the same day that Dole "could not hold his needlepoint tongue," while Mondale was serious and "played it for sincerity." A *New York Times* editorial on October 17 held that the Dole-Mondale debate was in many ways "more instructive than the two Presidential debates that had preceded it." Both candidates "helped clarify the philosophical differences between which the voter will have to choose." But Dole presented a "distinctly negative approach," while Mondale "took a characteristically activist position. . . ." Perhaps the most severe public assessment was written by columnist George F. Will in his post-debate column: "Until Dole took wing in his debate with Walter Mondale, it was unclear when this campaign would hit bottom. But surely it sank as low as it can sink" when Dole made Democrats responsible for wars and the death and wounding of 1.6 million Americans.[37]

Carter had good reason to express pride in Mondale's performance. First, Mondale bested Dole in the battle of images. Second, he simply looked and sounded good, quite independently of comparison with Dole. Third, his good showing added to the campaign momentum Carter had generated in his second debate with Ford. And finally, the contrasting images of Mondale and Dole would stick in the public mind and serve as evidence for what was to be one of Carter's best speeches in all the debates—his third-debate speech which cleverly fielded a hostile question in a way that made his choice of Mondale and Ford's choice of Dole a major test of prudence.

THE THIRD DEBATE

The final debate, at Williamsburg, Virginia, was held on October 22. The press billed it as "the rubber match"—as possibly decisive in the election. Carter needed to hold his roughly 6-point lead in the polls, and Ford needed an extraordinarily good showing to spur his already astonishing comeback. The press reported that Carter would be "more dignified, less on the attack," while Ford would be "more aggressive."[38] A few hours before the debate, CBS Television commentator Roger Mudd provided this insider's analysis: the Ford staff is "telling the President to be relaxed, less programmed, but never unpresidential. They thought him too stern during debate number two. The Carter people are telling their man to remain on the offensive, but avoid being strident. . . . Both sides are apprehensive about committing a last-minute mistake," and while both hope the last debate will not be crucial, "they are afraid it will be."

In the debate, Carter clearly was less vehement than in the second debate, although at times he talked tough—for example, on Ford's economic, civil rights, and environmental record. Ford was not aggressive; in fact, he was submissive, both to Carter and to the panelists. In the third debate, as we shall show, the panelists—Nelson, Maynard, and Kraft—did battle with the candidates, and in particular with President Ford who lost to the panel and to Carter. A Roper poll gave Carter the debate: 40 percent thought Carter won, 29 percent thought Ford the winner, and 31 percent called it a draw.

Notwithstanding his second- and third-debate victories, Carter's overall lead in the public opinion polls steadily decreased until a Harris poll on October 29 showed a virtual dead heat: Carter 45, Ford 44, and Ford still picking up—an election too close to call! The three broadcast networks did not declare a final outcome until the predawn hours on November 3 when it became certain that Jimmy Carter had won.

3.

Panelists
vs Candidates:
Analysis of the Questions

Walter Mears, national political correspondent for the Associated Press, was a panelist in the Dole-Mondale vice-presidential debate. Reflecting on the role of the panelists in the debates, Mears suggested that the reporters who posed questions to the candidates did not play a critical role:

I can testify that those of us who questioned the candidates were not nearly so important as we would like to think. Bruno, Hoge, and I made it a point to stop by a Texas League of Women Voters cocktail party to which we'd been invited after the debate. Nobody recognized us. Bruno hailed a taxi to the Houston airport Saturday morning. "Watch the debate last night?" the cabbie asked him. And The Associated Press reported that one Walter Wears was among the panelists. Just a typo, of course, soon corrected. But it could have stood for all the audience cared. They tuned in to see candidates, not reporters.[1]

The audience undoubtedly did tune in to see candidates and not reporters, but Mears' humility is not justified by fact. The panelists affected the prospects for well-focused clash between the candidates, and they set the tone of the debates. They engaged the candidates as adversaries and established issues of contention. Indeed, they played a third-party role in each debate, occupying a dominant position and significantly influencing the quality of the debates.

All of the panelists were members of the press. In the first debate, they were Frank Reynolds of ABC News, James Gannon of the *Wall Street Journal,* and Elizabeth Drew of the *New Yorker.* The panelists in the second debate were Max Frankel, editorial page editor of the *New York Times;* Henry Trewhitt, diplomatic correspondent for the *Baltimore Sun;* and Richard Valeriani, diplomatic correspondent for NBC News. In the third debate, they were Joseph Kraft, syndicated columnist; Robert Maynard, editorial writer for the *Washington Post;* and Jack Nelson, Washington bureau chief of the *Los Angeles Times.*

These nine panelists—all well-known reporters or columnists—could be expected to influence the character of the debates to some extent simply because of their unique personalities and interests. More important, as journalists they could be expected to use techniques and exhibit attitudes common to their profession—for instance, much attention to "the newsworthy," dogged persistence in pursuit of answers, skepticism toward politicians, and use of adversarial and argumentative techniques of questioning. In format each "debate" even resembled a televised joint press conference, a familiar setting which strongly invited the journalists to practice their normal craft. These factors and others noted later made it almost inevitable that the panelists would play conventional journalistic roles instead of functioning as catalysts of debate between Ford and Carter. Under these circumstances, it should be no surprise that the questioning by the panels was significantly defective.

Our examination of the role played by the panelists in the debates focused especially on the quality of the questions they chose to ask. In the first place, the questions often were not appropriate to high-level debate. Presidential candidates surely should be encouraged to address a range of critical issues if debate is to be valuable. Yet some questions asked by the panelists were narrow, some trivial, and some so low in priority that one wonders what motivated the questioner. Other questions were redundant, irrelevant, or founded in error. Many were highly tailored to the candidate to whom they were addressed, leaving the other candidate virtually free of any need to respond and thus clearly favored by the nature of the questions and the dynamics of the debate format.

Secondly, many of the panel questions lacked focus and clarity. Poorly stated questions tended to produce confusion; cosmic or unreasonably broad questions were frequently unanswerable; vague questions provided opportunities for candidates to serve up any one of numerous commonplace responses; and multiple questions packed into one question placed unreasonable burdens on candidates or allowed them to select and answer the less difficult question in the set.

A third and very serious defect was the adversarial tone and content in many of the questions. Panelists frequently did more than ask questions: they argued with the candidates and sought to refute them; they set forth charges and accusations; and they provided unfavorable characterizations of candidates and their actions or policies. This affected the temper of the debates and very probably influenced the public's perception of who "won." In the third debate, for example, panel members were almost brutal in their treatment of President Ford, implying that he had helped in limiting one of the original Watergate investigations, and that he was "hopeless" on environmental issues and had a "rotten record" on the economy.

THE APPROPRIATENESS OF THE QUESTIONS

What subjects did the panelists—by means of their questions— choose to place on the debate agenda? Were their questions appropriate to debates between presidential candidates? The following basic guidelines were used in evaluating the appropriateness of debate questions. Appropriate questions are significant, not trivial. They attempt to engage high-priority issues and do not introduce matters that are peripheral, irrelevant, short-lived, or local. Appropriate questions are likely to generate informative responses rather than stale material or wholly predictable speeches. They do not restate questions already asked and answered in the debates. Appropriate questions are so framed that both candidates are equally challenged to respond, with no distinct advantage given to either one. Finally, they are likely to produce debate between candidates rather than speeches devoid of clash on issues.

Among the sixty-three questions asked by the panelists, sixteen were excessively narrow, irrelevant, or had little potential for generating useful information. Two of James Gannon's questions, for example, concerned specific congressional bills on tax reform and public works jobs [I:D,P]. It is unlikely that more than 5 percent of the viewing public understood the bills or the consequences of their passage. Two questions by Valeriani and Trewhitt in the second debate, although not immaterial, were hardly of compelling significance at the time of the campaign. Valeriani asked Ford to defend his handling of the *Mayaguez* affair [II:S], which was not only a past issue but also a narrow one as a part of foreign policy. Trewhitt asked Ford whether he would be willing to reopen negotiations to restore relations with Vietnam if an accounting of the missing-in-action were received [II:U]. The question of relations with Vietnam was (and is) important, but Trewhitt sharply narrowed the question's significance with the condition he attached—an accounting of missing-in-action.

Seven of the sixty-three questions dealt with incidental or largely irrelevant matters instead of substantive issues. Frank Reynolds asked Ford to delineate causes of the anti-Washington attitude [I:S]. This matter was not an actual subject "at issue" between the candidates and the question did not invite meaningful clash. One could expect that Ford and Carter would condemn corruption, dishonesty, illegalities, and immorality, and that in all likelihood their responses would be of little value to the voting public. Questions by Valeriani and Nelson concerning Carter's presidential qualifications and the qualifications of his advisers probed "softness" in the Carter ethos rather than substantive issues [II:C, III:I]. Furthermore, Valeriani made a highly unorthodox proposal when he suggested that before the election Carter should state his preferences for key foreign policy positions. And Nelson's central question—

Will you bring into your administration people with the necessary background to run the federal government?—had to be answered with an obvious "yes," which at best could only express intentions. Maynard asked Carter two questions related to the campaign itself—one about the campaign's low level and digression from important issues [III:C] and the other about Carter's decline in the polls [III:T]. Neither concerned matters of government policy. Both were in fact press conference questions, not presidential debate questions.

After the debates, Maynard explained his rationale for asking the campaign-related questions:

I came away from our Oct. 22 meeting 'liking' Jimmy Carter less and respecting him more. I'd met him only once before, when he sat for more than an hour with our editorial conference at the *Post* in March of 1975. He was cordial, gracious, and in frightful command of his facts. I carried the residue of that first meeting with me to the debate. There, I found a colder and more calculating Jimmy Carter, and I responded accordingly by tossing him a hard political question as my last. My unarticulated purpose was to shake a human response from a man whose mind was a massive computer program. In retrospect, I should have stayed to my earlier course of exploring him on issues.[2]

Indeed, he should have! Maynard wished he had raised the issue of southern Africa, a far more appropriate subject for presidential debate. Note that during the debate Maynard was trying to evoke "a human response." This motive was articulated clearly by Kraft, who wrote that the questions should be designed to rip off the candidates' "mask of self awareness." (Kraft's viewpoint receives attention later.)

Three questions evoked highly predictable and not very informative responses. When Reynolds asked Ford if he would be able to get along with a Democratic Congress [I:T], Ford's reply was predictably affirmative. Valeriani asked Ford twice if he would provide military equipment to the mainland Chinese [II:I,J]. What prompted this question is unclear: supplying military equipment to the Peking government had not been mentioned publicly by national leaders, nor discussed publicly during the campaign. An affirmative answer to the question certainly would have astonished observers, departed radically from standard foreign policy, and been politically suicidal.

Eight of the panelists' questions were defective because of error, misinterpretation, or misunderstanding. Elizabeth Drew's questions contained three serious errors. Questioning Carter, she claimed that even with full employment, "there would not be anything more than a surplus of 5 billion dollars in 1981" [I:F]. Drew was referring to the Congressional Budget Office's "Five Year Budget Projections, Fiscal Years 1977-81," but her claim was inaccurate. The 5-billion-dollar figure was the projection under a weaker economic recovery, which assumed a 5 percent rate of economic growth and a 4 percent unemployment rate. The CBO projections indicated that under favorable economic circumstances the surplus would be much greater than 5 billion dollars: "Under path A—the stronger recovery assumption—the federal deficit would fall to $37 billion in 1977 and be entirely eliminated in 1979. By 1981 the budget shows a potential surplus of $92 billion. Under path B—the slower recovery assumption—the deficit would be $65 billion in 1977 and would not disappear until after 1981."[3] With a 6 percent rate of growth in the gross national product, the Congressional Budget Office projected total outlays of 560 billion dollars and total receipts of 652 billion dollars in fiscal year 1981. Carter correctly pointed out that Drew's figures were based upon an assumption of lower economic growth [I:8], to which she interjected, "No, they took that into account in those figures." In all likelihood Drew misunderstood rather than misrepresented the figures, but nevertheless she did a disservice to Carter by making him appear to be in error when the mistake was her own. It should be noted that Drew won high praise for her questioning.

Drew also failed to provide documentation for her claim that the programs outlined in the Democratic platform would cost 85 to 100 billion dollars by "conservative estimates" [I:F]. This was a key figure, and her failure to provide substantiation in the question was as serious a flaw as Ford's similar charge [I:17]. Finally, Drew's questioning of Ford on budget and tax policies exhibited what is commonly called "the black-white fallacy." She asked him to make a choice among what she apparently saw as exclusive options: ". . . would you try to reduce the deficit, would you spend money for these programs that you have just outlined, or would you, as you said earlier, return whatever surplus you got to the people in the form of tax relief?" [I:L] Drew did not acknowledge that other equally legitimate options might exist.

Two of Richard Valeriani's questions were based on questionable or weak premises. One question, directed to Carter, included the strongly implied premise that it is advisable for a presidential candidate to name the persons who will serve in key policy positions if he is elected [II:C]. Another Valeriani question, to Ford, was based on the premise that normalization of relations with mainland China necessarily means "establishing full diplomatic relations" [II:I]. Clearly, normalization may take forms other than full diplomatic relations.

Maynard and Nelson offered peculiar analyses of the expected low voter turnout and of Carter's standing in the public opinion polls. Maynard stated that one major reason for the fact that only an estimated one-half of the electorate intended to vote was "the low level at which this campaign has been conducted" [III:C]. He was apparently unaware that a 50 to 60 percent voter turnout has been typical voter participation in postwar elections.[4] There is very little probability that the claimed "low level of the campaign" had anything to do with the eventual turnout. Jack Nelson presented an unusual reason why "many Americans still seem to be uneasy" about Carter, claiming that Carter's staff members were "young and relatively inexperienced in national affairs" [III:I]. This causal relationship is surely doubtful: it assumes that the American electorate evaluates presidential candidates by the qualities of their staff members. It is unlikely that many voters pay any attention to a candidate's advisers; indeed most voters do not closely monitor the activities—or even know the names—of presidential advisers and cabinet members.

Another Maynard question, in which Carter was asked to explain his decline in the public opinion polls, contained an erroneous analysis. Maynard argued that Ford was just as much the incumbent in July when Carter was 20 points ahead as in October when it appeared that the race would be extremely close [III:T]. Carter correctly pointed out that he had just been nominated by the Democratic Party Convention at the time of his large lead in the polls, whereas the Republicans at that time were still sharply split between Ford and Reagan and their convention had not yet convened.

Ideally a debate question should be selected and phrased to place an equal burden of response on both speakers. Therefore, another measure of the appropriateness of a question for debate is whether it can be asked with equal relevance of both candidates. If a question is specifically tailored to one candidate, the prospects for clash are sharply limited. In addition, a one-sided question frequently places an excessive burden on the candidate to whom it is directed, leaving the other candidate in a favored position from which he can attack his opponent if the opportunity arises or otherwise advance his interests without the burden of responding to the question.

In the presidential debates, the question to one candidate in some instances was so one-sided that the other candidate simply could not have given a meaningful response. Eighteen of the sixty-three questions in the three debates could have been asked of either candidate. In addition, eight others could have been asked equally well of either candidate with slight rephrasing.[5] However, thirty-seven of the sixty-three questions asked by the panelists in the debates were significantly tailored to the candidate addressed.

Several questions could have been asked only of Ford, and the same is true of several questions to Carter. Ford was asked if he would sign specific bills, if he had acted responsibly in the *Mayaguez* affair, whether he could get along with a Democratic Congress, why he remained so adamant in his opposition to substantive gun control, and whether he would explain his role in Watergate. Carter was asked whether his proposed reorganization of the federal government would reduce the number of federal employees, whether he would fire Arthur Burns, whether he had consulted his foreign policy advisers before making a controversial statement on Yugoslavia, and what he meant in proposing an "open" foreign policy.

The one-sidedness of questions is also evident in the fact that fifteen of the questions addressed to President Ford called upon him to defend his record. Carter, a former governor of Georgia, was asked no questions requiring him to defend his record in government.[6] One consequence of this disproportion was that Carter could more easily take an aggressive stance, an advantage he used particularly in the second debate. The third debate panel asked Ford to defend his record in ten instances, each of which involved a hostile question. Panelists Kraft, Maynard, and Nelson seemed determined not only to examine Ford's record but to discredit it.

A review of one-sided questions, which comprise more than half of the questions asked, leads us to observe that the panelists by and large simply did not formulate and ask questions likely to produce excellent debate. Informative clash seldom occurred in response to questions on which only one candidate could offer a meaningful response.

An analysis of the twenty-three follow-up questions indicates that seven actually followed up on the original question, nine repeated the original question, four followed up on a candidate's diversion, and three introduced entirely new subject areas. Panelists occasionally interjected their own diversions and sometimes used follow-up questions to rebut or entrap the candidates.

Questions which pursued the same line of thought as the original questions were generally more specific than the originals. The follow-ups of Gannon and Drew on budgetary matters and taxes illustrate this. Gannon followed up two original questions by asking Ford if he would sign bills currently before him [I:D,P]. Drew twice presented specific figures on taxation [I:F,R]. Follow-up questions which merely repeated the original question seldom proved productive. Those which pursued a candidate's diversionary response clouded the issues in dispute or, worse yet, introduced entirely new subjects for debate.

The intended function of the follow-up questions was to

force the candidates to answer the original questions posed by the panels. The 1960 Kennedy-Nixon debates had not employed follow-ups and the candidates quickly discovered they could safely ignore panelists' questions. Douglass Cater, a panelist in the third Kennedy-Nixon debate, complained:

> The format of the Great Debate was neither fish nor fowl, not permitting the relentless interrogation of the "Meet the Press" type of quiz show or the clash of ideas that can occur in a genuine debate. The candidates had quickly mastered its special form of gamesmanship. No matter how narrow or broad the question, we could watch by the timing device the way each of them extracted his last second of allotted image projection in making his response. The panel's role was hardly more than to designate categories—animal, vegetable, or mineral—on which the two might or might not discourse.[7]

The inclusion of follow-ups in the 1976 debate format was intended to correct this defect: if Ford or Carter did not answer an original question fully and forthrightly, the panelist could take him to task by means of the follow-up.

Several follow-up questions were useful, fully justified, and served their intended purpose well. For example, Gannon asked Carter to detail the effects of government reorganization upon the number of federal employees. Carter's response was evasive, and Gannon's follow-up forced him back to the issue [I:I,J]. Ford did not answer Nelson's Watergate question in a straightforward manner, but instead cited the results of several investigations which gave him a "clean bill of health." In his follow-up Nelson rightly pointed out, "You still have not gone into details about what your role in it was. . . ." [III:D,E] Similarly, Trewhitt used a follow-up question to seek clarification of Carter's position on embargoes and human rights [II:H], and Max Frankel sought to determine Ford's precise position on American policy toward unrepresentative foreign governments [II:Q].

Numerous other follow-up questions were defective. Reynolds' follow-up to his question on amnesty for draft evaders was pointless, because Ford had already laid out his rationale for granting the limited pardon to draft evaders [I:G,H]. Follow-up questions in four instances pursued a diversion or an incidental point introduced by the candidate's original speech. For example, when Reynolds asked Ford to comment on the prevailing anti-Washington attitude, Ford responded that the Democratic Congress was largely to blame. Reynolds' follow-up then asked if Ford could get along with a Democratic Congress [I:S,T]. When Valeriani questioned Carter about his conception of the national interest and the role of the United States in world affairs, Carter's response included the claim that secrecy in the conduct of foreign affairs must be eliminated. Valeriani's follow-up pressed Carter to explain how he was going to bring the American people into the decision-making process in foreign policy [II:C,D]. Such questions in pursuit of a diversion or an incidental point decreased the possibility of clash on the principal issue.

In three other cases, panelists abandoned their original line of questioning and inserted new or modified subject areas, which tended to cloud the issues. Reynolds' first set of questions shifted from policies needed to reduce unemployment to the subject of wage and price controls [I:A,B]. Kraft's first question dealt with the "sacrifices" that would be required of the American people in coming years [III:A]. Ford answered that we would need to limit federal domestic spending, increase the defense budget, and take the long-overdue action of reducing taxes for middle income taxpayers. Kraft followed up by claiming that the "real" sacrifices of a second Ford administration would be the neglect of major national needs:

Could I be a little more specific, Mr. President? Doesn't your policy really imply that we're going to have to have a pretty high rate of unemployment over a fairly long time, that growth is going to be fairly slow, and that we're not going to be able to do very much in the next four or five years to meet the basic agenda of our national needs in the cities, in health, in transit, and a whole lot of other things like that?

This follow-up, which reveals Kraft's view of specific consequences, probably catches the essential import of his original question. Finally, Robert Maynard questioned Ford's opposition to substantive gun control in view of the fact that Ford was twice the intended victim of assassins. In his follow-up, Maynard introduced two new elements: (1) whether the mere availability of handguns contributes to the possibility of crimes being committed, and (2) whether a national handgun control law is needed in order to prevent the interjurisdictional transport of handguns [III:N,O].

A few other facts about the use of follow-up questions also deserve notice. Follow-ups were used more frequently in the first debate than in the second and third. The first panel's excessive use of them was widely criticized in press commentaries, and the League of Women Voters strongly encouraged later panels to use follow-up questions only when necessary. The number of follow-up questions addressed to Ford and Carter were equal in the first debate (five each). But in the second debate Ford was asked four follow-ups and Carter three, and in the third debate Ford was asked four and Carter two. All of the follow-up questions to Ford in the third debate were hostile: he was pressed by Kraft on the subject of prospective American sacrifices, by Nelson on the subject of Watergate, by Maynard on gun control, and by Kraft on his "rotten" economic record and his "obsession" with saving money. The two follow-up questions addressed to Carter in this same debate were not hostile. Many follow-ups wasted valuable time and detracted from what might otherwise have been clearer and sharper debate between the candidates. This was especially true when follow-ups repeated original questions unnecessarily, pursued candidate diversions or incidental points, or totally abandoned original lines of questioning.

In addition to sometimes posing the same or a similar question in their follow-ups, panelists also repeated themselves from one unit or one debate to another. Indeed, seven issues were covered in more than one round of questioning. The problem of unemployment was addressed by both Reynolds [I:A] and Gannon [I:P]. Tax reform was the subject of questioning by Gannon [I:D] and Drew [I:Q]. The subject of balancing the budget was introduced in three sets of questions: Gannon [I:C], Drew [I:E,F], and again Drew [I:K]. The subject of United States relations with the Soviet Union and the Communist world was introduced by Trewhitt [II:B] and by Frankel [II:E]. Both Valeriani [II:C] and Nelson [III:I] questioned Carter on his qualifications for office and the qualifications of his advisers. Kraft asked two sets of questions dealing with Ford's economic record [III:B,R,S]. Finally, Maynard twice asked Carter to defend and explain his conduct of the campaign [III:C,T].

In general, repetitive questions wasted time and restricted opportunities to place other more important issues on the debate agenda. They were sometimes justified because the candidates did not—or could not—adequately address issues in their two- to three-minute speeches. But an examination of candidate responses reveals that repetitious questions seldom produced deeper analysis of issues by the speakers. Indeed, they often received very nearly the same responses as given previously.

The responsibility for establishing a debate agenda of significant questions and topics rested with the three panels. Did the panelists fulfill this responsibility? They placed twenty-three highly important issues on the agenda in forty rounds of debate, each of which was initiated by one of their questions. Some of these issues were introduced almost incidentally by means of follow-up questions; others failed to generate debate between the candidates; and nine of the twenty-three were introduced by questions which actually focused on cognate topics or on the character of Ford or Carter. The failure of the panelists to raise issues of vital importance in an effective and consistent manner was a serious shortcoming in the debates.

High-priority subjects raised by the panelists in one way or another in the course of the debates included unemployment, balancing the budget, amnesty, government reorganization, tax reform and tax relief, safety of nuclear energy, mandatory energy conservation, the role of the Federal Reserve Board, regulation of intelligence agencies, the Republican foreign policy record, detente and relations with the Soviet Union and the Communist world, the role and strength of the United States in world affairs, trade embargoes and human rights, relations with mainland China, the size of the defense budget, SALT talks, sacrifices required to achieve national goals, the quality of the environment, the urban crisis, civil rights and desegregation, gun control, the Supreme Court, and the Ford economic record. The extent to which these panel-initiated issues led to clear and sharp debate is discussed in chapter 6.

The panelists asked at least fifteen relatively unimportant questions at the expense of other issues more truly worthy of presidential debate. It is instructive to sample a few issues not raised by the panelists and contrast these with some which were raised. The problem of world hunger, which directly affects two-thirds of the world population and has enormous implications for U.S. domestic and foreign policy, was not placed on the agenda; but panelist Valeriani did ask whether the United States is likely to provide military equipment to mainland China. The candidates were not challenged to address the role of the U.S. in arms proliferation; however, Frank Reynolds did ask about "the anti-Washington attitude" of 1976—surely an issue of little consequence as measured against the weapons question. And instead of placing on the agenda such issues as inflation, the Third World, welfare reform, crime, the Middle East, national health insurance, and other critical matters, the panelists chose to ask why General Brown was not fired for his derogatory comments about Great Britain, why Carter had lost ground in the public opinion polls, what responsibility Carter should accept for the low level of the campaign, and whether Averell Harriman and James Schlesinger were consulted before Carter commented on Yugoslavia.

The range and quality of issues discussed in the debates were the subject of numerous press commentaries, most of which blamed the candidates for the neglect of important topics. The *New York Times* editorialized that the foreign policy debate ignored several key questions:

The delicate balance between moral leadership and the limits of power was but superficially discussed. . . . The principles and standards that will motivate the Chief Executive in his relations with our democratic allies, with socialist states that may or may not be democratic, with Communist powers large and small, were but lightly explored; the broad relationship of America to the countries of the third world as a whole was hardly touched upon. The looming worldwide issue of exploration of the deep-sea bed was not even mentioned. . . . [8]

Another *New York Times* article, written by Harvard Professor of Government Stanley Hoffmann, likewise noted the failures of the *candidates:*

They should have talked about the Vietnam war, because if we do not examine its lessons we shall repeat its horrors. . . . They should have stated that in the Middle East (and southern Africa) both the risks for mankind and the difficulty of reaching a settlement are enormous. . . . They should have tried to warn an unprepared public about the need to take seriously—which does not mean to accept indiscriminately—the demands of the third world. . . . They should have pointed out that what plagues our alliances in Western Europe and Japan is the growing inability of many of these nations to provide themselves with governments supported by the bulk of their people. . . . They should have addressed the crucial issue of rebuilding a consensus at home behind a foreign policy devoid of the illusion of easy short-cuts to world order. [9]

What these and other critics apparently failed to recognize was that candidates Ford and Carter did not determine what issues should be addressed. Such matters as the balance between moral leadership and the limits of power, American values in dealing with democratic allies and Communist states, America's relationship to the Third World, exploration of the sea bed, the lessons of the Vietnam War, the Middle East, southern Africa, our relationship to our allies in Western Europe and Japan, and the need to build a consensus on foreign policy—*all were issues not raised because the panelists chose not to raise them.* Those who blamed the candidates misplaced their criticism: the agenda-setting function was the responsibility of the panelists, and not the candidates.

THE SHARPNESS OF THE QUESTIONS

A debate requires starting points consisting of issue statements, questions, or propositions selected and phrased to elicit informative exchanges and arguments between candidates. A good debate question should not be vague, meandering, ambiguous, cosmic, or cluttered. It should not include so many independent questions that the possibility of a cogent response in the allotted time is foreclosed. Yet many of the panel questions were flawed in these and other serious respects, and to an extent that should warrant a careful assessment of the function and utility of the panels and their questions.

The multiple question—that is, two or more questions presented as one—was the source of many faulty starting points in the debate rounds. Nineteen of the sixty-three questions asked in the debates were multiple: thirteen of these were double questions, four were triple, and two were quadruple.[10] Some multiple questions were so diffuse, complex, or otherwise defective that they could not have been answered at all in the time allowed, while others could not have been answered adequately without time for reflection.

The chance that a question would be answered completely was strikingly improved when it was single rather than multiple. Slightly more than half of the single questions (59 percent) but only three multiple questions (16 percent) were answered fully or completely in original and follow-up speeches. Many single questions were well phrased (though sometimes defective in other ways, as noted earlier). For example, the following question by Frank Reynolds has the virtues of brevity, clarity, and specificity:

Governor, in the event that you are successful and you do achieve a drastic drop in unemployment, that is likely to create additional pressure on prices. How willing are you to consider an incomes policy? In other words, wage and price controls? [I:B]

The multiple question had observable consequences on the quality of a candidate's response. Valeriani's first question to Carter in the second debate actually consisted of three separate and distinct questions. First, "What is your concept of the national interest?" Second, "What should the role of the United States in the world be?" And as if these two questions formed partnership with a third, Valeriani added, "And in that connection, considering your limited experience in foreign affairs,

and the fact that you take some pride in being a Washington
outsider, don't you think it would be appropriate for you to tell
the American voters, before the election, the people that you
would like to have in key positions, such as secretary of state,
secretary of defense, national security affairs adviser at the
White House?" [II:C] Valeriani's last question in this set was
very different from both the first and the second questions,
even though he asserted a relationship. This third question,
moreover, included a covert challenge—that Carter, as a Washington outsider presumably lacking necessary experience, had
a special obligation before the election to identify persons he
would appoint to key positions. The multiple question was diffuse because it harnessed three fairly independent topics: a definition of the national interest, a perspective on the role of the
country in world affairs, and the identification of prospective
top officials. In addition, it made preposterous demands on
Carter: under no circumstances could he have provided cogent
responses in three minutes to the three explicit questions which
were parts of the whole. Curiously, six months after asking this
question, Valeriani remained puzzled by the fact that Carter did
not define the national interest.[11]

In the third debate, Joseph Kraft questioned Carter on his
attitude toward constitutional amendments in general, and five
specific amendments in particular:

Governor Carter, in the nearly 200-year history of the Constitution,
there've been only, I think it's, twenty-five amendments, most of them
on issues of the very broadest principle. Now we have proposed
amendments in many highly specialized causes, like gun control, school
busing, balanced budget, school prayer, abortion, things like that. Do
you think it's appropriate to the dignity of the Constitution to tack on
amendments in wholesale fashion? And which of the ones that I
listed—that is, balanced budget, school busing, school prayer, abortion, gun control—which of those would you really work hard to
support if you were president? [III:M]

There were two basic parts to Kraft's question: first, are
amendments on "specialized" subjects appropriate to the
dignity of the Constitution; and second, which of the amend-

ments in Kraft's list would Carter support as president? However, if each of the five specific amendments is a discrete matter worthy of comment, then Kraft's query was actually a six-part question. The enormous scope of the question becomes evident when one considers that each of the five proposed amendments easily could command three-minute responses. In their speeches, Carter and Ford did not (and could not) treat in any detail the specific issues listed by Kraft. Carter provided a very short position statement on amendments and indicated that he would not work actively to support any of them [III:22]. Ford's rejoinder provided no general position on the propriety of the proposed amendments and dealt with two of the five mentioned by Kraft—abortion and school prayer [III:23]. Neither candidate chose to deal with gun control and school busing, which were particularly troublesome issues. Kraft's question was overloaded. Like numerous other multiple questions, it allowed the candidate to choose which issues to address or ignore.

Panelist Jack Nelson asked Carter a question that was both multiple and nebulous. He apparently sought clarification of Carter's stands on criminal rights and on the Supreme Court's decisions limiting those rights:

Governor, you've said the Supreme Court of today is, as you put it, moving back in a proper direction in rulings that have limited the rights of criminal defendants. And you've compared the present Supreme Court under Chief Justice Burger very favorably with the more liberal Court we had under Chief Justice Warren. So exactly what are you getting at, and can you elaborate on the kind of Court you think this country should have? And can you tell us the kind of qualifications and philosophy you would look for as president in making Supreme Court appointments? [III:P]

Nelson actually posed three discrete questions: (1) What do you mean when you compare the present Burger Court favorably with the more liberal Warren Court? (2) Can you elaborate on the kind of Court you think the country should have? (3) What kind of qualifications and philosophy would you look for as president when making Supreme Court appointments? Each of these questions was broad, and it was unreasonable to expect Carter and Ford to provide a cogent two- or three-minute response to all three. The triple question did not indicate any priority of its parts and thus failed to give direction to the candidates. Carter answered the last part first, devoting nearly half of his speech to a discussion of criteria and procedures to be used in the selection of judges, after which he discussed the Burger and Warren Courts [III:27]. Nelson's follow-up noted that Carter had not answered his question "about the kinds of people you would be looking for. . . ." Ford's rejoinder cited his John Paul Stevens appointment and the *Miranda* decision to touch lightly on the third and first questions [III:29]. The clash between candidates was minimal and provided very little useful information to voters—the result, in part, of an overloaded question that lacked sharp focus.

Ten of the nineteen multiple questions occurred in the third debate, with the third debate panel using approximately twelve minutes to ask questions—more time than either of the other panels. Jack Nelson, a member of the third panel, remarked that "my colleagues and I agreed that time was precious and we had to be as succinct as possible in our questioning. [Project director] Karayn suggested we hold the questions to a maximum of forty-five seconds. We shot for a thirty-second maximum and succeeded in most cases."[12] Nelson's statement runs counter to fact: twelve of the fourteen original questions and one of the six follow-ups took more than thirty seconds; none of Nelson's original questions were under thirty seconds; one of Kraft's questions took one minute and ten seconds. Wordiness seems to be linked with multiple questions, but it also suggests another relationship discussed later in this chapter. In the three debates, the questions by the third panel were the most hostile and accusatory: fourteen questions were "hostile," four were "slightly hostile," and only two could be clearly categorized as "non-hostile." It is possible that hostile questions require more time for the panelists to document charges against a candidate.

We have noted that about one-fourth of the questions were multiple and that these made excessive or unrealistic demands on the candidates because their parts were unrelated or only topically related and often individually global in scope. In addition, even some of the single questions invited double answers because they contained covert issues or challenges. It should come as no surprise, then, that candidates sometimes failed to respond directly and fully to panel questions, or that they elected to answer only one or two parts of a multiple question.

Experienced journalists serving as debate panelists could be expected to apply their skills in asking specific, direct, and explicit questions free of both ambiguity and obscurity. And indeed the majority of their questions were clear, even when flawed in other ways. There were notable exceptions, however. Twelve questions were marked by an absence of clarity and specificity.[13] Frank Reynolds was responsible for four of these. His question to Carter on nuclear energy is a case in point:

Governor Carter, I'd like to turn to what we used to call the energy crisis. Yesterday, a British government commission on air pollution, but one headed by a nuclear physicist, recommended that any further expansion of nuclear energy be delayed in Britain as long as possible. Now this is a subject that is quite controversial among our own people and there seems to be a clear difference between you and the President on the use of nuclear power plants, which you say you would use as a last priority. Why, sir? Are they unsafe? [I:M]

The question was cluttered by peripheral references—the energy crisis, a British air pollution commission, the controversy over nuclear energy, and the disagreement between Ford and Carter—before Reynolds reached his actual question about the safety of nuclear power plants. The breadth and fuzziness of these peripheral references allowed Carter to downplay the specific question—whether he believed nuclear power plants to be unsafe—and to use his response time as an opportunity to deliver a well-practiced commonplace on the need for a national energy policy [I:19].

Another question by Reynolds, in which he asked Ford's views on the prevalent "anti-Washington attitude," was the most nebulous question in the three debates:

I suspect that we could continue on this tax argument for some time, but I'd like to move on to another area. Mr. President, everybody seems to be running against Washington this year. And I'd like to raise two coincidental events and ask you whether you think perhaps this may have a bearing on the attitude throughout the country. The House Ethics Committee has just now ended its investigation of Daniel Schorr, after several months and many thousands of dollars, trying to find out how he obtained and caused to be published a report of the Congress that probably is the property of the American people. At the same time, the Senate Select Committee on Standards and Conduct has voted not really to begin an investigation of a United States senator because of allegations against him, that he may have been receiving corporate funds illegally over a period of years. Do you suppose, sir, that events like this contribute to the feeling in the country that maybe there's something wrong in Washington? And I don't mean just in the executive branch, but throughout the whole government. [I:S]

Apparently Reynolds, in his thinking, had already linked the two incidents with prevailing anti-Washington attitudes and was curious as to whether the President agreed. But his vague question had little potential for producing meaningful dialogue, and it allowed the President to say virtually anything related to anti-Washington sentiment. The quality of the response matched the quality of Reynolds' time-wasting question: Ford simply said that the sentiment is "misplaced"; it should be directed toward the Democratic Congress, for they spend too much money on themselves, they have too many employees, and "there's some question about their morality" [I:28].

The panelists had ample time before the debates to prepare clear and well-focused questions. Why then did they fail so badly at times? Why did they sometimes ramble? Why did they ask multiple and global questions which realistically could not be addressed well within the time constraints? And why did they pose several unclear questions? Undoubtedly one answer is that many questions were asked spontaneously and had not been given prior thought. Also, probably some panelists came to the debates prepared with topics, but not with finely honed questions; thus the phrasing of several questions was extemporaneous and less than precise. Finally, many of the questions, including the multiple ones, resembled the questions that are the stock-in-trade of journalists—for example, asking two questions in order to get one answered. The following review of other significant defects in the questions supports the conclusion that the panelists generally failed to place issues before the candidates in a manner that would stimulate informative debate.

THE PANELISTS AS ADVERSARIES

The peculiar format of the debates—in conjunction with professional tendencies of the panelists—promoted an adversary relationship between panelists and candidates. Both the argumentation and the hostility embedded in many questions demonstrate the adversary role assumed by the panelists. The candidate's antagonist frequently proved to be the panelist, not the other candidate.

More than half of the questions in the debates—thirty-five out of sixty-three—contain arguments, thus going well beyond the more limited role of simply placing issues on the debate agenda. In making arguments, the questioners sometimes tried to enhance the significance of the matter at issue; often, however, they also challenged the positions of the candidates. Argumentation by a panelist increased the probability that contention would occur between panelist and candidate, and indeed it did. Both Ford and Carter were often forced to refute the panelists rather than each other.

Jack Nelson's question to Ford about his civil rights record used argument both to highlight the importance of an issue and to challenge Ford directly with accusatory claims:

Mr. President, your campaign has run ads in black newspapers saying that, quote, "for black Americans, President Ford is quietly getting the job done." Yet, study after study has shown little progress in desegregation and, in fact, actual increases in segregated schools and housing in the Northeast. Now, civil rights groups have complained repeatedly that there's been lack of progress and commitment to an integrated society during your administration. So how are you getting the job done for blacks and other minorities, and what programs do you have in mind for the next four years? [III:L]

Note the accusations forming Nelson's argument: the claims in Ford's campaign ads are misleading and, moreover, are contradicted by "study after study"; there has been little progress in desegregation; there have been increases in segregation in the Northeast; civil rights groups have complained repeatedly about Ford's lack of progress and commitment to an integrated society. These several accusations form the "justification" for the two very broad questions asked in the final sentence. In the time available to him, Ford could not possibly refute the accusations about past performance and answer the questions about present accomplishments and future programs. The two specific questions were quite legitimate, and not hostile to Ford. But the accusations and the line of reasoning leading up to the questions were clearly hostile (although perhaps not intentionally so). Nelson could have raised the same two questions with no preliminary statement, or with one that did not display hostility and suspicion toward Ford's motives and record.

Elizabeth Drew and Robert Maynard, the most argumentative panelists, usually prefaced their questions with premises and evidence leading to substantive conclusions. Drew argued that both Ford and Carter were unrealistic in their taxation and spending goals, and that new laws are needed to govern America's intelligence agencies [I:E,F,K,Q,R,V]. Maynard argued that gun control is necessary, that General George Brown should have been fired, and that the presidential campaign had been conducted at a low level, for which Carter was partly responsible [III:N,O,H,C].

Henry Trewhitt's questions tended to be free of argumentation. He sought explanations of policy positions: Have we been successful in containing communism of late? How far are you willing to go to promote human rights? Will you turn over the Panama Canal to the Panamanians? Should the United States reopen negotiations for restoration of relations with Vietnam if we get an adequate accounting of our missing-in-action? [II:B,G,R,U]

Some arguments within questions made claims or implications strongly unfavorable to Ford or Carter: Reynolds implied that Ford would be unable to get along with a Democratic Congress [I:T]; Drew implied that both Ford and Carter were myopic, if not deceitful, in their budget-spending goals [I:E,F,K,L]; Frankel claimed that the Ford administration had allowed the Russians to get the best of us [II:E]; Richard Valeriani suggested that Carter's limited experience in foreign affairs would prevent him from competently executing American foreign policy [II:C]; and Joseph Kraft implied that Ford's record was "hopeless" on the environment and "rotten" on the economy [III:J,R].

Seven of the nine panelists—all except Trewhitt and Valeriani—engaged in direct refutation of Ford and Carter. In twelve follow-up questions, the panelists noted what either Ford or Carter had said and then attempted to refute it.[14] For example, Elizabeth Drew tried to discredit Carter's budget and tax reform goals. Twice, after asking Carter a very general original question, she followed up by producing specific figures which appeared to contradict Carter's position [I:F,R]. Frank Reynolds made it clear in a follow-up question that he did not accept Ford's justification for the disparate treatment of Richard Nixon and Vietnam draft evaders [I:H]. Kraft asked Ford what "sacrifices" he would ask of the nation if he had a second term [III:A], to which Ford responded that the United States would need to restrain domestic spending, while increasing military spending in order to keep the peace around the world. In his follow-up, Kraft charged that the "real costs" of a second Ford administration would be a stagnant economy and a neglect of our basic national needs. Jack Nelson accused Ford of not adequately explaining his role in limiting one of the original investigations of Watergate [III:D,E].

Certain strategies used by panelists in many of the questions were nearly inseparable from the argumentative character of those questions. First of all, the panelist displayed omniscience: in introducing and phrasing the question, an attitude of immense confidence and authority was used to lend weight to the question or challenge, convey an impression that the questioner was in control, and place the candidate in a subordinate position. Fourteen of the sixty-three questions strongly exhibited this attitude and twelve additional questions did so to a lesser degree.[15] Frank Reynolds, James Gannon, Henry Trewhitt, and Richard Valeriani did not use this strategy in phrasing their questions. On the other hand, the prize for "omniscient questioner" would have to go to Elizabeth Drew. Ready with figures from congressional budget committees, she challenged Carter's budget and tax reform goals [I:F,R]. Citing past campaign statements, she charged Ford with inconsistency on budgetary matters [I:K]. In another question she insisted, "The real problem with the FBI and in fact all of the intelligence agencies is there are no real laws governing them. Such laws as there are tend to be vague and open-ended" [I:V].

In addition to omniscience, the companion strategies of entrapment and dilemma were used to draw concessions from candidates. Entrapment as a strategy is very evident in eleven questions[16] and also appears in eight others, though less obviously. Six of Drew's seven questions sought to entrap Ford or Carter; and even her seventh [I:V] was not completely free of this strategy. In her first question, Drew reminded Carter that he had promised "a number of new or enlarged programs, including jobs, health, welfare reform, child care, aid to education, aid to cities, changes in Social Security, and housing subsidies." She pointed out that Carter had promised a balanced budget by the end of his first term in office, and then asserted that there would not be enough money to accomplish all of his goals, even allowing for full employment and economic growth. She concluded her remarks with the question, "So, in that case, what would give?" [I:E]. In her follow-up, Drew repeated the question but added specific budget forecasts which (according to her) indicated that Carter's goals were unrealistic. After presenting the damaging evidence, she asked, "So how do you say that you're going to be able to do these things and balance the budget?" The strategy used by Drew is clear: ask a general question, and then lay out specific figures in the follow-up question to contradict the candidate's answer or position. Her third set of questions employed the same strategem [I:Q,R].

Joseph Kraft also posed entrapping questions. Twice he began by asking general questions of Ford, then followed up with more specific ones. Kraft's first question was overly broad: he asked Ford what "sacrifices" he would ask the American people to make in coming years to achieve national objectives [III:A]. In his follow-up question, he then claimed that Ford's policies would involve substantial costs for the American people that Ford was not admitting:

Could I be a little bit more specific, Mr. President? Doesn't your policy really imply that we're going to have to have a pretty high rate of unemployment over a fairly long time, that growth is going to be fairly slow, and that we're not going to be able to do very much in the next four or five years to meet the basic agenda of our national needs in the cities, in health, in transit, and a whole lot of other things like that? Aren't those the real costs? [III:B]

Another set of questions by Kraft began by accusing the Ford Administration of compiling a "rotten" economic record [III:R]. After Ford disputed this contention, Kraft zeroed in on two specific concerns, wording his questions to entrap Ford whatever his answer:

Mr. President, let me ask you this: There has been an increase in layoffs, and that's something that bothers everybody because even people that have a job are afraid they're going to be fired. Did you predict that increase in layoffs? Didn't that take you by surprise? Hasn't your administration been surprised by this pause? In fact, haven't you been so obsessed with saving money that you didn't even push the government to spend funds that were allocated? [III:S]

The strategy of dilemma was used in fourteen questions.[17] Panelist Drew used it in six of her seven questions. Her second set of questions provides a good example. The original question in the set noted what she believed to be inconsistencies in past Ford statements on federal spending and taxation [I:K]. After Ford denied the existence of any inconsistency or dilemma, Drew then asked:

Sir, in the next few years would you try to reduce the deficit, would you spend money for these programs that you have just outlined, or would you, as you said earlier, return whatever surplus you got to the people in the form of tax relief? [I:L]

The omniscient panelist thus defined the available options for candidate Ford. If he accepted her definition, he was placed in a dilemma from which she apparently believed he could not escape.

In addition to arguing with the candidates, refuting them, and posing traps and dilemmas, the panelists often displayed hostility. This severely affected the tone of the debates, generated opposition between candidates and panelists, decreased the possibilities for clash between candidates, and worked to Ford's disadvantage.

Each debate question was analyzed and placed in one of three categories based on the extent of hostility present in the question—strongly hostile, slightly hostile, or non-hostile. Forty-one of the sixty-three questions were either strongly or slightly hostile.[18] Thirteen of the strongly hostile questions were directed to Ford and nine to Carter. Nine of the slightly hostile questions were directed to Ford and ten to Carter. The third debate was strikingly hostile, particularly toward Ford.

Several of the hostile questions contained implied or direct claims, charges, or challenges involving the ethos of the candidates—their character, honesty, judgment, qualifications. In her questions on budget balancing, Drew challenged each candidate's honesty [I:F,K,Q,R]. Reynolds questioned Ford's consistency in extending amnesty to Richard Nixon but not to all draft evaders [I:G]. Trewhitt implied possible recklessness in Carter's advocacy of an aggressive human rights policy [II:G,H]. Trewhitt also implied that Ford allowed domestic politics (the challenge from Ronald Reagan) to affect the SALT talks [II:M]. Joseph Kraft called on both candidates to be honest in outlining the sacrifices to be required of the American people in coming years [III:A]. Kraft also doubted Ford's sensitivity to the problems of the environment [III:J]. Jack Nelson appeared skeptical of Ford's claim that progress was being made in promoting civil rights and meeting the needs of minorities [III:L]. Nelson also suggested that Carter was not being specific in explaining his views on the Supreme Court [III:P,Q]. Robert Maynard seemed to doubt that Ford had even a rudimentary understanding of problems created by the existence of and easy access to handguns [III: N,O].

While the hostile questions just mentioned imply various character flaws in one or the other candidate, many other questions showed hostility in connection with decisions, present statements or actions, or future policies. Valeriani's question challenging Ford's past handling of the *Mayaguez* incident was typical of the hostile questions put to Ford. Valeriani cited a General Accounting Office report which (he said) suggested that Ford "shot from the hip" and "ignored diplomatic messages" in the *Mayaguez* affair. He then asked Ford if the White House tried to block the release of the report—implicitly raising the possibility of a cover-up [II:S].

In another instance, Jack Nelson implicitly accused Ford of being involved in a Watergate cover-up attempt:

Mr. President, you mentioned Watergate, and you became president because of Watergate. So don't you owe the American people a special obligation to explain in detail your role of limiting one of the original investigations of Watergate—that was the one by the House Banking Committee? [III:D]

Note that Nelson did not ask whether Ford was involved; his question, instead, implied that Ford's involvement was a fact and asked if there wasn't a special obligation on Ford's part to explain this involvement.

Robert Maynard—in assailing Ford's failure to fire General George Brown, who had made derogatory statements about Great Britain—prefaced his question by saying, "Sir, this question concerns your administrative performance as president"—thus directly challenging Ford's judgment [III:H]. In a different question, Maynard expressed astonishment that Ford did not share his own understanding of the problem of handguns and apparently could not recognize the need for national handgun legislation [III:N]. Perplexed at what he thought was Ford's failure to comprehend the relationship between guns and crime, he said, "But Mr. President, don't you think that the proliferation of the availability of handguns contributes to the possibility of those crimes being committed?'' [III:O]

Although Elizabeth Drew has quantitative superiority in the number of hostile questions asked, surely the most damaging hostility occurred in the questions of Joseph Kraft. He raised the issue of environmental protection, Ford's vetoes of the strip mining bill, his opposition to strong auto emission controls, and his absence of action to stop pollution of the Atlantic Ocean. Then, citing conclusions of an environmental interest group, Kraft asserted that the American people "want to know why a bipartisan organization such as the League of Conservation Voters says that when it comes to environmental issues, you are—and I'm quoting—'hopeless' '' [III:J]. Kraft's final set of questions described the consequences of the "economic pause," which he listed as low growth, high unemployment, a decline in take-home pay, lower factory earnings, and more layoffs. He then attributed these consequences to the Ford administration and charged Ford with compiling a "rotten record" on the economy [III:R].

Carter also was subjected to antagonistic questioning, although not to the same degree as Ford. His qualifications for the presidency were directly challenged twice. Valeriani, calling him a "Washington outsider" with "limited experience" in foreign affairs, implied that Carter was not capable of executing American foreign policy [II:C]. Nelson stated that many Americans still seemed "uneasy" despite the fact that Carter had been running for president for a long time. He then questioned whether Carter would have the ability to secure qualified people to run the government:

And one problem seems to be that you haven't reached out to bring people of broad background and national experience into your campaign or your presidential plans. Most of the people around you on a day-to-day basis are people you've known in Georgia. Many of them are young and relatively inexperienced in national affairs. And doesn't this raise a serious question as to whether you would bring into a Carter administration people with the necessary background to run the federal government? [III:I]

Joseph Kraft questioned the prudence of Carter's declaration that "I would not go to war in Yugoslavia, even if the Soviet Union sent in troops." He strongly suggested that such a statement was ill conceived and irresponsible:

Doesn't that statement practically invite the Russians to intervene in Yugoslavia? Doesn't it discourage Yugoslavs who might be tempted to resist? And wouldn't it have been wiser on your part to say nothing and to keep the Russians in the dark, as President Ford did, and as I think every president has done since President Truman? [III:F]

In the follow-up question Kraft asked if Carter had cleared the statement with his two foreign policy advisers, James Schlesinger and Averell Harriman. Kraft's tone in asking the question was clearly incredulous, as if he couldn't believe that a presidential candidate would make such a statement without first clearing it with his experienced advisers [III:G]. The clear implication in his follow-up was that Carter might make dangerous off-the-cuff statements on important matters without carefully weighing the possible consequences.

Twice in the third debate, Maynard asked Carter hostile questions about the campaign. He first claimed that the campaign had been conducted at a low level—"It has digressed frequently from important issues into allegations of blunder and brainwashing and fixations on lust and *Playboy*"—and then asked what responsibility Carter would accept for "the low level of this campaign for the nation's highest office?" [III:C] Not only was Maynard's reference to the *Playboy* interview hostile to Carter, but the whole import of his question was that Carter had become mired in irrelevant subjects instead of talking about important issues. Paradoxically, Maynard's question attempted to point out the small-mindedness of the campaign, but the question itself led to discussion of matters remote from an agenda of vital national issues. Maynard's final question asked Carter what had happened to his large lead in the public opinion polls and implied clearly that there must be something amiss with Carter or his campaign [III:T].

Hostile questions sometimes led to evasions and often to very defensive postures. By and large, hostility worked the most severe disadvantage to President Ford, who particularly bore the brunt of hostile questions from the third debate panel. Although not labelled as such, the impact of hostility on the candidates did not go unnoticed by some commentators. Columnist Bill Shipp of the *Atlanta Constitution* admired Jack Nelson's questioning: "As the night wore on, you could almost see Carter and Ford flinch when it came Nelson's turn to toss out a question, which for him was more like hurling a spear."[19] (The consequence of hostility upon candidate performance is discussed in chapter 4.)

Why were the panels so hostile? For that matter, why were they hostile at all? The most likely reason seems to be that the panelists identified with that part of the press for whom an adversary relationship with politicians is a habit or duty and were unable or unwilling to shed this role. The press is often called the Fourth Branch of Government, and many journalists hold that its proper function is that of a "watchdog" to keep government and politicians honest. The panelists earned acclaim from some quarters for their fulfillment of this role in the debates. Elizabeth Drew was praised for her tough questioning.[20] Jack Nelson's hard-hitting style was admired by Bill Shipp, who claimed that the real "winner" of Great Debate III was not Ford or Carter, but Nelson.[21]

A second possible explanation is that the panelists considered themselves in competition with the candidates and sought to upstage them. Media critic Marshall McLuhan commented that the panelists in the first debate were more imposing figures than Ford or Carter:

Why did Ms. Drew and Gannon and Reynolds look so much more impressive than the candidates? This is another medium trick. All those three sounded most authoritative and emphatic and they knew what they were talking about. . . . I mean the way they delivered themselves. It was authoritative, emphatic, like a good advertisement. Whereas, the candidates were groping around in the fog.[22]

If the panelists considered themselves to be fellow actors in a competitive performance, they might understandably seek good reviews by employing an effective strategy—that of appearing more knowledgeable and authoritative than the candidates.

The degree and direction of hostility changed over the three debates. The first panel, focusing on domestic and economic issues, was slightly more hostile to Carter than to Ford. Although the candidates received an equal number of questions showing some degree of hostility, Carter had to field four strongly hostile questions and Ford only two. The events of the campaign perhaps provide a partial explanation for this. At the time of the first debate, Carter held a commanding lead in the public opinion polls, but his position was slipping—in part because of his *Playboy* interview and an Associated Press interview in which he made some politically naive (and misinterpreted) statements about tax reform. In short, his campaign was floundering and he was under pressure to perform well in the first debate. Furthermore, he was still something of an unknown quantity to many Americans, including some members of the press, and the first debate—which Carter's campaign manager Hamilton Jordan had called "the big casino"[23]—would provide an opportunity for the press to examine and uncover Carter and his positions. For these and similar reasons, perhaps Carter was unintentionally targeted in the first debate. Ford's incumbency also may have had some influence on the first panel. As the first incumbent president to publicly debate his opponent, Ford may have received an extra measure of deference. Reynolds and Gannon in particular treated him with high respect.

The second debate panel, which posed questions on defense and foreign policy, was not as hostile as the first. Only two questions were strongly hostile, seven were slightly hostile, and twelve were non-hostile. The political positions of Ford and Carter may not have been conducive to hostile questioning. The foreign policy record of the Nixon and Ford administrations had been widely praised, which may have reduced the likelihood of hostile questions to Ford on foreign policy. The political position of Carter on foreign policy also seemed to shield him from hostile questioning: he had no record to defend, although he was open to charges of inexperience. By and large, Carter had not made foreign affairs a major campaign issue.

The third debate panel, which questioned the candidates on both domestic and foreign policy issues, was strongly hostile. Seven of nine questions put to Carter were strongly or slightly hostile. Ford, however, was under the greatest pressure: ten of the eleven questions to him were strongly hostile, and even the eleventh was slightly hostile. The extreme hostility of the third panel may be accounted for by several factors, listed according to increasing levels of plausibility. First, the novelty of an incumbent president debating his opponent had worn off, and consequently the third panel was far less reticent toward Ford than was the first panel.

Second, the last debate was held on October 22, only one and one-half weeks before the election. Because of the timing, panelists may have viewed the debates as the last opportunity to examine the president and his challenger closely. Such a viewpoint could result in tough questioning.

Third, the panel members may have sensed that viewers were dissatisfied with the relatively mild questioning styles of the earlier panels. Some observers had suggested that a good way to improve the debates would be to ask tougher questions:

Robert Hughes, Republican chairman of Ohio's Cuyahoga County . . . thought that . . . [the first] panel tossed too many soft questions at the candidates. "Where were the tough questions? Abortion. Busing. *Playboy*. The purpose of these debates is to challenge these two guys, and that wasn't done."[24]

It is reasonable to assume that Kraft, Maynard, and Nelson were aware of such suggestions. In fact, those very issues—abortion, busing and *Playboy*—were raised by the third panel. And the panel did "challenge these guys," for which it received acclaim. For example, William Greider in the *Washington Post* wrote:

. . . last night's questions from columnist Joseph Kraft, Robert Maynard of the *Washington Post*, and Jack Nelson of the *Los Angeles Times* were much tougher, more accusatory than in the previous shows. Kraft asked Ford at one point if his stewardship of the economy wasn't "rotten." All three took hard jabs at both men, though Ford seemed to get the worst of it. Those tough questions will be resented by some viewers, but they clearly improved the quality of the show—by putting sharp points on the areas of conflict between the two candidates. Their discussion of environmental issues, for instance, was a reasonable summary of two very different viewpoints.[25]

One of the reasons for the hostility of the third panel, therefore, may have been the desire of panelists to satisfy the expectations of some of the public—and some of their peers.

Fourth, the subject matter of the third debate was unfavorable to Ford. The panel decided to cover issues neglected in the first debate on the premise that the first panel had devoted inordinate time to economic and tax issues.[26] The neglected issues chosen by the panel would prove adverse to Ford—civil rights, Ford's possible role in Watergate, environmental issues, the problems of the cities, gun control, and the like.

Fifth, a partial explanation, perhaps, is that the panelists simply were tough questioners who would take a hostile attitude toward politicians almost instinctively, particularly toward Ford. Kraft had been a speechwriter for John Kennedy and is regarded as a moderately liberal columnist. Robert Maynard, as a representative of the *Washington Post* and the only black journalist on the debate panels, may have felt a special obligation to question Ford's record critically on matters of interest to black Americans and to live up to the *Post's* reputation for toughness. Jack Nelson is well known for his aggressive style. When Nelson wrote for the *Atlanta Constitution,* he was a thorn in the side of the then Governor of Georgia, Marvin Griffin, who later said to friends: "I used to wake up wondering what that little s.o.b. [Nelson] was going to try to do to me next."[27]

Finally, the hostile style of the third panel may have been conceived deliberately. According to Nelson, the panelists consulted before the debate. Their feeling was that "the previous questioners' failure to consult one another had limited their coverage of issues and caused some overlapping in questions."[28]

The panel's strategist may have been Kraft, who had written a column after the first debate in which he assessed the first panel and the character of the debate:

The debate between the presidential candidates on Thursday settled one matter, which is that the face-to-face televised encounters are almost surely not going to decide the presidential election. Those affairs are too managed, too heavily encumbered in advance planning, to yield a glimmer of spontaneity. . . . The questioners last Thursday were well briefed and serious. They asked about the big subjects—inflation, taxation, unemployment, energy. Inevitably the questions were complicated, and they could not have enlightened much of the American public. I found myself bored to the point of yawning and often confused. . . . The answers corresponded exactly with the questions. Both candidates had worked up pat positions, from which they varied hardly at all.

The column contains musings on the style and goals of questioning:

It takes a rare skill, a good deal of luck and not a little tricky editing to elicit an impromptu comment from any subject. It is significant that most of the very best television interviewers—David Frost in Britain, for example, or Mike Wallace in this country—generally ask offbeat questions, which in effect rip off the mask of self-awareness. But that approach is clearly inappropriate to debates between candidates for the White House.[29]

Kraft's disclaimer that offbeat questions are inappropriate to presidential debates is hardly convincing, however. In the third debate, he was the panelist who asked an incumbent president why his environmental record was regarded as "hopeless" and, in another question, asserted that Ford's economic record was "rotten." In the third debate, numerous questions from the panel appeared to be designed—in Kraft's words—to "yield a glimmer of spontaneity" and to "rip off the mask of self-awareness."

Kraft reiterated these views and added others in an article written during his own preparation for the final debate. Apparently, one of his goals was to reveal the "authentic" candidate:

The starting point is what Lionel Trilling . . . identified as the problem of "authenticity." Candidates and questioners alike are immensely self-conscious, and find it difficult not to play roles and indulge egos. Virtually all questions have been asked before and answered before. So a first objective is to find ways that break out President Ford and Jimmy Carter as human beings, that show them thinking on their feet, reacting spontaneously as they would have to in the White House.[30]

Kraft remarked in this column, as he did in the earlier one, upon the skill of such interviewers as David Frost and Oriani Fallaci, who "know how to penetrate poses and reach the core of personality." In addition, he indicated his own conviction that both candidates were reluctant to acknowledge the economic consequences of the policies they were advocating: "How does anybody get him [Carter] to acknowledge the risks and costs implicit in his policies?"; and, "How does one get Mr. Ford to acknowledge the risks he must know attend his own policies?" Kraft claimed that both candidates made "egregious errors" in the first and second debates that ought to be confessed: "The tone of the campaign would be heightened if both men would admit these and other errors. But how do you get political candidates to acknowledge mistakes in public, without seeming offensive or lacking in respect?" Kraft concluded his column by remarking that the debates, though imperfect, still seemed to him "the best way the public can develop insight into the character of the men who would be President."

Kraft's views, as revealed in his columns, provide interesting background for speculation about his own performance in the third debate. First, according to Kraft, good questions penetrate poses and reveal authentic or real human beings by forcing the candidates to think on their feet and react spontaneously—"as they would have to in the White House." In his opinion, almost all questions had been asked and answered before; thus the answers were less important than what happened in the process of answering—that is, what the candidates revealed to the public about their inner selves as they grappled with tough or unexpected questions. Kraft's own selection and hostile wording of questions may have been the end result of an attempt by him to reveal personality and spontaneous behavior. Second, Kraft believed that the candidates had been holding back—not telling all—and moreover, that they were guilty of errors which they ought to admit. Third, although he did not say so explicitly in the columns, his comments clearly imply that he believed the duty of the journalist-panelist was to unmask the genuine personalities of the candidates, get them to admit they were guilty of past errors, and force them to acknowledge the dangers inherent in their proposed policies. With this in mind, Kraft wondered before the debate what kind of questions were needed to achieve results.

It is significant that Kraft took upon himself a public role of unmasker, revealer, and task-setter. His concern was with the kind of questions he and his colleagues should ask in order to reveal insights for the public into "the character of the men who would be President." Not once did he ask how he and other panelists, through skillful questioning, might encourage the candidates *to debate each other* on national issues. Kraft's columns suggest that he saw himself in combat with the candidates. His performance in the third debate confirms this hypothesis.

Had we known before the third debate that the panel's questions would be so hostile to Ford both in substance and in tone, and had other factors in the debate remained constant, then we should have been able to predict the following outcomes with a strong degree of probability: (1) Ford would need to debate the panel—he did; (2) Carter would "win"—he did; and (3) the panel would play a large role in determining the outcome of the debate—which it did.

Clearly, the reporters in the 1976 presidential debates went far beyond the role of questioning the candidates. They argued, posed dilemmas, sought to entrap, assumed the posture of omniscient inquisitor, and raised hostile questions. Chiding, complaining, and making accusations, the panelists were adversaries of Ford and Carter, and the candidates probably had more to fear from them than from each other. The physical arrangement of the debates was symbolically accurate: the candidates stood on one side, and the panelists sat on the other. Gladiators Ford and Carter faced a common enemy.

This analysis and evaluation of the panels, their questions, and their role in the debates lead us to the following conclusions.

First, a substantial portion of the questions were inap-

propriate for various reasons—because of error, misinterpretation, triviality, irrelevancy, redundancy. Many questions
were specifically tailored to one candidate, thus limiting the
prospects for clear, well-focused debate, and often throwing the
advantage to the other candidate. Follow-up questions were
seldom useful. To the extent that inappropriate questions entered the debates, many compelling issues did not. The
responsibility for assuring that critical questions were placed
before the candidates—and before the public—rested with the
panelists. They failed badly in meeting this responsibility.

Second, many of the questions lacked focus and clarity.
There were many multiple, indirect, global questions—
sometimes coupled with accusations. Some questions placed
unreasonable demands on the candidates; some were so obscure
or so loaded with options that the candidate simply spoke to his
own interpretation of the question or responded to the less-
demanding of the alternatives. The presence of multiple
questions and of overt and covert charges clouded the issues and
sharply limited prospects for debate, as did questions which
lacked focus.

Third, panelists initiated an adversary relationship between
themselves and the candidates. They argued more often than not
from a substantive position, almost always unfavorable to the
candidate addressed, and sometimes used strategies designed to
elicit a particular response or concession. In some instances,
panelists went beyond mere "tough questioning": they sought
to outwit the candidates and put them in an unfavorable light.
Some accusations made by panelists were as serious as those
made by the candidates: Carter was accused, among other
things, of over-promising, of allowing his campaign to
degenerate, of being slightly reckless in foreign affairs
statements, and of being insufficiently qualified for the
presidency. Ford was subjected to even greater hostility—
accused of being an incompetent administrator, a party to an
early Watergate cover-up, a person "hopeless" on environmental issues, and a president responsible for a "rotten"
economic record. The adversary role played by the panelists
suggests that they believed the contest to be between the press

and the candidates, rather than between Ford and Carter. Or perhaps a more generous interpretation is that the panelists thought of themselves as select participants in a special joint press conference.

An argument could be made that there were three parties rather than two in the debates and that the journalists, including the moderators, actually amounted to the dominant "speaker"—enforcing the rules, keeping time on the candidates, opening and closing each debate, announcing when one candidate or another was entitled to speak—in short, controlling the situation. The journalists largely determined the topics; and they set the tone of the debate to a significant extent by the temper of their questions, the frequently accusatory character of their remarks, and the subjects they selected. The panelists and the moderators spoke more frequently, though not at greater length, than the candidates. In the three debates, the time consumed by panel questioning was thirty-two minutes and thirty-eight seconds—13 percent of the total debate time. The number of words spoken by the panelists (5,506 words) amounted to 15 percent of the total in the debates. The dominance of the journalists was reflected clearly in the deference shown to them by the candidates. Not once did a candidate reprimand or speak harshly to the panelists; on the other hand, the panelists chided the candidates and frequently treated them as if they were subservient. The panel members and the moderators enjoyed a privileged status and they used it. In the Lincoln-Douglas debates, there was no such third party.

We return, then, to the perspective of Walter Mears, who remarked that "those of us who questioned the candidates were not nearly so important as we would like to think." Mears was clearly mistaken; the panelists were every bit as important as they "would like to think." The audience surely was not fully aware of the role being played by the panels; and almost certainly the audience did not tune in to see and hear journalists. But journalists it got—and a heavy measure at that!

4. The Skills of Verbal Combat

Pre-debate commentary by members of the press included speculation on the debate abilities of Ford and Carter and the factors which would influence the final outcome. The public learned that the candidates were preparing for debate by studying position papers, and that both were confident. Some commentators pointed out that President Ford, because of his many years in the House of Representatives, might be a surprisingly good debater. On the other hand, although inexperienced in face-to-face debate, Carter could prove to be dangerously effective in using language. The public was reminded that Ford's position and long government experience would surely give him a good command of facts relevant to domestic and foreign issues and policies, and that Carter could use the debates to appear "decisive" and dispel talk that he "waffled" on issues. The general press consensus was that Ford must display competence in order to remove an unflattering part of his image as a "nice guy, but not too smart, and somewhat clumsy"; and further, that Carter had only to hold his own in the debates, whereas Ford needed a victory.[1]

These prognostications obviously included some elements of truth. The major reasons for Carter's victory over Ford in the debates bear little resemblance to pre-debate speculation, however. They rest instead upon important and mostly unforeseen factors. Who could have anticipated the extreme hostility that the third debate panel directed toward Ford? Or the blow that Ford dealt himself by asserting in the second debate that Eastern European countries are not under the domination of the Soviet Union? Carter, if untutored in debate, learned quickly how to score: by discovering and using the strategic possibilities of the chosen format, and by employing a wide range of argumentation skills, he battered Ford in round after round in the second and third debates. Ford debated ably enough in the first encounter to earn a slight edge in the public opinion polls. He faltered badly under Carter's attacks in the second debate, however, and fared very poorly in the third debate, when both the panelists and Carter pressured him severely. Even such elementary matters as skill in argument and rapidity of speech were rarely mentioned in pre-debate speculation, although both factors were instrumental in Carter's victory. Carter outscored Ford by a wide margin on initiative, aggressiveness, skill in attack and rebuttal, versatility of argument, quick wit and style—also factors scarcely recognized in pre-debate analyses.

In 1976, the public was not exposed to debates marked by penetrating thought, eloquent language, or rigorous argument. Discourse at that level may have been beyond reach of the candidates; and even if provided, it might have been tuned out by a vast and languid audience. Nevertheless, one conclusion is certain: superior debate was neither invited nor permitted by the chosen format, which channelled rhetorical skills toward the short answer, the worn commonplace, the quick argument, the hard-hitting charge, the strategic attack, the slogan, the image. Mundane rhetoric is the almost inevitable consequence of such a format.

INITIATIVE: BREAKING OUT OF THE FORMAT DILEMMA

In all likelihood, the speaker who initiates—who takes the lead in defining the debate terms and issues, capturing the most

favorable argumentative ground, and throwing his opponent on
the defensive—will gain some advantage in any debate format.
The Ford-Carter debate format, however, was so designed that
initiative became a necessary condition of the very act of
debating, as well as a key to victory. The format imposed a basic
dilemma—whether to answer or to debate. Carter's success in
breaking out of this dilemma by turning his answers into
initiative speeches was his springboard to other advantages.

Original and follow-up speeches, which accounted for 63 of
the 109 speeches in the three debates, were generally in the form
of answers. Each occurred in a highly constraining situation in
which the most powerful constraint was the question (or
questions) posed by the panelist. For example, Nelson's questions to Ford about possible Watergate involvement literally
demanded specific answers [III:D,E]. Drew's questions to
Carter about tax reform measures also called for specific answers [I:Q,R].

The fact that *answer* was the predominant form of
discourse used in the original and follow-up speeches may
appear at first to be insignificant. This form, however, runs
counter to the very idea of debate. In a debate, the essential
form of speech is *argument,* consisting of proposition and
proof. Debate requires a proposition which is in contention and
speeches offering arguments to support or oppose that
proposition. In the presidential debates, the panelists seldom
used propositions. Instead, they placed questions before the
candidates. In doing so, they created a serious dilemma: if the
candidates faithfully answered the questions and nothing more,
they failed to engage each other in debate; on the other hand, if
they tried to debate each other in their responses, they risked
inadequately answering the questions.

Did the candidates stay within the "sphere of influence"
delineated by the questions? Or did they free themselves from
the constraints of the questions and initiate different lines of
thought, new agenda issues, charges and criticisms against each
other? In short, to what extent did Ford and Carter use initiative
in order to debate, and how much were they controlled by the
questions?

An analysis of all of the original and follow-up speeches shows that forty-six of the total of sixty-three were controlled by the questions: that is, the form of each was essentially that of an *answer*. The remaining seventeen speeches displayed considerable initiative. The difference between Ford and Carter is striking. Ford nearly always stayed within the control of the question: only three of his thirty-three original and follow-up speeches could be regarded as displaying initiative; the remaining thirty were answers to questions. Carter frequently broke through the constraints of a specific question in order to make his "answer" serve duty as an initiative speech: he turned fourteen of his thirty original and follow-up responses into speeches which initiated charges and issues; the remaining sixteen were answers.

All three of Ford's initiative speeches occurred in the first debate. In one of these, after answering the question, he placed on the debate agenda a matter of importance to him—the extent to which his vetoes had reduced spending:

I think it's interesting to point out that in the two years that I've been president, I've vetoed fifty-six bills. Congress has sustained forty-two vetoes. As a result, we have saved over 9 billion dollars in federal expenditures. And the Congress, by overriding the bills that I did veto, the Congress has added some 13 billion dollars to the federal expenditures and to the federal deficit. Now, Governor Carter complains about the deficits that this administration has had, and yet he condemns the vetoes that I have made that have saved the taxpayer 9 billion dollars and could have saved an additional 13 billion dollars. Now he can't have it both ways. And, therefore, it seems to me that we should hold the lid, as we have to the best of our ability, so we can stimulate the private economy and get the jobs where the jobs are—five out of six in this economy. [23]

In another instance, after Reynolds had asked a vague question about causes of the anti-Washington feeling, Ford initiated criticism of the Congress [I:28]. In the third instance, he introduced a new line of thought after briefly answering the question—that in order to work properly, the nation's system of checks and balances required a Republican president to check a Democratic Congress [I:29]. Other Ford speeches included brief attacks and charges against Carter, but only these three speeches introduced lengthy units of discourse on matters outside the influence of the questions.

Four of Carter's original and follow-up speeches showing initiative occurred in the first debate, seven in the second, and three in the final debate.[2] For example, Carter used a somewhat vague question by Reynolds on the safety of nuclear power plants to initiate discussion of the need for a national energy policy [I:19]. He used Frankel's opening question in the second debate to initiate a broad attack on Ford's conduct of foreign policy [II:1]. In each of his seven initiative speeches in the second debate, Carter followed the same loose pattern: he provided a more-or-less-adequate answer to the question, and then carried the debate to his opponent by taking the offensive with criticism of Ford and of Ford's policies. In the third debate, two of Carter's initiative speeches followed this pattern—his speech on the issue of Mondale versus Dole [III:14], and the one on the issue of urban policy [III:18].

The following example illustrates Carter's technique of breaking away from the question in order to initiate agenda issues and to direct criticisms (mild ones, in this case) at his opponent:

REYNOLDS: Governor Carter, I'd like to turn to what we used to call the energy crisis. Yesterday, a British government commission on air pollution, but one headed by a nuclear physicist, recommended that any further expansion of nuclear energy be delayed in Britain as long as possible. Now this is a subject that is quite controversial among our own people and there seems to be a clear difference between you and the president on the use of nuclear power plants, which you say you would use as a last priority. Why, sir? Are they unsafe?

CARTER: Well, among my other experiences in the past, I've been a nuclear engineer and did graduate work in this field. I think I know the capabilities and limitations of atomic power. But the energy policy of our nation is one that has not yet been established under this administration. I think almost every other developed nation in the world has an energy policy except us.

We have seen the Federal Energy Agency established, for instance. In the crisis of 1973 it was supposed to be a temporary agency. Now it's permanent. It's enormous. It's growing every day. And I think the *Wall Street Journal* reported not too long ago, they have 112 public relations experts working for the Federal Energy Agency to try to justify to the American people its own existence.

We've got to have a firm way to handle the energy question. The reorganization proposal that I put forward is one first step. In addition to that, we need to have a realization that we've got about thirty-five years worth of oil left in the whole world. We're going to run out of oil. When Mr. Nixon made his famous speech on Operation Independence, we were importing about 35 percent of our oil. Now we've increased that amount 25 percent. We now import about 44 percent of our oil. We need to shift from oil to coal. We need to concentrate our research and development effort on coal burning and extraction that's safe for miners, that also is clean burning. We need to shift very strongly toward solar energy and have strict conservation measures; and then, as a last resort only, continue to use atomic power.

I would certainly not cut out atomic power altogether. We can't afford to give up that opportunity until later. But to the extent that we continue to use atomic power, I would be responsible as president to make sure that the safety precautions were initiated and maintained. For instance, some that have been forgotten: we need to have the reactor core below ground level; the entire power plant, that uses atomic power, tightly sealed and a heavy vacuum maintained; there ought to be a standardized design; there ought to be a full-time atomic energy specialist, independent of the power company, in the control room full-time, twenty-four hours a day, to shut down the plant if an abnormality develops.

These kinds of procedures, along with evacuation procedures, adequate insurance, ought to be initiated. So, shift from oil to coal; emphasize research and development on coal use and also on solar power; strict conservation measures; not yield every time that the special interest groups put pressure on the president, like this administration has done; and use atomic energy only as a last resort with the strictest possible safety precautions. That's the best overall energy policy in the brief time we have to discuss it. [I:19]

Notwithstanding Reynolds' fuzzy introductory material, his question was specific and narrow in scope: why would Carter use nuclear power plants only as a last priority? Carter answered the question in the last half of his speech. In the first half, he initiated an agenda issue—the need for a national energy policy.

As might be expected, the rejoinder speeches were less constrained by panel questions, mainly because an original, or both an original and a follow-up, speech intervened between each question and the rejoinder speaker's response. Ford presented seven rejoinders that showed initiative. In each, his typical pattern was first to attack Carter's positions and then to present his own view [for example, I:3,9,15,27]. Carter presented sixteen initiative rejoinders—more than twice as many as Ford. The Carter rejoinders usually were vigorous attacks and rebuttals. In the first debate, four severely attacked Ford [6,18,24,30] and one introduced a new issue—equity in the criminal justice system—after chiding Ford [12]. Carter was most aggressive in the second debate: three rejoinders were full-fledged attacks on Ford [16,22,27]; two were mild criticisms [31,35]; and two commenced with a brief self-defense and then attacked Ford [4,10]. In the final debate, three Carter rejoinders consisted entirely of refutation and attack—on Ford's record on the environment, civil rights, and the economy [17,21,32]—and two others included milder attacks [13,26].

Interestingly, seven rejoinder speeches were essentially "answers"—that is, responses controlled by panelists' questions. Two of these were by Carter and five by Ford.[3] These seven rejoinders share a common characteristic: each occurred immediately after the opponent had delivered a speech (or speeches) which failed to seriously challenge or attack the rejoinder speaker. Unconstrained by challenges from his opponent, the rejoinder speaker responded to the panelist's original or follow-up question. The remainder of the rejoinder speeches, by and large, engaged in attack and defense, charge and countercharge. Debate between the candidates occurred far more often in rejoinders than in the original and follow-up speeches.

Because a rejoinder speaker was seldom under the control of the panel question addressed to his opponent, rejoinders as a class were more free than original and follow-up speeches. Nevertheless, they were constrained to some extent when the preceding speech or speeches initiated issues, challenges, and charges to which the rejoinder speaker felt obliged to respond.

For this reason, eight rejoinders were essentially defensive, and all eight were delivered by Ford. In the first debate, when Ford was defending himself against the charge that his administration had done nothing to develop a national energy policy, his rejoinder was defensive from beginning to end [21]. In the second debate, Carter's aggressiveness prompted five defensive Ford rejoinders [7,13,19,24,33]. In the final debate, two Ford rejoinders were defensive: once, pressed by Carter, he defended his choice of Robert Dole as his running mate [15], and later, in response to Carter attacks, he defended his administration against the charge that it had no urban policy [19]. In all of the debates combined, Ford presented six aggressive rejoinders and eight defensive rejoinders; Carter presented sixteen aggressive rejoinders and no defensive ones.[4]

The rejoinder speaker occasionally enjoyed nearly absolute freedom. This occurred when two factors were present: the opponent had received a question so one-sided that it simply did not apply to the rejoinder speaker; and at the same time, the opponent had not issued any challenge to which the rejoinder speaker felt obliged to respond. The clearest instance occurred in the third debate when Nelson twice pressed Ford to explain his connection with an early Watergate investigation and Ford's replies were entirely defensive. Carter, who was left absolutely free in the rejoinder position, shrewdly chose to say nothing. In the three debates, Carter enjoyed a high degree of freedom in sixteen and Ford in ten rejoinders. In this respect, defective panel questions helped Carter to obtain a distinct advantage.

Why was Carter able to break through the constraints of the panelists' questions more than four times as often as Ford? And why, in rejoinder speeches, was Carter so much more initiative and aggressive in debating than Ford? We might conjecture that Ford responded with "answers" in the belief that this was more appropriate, more presidential; or that Carter decided to be initiative and aggressive in order to portray himself as bright and energetic, youthful and vigorous. Another explanation, no doubt equally plausible, is that Carter and Ford differed in talent, especially in creativity, cleverness, and quick wit.

The hostility of many questions seriously reduced the

possibility for initiative speeches. Carter had to defend himself three times under hostile questioning in the third debate. In the same debate the panelists asked Ford so many hostile questions that ten of his original and follow-up speeches were almost of necessity defensive.[5] The questions were particularly damaging to Ford because of their frequency and seriousness. It was extremely difficult for him to initiate debate with Carter while defending himself against so many hostile questions. As a result, Carter enjoyed a double advantage: first, the panelists hurt his opponent; second, and equally important, Ford's failure to initiate debate left Carter "free" in five rejoinder speeches from any burden of response. The freedom was put to good use: while the third panel was caging Ford with hostile questions, Carter landed punches on Ford in rejoinders as well as in his original and follow-up speeches, putting the beleaguered president on the defensive not only in virtually all of his original and follow-up speeches, but in two of his seven rejoinders as well.

Several conclusions may be drawn. The debate format placed candidates in a subordinate relationship to the panels: Ford and Carter were expected to answer whatever questions they were asked by the panelists. This, in turn, created a dilemma for the candidates—whether, or how much, they should depart from the questions in order to debate each other. This basic format deficiency could easily have been avoided by either eliminating the panels or assuring that panelists placed debatable propositions, instead of questions, before the candidates. Ford was significantly more submissive to panel influence; Carter evidently learned in the first debate that he could, and should, be less submissive. A comparison of Carter's speeches in the first and second debates shows a striking difference: in the second debate, his rejoinders as well as his original and follow-up speeches were highly initiative. Finally, the debater who initiates issues and challenges is more likely to gain an edge. To the extent that his speeches are well designed, the initiative debater can control the focus of debate by placing *his* issues on the agenda; he can attack with greater frequency and put his adversary on the defensive; and he can convey the image of a forceful, able speaker. Carter enjoyed all of these advantages and more.

AGENDA-BUILDING BY THE CANDIDATES

Primary responsibility for placing issues on the debate agenda rested with the panelists in the 1976 presidential debates. Ford and Carter initiated additional issues, however—sometimes because they thought the issues worthy of discussion, sometimes for tactical advantage, and at least once simply by accident. Some issues initiated by one speaker were never dealt with by the other, nor made the focus of a panelist's subsequent question. A few issues did result in clash. For purposes of this review, an agenda issue is defined as an issue which occurred in one or more speeches and received strong enough emphasis and amplification that an observant critic would judge that the candidate meant to underscore its importance and relevance.

Two classes of candidate-introduced issues occurred in the debates. The first class consisted of five general or thematic issues which were addressed in several speeches. Two of these issues were introduced by Ford and three by Carter. The second class included twenty-six specific issues which were introduced by the candidates—eleven by Ford and fifteen by Carter. Although these figures indicate no significant advantage to Carter, his aggressive initiation of issues gave them saliency and often placed Ford on the defensive. The best of Carter's issues also had greater substantive worth than the best of Ford's. Moreover, some Ford issues were almost futile—hardly issues on which he could "score." The "Eastern Europe" issue, which Ford himself initiated, may well have unnerved him and affected his second debate performance; there is little doubt that it severely damaged his credibility and threw his campaign off track.

THEMATIC ISSUES

Five issues introduced by the candidates appeared and reappeared in speeches throughout the three debates, as if to tell viewers that the candidates regarded these issues as the critical ones. One of the two initiated by Ford was an attack on Carter's ethos and the second was a traditional pocketbook issue.[6] Two of the three Carter issues directly challenged Ford's competence, and the third called for a higher measure of moral integrity in foreign affairs, at the same time chiding Nixon-Ford policies.

Carter is inconsistent, inaccurate, lacks specificity, and overpromises. There is reason to believe that Ford came into each debate prepared to underscore this issue. It was initiated at his first opportunity to speak and restated in several forms throughout the debates. His opening words in the first debate were, "I don't believe that Mr. Carter has been any more specific in this case than he has been on many other instances" [3]. His opening speech in the second debate commenced, "Governor Carter again is talking in broad generalities" [2]. And in the final debate, his last rejoinder concerning his and Carter's election prospects began, "I think the increase in the prospects as far as I'm concerned and the less-favorable prospects for Governor Carter reflect that Governor Carter is inconsistent in many of the positions that he takes. He tends to distort on a number of occasions" [III:34].

Variations on this theme occurred several times in other challenges to Carter's credibility. In one instance, after Carter had outlined in some detail the need for mandatory conservation and a national energy policy, and for safety precautions at nuclear power plants [I:19,20], Ford commented, "Governor Carter skims over a very serious and a very broad subject" [I:21]. After Carter had outlined proposed tax reform measures [I:25,26], Ford opened his rejoinder by saying, "Governor Carter's answer tonight does not coincide with the answer that he gave in an interview to the Associated Press a week or so ago." In the same speech, he later charged Carter with playing "a little fast and loose with the facts about vetoes" [I:27]. At the end of the first debate, he announced that "one of the major issues in this campaign is trust," and his subsequent remarks in the peroration bore clearly on the issue of Carter's character and competence: "A president should never promise more than he can deliver, and a president should always deliver everything that he's promised. A president should be the same thing to all people" [I:36]. In the second debate, Ford began a speech by noting, "Governor Carter again contradicts himself" [7]. Later, discussing possible cuts in the defense budget, he charged Carter with advocating conflicting cuts, one of which was 15 billion dollars, but "he's now down to a figure of 5 to 7 billion dollars" [II:19]. Carter never acknowledged that Ford's attack on his credibility and competence was a basic issue, of course. His strategy was to seek to display specificity, consistency, trust-worthiness, and command of factual material in his speeches.

Ford handled this issue intermittently and in fragments. He never developed a full-scale attack, although there were two major opportunities to do so. In the second debate Valeriani asked a triple question regarding Carter's conception of the national interest, his view of the United States' role in the world, and his possible key foreign affairs appointments. The question included a subordinate challenge—that Carter had limited experience and was a Washington outsider [C]. Carter responded to the challenge by devoting nearly all of his speech to a defense of his credentials [5]. In his rejoinder, Ford could have taken advantage of the Valeriani question and Carter's response by making a systematic assessment of Carter's preparation for the presidency. Instead, he addressed other aspects of Carter's original and follow-up speeches [7]. An even riper opportunity arose in the third debate when Nelson challenged both Carter's competence and that of his advisers [I]. In his response, Carter reviewed his contact with the public through twenty-one months of campaigning, affirmed the quality of his advisers, and gave an example of the care he would use in appointing persons of high merit. The example he cited was the careful procedure he used in selecting Walter Mondale as his running mate, a procedure he contrasted with Ford's method of selecting Robert Dole [14]. The Mondale-Dole comparison placed a burden of response on Ford, who used all of his rejoinder to defend Dole and mildly attack Mondale [15], thus losing another opportunity to challenge Carter on the basic issue.

This Ford-initiated challenge of Carter's competence and trustworthiness was a potentially strong debate issue for three reasons. First, the ground was already cultivated: Carter's opponents in the Democratic primary elections had charged him with waffling on issues, lack of specificity, and lack of preparedness for the presidency. Second, Ford's own radio and television advertisements had focused sharply on the issue of Carter's inconsistencies, inexperience, and status as an unknown quantity; the "man on the street" genre of commercials in particular had announced the issue to the public. Third, in the days just before the debates, Carter's campaign had been weakened by reaction to the *Playboy* interview and by inaccurate reporting of his remarks on tax reform in an Associated Press interview—events which raised doubts in the minds of some voters regarding his competence. Thus, Carter was vulnerable and the issue was ripe.

Ford never succeeded in treating this issue effectively, however. To forcefully articulate and set it in the public mind, he needed only to use two or three carefully chosen examples and well-amplified speech units, taking care that no doubts about his own competence were allowed to intervene and neutralize the issue. Instead, he usually challenged Carter's credibility and competence with a sentence or two here and there, even failing to take advantage of opportunities which arose when panelists themselves opened the issue. Furthermore, several of his efforts to underscore the issue were ill conceived. Charging that Carter had mismanaged state government in Georgia, Ford cited words of Carter's successor to prove his point [I:15]. The force of this example was diminished the next day when press reports noted that Ford had misinterpreted Georgia Governor Busbee's remarks. Some other examples used by Ford to discredit Carter's ethos were easy targets for rebuttal. For example, Ford's charge that Carter was inconsistent, as shown by his Associated Press interview [I:27], was quickly and sharply checked by Carter, who said, "Mr. Ford has misquoted an AP news story that was in error to begin with. . . . I'm sure that the president knows about this correction, but he still insists on repeating an erroneous statement" [I:30]. A Ford charge that Carter had called for different cuts in defense spending at different times [II:2] was dampened by Carter's denial, and by his countercharge that Ford had permitted the defense budget to become "a political football" [II:4]. In these and other instances, Ford's attack was weakened either by the use of unconvincing material or by Carter's responses. Ford should have set forth a systematic display of Carter's inaccuracies, waffling, inconsistencies, etc., but this was never done. Perhaps of even more importance, Ford weakened the issue by his own performance—particularly his Eastern European blunder in the second debate. He could hardly win on the issue of competence by creating more doubts about his own competence than about Carter's.

Carter is committed to excessive spending. Never the focus of a well-defined unit, this issue nevertheless was stated so many times that the message was clear: the election of Carter and his subsequent control of the federal government, in collaboration with a Democratic Congress, would sharply increase spending. Ford's very first speech claimed that the Humphrey-Hawkins bill (supported, he said, by Carter and the Democrats) would cost "10 to 30 billion dollars each year in additional expenditures" [I:3]. He later commented that the Congress had added "about 17 billion dollars in more spending . . . over the budget that I recommended" [I:5]. In addition, Ford claimed that Carter's record as governor of Georgia provided evidence of his excessive spending [I:15]; that Carter had indicated he would increase federal spending for education by 30 billion dollars [I:16]; that the Democratic platform would cost the taxpayers "100 billion dollars minimum and probably 200 billion dollars maximum each year" [I:17].

Numerous other examples of this issue occurred in the first debate: the Congress, by overriding Ford vetoes, added "some 13 billion dollars to the federal expenditures and to the federal budget" [23]; Carter would increase taxes "for roughly half of the taxpayers of this country" [27]; Congress spends too much money on itself—"the next Congress will probably be the first billion-dollar Congress in the history of the United States" [28]; if Carter were elected, the nation would have "a Democratic Congress next year and a president who wants to spend an additional 100 billion dollars a year or maybe 200 billion dollars a year with more programs," and that would mean greater deficits and greater danger of inflation [29]. Finally, Ford's peroration in the first debate specifically underscored the issue: ". . . Governor Carter has endorsed the Democratic platform, which calls for more spending, bigger deficits, more inflation, or more taxes. Governor Carter has embraced the record of the present Congress dominated by his political party. It calls for more of the same" [36]. Ford frequently made these charges against Carter within the context of discussing his own policies, which emphasized "holding the lid on spending," providing tax relief, and in general continuing a "responsible" fiscal policy.

This pocketbook issue, fleshed out in parts of several speeches, was Ford's most powerful issue. On his side was evidence that he could recite with ease—his vetoes of spending bills, Carter's support of programs likely to increase spending, high spending levels implicit in the Democratic platform, etc. Ford received aid on this issue from the first debate panel, which pressed Carter to explain how money could be saved by reorganizing government, how the budget could be balanced, and how tax reform would increase the treasury.[7] Carter's efforts to rebut Ford were less than convincing.

The strength of the issue is surely one reason for Ford's relatively good performance in the first debate when the subject was domestic affairs, and in particular, matters of taxation and budget. There was little opportunity to pursue the issue in the second debate, however, since the principal subject was foreign affairs. Furthermore, Ford had little chance to press the issue in the third debate—which was open to any topic—because he was so often shackled by the panel's questions. Thus, the strength of his best issue was limited mainly to the first debate.[8]

Ford has shown defective leadership and lack of vision and sensitivity. Running through all three debates was the fundamental issue of leadership in the Ford administration: Carter charged that the administration suffered from absence of vision, tendency to yield to pressure, standstill policy, and insensitivity to the needs of the unemployed, the underprivileged, the disadvantaged. Examples from each debate show how frequently, and in what guises, this issue appeared.

In the first debate, when discussing economic programs, Carter charged Ford with taking a "typical Republican attitude" just before elections of favoring programs he had earlier opposed, and with yielding to pressure from special interest groups [18,19]. Ford "doesn't seem to put into perspective the fact that when 500,000 more people are out of work than there were three months ago or we have two and a half million more people out of work than were when he took office, that this touches human beings." In the same speech, Carter said that Ford's "insensitivity in providing those people a chance to work has made this a welfare administration and not a work administration"; that current unemployment and inflation was a "travesty" which indicated a "breakdown in leadership" [24]; and that Ford had not accomplished any major programs [30]. "We've suffered because we haven't had leadership in this administration. We've got a government of stalemate, and we've lost the vision of what our country can and ought to be" [35].

In the second debate, Carter's first speech contained numerous barbed attacks: the administration's foreign policy had been "almost all style and spectacular, and not substance"; foreign policy had lost "the character of the American people"; the Soviet Union had been getting the best of us; and "Mr. Ford, Mr. Kissinger have continued on with the policies and failures of Richard Nixon. Even the Republican platform has criticized the lack of leadership in Mr. Ford. . . ." And Carter concluded, "As far as foreign policy goes, Mr. Kissinger has been the president of this country. Mr. Ford has shown an absence of leadership, and an absence of a grasp of what this country is and what it ought to be. That's got to be changed. And that is one of the major issues of this campaign of 1976" [1]. Carter charged that Ford had yielded to pressure from the Soviet Union in refusing to see Solzhenitsyn [10]; that the opportunity opened in 1972 for better relations with mainland China "has pretty well been frittered away under Mr. Ford" [16]; that the United States could not have stature and respect in foreign affairs under Ford [17]; and that Ford had made no progress on new SALT agreements, had yielded to pressure from industry, and exhibited "confusion and absence of leadership" [22]. Under the Ford administration, said Carter, America's economic and moral strength had deteriorated [23]. Ford administration officials, in permitting the Arab boycott of American businesses to continue, were allowing a foreign country to "circumvent or change our Bill of Rights"; and, "I think it's a disgrace that so far Mr. Ford's administration has blocked the passage of legislation that would have revealed by law every instance of the boycott. . . ." [32] Carter claimed that Ford had not worked aggressively to seek information about Americans missing in action in Vietnam—an "embarrassing failure" that "touches specifically on human rights" [35]. Carter's peroration announced specifically that one of the three basic issues is leadership [36].

Carter toned down his attack in the third debate, but the theme of poor leadership continued: for example, the aggressive leadership needed to help black Americans and other minorities has "been lacking in the last eight years" [21]; and the high unemployment rate tolerated by Ford "shows a callous indifference to the families that have suffered so much" [32]. Carter's closing statement at the end of the third debate underscored faults in Ford's leadership through the use of faint praise and a damning comparison: "Mr. Ford is a good and decent man, but he's been in office now more than eight hundred days, approaching almost as long as John Kennedy was in office. I'd like to ask the American people what—what's been accomplished. A lot remains to be done." The peroration was free of direct attack on Ford, but in listing failures and aspirations, Carter made it clear that the failures belonged to Ford and the aspirations to a Carter presidency [36].

This issue of leadership and vision was Carter's most powerful thematic issue. It was established in the first debate, reinforced heavily in the second, and carried through the third with the assistance of the third debate panelists. Carter supported it with examples not easily refuted by Ford, who was clearly at a severe disadvantage: in his brief presidency, he had not found solutions to major foreign or domestic problems and was vulnerable to charges of "standstill" policies and a "do-nothing" government. Moreover, Carter embroidered the issue with abstract but attractive sentiments which had become stock materials in his rhetoric—compassion, regaining the vision of the country, investing government with the virtues inherent in the people, etc. These are sentiments always difficult to argue against. Ford apparently lacked the capacity to deal verbally with lofty ideas and sentiment; for this reason, it was particularly hard for him to rebut Carter's moralistic characterization of goals and policies.

Ford conducts government in secrecy and excludes the people from processes of decision-making. Carter initiated this issue in the first debate and continued it into the third, but it was most evident in the second. His first peroration previewed the charges to be made in the second debate. The nation had been divided, and now was the time for unity—"to have a president and a Congress that can work together—with mutual respect, for a change; cooperating, for a change; in the open, for a change. . . ." And "for a long time our American citizens have been excluded, sometimes misled, sometimes have been lied to. . . . We ought not to be excluded from our government any more" [I:35]. In the second debate Carter repeated these charges and added others. "We've lost in our foreign policy the character of the American people," who have been excluded from "participation in the shaping of our foreign policy. It's been one of secrecy and exclusion" [1]. "Every time we've made a serious mistake in foreign affairs, it's been because the American people have been excluded from the process. . . . And I'm not going to exclude the American people from that process in the future as Mr. Ford and Kissinger have done" [5]; and past commitments, some of them "revealed later on to our embarrassment," were not made known to the people [6]; secret diplomacy dismayed America's allies [27]. Ford's secrecy extended even to his avoidance of the press [10]. The Carter peroration in the second debate emphasized again the secrecy theme: "Will we have a government of secrecy that excludes the American people from participation in making basic decisions . . . ?" [36]

This secrecy issue had only modest intrinsic merit, but no doubt sounded "right" to people who had come to distrust government. There was truth in some Carter charges: Ford had been at odds with Congress, and had minimized his contact with the working press. But the heavy charges—that Ford excluded the people from decision-making and conducted foreign policy in secrecy, as if secret negotiation violated sacred precept—lacked merit.

If Carter's arguments did not provide sure grounding for the secrecy issue—and they did not—why then did the issue exert force in the debates? The reason is that Ford failed to provide convincing counter-arguments. A clear case in point was Ford's rejoinder after Carter—charging that Ford and Kissinger had conducted foreign policy in secret—claimed that he would restore the fireside chat, work harmoniously with Congress, and conduct open diplomacy [II:6]. Ford could have responded that Carter deceived himself and the American people if he really believed that diplomacy on delicate matters could be conducted without confidentiality. He could have cited successful examples of cautious behind-the-scenes diplomacy, shown how his own conduct of foreign affairs involved consultation with appropriate parties, and demonstrated the absurdity of some Carter claims. But instead of attacking Carter's vulnerable position, Ford defended himself with feeble arguments. His rejoinder speech—quoted here in its entirety—missed the mark almost completely:

FORD: Governor Carter again contradicts himself. He complains about secrecy and yet he is quoted as saying that in the attempt to find a solution in the Middle East that he would hold unpublicized meetings with the Soviet Union, I presume for the purpose of imposing a settlement on Israel and the Arab nations.

But let me talk just a minute about what we've done to avoid secrecy in the Ford administration. After the United States took the initiative in working with Israel and with Egypt and achieving the Sinai II agreement—and I'm proud to say that not a single Egyptian or Israeli soldier has lost his life since the signing of the Sinai agreement—but at the time that I submitted the Sinai agreement to the Congress of the United States, I submitted every single document that was applicable to the Sinai II agreement. It was the most complete documentation by any president of any agreement signed by a president on behalf of the United States.

Now as far as meeting with the Congress is concerned: during the twenty-four months that I've been the president of the United States, I have averaged better than one meeting a month with responsible groups or committees of the Congress—both House and Senate. The secretary of state has appeared, in the several years that he's been the secretary, before eighty different committee hearings in the House and in the Senate. The secretary of state has made better than fifty speeches all over the United States explaining American foreign policy. I have made myself at least ten speeches in various parts of the country where I have discussed with the American people defense and foreign policy. [II:7]

Human rights must be assured for American citizens and promoted in a foreign policy exhibiting high moral purpose. This theme, sustained by Carter through all of the debates, appeared in connection with numerous topics. It was present in his commentary on both his own and Ford's programs for pardoning Vietnam draft evaders, as well as his call for equity in the criminal justice system [I:12]. The Carter rejoinder that was nearly lost in the first debate because of equipment failure called for protection of citizen rights [I:34]. In the second debate, he charged that the Ford administration had supported military dictatorships and ignored human rights of citizens in other countries [5,6]; that Ford had failed to enforce the part of the Helsinki Agreement "which insures the right of people to migrate, to join their families, to be free, to speak out" and had "refused to see a symbol of human freedom recognized around the world, Aleksandr Solzhenitsyn" [10]. These remarks led immediately to Trewhitt's question, which placed the matter of human rights more formally on the agenda: How far would Carter be willing to go to promote civil rights abroad? [II:G] In response, Carter outlined pressures he might exert, and then called for a greater measure of idealism in foreign policy [II:11]. He later stated that the country's strength lies in idealism, honesty, integrity, as well as in predictability and commitment [II:17]. These and similar comments prompted Valeriani's question: "Do you really believe that the United States is not the most respected country in the world? Or is that just campaign rhetoric?'' [II:O] Numerous statements in Carter's response touched the issue of higher moral purpose in foreign affairs, including his call for commitment to principles—''doing what's right, caring for the poor, providing food, becoming the breadbasket of the world instead of the arms merchant of the world. . . .'' [II:23] He cited Chile as ''a typical example, maybe of many others, where this administration overthrew an elected government and helped to establish a military dictatorship'' [II:27]. He denounced the Ford administration for permitting the Arab boycott of American businesses: ''This is the first time that I remember, in the history of our country, when we've let a foreign country circumvent or change our Bill of Rights. . . . It's not a matter of diplomacy or trade with me; it's a matter of morality'' [II:32]. Ford's failure to ''appoint a presidential commission to go to Vietnam, to go to Laos, to go to Cambodia and try to trade for the release of information about those who are missing in action'' was, said Carter, a failure that ''touches specifically on human rights'' [II:35]. The Carter peroration in the second debate echoed the theme: ''We ought to be a beacon for nations who search for peace and who search for freedom, who search for individual liberty, who search for basic human rights. We haven't been lately'' [II:36]. In the third debate, the issue appeared again when Carter contrasted the Ford record on civil rights with the achievements of Kennedy and Johnson, and affirmed his own commitment, and when he expressed his view that the Supreme Court should rule on the side of human rights rather than property protection when the two conflict [III:21,28].

The issue of human rights at home and abroad, as well as high moral purpose in foreign affairs, was attractive at face value. Unable to argue against the moral aspects of the issue, Ford could only defend himself against charges that his administration had not advanced this noble cause. His defense on this issue was not an able one. He suffered under Carter's repeated attacks in the second debate. The contrasting speeches of Carter and Ford on the subject of the Arab boycott of American businesses gave weight to the human rights issue

[II:32,33], as did Nelson's question about Ford's civil rights record and Ford's subsequent response [III:L,20].

All of Carter's thematic issues, at their core, called into question the ability, vision, leadership, sensitivity, compassion, and wisdom of the president. This is not to say that his arguments and charges failed to engage more specific issues and details; in fact they did. But each of them also touched upon the competence and character of his opponent. Whether Carter was wise to take this route is open to question, because he clearly risked being perceived as too harsh on a man whom most voters thought to be good and decent. His final peroration indeed reminded the audience that "Mr. Ford is a good and decent man, but. . . ." Perhaps sensing that he had been dangerously severe on Ford in the second debate, Carter softened his attacks in the third. There were two major advantages in attacking Ford's competence and character. First, Ford himself had made "trust" a major campaign issue; thus Carter's thematic issues met Ford's challenge. Second, it was advantageous to focus on Ford's competence and character rather than other more concrete issues which might be dangerous to Carter and divisive for his party. For example, he could have chosen to advocate the Humphrey-Hawkins "full employment" bill as a major issue in the debates, but he did not do so. In fact, even when challenged by Ford early in the first debate on this Democratic platform issue, Carter remained silent.

The contention that Carter and a Democratic Congress would sharply increase spending was the only thematic issue of a wholly substantive nature introduced by a candidate, and Ford probably scored with it in the first debate. Although one of his thematic issues challenged Carter's competence, Ford damaged his own credibility in the course of the debates on the matter of competence; at the same time, his ethos was hurt seriously by Carter's blows. On balance, Carter held the advantage on thematic issues.

SPECIFIC ISSUES

The candidates' speeches placed twenty-six specific issues on the debate agenda. The second debate was very active in terms of issues initiated, especially by Carter. The third debate was the most passive as well as cautious, with the candidates tending to be responsive to panelists' questions instead of initiating issues of their own. The following figures indicate the number of specific issues raised in debates:

	Debate I	Debate II	Debate III	Totals
Ford	5	5	1	11
Carter	4	8	3	15

Ford's Issues

Certain observations can be made with regard to Ford's specific issues. First, none set forth a challenge so serious as to put Carter on the defensive in an entire rejoinder, nor even in most of a rejoinder speech. Second, his issues as a set were of only modest tactical advantage to him: some were underdeveloped and thus lacked force; some were adequately checked by Carter's refutations; two lacked intrinsic merit; and one—his "blunder"—was disastrous to his campaign. Third, none was addressed substantively to a matter of critical national concern. Fourth, six of Ford's eleven issues were initiated in rejoinder speeches, four in original speeches, and one in a follow-up—a strong indication that his agenda-building efforts tended to be in response to his opponent. The following summary of Ford's issues begins with those of least intrinsic and strategic merit and proceeds to those which had the most merit as debate issues.

Eastern European countries are not under the domination of the Soviet Union [II:8,9]. Ford surely did not intend to create this issue in answering Frankel's question, which asked him whether the Soviet Union had been getting the best of us—although Frankel did observe that "we've virtually signed in Helsinki an argeement that the Russians have dominance in Eastern Europe" [E]. Ford's response touched several matters raised in Frankel's question, and in the final sentences, while defending the Helsinki agreement, Ford asserted, "There is no Soviet domination of Eastern Europe and there never will be under a Ford administration." Frankel immediately asked a follow-up question to clarify this statement, and probably to allow Ford to alter or withdraw it. But Ford's follow-up speech only cemented his adherence to the proposition [9]. This blunder was not ignored by Carter, who took issue with Ford in a 40-word unit of his rejoinder [10]. Although the panelists did not return to the issue after Carter's rejoinder, the press and the public did. No other issue raised in the debates received so much press coverage and public discussion, and probably no other debate issue had such serious consequences for the course of the campaign. It has been said that the Ford blunder set his campaign back as much as ten days—at a time when steady progress was being made in closing the gap between himself and Carter.[9]

Congress should be blamed for the anti-Washington feeling [I:28]. Reynolds' fuzzy question to Ford about possible causes of anti-Washington feeling [S] gave Ford occasion to make an issue of the Congress; and in doing so, he delivered one of the most feeble speeches in all three debates. The anti-Washington attitude was misplaced, said Ford; it ought to be directed not to the executive branch, but to the Congress. His whole speech, about 325 words, amplified his charges: Congress spends too much money on itself; it has hired "people by the droves"; "there is some question about their morality"; etc. No panelist kept the issue on the agenda, and Carter did not comment on Ford's charges against Congress, although he argued that Ford's problems with Congress were traceable to an absence of leadership [30]. Ford briefly repeated his claims in the third debate [5]. Ford's speech lacked merit and strategic value.

Low unemployment during Democratic administrations was the result of a wartime economy [II:24]. This issue also lacked merit and utility. Ford introduced it at the beginning of a rejoinder, apparently in answer to Carter's claim moments earlier that the economy was in "terrible disarray and getting worse by the month—we've got 500,000 more Americans unemployed today than we had three months ago; we've got two and a half million more Americans out of work now than we had when Mr. Ford took office" [23]. Ford immediately responded: "Governor Carter brags about the unemployment during Democratic administrations and condemns the unemployment at the present time. I must remind him that we're at peace, and during the period that he brags about unemployment being low, the United States was at war.'' Ford's comments were off target, since he claimed a comparison which Carter did not make. Carter responded briefly in a defective rebuttal in which he linked Ford's remarks with doctrines of Karl Marx—surely one of Carter's worst arguments. Ford restated the issue at greater length in his last rejoinder in the third debate [34].

Carter would raise taxes [*I:27*]. In a rejoinder following Carter's call for tax reform, Ford delivered a charge that his advisers probably thought would have strategic value: "Governor Carter's answer tonight does not coincide with the answer that he gave in an interview to the Associated Press a week or so ago. In that interview, Governor Carter indicated that he would raise the taxes on those in the medium [sic] or middle-income brackets or higher. . . . Governor Carter has indicated publicly, in an interview, that he would increase the taxes on about 50 percent of the working people of this country.'' No panelist moved this issue into sharper focus, but Carter responded in his next speech: "I might go back to one other thing. Mr. Ford misquoted an AP news story that was in error to begin with. That story reported several times that I would lower taxes for lower- and middle-income families, and that correction was delivered to the White House, and I'm sure that the president knows about this correction, but he still insists on repeating an erroneous statement'' [30]. The issue was not raised again and should not have been raised at all, for it had no genuine merit and could have generated tactical advantage for Ford only if Carter failed to refute it.

Carter's bad record as governor of Georgia [*I:15*]. This issue also lacked merit because Ford's amplification supported the charge with faulty evidence.[10] Tactically, however, the issue was effective. It was raised by Ford after Carter had advocated reorganization of the federal government and recited his own successes in state government reorganization. In a unit of about 140 words, Ford claimed that Georgia's expenditures under Carter rose by more than 50 percent; government employees increased over 25 percent; bonded indebtedness went up over 20 percent; and by the testimony of Carter's successor, Governor Busbee, the Medicaid program was left in "shambles." Carter's silence on these charges was a tactical error, because Ford's issue was cutting when left unchallenged.

The Humphrey-Hawkins bill would threaten the economy with high cost and "control" [I:3]. Ford initiated this issue in his first speech, apparently intending to link Carter to the bill. Carter did not answer Ford on the issue, and no panelist restated it in the first or later debates. Ford might well have given the issue fuller initial treatment than the 75-word statement he devoted to it. Moreover, in view of Carter's silence, he erred in not renewing it with greater force.

Prayer in the public schools [III:23]. In response to Kraft's question regarding the candidates' possible support of amendments to the Constitution, Ford stated that he supported an amendment that would "change the Court decision as far as voluntary prayer in public schools. It seems to me that there should be an opportunity, as long as it's voluntary, as long as there is no compulsion whatsoever, that an individual ought to have that right." Carter did not respond, nor did any panelist.

Ford's vetoes have saved taxpayers' money [I:23]. A Gannon follow-up question asked whether Ford would veto a public works jobs bill. In answer, Ford used half of his speech to argue that his fifty-six vetoes in two years, forty-two of which were sustained by Congress, had saved "over 9 billion dollars in federal expenditures." Ford specifically stated that the value of his vetoes was an issue between himself and Carter: "Now, Governor Carter . . . condemns the vetoes that I have made. . . ." Carter responded sharply by first attacking Ford's economic policies and then arguing in the last half of the speech that the vetoes not only did not save money, but displayed an absence of leadership [24]. Panelists did not take up the issue, but at his next opportunity to speak Ford defended himself against Carter's rebuttal [27].

America has made successful efforts to resolve conflicts in southern Africa [II:3]. In answer to a question from Trewhitt, Ford offered examples of recent successes in foreign affairs, giving the example of southern Africa his fullest treatment. The

United States "took the initiative in southern Africa," seeking to end bloodshed, assure self-determination, and preserve human dignity; and "in southern Africa today the United States is trusted by the black frontline nations and black Africa; the United States is trusted by the other elements in southern Africa." Carter immediately rejected these claims of success and clashed sharply with Ford [4]. Panelists did not return this matter to the agenda, but the candidates did [25,27].

Carter would welcome a Communist government in NATO [*II:3*]. Ford initiated this issue as an aside in his answer to Trewhitt, saying: "And may I make an observation on part of the question you asked, Mr. Trewhitt? I don't believe that it's in the best interest of the United States and the NATO nations to have a Communist government in NATO. Mr. Carter has indicated he would look with sympathy to a Communist government in NATO. I think that would destroy the integrity and the strength of NATO, and I am totally opposed to it." Carter responded immediately: "Now, Mr. Ford, unfortunately, has just made a statement that's not true. I have never advocated a Communist government for Italy. . . . I think that this is an instance of deliberate distortion. . . ." [4] No further references were made to this issue.

Carter advocates dangerous reductions in defense spending [*II:2*]. Ford undoubtedly came to the second debate prepared to make an issue of Carter's call for reduced spending for defense. He may have been preoccupied with this intention, because he challenged Carter on the issue without answering the scathing attack Carter had just made on his foreign policies [II:1]. In reality Ford made two charges: first and most important, Carter advocates reductions in the defense budget that will seriously damage the country's ability to defend itself; and second, Carter has been inconsistent. "Governor Carter again is talking in broad generalities. Let me take just one question that he raises: the military strength and capability of the United States. Governor Carter in November of 1975 indicated that he wanted to cut the defense budget by 15 billion dollars. A few months later he said he wanted to cut the defense budget by 8 or 9 billion dollars. And more recently he talks about cutting the defense budget by 5 to 7 billion dollars. There is no way you can be strong militarily and have those kind of reductions in our military appropriation.'' Panelists did not ask subsequent questions to encourage debate on the appropriate level of spending required to maintain a strong military defense. In a direct response to Ford's claim that Carter once advocated a budget cut of 15 billion dollars, Carter charged Ford with "deliberate distortion. As a matter of fact, I've never advocated any cut of 15 billion dollars in our defense budget."[11] Ford later repeated his charge [II:19].

Carter's Issues

The issues initiated by Carter were not only more numerous than Ford's but also more substantive: the need for a national urban policy, control of nuclear weapons and nuclear wastes, the need for a national energy policy, equity in the criminal justice system—these ranked higher in merit than Ford's best issues. At the same time, Carter was more often on the offensive: of his fifteen issues, twelve were set forth in original speeches and three in rejoinders. Most of the Carter issues were tactically advantageous. Furthermore, five issues initiated in original speeches were forceful enough to throw Ford on the defensive in his rejoinder speeches. In the summary which follows, we begin by noting these five issues—all substantive, tactically advantageous, and well developed.

The Arab boycott of American businesses [II:32]. Frankel asked Carter how he would handle a particular problem: "Governor Carter, if the price of gaining influence among the Arabs is closing our eyes a little bit to their boycott against Israel, how would you handle that?" [T] Carter used the question to initiate an issue he had mentioned earlier [II:10]. His speech in answer to Frankel is worth quoting in full, for it shows clearly how Carter often used his original speech position to put Ford on the defensive:

I believe that the boycott of American businesses by the Arab countries because those businesses trade with Israel or because they have American Jews who are owners or directors in the company is an absolute disgrace. This is the first time that I remember, in the history of our country, when we've let a foreign country circumvent or change our Bill of Rights. I'll do everything I can as president to stop the boycott of American businesses by the Arab countries. It's not a matter of diplomacy or trade with me; it's a matter of morality. And I don't believe that the Arab countries will pursue it when we have a strong president who will protect the integrity of our country, the commitment of our Constitution and Bill of Rights, and protect people in this country who happen to be Jews. It may later be Catholics, it may later be Baptists who are threatened by some foreign country. But we ought to stand staunch. And I think it's a disgrace that so far Mr. Ford's administration has blocked the passage of legislation that would have revealed by law every instance of the boycott, and it would have prevented the boycott from continuing.

Thrown on the defensive, Ford's rejoinder concluded by pledging, "I am going to announce tomorrow that the Department of Commerce will disclose those companies that have participated in the Arab boycott. This is something that we can do. The Congress failed to do it, and we intend to do it" [33]. This apparently impromptu decision caused some embarrassment subsequently. Administration officials announced the following day that Ford's pledge would not be carried out.[12]

Mondale versus Dole as vice-presidential candidates [III:14]. Panelist Jack Nelson began with several charges before posing his critical question to Carter: "Many Americans still seem to be uneasy about you. They don't feel that they know you or the people around you. And one problem seems to be that you haven't reached out to bring people of broad background and national experience into your campaign or your presidential plans. . . . And doesn't this raise a serious question as to whether you would bring into a Carter administration people with the necessary background to run the federal government?" In this manner, Nelson placed the burden of a hostile question upon Carter. During the first half of his speech, Carter said essentially that he had made contact with the American people while campaigning and added that his advisers were numerous and expert. But in the second half, Carter initiated the issue of vice-presidential qualifications in such a way as to make his choice of Mondale and Ford's choice of Dole a critical test of his judgment against Ford's. He amplified the issue in a 235-word statement. Ford devoted his entire rejoinder to the issue initiated by Carter and never commented on the original question raised by Nelson [15].

The nation lacks an urban policy [III:18]. Robert Maynard introduced the subject of the need for an urban development policy, but slanted the question specifically to Carter: "Could you please outline your urban intentions for us tonight" [K]. In response, Carter charged that "this administration has no urban policy," a theme which he then developed in about half of his speech. This effectively turned the challenge toward Ford, whose entire rejoinder defended his administration [19].

The nation needs an energy policy [I:19]. Frank Reynolds asked Carter whether his position that nuclear plants should be used "as a last priority" was based on considerations of safety. Only a quarter of Carter's speech discussed needed safety precautions; most of the speech argued for a national energy policy. Ford commenced his rejoinder by claiming that "Governor Carter skims over a very serious and a very broad subject" (though Carter in fact had been as specific as time allowed) and that he had already initiated "the first comprehensive energy program recommended by any president." Ford's entire rejoinder was responsive to Carter, not to Reynolds' question [21]. Panelists did not subsequently refer to this agenda item, but Carter restated it later when discussing other matters [II:11; III:17].

The federal government needs reorganization [I:13,14]. Gannon's original and follow-up questions asked whether Carter's reorganization plan would actually reduce federal spending and the number of federal employees. In his two speeches, Carter answered by recounting his achievements in reorganizing the Georgia government and argued for reorganization of the federal government. Ford's rejoinder attacked Carter's record as governor of Georgia, then cited his own successes in reducing federal employees and spending [15].

Four Carter issues went unanswered, or received only a late and fragmentary answer from Ford:

Control of nuclear weapons and nuclear waste [*II:22*]. Trewhitt directed two questions to Ford about progress of the SALT talks [M,N]. Ford discussed the agreements and some current problems related to them. Carter's rejoinder called for increased commitment to nonproliferation programs, a "complete moratorium on the testing of all nuclear devices," and greater control over waste materials that can be reprocessed into explosives. "I've also advocated that we stop the sale by Germany and France of reprocessing plants to Pakistan and Brazil. Mr. Ford hasn't moved on this." And he added, "If we continue under Mr. Ford's policy, by 1985 or '90 we'll have twenty nations that have the capability of exploding atomic weapons. This has got to be stopped. This is one of the major challenges and major undertakings that I will assume as the next president." Ford did not respond immediately to this issue and Carter restated it as a subordinate part of another speech [27]. In a rejoinder mainly devoted to his position on the Panama Canal issue, Ford finally responded briefly: "Let me take just a minute to comment on something that Governor Carter said. On nonproliferation: in May of 1975, I called for a conference of nuclear suppliers. That conference has met six times. In May of this year, Governor Carter took the first initiative, approximately twelve months after I had taken my initiative a year ago" [29]. This rebuttal was late and underdeveloped.

Ford has failed to secure an account of Vietnam missing-in-action [*II:35*]. Carter initiated this issue in his last rejoinder in the second debate, after Ford had already responded to Trewhitt's question concerning the missing-in-action and the Ford administration's willingness to move toward restoration of relations with Vietnam: "One of the most embarrassing failures of the Ford administration, and one that touches specifically on human rights, is his refusal to appoint a presidential commission to go to Vietnam, to go to Laos, to go to Cambodia and try to trade for the release of information about those who are missing in action in those wars." This issue—initiated in Carter's last speech before the closing statements in the debate—was not answered by Ford, although he delivered a very brief closing statement (only about 120 words in length) and had adequate time to respond.

The criminal justice system needs reform [*I:12*]. In a rejoinder speech, Carter stated his position on the pardon of draft evaders, and then in about half of his speech moved to a broader issue—the absence of equity and the need for reform in the criminal justice system. Ford did not answer this challenge, and no panelist reinstated it as an issue. In the last debate, Carter renewed it [27,28].

Carter's qualifications for the presidency [*II:5*]. We have noted already that a Valeriani question [C] made impossible demands on Carter, asking him to define the national interest, discuss the proper role of the United States in the world, and name the persons he would appoint to key foreign policy positions. In justifying the third part of the question, Valeriani remarked that Carter had only "limited experience in foreign affairs" and took "some pride in being a Washington outsider." Carter's speech did not define the national interest, and he said it was not appropriate at the time to name his cabinet. He indicated in a general way how foreign affairs should be conducted. But the greatest portion of his speech answered the subordinate challenge—whether he was well qualified for the presidency. Carter clearly interpreted this subordinate challenge to be the most important aspect of the question. By answering so extensively, he placed on the agenda the issue of his qualifications for the presidency. The same speech—as well as his follow-up—pressed attacks on Ford, who answered the attacks in his rejoinder but failed to challenge Carter's qualifications. The issue reappeared when Nelson, in the third debate, directly challenged Carter's qualifications, as well as those of his advisers [I].

The remaining Carter issues were met more or less adequately by Ford:

The need for tax reform [*I:25*]. Elizabeth Drew asked Carter to explain what kind of tax reforms, such as elimination of certain itemized deductions, would generate revenue sufficient "to provide an overall tax cut of any size" [Q]. Most of Carter's speech sought to answer Drew, but he began by calling for tax reform. Several subsequent questions to Ford and Carter probed taxation and the economy, but none specifically dealt with tax reform. And although Ford attacked specific Carter statements and proposals, he did not challenge the claim that tax reform was needed, except to imply that nothing more than additional "tax relief to the middle income people" was needed [27].

The Ford-Kissinger foreign policy has failed [II:1]. At his first opportunity to speak in the second debate, Carter placed on the agenda a set of charges forming an issue—in essence, that Ford's foreign policies were defective, and "as far as foreign policy goes, Mr. Kissinger has been the president of this country. Mr. Ford has shown an absence of leadership, and an absence of a grasp of what this country is and what it ought to be. That's got to be changed. And that is one of the major issues in this campaign of 1976." Ford's rejoinder attacked Carter's proposals for reducing spending for defense, but made no direct response to this issue [2]. The issue of foreign policy successes and failures was raised by several panelists [B,D,O], and both Carter and Ford returned to it [especially 5,6,23,24].

Economic weakness at home endangers other countries [II:17]. Frankel asked Carter how bad things would have to get before he made significant reductions in defense spending in order to address other problems [K]. Carter answered briefly that the United States historically had been able to maintain a strong domestic economy and at the same time strength and reputation in world affairs. He then asserted that the current domestic economic crisis was one of the failures of the Ford administration and a threat to the stability of other countries. "We have let our economy go down the drain. . . . And that terrible circumstance in this country is exported overseas. . . . And when we're weak at home, weaker than all our allies, that weakness weakens the free world." Ford answered by describing meetings with European leaders "for the purpose of seeing what we could do, acting together, to meet the problems of the coming recession. In Puerto Rico this year, I met with six of the leading industrial nations' heads of state to meet the problem of inflation so we would be able to solve it before it got out of hand" [19]. Carter restated the issue later in the same debate: "We'll never be strong again overseas unless we're strong at home" [23].

Ford's foreign policy has strained relations between the United States and our natural allies [II:17]. The Carter speech noted above was loaded with charges. In addition to the claim that weakness in the domestic economy leads to weakness overseas, he charged that the Ford administration had disturbed natural alliances, and that we should "reestablish the good relationships that we ought to have between the United States and our natural allies and friends. They have felt neglected. . . . Under this administration, we've had a continuation of the so-called balance of power politics. . . . Our allies, the smaller countries, get trampled in the rush." More than half of Ford's rejoinder sought to refute this charge [19].

The United States has faltered in its support of Israel [II:11]. Trewhitt asked Carter to comment on his appeal for a greater measure of idealism in foreign affairs, and in particular to indicate how much he would risk to promote civil rights in the world [G]. Carter answered the question, but at the same time accused the Ford administration of a "disturbing" shift—more arms to Arab countries, less to Israel; this, he said, was "a deviation from idealism; it's a deviation from a commitment to our major ally in the Middle East, which is Israel. . . ." There was little merit in this charge. Ford's rejoinder clashed directly with Carter's claims [13], and Carter, at his next opportunity to speak, responded to parts of Ford's rejoinder [16].

Abortion is wrong [III:22]. Kraft's question to Carter asked first about the appropriateness of several constitutional amendments—gun control, school busing, balanced budgets, school prayer, abortion—and then asked, "which of these would you really work hard to support if you were president?" [M] Most of Carter's speech stated his opposition to abortion.

Ford opened his rejoinder by stating his own position on abortion, as well as that of the Republican platform [23].

The format and rules of the debates made it awkward for candidates to place issues on the debate agenda, but they managed to do so—and usually by departing from the questions posed by panelists. Although it seems obvious that presidential rivals ought to have the power to initiate some or all issues in a formal way, this was not permitted by the debate format.

Both candidates were initiative—Carter to a greater extent than Ford. Together they placed on the agenda several issues of greater worth than many of the panel-initiated issues: for example, Carter introduced the issues of nuclear weapons and waste, comprehensive national energy policy, tax reform, reorganization of the federal government, reform of the criminal justice system, the relative merits of Mondale and Dole as vice-presidential candidates; and Ford introduced important issues related to the defense budget and to excessive government spending. It should also be noted that several candidate-initiated issues were low in priority or ill conceived and should not have entered the debates. Ford was responsible for most of these: Russia does not dominate Eastern Europe; Congress is responsible for the anti-Washington feeling; Carter favors a communist government in NATO; low unemployment during Democratic administrations resulted from wartime economies. Two Carter issues were ill conceived: Ford permitted U.S. support of Israel to falter; and Ford failed to get an accounting of the Vietnam missing-in-action.

Carter's issues proved to be strategically superior, in part because he initiated them in original speeches with fuller amplification, but also because Ford so often succumbed to their influence and responded ineffectively. In addition, for unknown reasons, Ford's choice of issues to initiate was usually defective; perhaps, before the debates, he formulated no conscious plan to introduce specific issues.

Ford's best thematic issue, which meshed with many specific issues raised by the panelists and the candidates, was his portrayal of Carter and the Democratic Congress as big spenders. On the issue of trust, competence, compassion, wisdom—initiated by Carter as well as Ford—the president lost. He was challenged both by the panels and by Carter on this issue, but he undoubtedly did more than his adversaries to undermine his own ethos.

AGGRESSIVENESS: PUTTING PRESSURE ON FORD

The chosen format sliced the debates into forty segments, each of which included an original speech and a rejoinder, and often a follow-up speech as well. Somewhat like boxing rounds, the short units had a beginning and ending, with limited time in which to score. And in all likelihood, judgments of "who won" were based largely on the number and severity of punches landed, the flurry of blows, the utility of tactical moves, and the aggressiveness or defensiveness of the contestants. But the boxing ring metaphor goes only so far. In the debate rounds, Candidate A had the opportunity to speak for two or three minutes (more, if he made a follow-up speech) and to do what he could to floor Candidate B, who could not dodge and deflect the attack during those minutes because he had to stand still. What is more, when the third party—the panelists—entered the ring with gloves on, the candidate found himself in the middle, pressed by both sides. The debate format was biased toward the candidate with most speed, agility, and cleverness; and it automatically handicapped the candidate who was an easier target, less adept at argument and countercharge, and slower to find the right tactic.

ARGUMENTS AND THEIR TARGETS

Who presented the most arguments and to whom were arguments directed? The evidence from the speeches points to two critical conclusions. First, Carter was an aggressive debater, whereas Ford was defensive and at times timid or overcautious. Second, Carter debated Ford, but Ford debated the panelists.

The phrase "argumentative unit" is used in presenting our analysis of the number, rapidity, and target of arguments. This phrase refers to either a single argument leading toward a conclusion or a cluster of closely linked arguments supporting one conclusion. An argumentative unit contains premises and evidence related to a conclusion; it is not simply a collection of assertions. In the second debate, for instance, two back-to-back speeches by Ford and Carter differ in the number of argumentative units each contains and in the "target" to which those units are directed. Noting that the United States had suffered setbacks in foreign relations, Trewhitt asked Ford, "What do you do about such cases as Italy, and secondly, does this general drift mean that we're moving back toward something like an old cold war relationship with the Soviet Union?" [II:B] Ford commenced his speech by declaring that the U.S. was not moving back to a cold war relationship, and most important, had achieved numerous recent successes in foreign policy. He then presented a single, long unit of argument consisting of examples to document those successes. His final paragraph initiated a brief additional argument—that Carter was sympathetic to the establishment of a Communist government in NATO [II:3]. The speech thus contained two units of argument: a justification directed to the panelist who asked the question, and an argument directed to Carter. Carter's rejoinder contained three argumentative units, all of which were directed to Ford: the first sought to refute Ford; the second argued that Ford played "political football" with the defense budget; and the third disputed Ford's account of the role of the United States in southern Africa [II:4]. The speeches differed in the number of units of argument, as well as in the target to which they were directed.

Inspection of argumentative units in all speeches indicates that Carter was responsible for 129 units and Ford for eighty-nine units. Furthermore, Carter held the advantage in each debate: in the first, forty-one to thirty-two; in the second, forty-four to twenty-eight; and in the third, forty-four to twenty-nine. This was due in part to Carter's more rapid speaking rate, discussed later in this chapter. But the most important reason for the difference is that Carter took advantage of opportunities better than Ford. He also moved swiftly within a speech from one unit of argument to another. Ford had a tendency to dwell on a point—sometimes so long that transition to another unit of argument was impossible.

Altogether, five Carter speeches contained five units of argument each. No Ford speech contained this many units. Nine Carter speeches and only two Ford speeches contained four argumentative units each. Eight Carter and six Ford speeches contained three units each; seventeen Carter and nineteen Ford speeches contained two units each; and ten Carter and twenty-five Ford speeches contained one unit of argument. Carter managed to pack forty more argumentative units into his speeches than did Ford in the course of the three debates.

These facts attest to Carter's speed and agility, but the most important aspect of his aggressive argumentation becomes evident only by contrasting the two speakers according to the *target* of their arguments—that is, to whom the arguments were addressed. Each unit was classified according to whether it was directed or responsive to the other candidate, or addressed primarily to the panelists and responsive to their questions and challenges. The accompanying table shows the total number of argumentative units by each candidate and the target of these units.

Argumentative Units Directed to Panel or Candidate

	Debate I		Debate II		Debate III		Totals	
	Ford	Carter	Ford	Carter	Ford	Carter	Ford	Carter
Total units of argumentation	32	41	28	44	29	44	89	129
Units directed to panelist	19	25	13	9	24	22	56	56
Units directed to other candidate	13	16	15	35	5	22	33	73

In the first debate, twenty-five of Carter's forty-one units were directed to the panel and sixteen to Ford; nineteen of Ford's thirty-two units were directed to the panel and thirteen to Carter. The ratios were about the same, with both candidates addressing more units of argument to the panel than they did to each other: combined, they directed forty-four units to the panel members and twenty-nine to each other.

A sharp departure from this pattern occurred in the second debate: thirteen of Ford's twenty-eight units of argument were directed to the panel members and fifteen to Carter; only nine of Carter's forty-four units were directed to the panelists, while thirty-five were aimed at Ford. The panelists and Carter were almost equal targets of Ford's arguments, whereas Ford was the target of about 80 percent of Carter's units of argument. This analysis clearly points up Carter's strategy of "attack" in the second debate. Ford, whose argumentation had been rather aggressive in the first debate, became noticeably more subdued and timid in the second.

The figures for the third debate reveal even more dramatically the extent of Ford's timidity. One of the reasons for his timidity is very apparent: the hostile questioning of the third debate panel forced Ford not only to respond to panel members rather than debating Carter but also to face the panel as an adversary. In Ford's argumentation, twenty-four of his twenty-nine units (83 percent) responded to the panelists, while only five units attacked or responded to Carter. On the other hand, Carter's forty-four units of argument in the third debate were evenly distributed—twenty-two were directed to the panelists and twenty-two attacked or rebutted Ford. Carter was less vehement in this debate than in the second one. Either he came into the debate resolved to be less abrasive or he recognized very quickly that the panelists in the third debate were doing his work for him. If the direction of the argument indicates the location of the opponent, then Ford's principal opponent in the third debate clearly was the panel.

A Ford tactic in the third debate (perhaps decided in advance) was to speak directly to the panelist who questioned him. He had spoken directly to panelists before, but in the third debate—as if to emphasize his intended "directness"—he addressed the questioner by name in most of the speeches in which he answered questions. This strategy played into the hands of a hostile panel: his apparent willingness to be very responsive to the panel was reinforced by the panel's hostility, which practically demanded responsiveness. Ford erred in two ways. First, he allowed the panel to hammer him with hostile questions, instead of objecting as soon as he sensed excessive hostility. He might well have chastised the panel by saying, in effect, "If you won't place fair and important questions on the debate agenda, I will"; instead, he remained submissive. Second, he failed to carry the debate to Carter. The result was that he essentially debated the panel, whose questions constantly placed him on the defensive. He was seldom able to employ the tactic mastered by Carter in the second debate: respond to questions, hostile or not, in such a way as to shift the burden to the other candidate.

In the first debate, both Ford and Carter used their time in original speeches to respond directly to panel questions and to address arguments to the panel. Only one of the original speeches in this debate contained a unit of argument directed to the opponent. The pattern shifted in the second debate. Carter in particular was quick to initiate dispute, directing fourteen out of twenty-one units of argument at Ford in his original speeches. Nine of Ford's eleven units were directed to the panelists. In the third debate, Carter was less aggressive toward Ford; fourteen of seventeen units in his original speeches were directed to the panel. Ford addressed all eleven units in his original speeches to the panel. In all of the original speeches combined, Carter directed thirty-three argumentative units to the panels and eighteen to Ford; Ford directed thirty to the panels, but only two to Carter. (For distribution of all argumentative units including those in follow-ups, rejoinders, and perorations, see table in note 13.)

Debate between the candidates occurred chiefly in rejoinder speeches. Out of 218 units of argument in all debates, ninety-six (44 percent) occurred in rejoinder speeches, whereas eighty-three (38 percent) occurred in original speeches. More important, rejoinder speeches were very argumentatively "active," with 81 percent of the units of argument in rejoinder speeches directed by one candidate to the other. A comparison of rejoinders with other speeches illustrates even more the importance of the rejoinders: in rejoinders seventy-eight out of ninety-six argumentative units were directed to the speaker's opponent; in all other speeches combined—originals, follow-ups, and perorations—

only twenty-eight of 122 argumentative units (23 percent) were directed to the opposing candidate. These facts support a conclusion that it was primarily the rejoinder speeches which carried the direct "debate" between the candidates. Ford and Carter clearly needed more time in rejoinders. In nearly every one, each candidate pressed to his time limit, or exceeded it—struggling, as it were, to debate.[14]

Carter's ability to pile up more arguments than Ford is evident in the rejoinders: his total accumulation of arguments in rejoinders was fifty-eight to Ford's thirty-eight. His second-debate aggressiveness is also clearly demonstrated in the rejoinders, where all of his nineteen units of argument were aimed at Ford. Ford's timidity in argumentation shows up in his third-debate rejoinders, which contained only eleven units of argument, with only five of these attacking or rebutting Carter. In the same debate, Carter's rejoinders included twenty-two units of argument, seventeen of which attacked or rebutted Ford.

The following generalizations seem fully warranted. First, the candidates presented a high degree of argumentation in their speeches—about as much as could reasonably be expected in a debate format which fostered panel questions soliciting information and position statements rather than debate. The fact that several speeches contained little or no argumentation is related more to the nature of the panel questions than to deficiencies in the candidates.[15]

Second, the debate format, the presence of panelists, and the manner of questioning militated against actual face-to-face debate between opponents. Both candidates directed a large proportion of their units of argument to the panelists. Ford debated the panelists very frequently, directing 63 percent of his arguments to them and 37 percent to Carter. Carter directed more than half of his arguments (57 percent) to Ford.

Third, the most active argumentation between Ford and Carter took place in the rejoinder speeches. The candidates had too little time in rejoinders, however, to refute charges and provide well-argued positions.

Fourth, several changes occurred from the first to the third debates. Although Ford argued aggressively in the first debate and maintained an aggressive style and delivery in the second and third debates, he steadily deteriorated in "content aggressiveness," becoming timid in the third debate. Carter clearly came to the second debate resolved to make a better showing than in the first debate.[16] He succeeded in part because he mounted more arguments than Ford, but also because Ford himself faltered. Ford was practically forced to use his debate time for the purpose of responding to the panel in the third debate because of the panel's hostility—a factor to be examined shortly in more detail.

Finally, Carter was the more aggressive debater; he created more arguments and packed more arguments into individual speeches than did Ford. He learned quickly how to use the format, targeting Ford repeatedly with his arguments in the second debate and continuing an aggressive approach in the third debate.

LIGHT JABS AND BODY BLOWS

Both candidates made charges, criticisms, and attacks against each other—sometimes within and sometimes outside of argumentative units. The number and severity of these challenges serve as measures of speed and aggressiveness. It does not strain the metaphor of the prize fight to say that Carter outslugged Ford by a wide margin.

Carter's opening speech of the first debate did not argue directly against Ford, but did contain one *mild* charge: the Ford administration failed to take a number of steps that would have reduced unemployment. After identifying them, Carter said: "These kinds of specific things, none of which are being done now, would be a great help in reducing unemployment." This charge—a mild one—was the only one in his first speech [I:1]. His next speech, a follow-up, contained no charges against Ford. Ford's rejoinder began with a paragraph containing two *severe* charges. First, Carter had not been "any more specific in this case than he has been in many other instances." Secondly,

Carter had not mentioned the Humphrey-Hawkins bill which he endorsed previously (implying that Carter was avoiding the subject). This bill, according to Ford, would not only be expensive but would "control our economy." Thus at his first opportunity to speak—and before setting out to answer Reynolds' question—Ford struck two damaging blows to Carter [I:3].

A few additional examples illustrate the variety of "charges" in the debates. The second round of the first debate contained three speeches—an original and a follow-up speech by Ford, both of which were free of attacks on Carter, and a Carter rejoinder [6] organized on the basis of the following six severe attacks: (1) Ford is "changing considerably his previous philosophy"—that is, he is inconsistent; (2) the present tax structure is a disgrace; (3) Ford seeks to increase taxes "in the midst of the heaviest recession since the Great Depression . . ."; (4) he promotes tax increases for low- and middle-income taxpayers, but tax decreases for "the corporations and the special interests"; (5) he vetoed a bill that would have provided an 18 to 20 billion dollar tax reduction; and (6) "the whole philosophy of the Republican party, including my opponent, has been to pile on taxes on low-income people. . . ." The charges in this speech were the central points—the theses of argument. At other times, attacks or charges were independent of the argumentation.

A final example of charges, drawn from the first debate, occurred in the round initiated by Reynolds' question on pardon or amnesty [I:G]. In his original speech, Ford made a single mild attack on Carter, remarking almost as an aside, "I am against an across-the-board pardon of draft evaders or military deserters" [10]. In the context of campaign rhetoric, this amounted to a criticism of Carter, who had earlier called for a pardon. Ford then made a severe charge in his follow-up speech: he identified Carter with "blanket pardon" for all draft evaders and underscored his own opposition to that position [11]. Carter's rejoinder contained three moderate charges: first, Ford's explanation of why his rationale for the pardon of Nixon did not extend to the pardon of draft evaders was not quite satisfying; second, Ford's amnesty program was defective; third, the Ford administration had not adequately addressed a larger problem, that of equity in the criminal justice system [12].

An analysis of all speeches shows that Carter was the aggressive candidate, a turning point occurred in the second debate when Carter pounded Ford repeatedly and Ford failed to return in kind, and Ford's performance in the third debate was submissive.

Carter's aggressiveness can be demonstrated in three ways. First, he made more speeches containing charges against his opponent than did Ford. Sixty-five of the 109 speeches in the debates contain one or more charges; Carter made thirty-eight of these sixty-five speeches and Ford made twenty-seven. Second, based on sheer numbers of specific attacks, charges, and criticisms, aggressiveness weighed heavily in favor of Carter, who made 73 percent of the total attacks, charges, and criticisms leveled by one candidate against the other. Out of a total of 175 specific attacks and charges, Carter was responsible for 127 and Ford for forty-eight. (In the second debate alone, Carter made sixty such attacks.) Third, Carter made the greatest number of "severe" attacks—almost three times as many as Ford.

Attacks, Charges, and Criticisms by One Candidate Against the Other

| | Debate I | | Debate II | | Debate III | | Totals | | |
	Carter	Ford	Carter	Ford	Carter	Ford	Carter	Ford	Both
Severe	29	25	53	12	18	1	100	38	138
Moderate	7	2	5	4	11	2	23	8	31
Mild	1	1	2	0	1	1	4	2	6
Totals	37	28	60	16	30	4	127	48	175

The second debate was a turning point. Carter battered Ford with charge after charge and Ford did not strike back, a pattern which carried into the third debate as well. Comparing the candidates' performances in the first and second debates helps make this clear. In the first debate, Ford and Carter made eighteen speeches each, with a nearly equal number of speeches containing attacks on each other: eleven of Carter's speeches made charges against Ford; thirteen of Ford's speeches made charges against Carter. The number of attacks in the first debate indicates no sizeable difference between the candidates: Ford made twenty-eight attacks on Carter, and Carter made thirty-seven on Ford. They were even more equally matched in terms of the number of severe charges—Ford issued twenty-five and Carter twenty-nine. Ford's aggressive intent was clear not only in the content of his speeches but in his manner—his stance, facial expression, and delivery. Indeed, he was judged by the press and the public to have bested Carter in the first debate.

Why was Ford given the edge in this debate, when the figures show that Carter actually was more aggressive in content? Ford succeeded in establishing momentum at the very beginning, when he made two severe charges against Carter at his first chance to speak. He then maintained a steady attack on Carter throughout the debate, concluding with five severe attacks in his peroration. In addition, his charges were designed to do considerable damage: he accused Carter of inconsistency, lack of specificity, fuzziness, contradiction; and he linked Carter to costly programs and tax increases. At the same time, Carter's speech style in the first debate was mild and hesitant, even when attacking Ford. He permitted many of Ford's charges to go unanswered. And in his last three speeches, including his peroration, he made no attacks on Ford. In fact, he attacked Ford only once in his last five speeches. These factors, taken together, very likely conveyed an impression to the audience that Ford had "out-slugged" Carter—even though Carter actually initiated more charges than Ford.

The situation changed radically in the second debate. Carter was clearly on the attack, making charge after charge—and severe ones at that. He pressed attacks on Ford in sixteen of his eighteen speeches, while Ford attacked him in only nine out of nineteen speeches. The shift which occurred in the second debate is revealed even more clearly when one looks at the number and severity of attacks, charges, and criticisms. Carter made sixty attacks on Ford in this debate—more than Ford leveled against Carter in all three debates. Fifty-three of his attacks were severe. Ford attacked Carter only sixteen times in the second debate, and twelve of his attacks were severe. Carter surely entered this debate with a resolve to initiate serious charges at every opportunity. For reasons still unclear, Ford did not answer in kind. His Eastern Europe "blunder" early in the second debate may have unnerved him, making him cautious. Perhaps too, Carter's steady attack simply forced him into a defensive posture from which he could not easily initiate criticisms.

In the third debate, Ford was submissive, passive, and nearly always on the defensive—partly because of Carter's attacks and argumentative strategies, but also because of the hostile panel questions. He made only four charges against Carter in the entire debate, and only one could be considered severe [34]. At the same time, Carter continued to pressure Ford, although less aggressively than in the second debate: he leveled charges against Ford in eleven of his seventeen speeches, and eighteen of his thirty charges were severe in content. It should be noted that the speakers' references to each other—by name or by some descriptive word—matched the aggressive patterns already noted.[17]

In summary, Ford was aggressive in the first debate, weak in the second, and literally submissive in the third. From a strong start, he declined steadily as the debates progressed. In the first debate, Carter matched Ford's aggressiveness in substance, although his manner was milder. Aggressive in both substance and style in the second debate, he pounded the president in round after round. He relaxed somewhat in the third debate, perhaps because the panel took the role of Ford's adversary.

The advantage enjoyed by Carter over Ford was not simply one of numbers. The candidate who was ready with quick charges and attacks could increase his advantage by using the debate format cleverly. The feature of the 1976 presidential debates format which made this possible is easily explained: in twenty-one instances, a candidate delivered three speeches in succession—a rejoinder closing one debate round, plus an original and a follow-up speech in the next. These three successive speeches, which could total six or seven minutes, created an opportunity for a speaker to pile up a large number of charges and criticisms—so many that the other candidate might find it impossible to respond completely in his rejoinder. In fact, even trying to answer everything could easily force the other candidate into a highly defensive rebuttal position.

In the first debate, Ford had five opportunities to take advantage of the format in this manner, two of which he used fully by making charges against Carter in each speech of the set—four charges in one set and seven in the other [9,10,11;15,16,17]. Carter had four opportunities in the first debate, two of which he used in the same fashion—six charges against Ford in one set of three speeches and seven charges in another [12,13,14;18,19,20].

Ford had four similar opportunities in the second debate, but used none of them. On the other hand, Carter used two of his three opportunities to mount heavy attacks, issuing seven charges in one set of speeches and nine in another [4,5,6;16,17,18]. Even his third opportunity was used advantageously: in a rejoinder speech and the following original speech, he made twelve charges against Ford [10,11]. In the third debate, Ford had three opportunities and Carter had two, but neither candidate used them fully. In the three debates combined, Ford used two out of twelve opportunities to take advantage of the format for piling up charges and Carter used four out of nine.

The effect of piling up charges in successive speeches can be seen in three back-to-back speeches by Carter in the second debate [16,17,18]. He made a total of nine charges: (1) Ford presented erroneous statistics regarding aid to Israel; (2) administration policies made Israel "the scapegoat for the problems in the Middle East" and "weakened our relationships with Israel"; (3) the Ford administration has "frittered away" the opportunity for improved relations with the People's Republic of China; (4) U.S. influence and strength have been endangered under Ford's leadership; (5) the administration has erred with its "Lone Ranger-type diplomatic efforts" in foreign affairs; (6) Ford has let the domestic economy "go down the drain," weakening the country at home and abroad; (7) the administration erroneously continues to pursue "balance of power" world politics; (8) the country has lost the world respect it once commanded, a respect it will not regain "if Gerald Ford is reelected and this present policy is continued"; and finally, (9) the inflation rate under the Ford administration is vastly higher than it was under the Kennedy and Johnson administrations. In these three successive speeches, Carter made nine charges or attacks in a speaking time of five minutes and twelve seconds. Ford had an impossible burden in his two-minute rejoinder; speaking eight seconds beyond his time, he could only begin to answer the charges. He commenced by attacking Carter's proposals for cutting defense spending, and then argued that his own efforts had led to stronger relations with other countries. His speech showed hardly any relationship to Frankel's question, and he answered only two of Carter's nine charges [II:19].

A similar effect occurred when a candidate who had two speeches in sequence used both to level charges against his opponent. In the first debate, Ford had one such opportunity and Carter three, but none were used. In three opportunities in the second debate, Ford used only one—a set of back-to-back speeches in which he made four charges [2,3]. Carter used three of four opportunities to full advantage, issuing eight charges in one sequence [22,23], eight in another [27,28], and three in the third [31,32]. In the final debate, Ford made no attacks on Carter in any of his five sets of back-to-back speeches. Carter used three of his five sets, issuing three charges against Ford in each of two sets [3,4, and 13,14], and ten charges in the last set [17,18]. In all, Ford used only one out of nine opportunities; Carter used six out of twelve opportunities.

The effect of accumulated attacks shows up clearly in two back-to-back Carter speeches in the third debate—a rejoinder in answer to Ford [17] and an original speech in answer to a question by Maynard [18]. Kraft commenced a unit by asking Ford to justify his "hopeless" record on environmental issues. In providing a rationale for his question, Kraft noted that Ford vetoed a strip-mining bill, worked against strong controls on auto emissions, and did nothing about pollution of the Atlantic Ocean [J]. Burdened by this very hostile question, Ford explained his reasons for vetoing the mining bill and opposing stronger auto emission controls. He then argued that his efforts had brought about increased funding for water treatment plants, funding for land and water conservation programs, and expansion of the national parks and wilderness areas [16]. Carter began his rejoinder by reaffirming and agreeing with Kraft's charge that Ford's record on the environment was indeed "hopeless." Then, systematically rejecting Ford's explanations and claims, he piled charge upon charge: (1) Ford's reasons for vetoing the strip-mining bill are unsound; (2) Ford has consistently sought to lower or delay enforcement of pollution standards; (3) both Ford and Nixon impounded funds that were to be used to control water pollution; (4) the nation has no energy policy; (5) Ford's claim that he has made significant additions to the nation's parks and wilderness areas is exaggerated; (6) there has been no "strong position in the control of pollution of our oceans"; and (7) the administration has not taken "strong and bold action to stop the proliferation of nuclear waste around the world" [17]. This rejoinder speech came at the conclusion of a round of debate. Consequently, Ford had no chance to respond except by taking time from a subsequent speech on another topic. Before he had such an opportunity, however, Carter spoke again in response to Maynard's question [K], which asked him to outline an urban policy. In responding to this question, Carter increased the burden on Ford by adding three more attacks: (1) the Ford administration has no urban policy; (2) the administration's attitude toward the problems of the large cities is reflected in the *Daily News* headline that says (according to Carter), "Ford to New York: Drop Dead"; and (3) the Ford administration has contributed to a 30 percent reduction in federal aid to education. These charges and criticisms were included in Carter's statement outlining solutions to urban problems [18]. How did Ford respond to the blistering attack mounted in Carter's two speeches? Arguing defensively, he tried to show that his administration had made progress toward helping "our major metropolitan areas." His rejoinder never addressed the charges about his environmental record, and his speech made no criticism of Carter's position [19].

The debate format gave a significant advantage to a candidate who could quickly and ably build arguments and charges in sequence. Because Carter was more adept at doing this, the light jabs and body blows—all the attacks, charges, and criticisms made by one candidate against the other—were stacked disproportionately on his side (127 to 48). The debate audience—journalists, as well as the public—probably scored the events largely by noting which candidate was more aggressive, on the move, and landing punches. By this yardstick, Carter came out ahead.

WITH THE HELP OF THE PANELISTS

Hostile questioning by the panels was a third force operating in the debates. During approximately twelve minutes of questioning in the third debate, the panel made at least nine serious charges against Ford and four against Carter. The four charges by the panel against Carter were more serious than any initiated against him by Ford. Some of the charges by the panel against Ford certainly were as serious as any initiated against him by Carter—for example, the implied connection between Ford and Watergate, and the charges in regard to his "hopeless" environmental and "rotten" economic records. In seventy minutes of speaking in the third debate, Ford and Carter made thirty-four specific attacks or charges against each other—about one charge for each two minutes. The panelists made at least thirteen specific charges or attacks against the candidates in just under twelve minutes—about one charge per minute.

Two general conclusions can be documented easily: first, hostile questioning was more often directed to Ford than to Carter; and second, Carter handled hostility more skillfully than Ford, both in responding directly to a hostile question and in responding to an answer given by Ford to a hostile question. In chapter 3 we pointed out that Ford received thirteen and Carter nine strongly hostile questions in the three debates. The third and toughest of the debate panels directed ten strongly hostile questions to Ford and only four to Carter, requiring Ford to defend himself more than twice as often as Carter. Carter was challenged to explain why he didn't "clear" his statement on Yugoslavia and to defend the quality of his presidential campaign, his lack of experience, and his trustworthiness in making future appointments to key positions [F,C,T,I]. Hostile panel questions to Ford included charges of defective economic policies and a hopeless environmental record, involvement in an early effort to cover up the Watergate affair, failure to fire General Brown, a bad record on civil rights, and a confused stand on handgun control [A,R,J,D,B,L,N].

An account of the hostile questions directed to Ford and Carter is very revealing, but alone does not enable us to understand fully the extent of the harm done to Ford and the advantage given to Carter. Several effects of the panelists' hostility must also be considered. First, hostile questions and challenges pressured the candidates to react to the panelists instead of debating each other. Occasionally one of the candidates actually debated a panelist—for instance, when Ford was twice challenged by Nelson regarding his connection with Watergate [III:6,7]. Carter managed to initiate only six issue-oriented charges or criticisms of Ford's programs and policies in the nine speeches in which he had to respond to strongly hostile panel questions. Ford was able to initiate only three challenges or policy attacks during speeches which required his response to thirteen strongly hostile panel questions. Both men addressed their arguments almost totally to the panelists in these same speeches.[18]

Panel questions and challenges that were more or less hostile led to speeches directed mainly to the panelists in twenty-three of the forty rounds constituting the three debates. This happened six times in both the first debate and the second debate.[19] For example, Reynolds challenged Ford in the first debate to justify his pardon of Richard Nixon and show why the same rationale for pardon should not extend to Vietnam draft evaders [G]. Ford's entire speech was directed to Reynolds and dominated by that challenge. In the second debate, Valeriani's question to Ford about the *Mayaguez* affair [S] practically compelled Ford to justify his actions to Valeriani. This left Carter completely free to criticize Ford in his rejoinder. Valeriani also challenged Carter to defend his claim that America had lost respect and strength [O]; but in this instance, Carter shifted from a defense of his claim to an attack on Ford rather than respond submissively to the question [23]. Ford was then forced to defend his administration in his rejoinder [24]. The third debate panel was by far the most domineering one; it posed questions containing challenges, propositions, or claims— almost always hostile—which drew the candidates into debate with the panel in eleven rounds. [20]

The second effect of hostile questions was to force the candidates into defensive postures—Ford to a greater extent than Carter. In responding to thirteen strongly hostile questions, Ford was essentially defensive in seven responses. Carter was defensive in two of eight speeches in which he had to respond to hostility. [21] This difference between Ford and Carter was in part a result of the number and severity of the questions; but it was also due to Carter's ability to turn a hostile question to his advantage.

The victim of a hostile question could turn it to his advantage occasionally—but only if he hit upon the right strategy. Carter was more skillful at this than Ford. The best example is his speech in response to one of Nelson's questions in the third debate, a question that was hostile and one-sided. Carter used the original speech position to "shift the burden" onto Ford, who was in the rejoinder position. Nelson asked:

Governor, despite the fact that you've been running for president a long time now, many Americans still seem to be uneasy about you. They don't feel that they know you or the people around you. And one problem seems to be that you haven't reached out to bring people of broad background and national experience into your campaign or your presidential plans. Most of the people around you on a day-to-day basis are people you've known in Georgia. Many of them are young and relatively inexperienced in national affairs. And doesn't this raise a

serious question as to whether you would bring into a Carter administration people with the necessary background to run the federal
government? [III:I]

Carter responded to this question by recounting the ways in
which his campaign had made contact with a broad range of the
public, and he claimed to have acquired a wide circle of expert
advisers. The burden created by the question was on Carter. At
this point in his speech, and in response to the sense of Nelson's
question, Carter offered an example of the exacting criteria he
would use to find and appoint people to important positions in
his administration:

> The one major decision that I have made since acquiring the
> nomination, and I share this with President Ford, is the choice of the
> vice-president. I think this would be indicative of the kind of leaders
> that I would choose to help me if I am elected. I chose Senator Walter
> Mondale. And the only criterion that I ever put forward in my own
> mind was who among the several million people in this country would
> be the best person qualified to be president, if something should
> happen to me, and to join me in being vice-president if I should serve
> out my term. And I'm convinced now, more than I was when I got the
> nomination, that Walter Mondale was the right choice.

This choice, said Carter, is a "good indication of the kind of
people I would choose in the future." He then skillfully trans-
ferred the burden to Ford:

> Mr. Ford has had that same choice to make. I don't want to say
> anything critical of Senator Dole, but I've never heard Mr. Ford say
> that that was his primary consideration—who is the best person I could
> choose in this country to be president of the United States? [III:14]

Carter's response to Nelson's question was well-nigh
perfect. He dealt adequately with a one-sided and hostile
question, and at the same time shifted the burden to Ford. And
significantly, he also introduced a new agenda issue—Mondale
versus Dole. Ford's rejoinder was not responsive to Nelson's
question, in spite of the fact that the question raised doubts
about Carter's political judgment—doubts that Ford surely
would wish to reinforce in the public consciousness. Carter's
strategy, however, prompted Ford to defend his selection of

Dole and placed him on the defensive in his rejoinder speech [III:15].

The significance of Carter's strategy under the pressure of hostile questions should not be underestimated. Not only did he succeed in reducing his own burden, but by shifting the burden to Ford, he forced the president to defend himself and deprived him of an opportunity to debate on affirmative grounds. In the next chapter, this strategy is discussed at length. For the moment, it is sufficient to underscore one fact: in four of the nine rounds in which questions from panelists would otherwise have dominated his responses, Carter succeeded in throwing the burden onto Ford.[22] This strategy increased the number of speeches in which Ford was forced to be defensive and, as a consequence, magnified his problems.

Finally, a hostile question produced a double advantage for the candidate in the rejoinder position: first, it pressured his opponent and perhaps hurt him; second, it left the rejoinder speaker practically free of any constraints in his response. A clever rejoinder speaker, in effect, could ally himself with the hostile questioner and increase the damage to his opponent. Carter used this double advantage in several instances, joining forces with the panelist when his opponent was weakened by a hostile question. For example, both Ford and Carter responded to a hostile and one-sided question by Maynard, who asked Ford why he had not fired General George Brown for making derogatory remarks about Great Britain [III:H]. Ford's entire response was apologetic and defensive. Carter's rejoinder simply endorsed and amplified the charges in the question. He could not really "answer," because Maynard's question was so one-sided and accusatory that it placed no burden of response on him. However, he could—and did—ally himself cleverly with the question, producing additional examples of General Brown's inept statements and renewing the theme of Ford's failures in leadership [13]. Other examples of this strategy are detailed in the next chapter.

While it is difficult to give exact weight to the influence of the panels' hostility, the evidence is conclusive that hostile questions favored Carter, especially those of the third panel.

The evidence also shows that Carter increased this advantage through his strategies in dealing with hostile questions addressed to himself and to Ford. It is reasonable to hold that a format for future debates should be devised which altogether eliminates the hostility injected by the panels.

UNMATCHED OPPONENTS

With respect to skills already discussed, Ford and Carter were not evenly matched. Nor were they matched in three other important areas—preparedness, rate of speech, and style. Although considerable pre-debate talk made note of Ford's good command of information and issues, he entered the debates less prepared than Carter who had developed his "commonplaces" during two years of campaigning. In addition, Ford's extemporaneous speech rate was so much slower than Carter's that he actually needed almost thirty minutes extra debate time to allow him to match Carter's total number of words uttered. And, not least important, the Ford and Carter styles differed in ways that gave the challenger several advantages.

COMMONPLACES

Moderator Edwin Newman made an announcement in the first debate that other moderators would repeat: "President Ford and Governor Carter do not have any notes or prepared remarks with them this evening." Newman's language was inaccurate, but his meaning was clear. Ford and Carter did not bring notes or manuscripts to the debates. They did bring something considerably more effective—their well-rehearsed remarks or "commonplaces." Carter in particular used these prepared remarks abundantly and with profit.

Both candidates studied briefing books before the debates and considered how to answer questions that were likely to be asked. Ford rehearsed answers during mock debates. Carter's rehearsal was probably equally serious, even if less formal. However, pre-debate rehearsal and study of briefing books cannot substitute for months of campaigning in which common-places are developed and refined.

A commonplace is a unit of discourse—a "mini-speech" on a topic. It is given again and again during stump speeches, radio and television interviews, caucuses, and news conferences—literally hundreds of times. After much repetition, the commonplace acquires refinements and subtle touches that render it more effective. It can be shortened or lengthened as time permits, it comes readily to mind when needed, and it can be adapted to attack or defense.

Commonplaces in the Ford and Carter debates carry no marks of identification. They are recognizable only by reference to previous speeches in which they appear. During the primary and presidential campaigns, the authors observed and listened to far more Carter speeches than Ford speeches, both first-hand and through audio and video tapes. Carter campaign speeches were simply more numerous and available. For this reason, we approach the identification of commonplaces with greater confidence in regard to Carter's speeches than in regard to those of Ford. Even allowing for some error in identifying the number and variety, however, it is possible to estimate the extent to which Carter and Ford used commonplaces and the probable advantage given to Carter.

At least forty-one of Carter's fifty-three speeches contain commonplaces; in twenty-one speeches more than 50 percent of the content is made up of commonplaces,[23] and in nine the commonplace content is higher than 75 percent.[24] At least nineteen of Ford's fifty-six speeches contain identifiable commonplaces; but 75 percent of the content is made up of commonplaces in only two speeches[25] and about 50 percent in eight speeches.[26] An estimate—more an educated guess than a calculation—is that Carter used commonplaces twice as often as Ford.

For example, Carter delivered this well-traveled commonplace in his rejoinder to Ford's speeches justifying his pardon of Richard Nixon and his unwillingness to pardon Vietnam War draft evaders:

As a matter of fact, I don't advocate amnesty; I advocate pardon. There's a difference, in my opinion, and in accordance with the ruling of the Supreme Court and according to the definition in the dictionary. Amnesty means that what you did was right; pardon means that what you did, whether it's right or wrong, you're forgiven for it. And I do advocate a pardon for draft evaders. [I:12]

Minutes later, in response to a question regarding the safety of nuclear power plants, Carter first delivered a commonplace on the need for a national energy policy, followed by another commonplace intended to meet the question:

I would certainly not cut out atomic power altogether. We can't afford to give up that opportunity until later. But to the extent that we continue to use atomic power, I would be responsible as president to make sure that the safety precautions were initiated and maintained. For instance, some that have been forgotten: we need to have the reactor core below ground level; the entire power plant, that uses atomic power, tightly sealed and a heavy vacuum maintained; there ought to be a standardized design; there ought to be a full-time atomic energy specialist, independent of the power company, in the control room full-time, twenty-four hours a day, to shut down the plant if an abnormality develops. [I:19]

Why was Carter better prepared than Ford? The most obvious answer is that he had been campaigning for nearly two years as a challenger for office. In literally hundreds of campaign events, Carter had discussed such topics as pardon or amnesty for Vietnam draft evaders, government reorganization, equity in criminal justice, his commitment to civil rights, the selection of judges and diplomats, the need for a national energy policy, etc. He entered the debates well prepared with scores of finely honed commonplaces, and he used them. Ford had not campaigned extensively and vigorously during the primaries, and he did not commence daily full-scale campaign speaking until five weeks before the election. Consequently Ford simply had fewer opportunities than Carter to develop campaign commonplaces.

In any debate format, it is likely that Carter would have gained some degree of advantage from his easy access to a stock of commonplaces. The chosen format, however, invited the use of commonplace materials and gave him a large advantage. His commonplaces fit neatly into the two- or three-minute speeches. Furthermore, the three debates were chopped into forty rounds, each initiated by a panelist's question, with the result that there were actually forty short debates involving nearly as many topics. Because of his long campaign, Carter had a commonplace for nearly every standard topic. It is also worth noting that the debate format closely resembled a press conference format—the very setting in which the commonplaces had been so frequently invented, used, and refined. Reporters covering Carter during the primary campaign had heard his commonplaces dozens of times.

The frequent use of well-rehearsed commonplaces gave Carter several advantages. First, he was able to use a more rapid rate of delivery, since he did not need to create at the moment of speaking. Second, his speeches had a more finished quality, because the commonplaces exhibited unity and coherence. Third, he could adapt the commonplaces to his immediate purpose—whether answering a question, initiating an issue, or challenging his opponent. Fourth, the commonplaces provided him with a practiced array of facts, examples, and arguments that conveyed to the audience his apparent command of material. Finally, he could convey compassion and other personal qualities by using commonplaces invested with moral flavor, and sometimes emotion.

SPEED

The original speeches usually stayed within the agreed upon time limits. For example, in the first debate when candidates had up to three minutes for their original speeches, Carter's times for his six speeches were 2:55, 2:34, 1:32, 2:42, 3:05, and 1:36. Ford's times were 2:57, 2:24, 2:33, 2:07, 2:19, and 1:37. The last speech in each sequence was well under three minutes at the urging of the moderator, who had noted that time was running out.

The candidates often exceeded their time limits in the two-minute rejoinders. Carter's first-debate rejoinder times were 2:13, 1:50, 2:09, 2:05, 2:12, and 0:20 (the last one was shortened because of equipment failure). Ford's rejoinder times were 2:02, 2:10, 2:10, 2:05, 2:16, and 0:59. These time patterns were generally characteristic of the second and third debates too, except that original speeches in the third debate were cut from three minutes to two and one-half minutes.

Follow-up speeches showed considerable variation. For example, with a two-minute time limit, Carter's follow-ups in the first debate actually used 0.52, 2:05, 1:36, 1:44, and 1:08; Ford's used 1:48, 1:31, 1:48, 0:34, and 1:38.

Each debate closed with perorations which had four-minute limits in the first and third debates and three-minute limits in the second. Although the first-debate perorations were almost exactly equal in number of words (Carter 485, Ford 487), Carter was fifty-five seconds under the four-minute limit and Ford exceeded it by seventeen seconds. In the third debate, Carter exceeded the four-minute limit by fifteen seconds and Ford was ten seconds under it. In the second debate, Carter spoke seventeen seconds over the three-minute limit, but Ford used only one minute and sixteen seconds of his time (117 words in contrast to Carter's 460 words). Analysis of both videotape and text of this speech leads us to surmise that Ford lost his way and perhaps forgot a portion of a speech roughed out in advance.

The format of the debates assured nearly equal opportunity to speak in terms of number of speeches and time available to the speakers. In theory this would appear to provide equality in regard to how much can be said. However, the difference is considerable between such theoretical equality and what actually occurred in the debates.

Ford and Carter were not equal in actual speaking time in the first and second debates, but they were not much out of balance. In both debates Ford exceeded Carter in total speaking time—by a minute and a half in the first and about one minute in the second. The difference was much greater in the third debate: Ford spoke thirty-eight and one-half minutes and Carter thirty-one and three-quarters minutes, giving Ford a time advantage of about seven minutes. In the total for the three debates, Carter spoke about 103 minutes and Ford 112, giving Ford a time advantage of over nine minutes. There are two principal reasons for this difference. First, Carter said very little in three of his opportunities to speak: one rejoinder in the first debate was practically lost because of equipment failure [I:34]; a rejoinder in the third debate consisted of five words, "I don't have any response," after Ford had defended himself against Nelson's Watergate questions [III:8]; and an answer to a Kraft follow-up question was a four-word response, "No, I did not" [III:10]. Second, Ford had three extra speeches because he received three more follow-up questions than Carter.

In spite of his advantage in total speaking time, Ford said far less than Carter. The difference is striking. In the first debate, he spoke one and one-half minutes longer than Carter, but Carter uttered about 885 more words. Carter's total also exceeded Ford's in the second debate—by about 985 words. In the third debate, even when Ford had a time advantage of approximately seven minutes, Carter outdistanced him by about 735 words. Altogether, Carter spoke about 2,600 more words than Ford in nine minutes less speaking time. The explanation for this difference, of course, lies in the speaking rate of the two men, which is summarized in the following table.

Speaking Time, Number of Words, and Rate per Minute, for All Debates

	Carter			Ford		
	Time	Words	Rate	Time	Words	Rate
Debate I	35:43	5,756	161	37:15	4,872	131
Debate II	35:22	5,642	160	36:32	4,657	127
Debate III	31:43	5,446	172	38:26	4,712	123
Totals	102:48	16,844	164 (av.)	112:13	14,241	127 (av.)

Total time, Ford plus Carter: 215:01 minutes
Total words, Ford plus Carter: 31,085

The significance of the difference in speaking rate which enabled Carter to gain a 2,600-word advantage may be appreciated better through several illustrations. First, this total word advantage matches almost exactly the number of words spoken by Carter in all of his original speeches in the third debate (2,627 words in about fifteen and one-half minutes). Measured by his rate of speaking in the third debate, Carter's extra 2,600 words gave him the equivalent of a fifteen-and-one-half-minute advantage over Ford. Or stated another way, Ford actually spoke nine minutes and twenty-five seconds longer than Carter; given his own speaking rate, he would also need an additional twenty minutes—that is, a total of thirty minutes more than Carter—in order to match Carter's total number of spoken words.

It might be argued that the difference in speaking rate would not matter if Ford's language style were richer and more compact than Carter's. Ford's style, however, was loose and often redundant and displayed neither compactness nor richness. He was slow in speech and also in content.

The panelists in the three debates together spoke about 5,500 words in thirty-two minutes and thirty-eight seconds, at an average speaking rate of 169 words per minute—very close to Carter's rate. Their total time and number of words were almost identical to the time and words spoken by Carter in the entire third debate. Joseph Kraft spoke at greatest length (five minutes, ten seconds) and Richard Valeriani's questions used the least time (one minute, forty-nine seconds). The panels were responsible for 15 percent of the words spoken in the debates. Had there been no panelists, each candidate could have had an additional sixteen minutes of prime time.

STYLE

Ford's acceptance speech at the Republican National Convention was rousing, aggressive, well polished, and much rehearsed. He delivered it well. The press reported that Jerry Ford showed a new, tough, dynamic style and that this style would be continued. On September 15, just eight days before the first debate, Ford delivered his official campaign kick-off speech at his alma mater, the University of Michigan, and his address employed the aggressive "new" style of his acceptance speech. In the debates, he tried to convey toughness and dynamism by visual image—an always erect and commanding posture, jutting jaw, stern visage—and by decisive statements and well-measured utterances. In several speeches in the first debate his aggressive manner matched the content of his speeches. However, the new style could not be sustained. Although continuing to project the stern visual image throughout the debates, he became submissive and timid in speech content. Why did Ford not maintain the tough style demonstrated so ably in his acceptance speech and repeated in the speech at Michigan?—primarily because the new style required a manuscript, and in the debates he had none.[27]

Carter was hesitant and nervous in opening the first debate, but gained confidence and steadiness as the debates progressed. After the initial nervousness, there was no detectable hiatus between manner and matter: speaking naturally and comfortably, he was in his element. The months of press conference sparring and stump speaking had prepared him for debates of just this kind. He needed no formal manuscript because he had large chunks of well-polished material at the tip of his tongue. In campaigning, he had been at his best when speaking extemporaneously and at his worst when a script was in hand. He did not (and still cannot) read well from a prepared text. But in the debates, free from a text and relying on his ability to fashion speeches in large part from stored commonplaces, Carter was in a setting exactly right for him—that is to say, right for his style. The format played to his strengths, and against Ford's. Had the format called upon Ford and Carter to present formal manuscript addresses on policy matters, the fortunes of the candidates probably would have been quite different.

Ford's language, by and large, was highly repetitious; some of his speeches could be edited down to half their length with no loss of content. For example, the following short speech deserves a prize for redundancy:

There is no policy of this government to give to the People's Republic, or to sell to the People's Republic of China, military equipment. I do not believe that we, the United States, should sell, give, or otherwise transfer military hardware to the People's Republic of China, or any other Communist nation, such as the Soviet Union and the like. [II:15]

He reminded his audience no less than ten times in one speech that "I made the recommendation," "I have proposed," "I submitted to the Congress,'' etc. [I:4] Lacking speed of thought and expression, and tending to dwell overlong on a matter, he said less than his time allowed. In general, precision was not a quality of his style. Most of his debate speeches contained one or more awkward expressions, or meanings that failed to match up with what he meant to say. His sentences, usually simple and declarative, linked ideas serially; he seldom showed complexity of thought by use of subordination and complex structures. Because he depended heavily on nouns and focused on matters of fact, his prose was sluggish and wooden. Emotion seldom entered his speeches; nor did humor or clever play on words enliven his style. Ford was most impressive when questions from panelists or challenges from Carter permitted him to speak ''presidentially'' about documents, events, and policies which had a history that he could recite with ease. He was least impressive when handling a vague question or speaking in the absence of questions and challenges, as in his closing statements—in other words, when his discourse had to be fashioned without the help of guiding topics.

In contrast, Carter usually said exactly what he meant to say—with few wasted words, little repetition, and only occasional awkwardness. He moved speedily within a speech from topic to topic, argument to argument, rebuttal to position statement. His speeches usually were composed of natural units. (For this reason, they yielded readily to editorial paragraphing efforts.) Carter made far greater use than Ford of subordination, contrast, and balanced clauses: because his thought employed distinctions and hierarchies, his style was more complex. He frequently used active verbs, qualifiers attached to nouns, expressions of feeling, and sometimes a series of clauses or sentences moving in qualitative as well as logical progression. As a result, his style was sometimes vivid, and almost always lean and rapid. Many Carter speeches, especially the speeches concluding each debate, contained vision statements—those passages expressing lofty aspiration, reciting the virtues of the American people, prescribing the proper role of government, etc. Words rich in symbolic value appeared in most of the vision statements; and in some, ideas found expression through well-framed metaphors. The vision statements were earnest, at times evangelical. Whereas Ford's strength was exposition, Carter's strength was exhortation and argument; his best passages appeared in the perorations and in those speeches which sharply rebutted Ford and advanced his own cause; his least impressive speeches occurred in the first debate when he was forced to explain and defend budget proposals and tax reforms. Carter's hyperbole, the most serious fault in his style, went beyond the license we willingly give political speakers. Hyperbole was also a defect in his argumentation.

Ford's style was literal, and stolid declarations were his stock in trade. He seldom conveyed meanings by suggestion, implication, subtle nuance, or metaphor. Instead of letting his audience infer his presidential authority, he repeated "I recommended," "I submitted," etc. His portrayal of Carter consisted of flat, straightforward statements which gave the imagination no room for play: Carter is inconsistent; he tends to distort; he will add costly programs and increase the budget deficit. Ford's slogans were conventional: "hold the lid on spending"; "expand the private sector"; "we've turned the economy around"; we need an "additional tax cut"; and "America is at peace with freedom." Nowhere did figuration or lofty thought impart dignity, even when he treated a subject singled out for special praise—the "new spirit in America" evident in the Bicentennial Year. His sentences on this topic echoed his television commercials, which linked Ford to the Bicentennial "good feeling." He used no themes or symbols to touch deep chords in the psyche. If he did think metaphorically at times, that fact was hidden by his style. If he was sometimes profoundly moved by noble causes, human suffering, or truths beyond the range of fact, his speeches gave no hint. Very literal language emanated from an apparently very literal man.

Carter's language, though often direct and literal, was also sometimes coded and metaphoric. Thus it was richer in appeals, and it threw out a wider net. His frequent references to the "needs in the central cities" and to the plight of the unemployed, poor, and disadvantaged were calculated for broad appeal; and he cemented the appeal to black voters with a sentence he had repeated scores of times: "The greatest thing that ever happened to the South was the passage of the Civil Rights Act. . . ." Carter stated some of Ford's own slogans, but simultaneously sent signals to the other side. Almost as frequently as Ford, he called for a "balanced budget" and "control of the inflationary spiral," while at the same time calling for new programs to "get our people back to work." He committed himself to many new programs, but cautioned that he might have to phase them in slowly. The nation, he said, is in terrible economic disarray, the "tax structure is a disgrace," and we have become weak economically. Yet he assured his audience of the "tremendous economic strength of this country"— we are still strong, "still the best system of government on earth." The present government is bureaucratic, aloof, confused, mismanaged, secretive, linked to big business and corporations, wasteful; yet it can be transformed through strong leadership, cooperation, vision, and can be made again "economical, efficient, purposeful, manageable." Thus there was a remedy for every ill. The worst ill, he implied, was spiritual—a wounding of the spirit caused by disillusionment, division, and disappointment. He spoke repeatedly of the "deep discouragement of the American people" who have been hurt by "Vietnam and Cambodia and Watergate and the CIA revelations," "have felt they've been betrayed by public officials," and have been "excluded, sometimes misled, lied to." "We've been drifting too long. We've been dormant too long. We've been discouraged too long." "Now is the time to heal our country"; "we have been divided" and "now is a time for unity." How heal? How cure division? By drawing inspiration and virtue from the good character and hearts of the people, and by employing their "intelligence, ability, sound common sense, good judgment." Then we can "once again have a government as good as our people." Carter's "healing" metaphors tapped deep motives—deception and truth, division and unity, the wound and the cure, decay and rebirth, suffering and redemption. He would lead, but his own strength and virtue, he said, came from "the people."

The image projected by Ford was sharply defined and easily understood. He was The President, a fact he underscored time after time. He would provide fiscal responsibility and check a spending Congress. There were problems, to be sure, but of modest proportions; and we need only keep to the steady course already charted. The image rounds out: a good and decent man who did not seek the presidency but took it in troubled times; a man who had done a good job in restoring dignity to the White House and in bringing the country together in the aftermath of Vietnam and Watergate. He saw a new spirit in America, and had earned a full term.

The Georgian's image was more complex; in crafting it, he chose to provide multiple definitions of himself. He was a farmer, nuclear engineer, planner, military man, southerner, school board member, Christian, governor, Democrat, reformer, scientist. And, he reminded us, he was not a lawyer, bureaucrat, or establishment politician, and was not controlled by special interests. He drew moral strength and wisdom from the people on the one hand, and from his religious heritage on the other; yet he was master of technical skills and scientific facts. One side of him was a visionary, the other side an engineer: the former was reflective, compassionate, capable of the distant view; the latter was calculative, decisive, occupied with present details. The country's problems were severe and their solutions perhaps would require sacrifice, but they most certainly would yield to comprehensive planning, cooperation, and good government. His connection with past figures of the Democratic party—Roosevelt, Kennedy, Johnson—was symbolic rather than ideological; he preached no party line. His ideology was moral rather than political; his "platform" was not the party's document, but his own position statements coupled with his image. For many voters, the Carter image was primary: it was complex, ambiguous, unclear, uncertain—and it was therefore fresh and promising, but also puzzling and suspect to many Democrats and independents. The image was vulnerable, and the Ford campaign bad-mouthed it in commercials and jabbed at it steadily until election day—wishing mightily that Carter would either discredit himself with blunders or define himself sharply enough to cause some portion of his lukewarm supporters to change allegiance.

The format of the debates was altogether wrong for Ford. As the incumbent with a record to defend, he was a large target for panelists' questions and Carter's attacks. Lead-footed in the ring, he was also an easy target: in round after round, he was punched and forced to defend, then driven to a new topic without time to conceive a strategy. Relatively unprepared with commonplaces and unskilled in rapid verbal combat, Ford lost. A ringside commentator, sketching notes for his post-debate analysis, might have jotted: "A mis-match. The challenger has speed, agility, know-how in the ring. Ford—slow, clumsy, doesn't know how to score. Carter—on the attack, initiative, aggressive, delivers flurry of punches. Ford backing away, defensive, sluggish, hurts himself with a self-inflicted blow. The panelists, too, are hitting Ford! No time for rest and reflection! *Forty rounds!* This is a peculiar way to conduct presidential politics."

5.   The Argumentation

Barbara Walters, moderator of the final Ford-Carter debate, announced that the debate should pursue truth. After introducing the candidates, she linked lofty aims with historic setting:

This debate takes place before an audience in Phi Beta Kappa Memorial Hall on the campus of the College of William and Mary in historic Williamsburg, Virginia. It is particularly appropriate in this Bicentennial year that we meet on these grounds to hear this debate. Two hundred years ago, five William and Mary students met at nearby Raleigh Tavern to form Phi Beta Kappa, a fraternity designed, they wrote, to search out and dispel the clouds of falsehood by debating without reserve the issues of the day. In that spirit of debate, without reserve, to dispel the clouds of falsehood, gentlemen, let us proceed.

Walters' hope was hardly realized. Some "clouds of falsehood" were dispelled, but others remained, and some new ones were created. Ford and Carter sometimes presented speeches which removed doubts about their positions or threw light on murky subjects; but at times their speeches clarified nothing. Frequently, both candidates used defective evidence and shallow arguments; if they sometimes dispelled clouds of falsehood, they also generated new ones. Lofty, rigorous, error-free speeches did not mark the debates.

The format did not invite lofty debate of course, or even debate; it invited answers to questions. And most certainly, it did not permit the sort of painstaking scrutiny of issues envisioned by those students at William and Mary two centuries ago. Indeed, the injunction mouthed by Barbara Walters was both false and foolish: "Let us, gentlemen, debate, without reserve, the issues of the day, and so dispel falsehood." It called on the candidates to do what the format, time limits, and the panelists would not permit. Walters seemed wholly unaware of its impossibility.

In assessing the argumentation, three main questions are considered. What strategies of argumentation enhanced the chances for victory by either candidate? What was the quality of the argumentation—the quality of the evidence and reasoning? And finally, what could an attentive audience have learned about the candidates' tendencies of thought and expression which might provide grounds, however tentative, for estimating presidential potential?

STRATEGIC ARGUMENTATION

We have already noted important differences which indicate that Carter debated more ably than Ford. Carter presented more units of argument than Ford (129 to 89), and packed numerous argumentative units into individual speeches. He directed his arguments more often to Ford than to the panels (73–56), while Ford did the opposite (33–56). Carter heavily outscored in the use of charges, attacks, and criticisms against his opponent (127–48), often using back-to-back speeches to stack up numerous charges which would burden Ford's rejoinder speeches.

We turn now to additional skills which help account for Carter's victory. In the first place, he hit upon the key strategies to be employed in original and rejoinder speeches. Secondly, he displayed greater versatility than Ford: his speeches often exhibited principle and quality, while Ford's tended to be starkly factual.

The key formula for a speaker's strategic response to a panelist's question was to use the original and follow-up speeches to answer the question more or less adequately, and then go on the offensive to initiate issues and attack the opposition. The effect was to tie the hands of the opponent who had yet to speak in the rejoinder position. The previous chapter noted the effects of Carter's use of the formula: Ford was essentially defensive in eight rejoinders, but Carter in none; and Carter was the more aggressive debater. But we need to observe a particular tactic—"shifting the burden"—which Carter used more often than Ford.

Shifting the burden occurs when the speaker in the original and follow-up position responds to a question, hostile or not, in such a way that he escapes somewhat the challenge of the question and transfers that challenge plus additional charges to his opponent, who will speak in the rejoinder position. In all debates, Ford employed this strategy three times—all in the first debate [17, 23, 29]. The best of Ford's three was his speech in response to Gannon's follow-up question which asked whether Ford would veto a bill providing for a public works jobs program. After briefly responding to the question, Ford issued this challenge to Carter:

FORD: I think it's interesting to point out that in the two years that I've been president, I've vetoed fifty-six bills. Congress has sustained forty-two vetoes. As a result, we have saved over 9 billion dollars in federal expenditures. And the Congress, by overriding the bills that I did veto, the Congress has added some 13 billion dollars to the federal expenditures and to the federal deficit. Now, Governor Carter complains about the deficits that this administration has had, and yet he condemns the vetoes that I have made that saved the taxpayer 9 billion dollars and could have saved an additional 13 billion dollars. Now he can't have it both ways. And, therefore, it seems to me that we should hold the lid, as we have to the best of our ability, so we can stimulate the private economy and get the jobs where the jobs are—five out of six in this economy. [I:23]

Ford addressed the question, but at the same time he issued a challenge which burdened Carter in the rejoinder position. Carter responded to Ford in his rejoinder, but not defensively. In fact, no Ford speech succeeded in throwing Carter completely on the defensive in a rejoinder speech.

Carter employed the "shift the burden" strategy in nine speeches, none of which occurred in the first debate—the debate Carter "lost." He used the strategy seven times in the second debate [1, 5, 6, 11, 17, 23, 32], and two times in the third [14, 18]. What is most important, however, is that Carter's use of this strategy generally got results, either by leading Ford to present rejoinders essentially defensive throughout, or by throwing him off stride and depriving him of a strong and effective rebuttal.

For example, Carter charged, in both an original and a follow-up speech, that the Ford administration had excluded the people from processes of decision-making, conducted foreign policy in secrecy, and thus departed from important principles [II: 5, 6]. Ford opened his rejoinder with a brief attack on Carter, but the rejoinder was essentially a defense of himself and his administration:

FORD: Governor Carter again contradicts himself. He complains about secrecy and yet he is quoted as saying that in the attempt to find a solution in the Middle East that he would hold unpublicized meetings with the Soviet Union, I presume for the purpose of imposing a settlement on Israel and the Arab nations.

But let me talk just a minute about what we've done to avoid secrecy in the Ford administration. After the United States took the initiative in working with Israel and with Egypt and achieving the Sinai II agreement—and I'm proud to say that not a single Egyptian or Israeli soldier has lost his life since the signing of the Sinai agreement—but at the time that I submitted the Sinai agreement to the Congress of the United States, I submitted every single document that was applicable to the Sinai II agreement. It was the most complete documentation by any president of any agreement signed by a president on behalf of the United States.

Now as far as meeting with the Congress is concerned: during the twenty-four months that I've been the president of the United States, I have averaged better than one meeting a month with responsible groups or committees of the Congress—both House and Senate. The secretary of state has appeared, in the several years that he's been the secretary, before eighty different committee hearings in the House and in the Senate. The secretary of state has made better than fifty speeches all over the United States explaining American foreign policy. I have made myself at least ten speeches in various parts of the country where I have discussed with the American people defense and foreign policy. [II:7]

The defensiveness in this rejoinder also appeared in other Ford rejoinders after Carter had shifted the burden—especially in rejoinder speeches 13, 19, and 33 in the second debate. One last example in the third debate shows how Carter fielded a question from Robert Maynard in such a way as to place Ford on the defensive:

MAYNARD: Governor, federal policy in this country since World War II has tended to favor the development of suburbs at the great expense of central cities. Does not the federal government now have an affirmative obligation to revitalize the American city? We have heard little in this campaign suggesting that you have an urban reconstruction program. Could you please outline your urban intentions for us tonight? [III:K]

CARTER: Yes, I'd be glad to. In the first place, as is the case with the environmental policy and energy policy that I just described, and the policy for nonproliferation of nuclear waste, this administration has no urban policy. It's impossible for mayors or governors to cooperate with the president, because they can't anticipate what's going to happen next. A mayor of a city like New York, for instance, needs to know eighteen months or two years ahead of time what responsibility the city will have in administration and in financing in things like housing, pollution control, crime control, education, welfare, and health.

This has not been done, unfortunately. I remember the headline in the *Daily News* that said, "Ford to New York: Drop Dead." I think it's very important that our cities know that they have a partner in the federal government.

Quite often Congress has passed laws in the past, designed to help people with the ownership of homes and with the control of crime and with adequate health care and better education programs and so forth. Those programs were designed to help those who need it most. And quite often this has been in the very poor people and neighborhoods in the downtown urban centers. Because of the greatly advantaged persons who live in the suburbs—better education, better organization, more articulate, more aware of what the laws are—quite often this money has been channelled out of the downtown centers where it's needed.

Also I favor all revenue sharing money being used for local governments, and also to remove the prohibitions in the use of revenue sharing money so that it can be used to improve education and health care. We have now, for instance, only 7 percent of the total education cost being financed by the federal government. When the Nixon-Ford administration started, this was 10 percent. That's a 30 percent reduction in the portion that the federal government contributes to education in just eight years. And, as you know, the education costs have gone up tremendously.

The last point is that the major thrust has got to be to put people back to work. We've got an extraordinarily high unemployment rate among downtown urban ghetto areas, particularly among the very poor and particularly among minority groups, sometimes 50 or 60 percent. And the concentration of employment opportunities in those areas would help greatly not only to reestablish the tax base, but also to help reduce the extraordinary welfare cost.

One of the major responsibilities on the shoulders of New York City is to finance welfare. And I favor the shifting of the welfare cost away from the local governments altogether. And over a longer period of time, let the federal government begin to absorb part of it that's now paid by the state governments. Those things would help a great deal with the cities, but we still have a very serious problem there. [III:18]

FORD: Let me speak out very strongly. The Ford administration does have a very comprehensive program to help our major metropolitan areas. I fought for, and the Congress finally went along with, a general revenue sharing program whereby cities and states—the cities two-thirds and the states one-third—get over 6 billion dollars a year in cash for which they can provide many, many services, whatever they really want. In addition, we in the federal government make available to cities about 3 billion, 300 million dollars in what we call community development.

In addition, as a result of my pressure on the Congress, we got a major mass transit program over a four-year period: 11 billion, 800 million dollars. We have a good housing program that will result in cutting the down payments by 50 percent and having mortgage payments lower at the beginning of any mortgage period. We're expanding our homestead housing program.

The net result is, we think under Carla Hills—who's the chairman of my Urban Development and Neighborhood Revitalization Program—we will really do a first-class job in helping the communities throughout the country. As a matter of fact, that committee under Secretary Hills released about a seventy-five-page report with specific recommendations so we can do a better job in the weeks ahead. And in addition, the tax program of the Ford administration, which provides an incentive for industry to move into our major metropolitan areas, into the inner cities, will bring jobs where people are and help to revitalize those cities as they can be.

Maynard's question was not hostile, although it did suggest that Carter had said precious little in the campaign about urban revitalization. Carter's speech covered numerous topics relevant to the question, but also sharply attacked the Ford administration's failure to institute an urban policy. Ford's rejoinder was defensive throughout, containing not one phrase critical of Carter's proposals.

There are three obvious strategies to be employed in rejoinders. First, the rejoinder speaker should be aggressive, and not defensive. Six of Ford's and sixteen of Carter's rejoinders were aggressive; none of Carter's rejoinders, but eight of Ford's, were essentially defensive. The aggressive rejoinder should actively rebut the opponent's arguments and positions, setting out new issues, and offering charges and counter-arguments. Ford did this, for example, after Carter had been pressured by Drew as to how he would manage to balance the budget. Carter's speeches answering Drew did not burden Ford, who was essentially free in his rejoinder:

FORD: If it is true that there will be a 60 billion dollar surplus by fiscal year 1981, rather than spend that money for all the new programs that Governor Carter recommends and endorses and which are included in the Democratic platform, I think the American taxpayer ought to get an additional tax break, a tax reduction of that magnitude. I feel that the taxpayers are the ones that need the relief. I don't think we should add additional programs of the magnitude that Governor Carter talks about. It seems to me that our tax structure today has rates that are too high.

But I am very glad to point out that since 1969, during a Republican administration, we have had 10 million people taken off of the tax rolls at the lower end of the taxpayer area, and at the same time, assuming that I sign the tax bill that was mentioned by Mr. Gannon, we will, in the last two tax bills, have increased the minimum tax on all wealthy taxpayers. And I believe that by eliminating 10 million taxpayers in the last eight years and by putting a heavier tax burden on those in the higher tax brackets, plus the other actions that have been taken, we can give taxpayers adequate tax relief.

Now, it seems to me that as we look at the recommendations of the budget committees and our own projections, there isn't going to be any 60-billion-dollar dividend. I've heard of those dividends in the past. It always happens. We expected one at the time of the Vietnam War, but it was used up before we ever ended the war and taxpayers never got the adequate relief they deserved. [I:9]

The same pattern and the same reasons for Ford's easy "score" on Carter are evident in three other Ford rejoinders [I:27; II:2; III:34].

By comparison, Carter was more frequently on the attack and initiating issues in rejoinders; and, not of least importance, he did so not only when his rejoinder was free, but also when he had been challenged by Ford's just concluded speech. In the first debate, after Ford had presented two speeches free of any serious challenge to his opponent, Carter made this essentially free rejoinder speech, aggressive from beginning to end:

CARTER: Well, Mr. Ford is changing considerably his previous philosophy. The present tax structure is a disgrace to this country. It's just a welfare program for the rich. As a matter of fact, 25 percent of the total tax deductions go for only 1 percent of the richest people in this country. And over 50 percent of the tax credits go for the 14 percent of the richest people in this country. When Mr. Ford first became president in August of 1974, the first thing he did in October was to ask for a 4.7-billion-dollar increase in taxes on our people in the midst of the heaviest recession since the Great Depression of the 1940s. In January of 1975, he asked for a tax change—a 5.6-billion-dollar increase on low- and middle-income private individuals, a 6½-billion-dollar decrease on the corporations and the special interests. In December of 1975, he vetoed the roughly 18- to 20-billion-dollar tax reduction bill that had been passed by the Congress. And then he came back later on in January of this year and he did advocate a 10-billion-dollar tax reduction, but it would be offset by a 6-billion-dollar increase this coming January in deductions for Social Security payments and for unemployment compensation. The whole philosophy of the Republican party, including my opponent, has been to pile on taxes on low-income people, to take them off on the corporations. As a matter of fact, since the late sixties when Mr. Nixon took office, we've had a reduction in the percentage of taxes paid by corporations from 30 percent down to about 20 percent. We've had an increase in taxes paid by individuals—payroll taxes—from 14 percent up to 20 percent, and this is what the Republicans have done to us. And this is why tax reform is so important. [I:6]

Virtually the same conditions and the same strategy occurred in nine additional Carter rejoinders.[1] In each case, Ford's preceding speeches placed no significant challenge upon Carter, nor did the panelists' questions burden him. Thus Carter was left free in his rejoinders to attack, criticize, provide a counterposition—indeed, free to do whatever his political savvy suggested was appropriate. It was necessary in only two instances for Carter to present a rejoinder speech while feeling some sting from Ford's just concluded speech [I:18, II:4].

The following short and contrasting speeches show clearly that Ford was an easy mark for Carter's rejoinder speech. This exchange is the final one of the second debate.

TREWHITT: Mr. President, if you get the accounting of missing-in-action you want from North Vietnam—or from Vietnam, I'm sorry—now, would you then be prepared to reopen negotiations for restoration of relations with that country?

FORD: Let me restate our policy. As long as Vietnam—North Vietnam—does not give us a full and complete accounting of our missing-in-action, I will never go along with the admission of Vietnam to the United Nations. If they do give us a bona fide, complete accounting of the 800 MIAs, then I believe that the United States should begin negotiations for the admission of Vietnam to the United Nations, but not until they have given us the full accounting of our MIAs.

CARTER: One of the most embarrassing failures of the Ford administration, and one that touches specifically on human rights, is his refusal to appoint a presidential commission to go to Vietnam, to go to

Laos, to go to Cambodia, and try to trade for the release of information about those who are missing in action in those wars. This is what the families of MIAs want. So far, Mr. Ford has not done it. We've had several fragmentary efforts by members of the Congress and by private citizens. Several months ago the Vietnam government said we are ready to sit down and negotiate for release of information on MIAs. So far, Mr. Ford has not responded. I also would never normalize relationships with Vietnam, nor permit them to join the United Nations, until they've taken this action. But that's not enough. We need to have an active and aggressive action on the part of the president, the leader of this country, to seek out every possible way to get that information which has kept the MIA families in despair and doubt, and Mr. Ford has just not done it.

Ford answered the question—and nothing more. Carter answered the question *and* attacked Ford. Because Carter's speech closed the last unit of debate, Ford had no opportunity to answer Carter's attack unless he used some of the time assigned for his peroration—and he did not.

A second basic strategy in rejoinder speeches is the speaker's selection of the most advantageous subjects for rebuttal or criticism. One must keep in mind that the question posed originally by the panelist and the several topics discussed in the original speech are all transitory. The rejoinder speaker has a striking advantage in that he can give saliency to one matter rather than another, as suits his purpose. In the first debate Ford gave saliency rather skillfully to some matters that were advantageous to him.[2] The best of these is worth quoting in full. It came after Carter delivered two speeches covering inequities in the tax system, Ford's advocacy of tax reductions for special interest groups and the wealthy, needed changes in tax deductions and exemptions, elimination of certain business deductions, and the need to provide tax relief to middle- and lower-income families.

FORD: Governor Carter's answer tonight does not coincide with the answer that he gave in an interview to the Associated Press a week or so ago. In that interview, Governor Carter indicated that he would raise the taxes on those in the medium- or middle-income brackets or higher. Now if you take the medium- or middle-income taxpayer, that's about

14,000 dollars per person. Governor Carter had indicated publicly, in an interview, that he would increase the taxes on about 50 percent of the working people of this country.

I think the way to get tax equity in this country is to give tax relief to the middle-income people, who have an income from roughly 8,000 dollars up to 25,000 or 30,000 dollars. They have been short-changed as we have taken 10 million taxpayers off the tax rolls in the last eight years, and as we have added to the minimum tax provision to make all people pay more taxes. I believe in tax equity for the middle-income taxpayer, increasing the personal exemption. Mr. Carter wants to increase taxes for roughly half of the taxpayers of this country.

Now, the governor has also played a little fast and loose with the facts about vetoes. The records show that President Roosevelt vetoed on an average of fifty-five bills a year. President Truman vetoed on the average, while he was president, about thirty-eight bills a year. I understand that Governor Carter, when he was governor of Georgia, vetoed between thirty-five and forty bills a year. My average in two years is twenty-six, but in the process of that we have saved 9 billion dollars.

And one final comment. Governor Carter talks about the tax bills and all of the inequities that exist in the present law. I must remind him: the Democrats have controlled the Congress for the last twenty-two years, and they wrote all the tax bills. [I:27]

Ford used this tactic four times in the first debate, in which he was at his best. He faltered in the second and third debates, when he succeeded in using it in only two rejoinders [II:24 and III:11].

Thus the strategy of selecting issues for strategic attack and rebuttal was ably employed by Ford in six rejoinders. In contrast, fourteen of Carter's rejoinders clearly employed this strategy.[3]

The third and perhaps the most clever tactic is "joining forces with the questioner" when the question is one-sided and more or less hostile to the speaker in the original position. In essence, the rejoinder speaker says to the panelist, "You're right," and then adds fuel to the fire started by the panelist. Carter used this tactic five times—once in the second debate, and four times in the third debate, when panelists created numerous opportunities for him. In every instance, Ford had responded defensively to a one-sided and hostile question—on the *Mayaguez* incident [II:31], his failure to fire General Brown [III:13], his environmental record [III:17], his record on civil rights [III:21], and his economic record [III:32]. The following example serves as a model:

KRAFT: . . . one main subject on the minds of all of them [the public] has been the environment. They're particularly curious about your record. People really want to know why you vetoed the strip-mining bill. They want to know why you worked against strong controls on auto emissions. They want to know why you aren't doing anything about pollution of the Atlantic Ocean. They want to know why a bipartisan organization such as the National League of Conservation Voters says that when it comes to environmental issues, you are—and I'm quoting—"hopeless."

FORD: First, let me set the record straight. I vetoed the strip-mining bill, Mr. Kraft, because it was the overwhelming consensus of knowledgeable people that that strip-mining bill would have meant the loss of literally thousands of jobs, something around 140,000 jobs. Number two, that strip-mining bill would have severely set back our need for more coal, and Governor Carter has said repeatedly that coal is the resource that we need to use more in the effort to become independent of the Arab oil supply. So, I vetoed it because of a loss of jobs and because it would have interfered with our energy independence program.

The auto emissions: it was agreed by Leonard Woodcock, the head of the UAW, and by the heads of all of the automobile industry—we had labor and management together saying that those auto emissions standards had to be modified.

But let's talk about what the Ford administration has done in the field of environment. I have increased, as president, by over 60 percent, the funding for water treatment plants in the United States—the federal contribution.

I have fully funded the land and water conservation program—in fact, have recommended, and the Congress approved, a substantially increased land and water conservation program. I have added in the current-year budget the funds for the National Park Service. For example, we proposed about 12 million dollars to add between four and five hundred more employees for the National Park Service.

And a month or so ago, I did likewise say over the next ten years, we should expand—double—the national parks, the wilderness areas, the scenic river areas. And then, of course, the final thing is that I have signed and approved of more scenic rivers, more wilderness areas since I've been president than any other president in the history of the United States. [III:16]

CARTER: Well, I might say that I think the League of Conservation Voters is absolutely right. This administration's record on environment is very bad.

I think it's accurate to say that the strip-mining law which was passed twice by the Congress—and only lacked two votes, I believe, of being overridden—would have been good for the country. The claim that it would have put 140,000 miners out of work is hard to believe, when at the time Mr. Ford vetoed it, the United Mine Workers was supporting the bill. And I don't think they would have supported the bill had they known that they would lose 140,000 jobs.

There's been a consistent policy on the part of this administration to lower or to delay enforcement of air pollution standards and water pollution standards. And under both President Nixon and Ford, monies have been impounded that would have gone to cities and others to control water pollution.

We have no energy policy. We, I think, are the only developed nation in the world that has no comprehensive energy policy to permit us to plan in an orderly way how to shift from increasingly scarce energy forms—oil—and have research and development concentrated on the increased use of coal, which I strongly favor—the research and development to be used primarily to make the coal burning be clean.

We need a heritage trust program, similar to the one we had in Georgia, to set aside additional lands that have geological and archeological importance, natural areas for enjoyment. The lands that Mr. Ford brags about having approved are in Alaska, and they are enormous in size, but as far as the accessibility of them by the American people, it's very far in the future.

We've taken no strong position in the control of pollution of our oceans. And I would say the worst threat to the environment of all is nuclear proliferation; and this administration, having been in office now for two years or more, has still not taken strong and bold action to stop the proliferation of nuclear waste around the world, particularly plutonium. Those are some brief remarks about the failures of this administration. I would do the opposite in every respect. [III:17]

This Carter speech has all the virtues of a strategic rejoinder: it joins forces with Kraft, amplifies the criticism of

Ford, refutes Ford's claims, and adds other charges. In addition, it is cogent, well structured, and soundly argued.

In addition to the five instances already noted in which he joins forces with the questioner, Carter had another opportunity to do the same, but chose instead to remain silent. In the third debate, Nelson posed two questions to Ford about his possible involvement in an early Watergate cover-up. Ford struggled through two speeches, arguing that he had been cleared of involvement. When moderator Barbara Walters asked Carter for his response, he said only, "I don't have any response." His silence was wise tactically: little could have been gained by adding to the issues Nelson had raised; on the other hand, a somewhat strident rejoinder by Carter might have risked "over-kill" and gained audience sympathy for Ford.

Ford employed the tactic of joining forces with the questioner in only one rejoinder. The last question of the third debate, posed by Robert Maynard, challenged the efficiency and perhaps the conception of Carter's campaign. It was strikingly one-sided, and it was hostile.

MAYNARD: Governor Carter, you entered this race against President Ford with a 20-point lead or better in the polls. And now it appears that this campaign is headed for a photo finish. You've said how difficult it is to run against a sitting president. But Mr. Ford was just as much an incumbent in July when you were 20 points ahead as he is now. Can you tell us what caused the evaporation of that lead, in your opinion?

Carter's speech answered that Maynard's analysis of the polls was somewhat misleading, denied that the polls were of much significance to him, reviewed briefly his manner of campaigning and the strength of his support, and concluded with his hope for victory. Carter's speech addressed no argument or charge to Ford. Neither Maynard's question nor Carter's speech put any challenge to the president, who said in his rejoinder:

FORD: I think the increase in the prospects as far as I'm concerned and the less-favorable prospects for Governor Carter reflect that Governor Carter is inconsistent in many of the positions that he takes. He tends to distort on a number of occasions.

Just a moment ago, for example, he was indicating that in the 1950s, for example, unemployment was very low. He fails to point out that in the 1950s, we were engaged in the war in Vietnam—I mean in Korea. We had 3,500,000 young men in the Army, Navy, Air Force, and Marines. That's not the way to end unemployment or to reduce unemployment.

At the present time we're at peace. We have reduced the number of people in the Army, Navy, Air Force, and Marines from 3,500,000 to 2,100,000. We are not at war; we have reduced the military manpower by 1,400,000. If we had that many more people in the Army, the Navy, the Air Force, and Marines, our unemployment figure would be considerably less. But this administration doesn't believe the way to reduce unemployment is to go to war, or to increase the number of people in the military. So you cannot compare unemployment, as you sought to, with the present time, with the 1950s, because the then administration had people in the military, they were at war, they were fighting overseas. And this administration has reduced the size of the military by 1,400,000; they're in the civilian labor market, and they're not fighting anywhere around the world today. [III:34]

This Ford rejoinder was essentially free of constraints from both questioner and opponent. It joined forces with Maynard's question to state, in effect, "here is the reason for the Governor's quick drop in the polls—his inconsistencies and distortions." Ford belabored this single point, however, and, in doing so, missed the opportunity to pinpoint numerous reasons for Carter's decline in the polls. He might well have "reminded" the audience of the public's loss of confidence in Carter because of the *Playboy* interview and the "fuzzy" Carter image; and he could have cited reasons for the public's growing confidence in and respect for the record and policies of the Ford administration. Ford's argumentation in this rejoinder signals a characteristic flaw in his rebuttal skills: he apparently believed that he was making a strong argument, when in fact he was not.

In five other rejoinders, Ford had obvious opportunities to "join forces" and deal damaging blows to his opponent, but he failed to recognize them. For example, Frankel's opening question to Carter in the second debate listed several foreign policy successes, and then asked, "Do you really have a quarrel with this Republican record?" Carter delivered a blistering and diffuse attack on the Nixon-Ford record. In his rejoinder, Ford argued that Carter's proposed cuts in defense spending would impair the national security [2]. He should have returned to the sense of the question and reaffirmed Frankel's account of his successful record. In two other rejoinders in the same debate, Ford missed similar opportunities to join forces with Valeriani, who challenged Carter's credentials for the presidency [7] and later suggested that Carter's charge of secrecy in the Ford administration was "just campaign rhetoric" [24]. In the third debate, after Maynard charged (in a question directed to Carter) that the campaign was being conducted at a low level, Carter responded with apologies for the *Playboy* interview, an admission of mistakes, and a pledge to conduct the campaign at a high level during the remaining days. In his rejoinder, Ford missed the opportunity to identify specific defects in Carter's campaign and, what might have proved most effective, to recite Carter's several campaign gaffes [5]. Finally, Nelson questioned whether Carter would bring able people into his administration; in reply, Carter "shifted the burden" by comparing his choice of Mondale with Ford's choice of Dole. Instead of endorsing and amplifying Nelson's challenge to Carter, Ford used his rejoinder to defend Dole [15].

Based upon the evidence, it is clear that Carter's tactical skills in debate exceeded Ford's. Surely, this can be traced largely to ability: Carter was quicker than Ford to see opportunities, adept at piling up charges and criticisms, able to fashion speeches containing new issues and sharp rebuttals, and clever in taking advantage of the strategic possibilities of the debate format. At the same time, the debate format favored Carter in that it enabled him to capitalize on his talents. And the panels, especially the third one, contributed to Carter's success because they so often placed Ford on the defensive with hostile and one-sided questions. Finally, Ford's performance in the second and third debates deteriorated as he became more and more submissive to the panels; his failure to initiate charges and criticisms also worked to Carter's advantage.

One additional facet of argumentative technique requires discussion. Ford argued mainly on the basis of *the facts* and provided relatively few arguments based on principle and quality. Carter displayed far greater versatility. The difference between the two was more an indication of Ford's severe argumentative limitation than of particular excellence in Carter, but the consequence was a distinct advantage for Carter.

The type of argument most frequently used was argument to or from *consequences,* a type ordinarily used to establish that desirable or undesirable consequences will or won't follow upon certain attitudes, circumstances, policies, etc. Arguments of this type occurred no less than sixty-five times, with the candidates using them almost equally. A Carter speech provides an obvious instance: President Ford "says we have to move from one area of the world to another. That's one of the problems with this administration's so-called shuttle diplomacy. [The undesirable consequence is:] While the secretary of state's in one country, there are almost 150 others that are wondering what we're going to do next. What will be the next secret agreement?" [II:27]

Arguments from *example* appeared at least fifty times, again used frequently by both speakers. Seeking to show that U.S. foreign policy had expressed "the very highest standards of morality," Ford stated in the second debate that "the initiatives that we took in southern Africa are the best examples of what this administration is doing and will continue to do in the next four years." Ford's speech amplified his examples [25].

Arguments stating a *causal relation* occurred at least thirty-seven times, with Carter using this technique more often than Ford. Argument from example joins a causal argument in the speech just mentioned: Ford claims that his administration's leadership led to (was the cause of) agreements reached in the Middle East. In the first debate, both candidates often argued that a policy or legislative program did or would produce higher taxes, lower taxes, more or less unemployment.

Arguments from the *testimony* of authorities appeared no less than twenty-four times, with Ford using this type more often than Carter. For example, Ford cited the testimony of the ship's captain in order to document the prudence of his action in the *Mayaguez* incident [II:30]. He cited testimony of Georgia's

Governor Busbee to lend weight to his criticism of Carter's record as governor of Georgia [I:15]. Carter called upon the testimony of advisers Schlesinger and Harriman [III:9].

Other types of argument employed often, although less frequently than those already mentioned, were arguments based on *statistics;* on *inconsistency, contradiction,* and *dilemma;* on *comparison* and *analogy;* and on *historical parallel* and *precedent.* Many speeches also contained what might be called *counterclaim*—the rejection of a proposition offered by the opponent, coupled with an assertion of "what is the case."

A feature that almost all of the previous types of argument have in common is a factual base; that is, they are grounded in what is thought to be "fact." In nearly all instances, arguments from consequences, causes, examples, statistics, testimony, comparisons, analogies, and precedents related essentially to the facts. The candidates presented roughly equal numbers of "factual" arguments.

There is yet another broad category, however—argument from *principle*— which engages criteria, aspirations, definitions, conceptions, or principles. Unlike argument that is essentially factual, argument based on principle begins with a premise having the character of a principle ("All men are created equal"), or a definition ("A moral government is . . ."), or a criterion ("The duty of a president is to . . ."). Arguments based on principle occurred at least fifty-seven times, with Carter using them more than twice as often as Ford (40–17). The numerical difference hardly tells the full story, however, because Ford's arguments were usually short and underdeveloped.

In only a few speeches did Ford develop an extended argument based on principle. Answering Reynolds' question in the first debate about whether he could get along with a Democratic Congress, Ford replied that *on principle* a Republican president is needed to check a Democratic Congress:

I think it would be contrary to one of the basic concepts in our system of government, a system of checks and balances. We have a Democratic Congress today, and fortunately, we've had a Republican president to check their excesses with my vetoes. If we have a Democratic Congress next year and a president who wants to spend an additional 100 billion dollars a year or maybe 200 billion dollars a year with more programs, we will have, in my judgment, greater deficits with more spending, more dangers of inflation. I think the American people want a Republican president, to check on any excesses that come out of the next Congress if it is a Democratic Congress. [I:29]

This unit contains mixed lines of argument, of course, including cause and consequences. But the chief point to note is the prominence of the principle Ford lays down as an operating premise, or a leading concept, in his conception of the system of checks and balances. Again, in answer to one of Valeriani's questions in the second debate, Ford provided a speech based largely on principles contained in the Shanghai Communiqué—especially the principle that normalization of relations with Mainland China should proceed in such a way that disputes between China and Taiwan are resolved by peaceful means [II:14]. Similarly, his speech in answer to a question about his administration's civil rights record sought to show that his achievements and programs have operated upon principles [III:20].

Even when panelists' questions appeared to seek justifications anchored in principles and criteria, Ford tended to ground his speech in fact. For example, after Carter was asked by Nelson to explain his views on the Supreme Court and his criteria and philosophy in making appointments to the Court, Ford's rejoinder—addressing roughly the same questions—went directly to factual grounds. Instead of stating criteria and principles, he cited an example:

Well, I think the answer as to the kind of a person that I would select is obvious. I had one opportunity to nominate an individual to the Supreme Court and I selected the Circuit Court of Appeals judge from Illinois, John Paul Stevens. I selected him because of his outstanding record as a Circuit Court of Appeals judge, and I was very pleased that an overwhelmingly Democratic United States Senate, after going into his background, came to the conclusion that he was fit and should serve, and the vote in his behalf was overwhelming. So, I would say somebody in the format of Justice Stevens would be the kind of an individual that I would select in the future, as I did him in the past. [III:29]

In short, Ford seldom argued from principles. When he did, the arguments were often brief or underdeveloped. Even when there was a strong invitation to argue from principle, his inclination was to argue from fact. This "factual" tendency or strategy sharply limited the range and quality of his speeches. In contrast, Carter argued much more frequently from criteria, principles, and definitions. Moreover, he sometimes made extended arguments of this sort. In the first debate, clear examples occurred in his speeches on "amnesty" and "pardon" and in his objections to the criminal justice system [I:12]; in his statement of goals of government reorganization [I:13]; in his characterization of the present tax structure as unfair [I:25]; in the qualities or criteria of presidential leadership [I:30]; and in his peroration which stated principles and definitions he believed to be central to a proper conception of American government, of the people, and of the relation between the two [35].[4] In the second debate, the grounds of Carter's arguments were even more heavily weighted toward principles and criteria. For example, many moral principles and criteria appeared in his lengthy speeches on foreign policy aims, human rights, and openness in government [II:5,10]. According to Carter, Ford's policies amounted to a "deviation from idealism" and a "yielding to pressure" which were contrary to principles and commitments [II:11], whereas the nation's strength—defined by Carter in a lengthy unit—rested on grounds of moral principle and vision as well as on economic and military prowess [II:23]. Carter objected on principle to the Arab boycott of American businesses [II:32]; and his peroration was liberally sprinkled with aspirations and statements exhibiting principles and definitions, particularly definitions of "what should be" [II:36]. In the third debate, Carter engaged principles in numerous speeches: for example, his justification of selecting Mondale as his running mate [14], his position on civil rights [21], and his criteria for the selection of Supreme Court judges [27].

The intention here is not to suggest that Carter regularly argued from principle, nor that his argumentation was less based in fact than Ford's. He did, however, ground a much larger proportion of his argumentation in principle than did Ford.

This conclusion, reached through an analysis of specific types of arguments, appears again if one examines the general character of the speeches. All speeches were classified as essentially factual, definitional, or qualitative—or as showing some combination of these three grounds of disputes, or points of issues. This classification has roots in the writings of the classical rhetoricians, who held that any simple (non-complex) dispute or issue depends on, or establishes, a matter of fact, definition, or quality. Thus, a matter of fact is at issue in debate about the causes of unemployment: something is or is not a cause. At issue in debate about the health of the economy is not merely certain facts, but also a definition—what "healthy economy" means. And at issue in debate about the seriousness of unemployment is not simply facts, but a value, a judgment of quality, or a certain feeling or appreciation (for example, sympathy for the plight of the unemployed) which invests facts with quality. Speeches often treat complex disputes which combine issues of fact, definition, and quality; in addition, some speeches contain more than one unit of argument, each of which may engage a different argumentative ground. For these reasons, many speeches exhibit a combination of fact and quality, or fact and definition, etc.

The factual ground was dominant throughout the debates: of 109 speeches, 56 were essentially based in fact. But the difference between the speakers is significant: 71 percent of Ford's 56 speeches were grounded in fact, while 30 percent of Carter's 53 speeches were similarly grounded. Moreover, 6 additional Ford speeches and 9 additional Carter speeches exhibit combinations in which the factual ground is primary. This means that 82 percent of Ford's speeches and 47 percent of Carter's were either wholly or primarily factual. Ford presented only 7 speeches—in contrast to 25 by Carter—in which the factual ground was combined equally with definition or quality, or in which definition or quality was the single or primary ground.

Ford rarely presented speeches which were thoroughly definitional or qualitative. The single instance of a Ford speech which attempted, through extended discourse, to provide a broad conception (mainly by way of definition) was his peroration at the close of the first debate. For example, the middle paragraphs provide, in broad strokes, a notion of stages in the development of the country:

On the Fourth of July we had a wonderful two-hundredth birthday for our great country. It was a superb occasion. It was a glorious day. In the first century of our nation's history, our forefathers gave us the finest form of government in the history of mankind. In the second century of our nation's history, our forefathers developed the most productive industrial nation in the history of the globe. Our third century should be the century of individual freedom for all our 215 million Americans today and all that join us.

In the last few years government has gotten bigger and bigger. Industry has gotten larger and larger. Labor unions have gotten bigger and bigger. And our children have been the victims of mass education. We must make this next century the century of the individual. We should never forget that a government big enough to give us everything we want is a government big enough to take from us everything we have. The individual worker in the plants throughout the United States should not be a small cog in a big machine. The member of a labor union must have his rights strengthened and broadened. And our children in their education should have an opportunity to improve themselves based on their talents and their abilities. [I:36]

The idea of developmental stages is present, but unamplified; and the concept of the "century of individual freedom" remains obscure. Ford only rarely brought quality, sentiment, and valuation to the surface. Perhaps the speech in which he succeeded best was his rejoinder after Carter had charged that foreign affairs are secretive and lack moral principle. Ford's rejoinder contained this paragraph:

The governor also talks about morality in foreign policy. The foreign policy of the United States meets the highest standards of morality. What is more moral than peace? And the United States is at peace today. What is more moral in foreign policy than for the administration to take the lead in the World Food Conference in Rome in 1974 when the United States committed 6 million metric tons of food— over 60 percent of the food committed for the disadvantaged and underdeveloped nations of the world? The Ford administration wants to eradicate hunger and disease in our underdeveloped countries throughout the world. What is more moral than for the United States, under the Ford administration, to take the lead in southern Africa, in the Middle East? Those are initiatives in foreign policy which are of the highest moral standard, and that is indicative of the foreign policy of this country. [II:24]

This was one of Ford's best speeches. In the part quoted, there is expression of feeling, there is moral quality, there is a flash of indignation. But such speeches were infrequent. Unable or unwilling to develop arguments displaying principle and definition on the one hand, or quality on the other, his speeches by and large were starkly factual. It is possible that his use of factual matter was deliberate and intended to display command of information. A more likely hypothesis is that his factual bias reflected the natural tendency of his thought.

Several Carter speeches, including all three perorations, displayed a balance of positions—definition, quality, and fact. His speech in answer to a question by Valeriani is a clear example: "Governor Carter, earlier tonight you said, 'America is not strong anymore,' 'America is not respected anymore'; and I feel that I must ask you, do you really believe that the United States is not the most respected country in the world? Or is that just campaign rhetoric?" [II:0] In response, Carter referred to matters of fact, but also sought to define his meaning and, at the same time, to express aspirations and ideals. The first half of the speech reads:

No, it's not just campaign rhetoric. I think that militarily we are as strong as any nation on earth. I think we've got to stay that way and continue to increase our capabilities to meet any potential threat. But as far as strength derived from commitment to principles; as far as strength derived from the unity within our country; as far as strength derived from the people, the Congress, the secretary of state, the president sharing in the evolution and carrying out of our foreign policy; as far as strength derived from the respect of our own allies and friends, their assurance that we will be staunch in our commitment, that we will not deviate, and that we'll give them adequate attention; as far as strength derived from doing what's right, caring for the poor, providing food, becoming the bread-basket of the world instead of the arms merchant of the world: in those respects, we're not strong. [II:23]

Similarly, Carter's answer to Frankel's question about the Arab boycott of Israel exhibits valuation, and emotion as well [II:32]. Other Carter speeches show dominance of either definition or quality—for example, his speech on what should be done to obtain an accounting of the missing-in-action in Vietnam [II:35], his speech criticizing the Ford record on civil rights [III:21], a speech dealing with amendments to the Constitution [III:22], and two speeches outlining criteria and philosophy relating to Supreme Court appointments [III:27,28].

What conclusions may be drawn from these observations? First, and most apparent, the range of possible arguments is sharply restricted if a speaker, whether from choice or nature, is strongly biased toward use of the factual ground. Argumentation to establish concepts, principles, moral frameworks, and notions of *what should be* cannot be made on facts alone. Nor can argumentation designed to evoke feeling be built of pure fact; it requires, instead, the engaging of principles, sentiments, emotion, and sympathy. Whatever the cause, Ford's argumentation showed a strong factual bias; only rarely did he present arguments displaying principles and expressing emotion.

Second, audiences "read character" in what speakers say and how they say it. Aristotle wrote that the most effective speeches reveal the virtues of the speaker—wisdom, high moral character, and good will. Furthermore, the impression conveyed by the speaker's virtues—his ethos—often provides a stronger proof than the arguments. How are wisdom, moral character, and good will displayed? Not by means of a steady recital of facts, even though this may show the speaker's command of "information." Wisdom, moral character, and good will are displayed through speeches containing a right mixture of lofty ideas, complexity of thought, moral maxims, dignity in thought and style, appropriate expressions of emotion, and communication of a sense of genuine concern. The result is discourse that is judged to be "principled" and earnest, reflecting the good character of the speaker. Ford's strong dependence on the factual ground and on factual arguments significantly reduced his opportunity to reveal virtues of character. Carter was more able than Ford to enhance his ethos by means of his speeches. [5]

The evidence shows that Carter was by far the more skillful and versatile debater. After a shaky start in the first debate, he made good use of the strategic possibilities of the debate format and exploited Ford's failure to do the same. At the same time, he was able to argue from principle as well as fact, to invest his speeches with moral flavor, and to communicate emotion. Ford, on the other hand, argued regularly at the level of fact and thus limited his argumentative range and reduced his opportunity to present a persuasive ethos.

THE QUALITY OF THE ARGUMENTS

Severe limitations restricted the possibility that Ford and Carter could present excellent speeches and argumentation. They did not know what questions would be asked; they had to speak at once; and they could only speak two or three minutes regarding even momentous issues. Under these conditions, eloquence could not be expected; one should be satisfied if the speeches by and large were free of defects and sound in argument. In view of the limitations, one should also be surprised if as many as a dozen or so speeches succeeded in presenting excellent argumentation. Actually, a handful of speeches were excellent, and many more than that were defective.

A careful reading and comparison of speeches in every round of debate was undertaken in order to assess each speech on the basis of such factors as the presence or absence of proper evidence, sound reasoning, effective argumentative tactics, and relevance of matter to the question at issue.[6] For example, two back-to-back speeches which answered a question by Nelson show sharp contrast: Ford's is significantly defective; Carter's is much better than Ford's but not unflawed:

NELSON: Mr. President, your campaign has run ads in black newspapers saying that, quote, "for black Americans, President Ford is quietly getting the job done." Yet, study after study has shown little progress in desegregation and, in fact, actual increases in segregated schools and housing in the Northeast. Now, civil rights groups have complained repeatedly that there's been lack of progress and commitment to an integrated society during your administration. So how are you getting the job done for blacks and other minorities, and what programs do you have in mind for the next four years? [III:L]

FORD: Let me say at the outset, I'm very proud of the record of this administration. In the cabinet I have one of the outstanding, I think, administrators as the secretary of transportation, Bill Coleman. You're familiar, I'm sure, with the recognition given in the Air Force to General James, and there was just approved a three-star admiral, the first in the history of the United States Navy. So, we are giving full recognition to individuals of quality in the Ford administration in positions of great responsibility.

In addition, the Department of Justice is fully enforcing, and enforcing effectively, the Voting Rights Act, the legislation that involves jobs, housing for minorities, not only blacks but all others. The Department of HUD is enforcing the new legislation that outlaws—that takes care of red-lining.

What we're doing is saying that that there are opportunities—business opportunities, educational opportunities, responsibilities—where people with talent, black or any other minority, can fully qualify. The Office of Minority Business, in the Department of Commerce, has made available more money in trying to help black businessmen or other minority businessmen than any other administration since the office was established. The Office of Small Business, under Mr. Kobelinski, has a very massive program trying to help the black community. The individual who wants to start a business or expand his business as a black businessman is able to borrow, either directly or with guaranteed loans. I believe, on the record, that this administration has been responsive and we have carried out the law to the letter, and I'm proud of the record. [III:20]

In this speech, the argumentation is shallow: the examples of Mr. Coleman, General James, and an unnamed admiral will not produce satisfying evidence for the generalization Ford announces; and some claims in the remainder of the speech are overblown, while others need evidence. In addition, the speech does not come to grips with Nelson's request that the president outline or describe the future programs that would meet the problem. Perhaps most telling is what one must read between the lines: that apparently Ford did not fully appreciate or understand the dimensions of the problems Nelson called to his attention, and one may surmise that the shallowness of his speech is in part due to his misapprehension.

Carter responded in his rejoinder:

CARTER: The description just made of this administration's record is hard to recognize. I think it's accurate to say that Mr. Ford voted against the Voting Rights Acts, and against the Civil Rights Acts in their debative stage. I think once it was assured they were going to pass, he finally voted for it.

This country changed drastically in 1969 when the terms of John Kennedy and Lyndon Johnson were over and Richard Nixon and Gerald Ford became the presidents. There was a time when there was hope for those who were poor and downtrodden and who were elderly or who were ill or who were in minority groups, but that time has been gone.

I think the greatest thing that ever happened to the South was the passage of the Civil Rights Acts and the opening up of opportunities to black people of the chance to vote, to hold a job, to buy a house, to go to school, and to participate in public affairs. It not only liberated our black people, but it also liberated the whites.

We've seen in many instances in recent years in minority affairs section of Small Loan Administration—Small Business Administration—lend a black entrepreneur just enough money to get started and then to go bankrupt. The bankruptcies have gone up in an extraordinary degree.

FHA, which used to be a very responsible agency that everyone looked to to help own a home, lost 600 million dollars last year. There have been over 1,300 indictments in HUD, over 800 convictions, relating just to home loans. And now the federal government has become the world's greatest slum landlord.

We've got a 30 percent or 40 percent unemployment rate among minority young people, and there's been no concerted effort given to the needs of those who are both poor and black, or poor and who speak a foreign language. And that's where there's been a great generation of despair and ill health and lack of education, lack of purposefulness, and the lack of hope for the future. But it doesn't take just a quiet, dormant, minimum enforcement of the law. It requires an aggressive searching out and reaching out to help people who especially need it. And that's been lacking in the last eight years. [III:21]

This speech is above average, but not among the best-uttered in the debates. It is strategically sharp, beginning with a cutting attack on Ford's voting record; and it exhibits a seemingly genuine and accurate concern about the problems of black Americans and other minorities which was not present in Ford's speech.[7] The speech is flawed by overstatement, however, mainly in the second paragraph; and it fails, as did Ford's speech, to treat the question of new programs.

Among the Carter speeches which exhibited excellent argumentation, the best was his attack on Ford's environmental record. In this rejoinder, he combined forces with the questioner, Kraft, adding charges and refutation in an artistic structure unmatched by any other speech in the three debates [III:17]. Among other speeches by Carter showing excellent argumentation were: in the second debate, his rejoinder following the two Ford speeches which contended that Eastern European countries were not dominated by the Soviet Union [10], and his speech defining America's strength in largely moral terms [23]; in the third debate, his "apology" in response to Maynard's claim that the campaign had been conducted at a low level [4], his rejoinder regarding General Brown's statements [13], the original speech in which he defended his credentials and challenged Ford to defend his selection of Robert Dole as a running mate [14], and his rejoinder regarding Ford's poor civil rights record [21]. Only two speeches by Ford used excellent argumentation: in the second debate, his refutation of Carter's claims that the United States is weak and fails to uphold moral principles [24]; and in the third debate, the rejoinder in which he sets forth his view that a president should not publicly announce the options he might exercise in foreign affairs [11].

Each candidate presented some speeches that were poor in quality—shallow in conception, weak in argumentation and evidence, strategically unwise, or evasive. Mediocre speeches by Ford far outnumbered those by Carter, however. One of Ford's worst speeches was surely his attack on the Congress in the first debate: when asked to account for the anti-Washington feeling, he placed all blame on the Congress [I:28].

His original speech in answer to Valeriani's question about the *Mayaguez* incident was almost as defective. Defending his actions, he offered the testimony of the *Mayaguez* captain as "the best evidence" of a correct decision: "This morning, I got a call from the skipper of the *Mayaguez*. He was furious, because he told me that it was the action of me, President Ford, that saved the lives of the crew of the *Mayaguez*. . . . Captain Miller is thankful. The crew is thankful. We did the right thing" [II:30]. Ford's speeches on the environment [III:16], on civil

rights [III:20], on gun control [III:24,25], and his two speeches
disputing the domination of Eastern European countries by the
Soviet Union [II:8,9] were also defective speeches. Into the same
class should be placed his three perorations—especially the one
concluding the second debate, which wasted the "primest" of
prime time.

Carter's response to a question by Reynolds on wage and
price controls [I:2], his feeble attempt to argue that tax reforms
would produce significant amounts of money [I:26], his two
back-to-back speeches answering Frankel's request to justify
high defense budgets and at the same time explain how the
nation could meet the demands of pressing domestic problems
[II:17,18], and his rejoinder on gun control [III:26] were his
worst speeches. In most of these instances, it appears that he was
deliberately evasive or fence-straddling.

The general argumentative strength or weakness of speeches
is but one measure of the quality of the candidates' argumentation, of course. Another and perhaps more revealing measure
is the number and kind of specific defects or errors in reasoning
and in the use of evidence. No less than 226 such defects and
errors occurred, by our count; other critics might find a larger
number, particularly if every instance of exaggeration were
cited. Of the total, Ford was responsible for 138, and Carter for
88. The first debate, on domestic problems, shows the largest
number of errors (111), perhaps because the ocean of statistics,
the claims about causes of inflation, unemployment, and higher
taxes, and the interpretations of legislation and economic forces
were fertile grounds for mistakes. In the second debate there
were no fewer than 69 errors, and in the third debate, 46.

All defects of evidence and reasoning were placed in three
categories: (1) *misuse of evidence,* including distortions,
selective facts and statistics, inconsistencies, and questionable
premises or claims; (2) *errors of reasoning,* including false
causes, false alternatives, false analogies, and instances of
begging the question; and (3) *sophistries,* including arguments
ad hominem, arguments ad populum, hyperboles, persuasive
definitions, and instances of vagueness. The 226 defects can only
be summarized here and illustrated by reference to several

speeches. We should note that one valuable contribution of the press was the publication of newspaper articles identifying many of these defects.[8]

Misuse of evidence was the most common flaw. Of 133 such errors, there were 44 distortions, 7 instances of selective statistics, 12 inconsistencies, and 70 instances of questionable premises or claims. Ford was responsible for 93 and Carter for 40 misuses of evidence.

Ford's speeches contained 27 of the 44 distortions. The one receiving the most attention was his claim that "there is no Soviet domination of Eastern Europe and there never will be under a Ford administration":

> If we turn to Helsinki—I'm glad you raised it, Mr. Frankel. In the case of Helsinki, thirty-five nations signed an agreement, including the secretary of state for the Vatican. I can't under any circumstances believe that His Holiness the Pope would agree by signing that agreement that the thirty-five nations have turned over to the Warsaw Pact nations the domination of Eastion Europe. It just isn't true. And if Mr. Carter alleges that His Holiness by signing that has done it, he is totally inaccurate. Now, what has been accomplished by the Helsinki agreement? Number one, we have an agreement where they notify us and we notify them of any military maneuvers that are to be undertaken. They have done it in both cases where they've done so. There is no Soviet domination of Eastern Europe and there never will be under a Ford administration. [II:8]

Jules Witcover reported that a Ford associate said that the President, before the debates,

> "was convinced he'd get questioned on the Helsinki Agreement and its relationship to Eastern Europe and Soviet domination, and/or about the Sonnenfeldt Doctrine." The Sonnenfeldt Doctrine was a reported position enunciated by one of Kissinger's deputies, Helmut Sonnenfeldt, to the effect that the Soviet sphere of control in Eastern Europe was a fact of life; that American policy ought to proceed from an acceptance of it. The Ford Administration steadfastly insisted that no such doctrine existed and was certainly not a part of official American policy. These matters were brought up now with Ford, and the President seemed clear about both the facts and the policy. "He knew that subject very well," one participant said.[9]

On this interpretation, Ford was briefed and ready to discuss Eastern Europe—but he blew his lines. According to Witcover, panelist Max Frankel later recognized that Ford's statements on the Sonnenfeldt Doctrine issue—excluding, of course, the assertion of "no Soviet domination"—was

identical to a response Kissinger had given him months earlier in a discussion of the same matter. Kissinger had defended the Helsinki Agreement by saying the United States would not agree to anything that was not already a fact of life, observing—twice—that the Pope certainly would not have agreed unless that was so. It was clear to him, Frankel said, that Ford's answer had come from a Kissinger briefing or briefing paper. Except, of course, the President did not quite get it right.[10]

A complementary explanation is that Ford's statement was simply the result of an inartistic conclusion to his speech. Ford defended the Helsinki Agreement, saying that he was "glad" Frankel raised the issue. After pointing out that thirty-five nations had signed the agreement, including the secretary of state of the Vatican, he began a recitation of the benefits of the agreement, saying, "Number one, we have an agreement where they notify us and we notify them of any military maneuvers that are to be undertaken. They have done it in both cases where they've done so. There is no Soviet domination of Eastern Europe and there never will be under a Ford administration." At this point, Ford's time expired and he stopped. Ford may have had in mind a "number two"—another point that would have rounded out an unobjectionable explanation. Ford's number one argument was that the Soviet Union was not conducting massive, secret military maneuvers in Eastern Europe—that this was evidence that the Russians were not dominating Eastern Europe. Perhaps, when his speaking time expired, he simply produced an awkward conclusion. Conceivably, the "blooper heard round the world" was merely an awkward and incorrectly stated conclusion to an otherwise defensible position. However, when Frankel asked in his follow-up if Ford actually meant what he had just said, Ford missed the opportunity to correct himself. Instead, he stuck to his claim, and the distortion—whether caused by ignorance, confusion, accident, or inartistic utterance—became perhaps the most costly mistake of his political career.

Among other Ford distortions were several inaccurate characterizations of Carter's record and position on issues. For example, he charged that Carter advocated the Humphrey-Hawkins full-employment bill [I:3]. This was not quite accurate. Throughout the campaign, when questioned about the bill, Carter gave it lukewarm support and ordinarily discussed the need for substantial modifications. On three other occasions Ford grossly misrepresented Carter's positions. He claimed that Carter advocated a federal expenditure of 30 billion dollars for education [I:16]; no such Carter proposal was on the record. He repeated statements from an erroneous Associated Press interview which quoted Carter as favoring tax increases for the middle class [I:27], even though the Associated Press had already acknowledged its error and corrected it. Also, Ford charged Carter with "looking with sympathy" upon a Communist government in Italy, or in the North Atlantic Treaty Organization [II:3]. But Carter's position was that the United States should not automatically withdraw its support and diplomatic relations from a newly elected Communist government, since such action would only force that nation into the Soviet camp.

In several instances, Ford distorted or misapplied statistical data. He claimed inaccurately that his proposed increase of the personal exemption for income tax purposes would provide an additional $1,000 to a family of four [I:5]. He claimed that James Schlesinger had calculated the serious effects of a 3- to 5-billion-dollar reduction in the defense budget [II:2]; in reality, Schlesinger's projections were based on a reduction of 10 billion dollars. Finally, Ford grossly exaggerated certain facts in justifying his 1975 veto of a strip-mining bill. He claimed that "it was the overwhelming consensus of knowledgeable people that that strip-mining bill would have meant the loss of literally thousands of jobs, something around 140,000 jobs" [III:16]. Ford himself had made a far less extravagant claim in his veto message of May 20, 1975, when he said that 36,000 jobs would be lost.

Consistency in statement, argument, and position is clearly a virtue. During the campaign, Carter had been accused of inconsistency, fuzziness on issues, and "waffling." Campaigner Ford told a Pontiac, Michigan, audience that Carter "changes his accent" when appearing before different groups of voters; and in a finely tuned alliterative sentence, he charged that Carter "wavers, he wanders, he wiggles, and he waffles, and he shouldn't be the president of the United States." Whatever the truth of these campaign charges, it was Ford who was inconsistent in the three debates. Among the twelve inconsistencies which appeared in Ford's debate discourse, the following are clear examples.

Ford argued in one instance that adequate tax relief had been provided to middle-income taxpayers, and later argued that the middle class had been short-changed and deserved lower taxes [I:9,27]. In several speeches he claimed credit for reducing taxes, and expressed satisfaction that tax cuts had occurred under his Republican administration; but later he placed responsibility on the Democratic Congress for all tax bills, reminding Carter that Democrats had controlled Congress for the last twenty-two years and that "they wrote all the tax bills" [I:27]. Ford argued that it was not in the best interests of the United States to enter into a cold war relationship with the Soviet Union, but subsequently appeared to reverse himself as he talked of ways the United States was getting the upper hand in cold war diplomacy [II:3].

Another misuse of evidence consists of explicitly or implicitly using premises or claims which are extremely questionable, though not clearly false. Ford's justification for lowering auto emission standards implied a dubious premise. In response to Kraft's inquiry on his environmental record, Ford stated: "The auto emissions: it was agreed by Leonard Woodcock, the head of the UAW, and by heads of all the automobile industry, that those auto emission standards had to be modified." This argument hinges on the premise that what these "authorities" decide regarding auto emission standards must be the case [III:16]. Ford also presented a questionable economic analysis when he claimed, in numerous speeches, that the nation should "hold the lid" on federal spending because this action would "stimulate" the economy. "Holding the lid" on spending and inflation is generally regarded as a restrictive economic policy, and is intended to reduce economic activity, not stimulate it. Ford often asserted that "inflation destroys jobs," a claim likewise at odds with standard economic theory. Inflation may affect real earning power, but it often improves prospects for employment when associated with an expansion of the economy.

The misuses of evidence committed most frequently by Carter were distortion of the record and use of questionable claims. For example, in the first debate he claimed that fewer people were employed in private non-farm jobs in September of 1976 than when Ford assumed office [I:24]. This statement, however, is contradicted by data from the Bureau of Labor Statistics. In the second debate, when arguing that Ford's foreign policy did not meet high standards of morality, Carter misstated the nature of American aid to the government of Chile: "Last year under Mr. Ford, of all the Food for Peace that went to South America, 85 percent went to the military dictatorship in Chile" [II:27]. It is true that approximately 85 percent of U.S. *sales* in South America went to Chile, but less than 10 percent of the *donations* for Latin American countries went to Chile. The aggregate figure for both sales and donations to Chile was around 60 percent. In another instance, Carter made a claim not supportable by facts, that under Ford there had been "absolutely no progress" toward a new SALT agreement [II:22]. Finally, in the third debate, Carter presented evidence that even his campaign manager Hamilton Jordan was unable to explain. To document his claim that a second Ford administration would require serious sacrifices of the American people, Carter asserted that "Mr. Ford's own environmental agency has projected a 10 percent unemployment rate in 1978 if he's president" [III:3]. The President's Council on Environmental Quality had made no such projection. In its seventh annual report, issued in September, 1976, the council's only comment on unemployment was to claim that federal environmental regulations *increase* the number of jobs.

Among Carter's most questionable premises and claims were several concerning taxation, government reorganization, and unemployment. He promised, "I would never do anything that would increase the taxes for those who work for a living or who are presently required to list all their income" [I:26]. Should an audience believe that Carter would never support a tax increase for workers—even in a time of national emergency when a tax increase could avert disaster? Misleading claims were involved in Carter's account of how he reduced the Georgia bureaucracy: "And we cut those 300 agencies and so forth down substantially. We eliminated 278 of them" [I:13]. The assertion that 278 agencies were eliminated is misleading, because the thrust of his government reorganization effort in Georgia was consolidation of smaller agencies into larger ones, not abolition of government programs and functions. Finally, Carter repeatedly claimed that a decrease in unemployment would decrease the inflationary spiral, surely an unusual view of economic forces.

Errors in reasoning, the second category of defects, included false cause, false alternatives, false analogies, and begging the question. Ford committed twelve such errors and Carter six.

Ford drifted easily into "false cause" when he argued that his leadership had brought peace: "In the last two years, I have made policy decisions involving long-range difficulties and policies and made day-to-day judgments not only as president of the United States but as the leader of the free world. What is the result of that leadership? America is strong. America is free. America is respected. Not a single young American today is fighting or dying on any foreign battlefield. America is at peace, with freedom" [II:37]. Ford can hardly claim that his decisions and his leadership caused these conditions, as America was "strong," "respected," and "at peace, with freedom" when he took office. Ford presented a false alternative when he criticized Carter's position on budget deficits and presidential vetoes:

"Now, Governor Carter complains about the deficits that this administration has had, and yet he condemns the vetoes that I have made that have saved the taxpayer 9 billion dollars and could have saved an additional 13 billion dollars. Now he can't have it both ways" [I:23]. Surely Carter could. Carter opposed vetoes of jobs bills, on the view that the programs would reduce federal expenditures for welfare and unemployment compensation in addition to generating increased tax revenue. Ford obviously committed the error of false analogy when he noted that Carter, as Georgia governor, vetoed "between thirty-five and forty bills a year" [I:27]. The analogy, comparing the vetoes of a president and those of a governor, was faulty: Carter as governor did not veto the same sorts of bills that Ford vetoed. None of Carter's vetoes dealt with such national issues as job creation, health care, or housing. Rather, many concerned "private" bills and "special interest" legislation. Finally, Ford offered circular reasoning four times in three speeches [I:3,22,23]; actually, he simply repeated the same defective argument: "In my judgment, the best way to get jobs is to expand the private sector, where five out of six jobs today exist in our economy." The reasoning is circular. Simply because five-sixths of the current jobs are in the private sector does not mean that that is where the unemployed will find jobs.

Some Carter arguments also suffered from errors in reasoning. In the second debate, he inaccurately located the blame for alleged failures in foreign policy: "Every time we've made a serious mistake in foreign affairs, it's been because the American people have been excluded from the process" [II:5]. To say that the exclusion of the public from policy formation was the cause of unnamed failures is unbelievable, and a clear instance of single-cause analysis. Twice Carter offered inaccurate analogies between Ford's budget deficits and those of earlier administrations. He criticized Ford for having in 1975 "more of a deficit spending than we had in the entire eight-year period under President Johnson and President Kennedy" [I:18]. Carter's argument was based on a comparison of conditions lacking genuine similarity: the economy in 1976 was twice as large as it was in the 1960s, and budgets and deficits must be judged accordingly. Finally, Carter, in arguing that "Mr. Ford, Mr. Kissinger have continued on with the policies and failures of Richard Nixon" [II:1], *assumed* what needed proof—that Nixon's policies failed.

Sophistries are a final classification of defects in argumentation. An ad hominem argument centers on the defects of the person—an opponent's view is incorrect or should be discounted because of some personal deficiency; ad populum arguments make appeals to popular conceptions or prejudices; hyperbole consists of extravagant claims; persuasive definitions appeal to slogans, glittering generalities, or slanted language; and candidates' statements are regarded as vague—a sophistry rather than a mere defect in style—when the candidates appear to intentionally obscure their meaning for tactical reasons. Carter "outscored" Ford in the sophistry category forty-two to thirty-three, primarily because of his peculiar tendency toward hyperbole.

Ford's ad hominem arguments centered on Carter's supposed inconsistency, lack of specificity on issues, and lack of detailed knowledge on matters of importance. Said Ford, "I don't believe that Mr. Carter has been any more specific in this case than he has been on many other instances" [I:3]; "Governor Carter again contradicts himself" [II:7]. "Governor Carter apparently doesn't know the facts" [II:19]; and "Governor Carter is inconsistent in many of the positions that he takes. He tends to distort on a number of occasions" [III:34]. Ford was hyperbolic in his criticism of Carter's proposed defense budget cuts, claiming that Carter's suggested reductions would leave the nation virtually defenseless: "Let me tell you this straight from the shoulder: You don't negotiate with Mr. Brezhnev from weakness, and the kind of a defense program that Mr. Carter wants will mean a weaker defense and a poorer negotiating position" [II:2]. Ford employed persuasive definition in his portrayal of the Humphrey-Hawkins bill, which would "control our economy" [I:3], and in accusing Carter of favoring "more and more programs, which means more and more government" [I:36].

Several ad hominem arguments by Carter were quite

abusive. He chided Ford for his "insensitivity" to the problems of the unemployed: "I think this shows a callous indifference to the families that have suffered so much" [III:32]; and "Mr. Ford doesn't seem to put into perspective the fact that . . . [unemployment] touches human beings" [I:24]. He also claimed that Ford was simply not up to the task of being president: "As far as foreign policy goes, Mr. Kissinger has been the president of this country. Mr. Ford has shown an absence of leadership, and an absence of a grasp of what this country is and what it ought to be" [II:1]. Also, Carter said with sarcasm, "Well, Mr. Ford acts like he's running for president for the first time," and Ford "has learned the date of the expiration of SALT I, apparently" [II:22]. Both comments came in the second debate, throughout which Carter was extremely aggressive and caustic.

Carter's hyperbole was a characteristic of his argumentation as well as his style. He made at least twenty-two hyperbolic statements, including these: "Our country's not strong anymore"; "We're not respected anymore"; "I think this Republican administration's been almost all style and spectacular and not substance"; "We've become fearful to compete with the Soviet Union on an equal basis." Describing federal domestic policy: "The present tax structure is a disgrace to this country. It's just a welfare program for the rich"; and "the whole philosophy of the Republican party, including my opponent, has been to pile on taxes on low income people, to take them off on the corporations."

Finally, Carter's position on several proposed constitutional amendments remained obscure—probably for strategic purpose. "I honor the right of people who seek the constitutional amendments on school busing, on prayer in the schools, and on abortion" [III:22]. How could a president *not* "honor the right" of citizens to seek amendments? Carter apparently sought to satisfy those on both sides of several issues.

Before concluding this overview, we should notice how frequently the defects appear in some speeches. For example, the first two speeches of the second debate were severely flawed. Defects are indicated by use of parentheses, and the defects are named in the margin.

CARTER: (Well, I think this Republican administration's been almost all style and spectacular, and not substance.) (We've got a chance tonight to talk about, first of all, leadership, the character of our country, and a vision of the future. In every one of these instances, the Ford administration has failed), and I hope tonight that I and Mr. Ford will have a chance to discuss the reason for those failures. *(right margin: Ad hominem)* *(right margin: Hyperbole)*

(Our country's not strong anymore. We're not respected anymore.) We can only be strong overseas if we're strong at home, and when I become president we'll not only be strong in those areas but also in defense, a defense capability second to none. *(right margin: Hyperbole)*

We've lost in our foreign policy the character of the American people. (We've ignored or excluded the American people and the Congress from participation in the shaping of our foreign policy. It's been one of secrecy and exclusion.) In addition to that, we've had a chance to become now, contrary to our longstanding beliefs and principles, the arms merchant of the whole world. We've tried to buy success from our enemies, and, at the same time, we've excluded from the process the normal friendship of our allies. *(right margin: Hyperbole)*

(In addition to that, we've become fearful to compete with the Soviet Union on an equal basis. We talk about detente. The Soviet Union knows what they want in detente and they've been getting it. We have not known what we've wanted, and we've been out-traded in almost every instance.) *(right margin: Hyperbole)*

The other point I want to make is about our defense. We've got to be a nation blessed with a defense capability that's efficient, tough, capable, well organized, narrowly focused fighting capability. The ability to fight if necessary is the best way to avoid the chance for, or the requirement to fight.

And the last point I want to make is this. (Mr. Ford, Mr. Kissinger have continued on with the policies and failures of Richard Nixon.) Even the Republican platform has criticized the lack of leadership in Mr. Ford and they've criticized the foreign policy of this administration. This is one instance where I agree with the Republican platform. *(right margin: Circular reasoning)*

I might say this in closing, and that is, that (as far as foreign policy goes, Mr. Kissinger has been the president of this country. Mr. Ford has shown an absence of leadership, and an absence of a grasp of what this country is and what it ought to be.) That's got to be changed. And that is one of the major issues in this campaign of 1976. [II:1] *(right margin: Ad hominem)*

FORD: (Governor Carter again is talking in broad generalities.) Let me take just one question that he raises: the military strength and *(right margin: Ad hominem)*

Questionable claim[11] capability of the United States. (Governor Carter in November of 1975 indicated that he wanted to cut the defense budget by 15 billion dollars.) A few months later he said he wanted to cut the defense budget by 8 or 9 billion dollars. And more recently he talks about cutting the defense budget by 5 to 7 billion dollars. There is no way you can be strong militarily and have those kind of reductions in our military appropriation.

Now let me just tell you a little story. (About late October of 1975, I asked the then Secretary of Defense, Mr. Schlesinger, to tell me what **Distortion[12]** had to be done if we were going to reduce the defense budget by 3 to 5 billion dollars.) A few days later, Mr. Schlesinger came back and said, (if we cut the defense budget by 3 to 5 billion dollars, we will have to cut **False alternatives** military personnel by 250,000, civilian personnel by 100,000, jobs in America by 100,000. We would have to stretch out our aircraft procurement; we would have to reduce our naval construction program; we would have to reduce the research and development for the Army, the Navy, the Air Force, and Marines by 8 percent; we would have to close twenty military bases in the United States immediately.) That's the kind of a defense program that Mr. Carter wants. (Let me tell you this straight from the shoulder: you don't negotiate with Mr. Brezhnev from weakness, and the kind of a defense **Hyperbole** program that Mr. Carter wants will mean a weaker defense and a poorer negotiating position.)

The candidates seldom called attention to errors of evidence and reasoning in each other's speeches. At times, this was no doubt due to the swift movement from one round to the next, which made refutation difficult. Sometimes, too, the candidates may have perceived certain errors as inconsequential. In some instances, they probably recognized defects, but had no corrective information and argument at hand. Sometimes, of course, they simply failed to detect faults.

Obviously, the presence of factual distortions, logical fallacies, and sophistical techniques is objectionable—first, because presidential debates ideally ought to be free of such defects, and second, because some defects very probably influenced the judgment of members of the audience. The candidates' errors in some degree amount to no more than testimony of their membership in the human community. But the high number of errors detectable in the debates does provide grounds to consider whether some other format for presidential debate might reduce the occurrence of errors so serious and numerous.

ASSESSMENT OF PRESIDENTIAL POTENTIAL

The evidence presented in this and the previous chapter shows that Carter undoubtedly was the more able debater, which does not mean necessarily that he would prove to be the more able president. A primary reason for conducting presidential debates stems from a belief that debate will somehow reveal traits of thought and character, as well as positions and policies, and that this in turn will assist the audience in making an informed judgment about the candidates' presidential qualities. Let us turn, then, to the question of what an attentive and critical audience could have learned about Ford and Carter that might count as grounds for judgment. Quite apart from the fact that Carter outslugged Ford, could we have learned anything about the candidates that would help us cast an informed vote?

In the first place, Ford was less skilled than Carter in verbal confrontation. Carter was quicker in thought and expression, more creative, sharper in rebuttal, and more clever in the sense that he easily saw opportunities and usually knew how to use them to his purpose. These traits of thought and expression cannot be invented or taught to a candidate just for the debates. What we observed of these rather stable elements would probably carry over into a presidency.

Second, Ford was more prone to verbal and factual errors than Carter, and contrary to pre-debate prognostications, he did not have a ready command of vast information. His Eastern Europe blunder called into question his basic political knowledge; and his inability to extricate himself from the blunder prompted some to wonder whether he was "bullheaded." Carter, on the other hand, made no obvious or serious blunders in the debates; and he displayed more factual detail than Ford, in spite of being an "inexperienced Washington outsider." We could conclude that Ford either did not remember well what he had learned or that he did not have a firm knowledge of government and world affairs, and that Carter learned faster and remembered more.

Third, Ford was limited in his powers of expression: he could only very minimally address matters of principle, definition, and quality; he could not or would not display feeling and compassion; and there was not a single Ford speech showing more than ordinary powers of conception. Carter was not limited in these ways: his speeches frequently argued to and from definitions and principles, frequently displayed emotion, and his best speeches revealed a mind of more than ordinary talent.

Fourth, a very serious flaw in Ford's performance was his tendency to present shallow argument—shallow not simply because of weak evidence and shaky reasoning, but also because of his thin apprehension: he seemed not to fully understand and appreciate certain substantive issues. He appeared to misconceive the seriousness of the energy problem and offered a defense of his Nixon pardon that could not have satisfied reasonable people even mildly sympathetic to the plight of young people who resisted military service during the Vietnam War. He seemed unable to comprehend the relationship between the availability of handguns and the incidence of their criminal use, heaped the entire blame on Congress for the anti-Washington feeling, and seemed genuinely satisfied with his response to Nelson's questions about his achievements in the area of civil rights. With respect to these and other matters, he did not display depth and sensitivity.

Fifth, Ford provided inaccurate or highly questionable analyses on specific and important public policy matters which could well influence his decision-making as president. For example, he announced a questionable economic interpretation which, if adhered to, could affect his actions as president. He defended "holding the lid" on federal spending by claiming that such action would stimulate the economy. A related argument, also questionable, was that "inflation destroys jobs." While Ford claimed that his policies were intended to increase employment, their more likely effect would be to control inflation.

Sixth, some of Carter's positions were ill conceived, and deep analytical thought was missing on some subjects. His analysis of the relationship between inflation and unemployment was surely questionable. Whereas Ford claimed that "inflation kills jobs," Carter claimed that reducing unemployment would reduce inflation: "We'll never have an end to the inflationary spiral . . . until we get our people back to work." During the campaign, Carter made reductions in unemployment a priority, apparently in the belief that this policy would stem inflation as well—an unlikely economic hypothesis. Again, Carter's analysis of the federal deficit was questionable. Throughout the first debate, he referred to the 65-billion-dollar federal deficit as an indication of Ford's economic "mismanagement." In actuality, the deficit occurred largely because of the economic recession of 1975: federal revenues fell off, and spending for unemployment compensation and welfare increased. Another prime example of shallow analysis by Carter was his recitation of causes of recent failures in American foreign policy: "Every time we've made a serious mistake in foreign affairs, it's been because the American people have been excluded from the process." To suggest that all serious mistakes in American foreign policy were caused by the exclusion of the American people from the process is sheer fiction.

Seventh, the debate audience might have noticed, in Carter's language and argumentation, a disturbing tendency toward overstatement—a hyperbolic quality that went beyond excusable stylistic embellishment and called his prudence into question. For example, arguing the need for justice in the penal system, Carter declared, "We've got a sharp distinction drawn between white-collar crime: the big shots who are rich, who are influential, very seldom go to jail; those who are poor and who have no influence quite often are the ones who are punished." This inclination to exaggerate the magnitude of problems was also evident in his closing statement in the first debate: "Our nation in the last eight years has been divided as never before. It's a time for unity." While the Vietnam-Watergate era was certainly divisive, it does not compare in seriousness to the Civil

War era, for example. In the foreign policy debate, he asserted that "our country's not strong anymore. We're not respected anymore"; and "we've become fearful to compete with the Soviet Union on an equal basis. We talk about detente. The Soviet Union knows what they want in detente and they've been getting it. We have not known what we've wanted, and we've been out-traded in almost every instance." Similarly, he stated that "every time we've made a serious mistake in foreign affairs, it's been because the American people have been excluded from the process." In the first debate he said that the tax structure is "just a welfare program for the rich," and that "the whole philosophy of the Republican party, including my opponent, has been to pile on taxes on low-income people, to take them off on the corporations."

In these examples, the claims made by Carter included elements of truth—more in some and less in others; but the truth was masked and discredited by his grossly inflated statements. Moreover, his hyperbolic utterances were self-defeating, because there is obvious inconsistency: on the one hand, Carter committed himself to total honesty and integrity (one of his most-quoted phrases was "I'll never lie to you"); on the other hand, he reverted to overstatement so frequently as to give an audience cause for alarm, especially because he drifted so often into hyperbole when an accurate description or assessment would have made his case successfully. Perhaps this unnecessary, inconsistent, and self-defeating tendency reflected slippage in his sense of propriety; or perhaps it signalled a willingness to substitute effect for accuracy. In any case, Carter's hyperbole was a serious defect.

Eighth, Carter's stylistic and argumentative hyperbole accompanied an inflated conception of the powers of the presidency. He portrayed himself as an extraordinarily strong leader, "someone who can analyze the depths of feeling in our country, to set a standard for our people to follow, to inspire our people to reach for greatness, to correct our defects, to answer difficult questions, to bind ourselves together in a spirit of unity." Time and again, he called for "strong leadership" as a key to a successful presidency and, significantly, offered to take upon himself the responsibility: "I hope to have a complete responsibility on my shoulders to help bring about a fair criminal justice system and also to bring about an end to the divisiveness that has occurred in our country as a result of the Vietnam War"; and, "when I get to Washington, coming in as an outsider, one of the major responsibilities that I will have on my shoulder is the complete reorganization of the executive branch of government." A "complete responsibility on my shoulder"—this stock phrase in Carter's rhetoric was usually linked to inordinately high estimations of his presidential power: he would restore efficiency, competence, and virtue to the federal government; he would be the knowledgeable citizen-president, capable of overcoming an intransigent bureaucracy and a Congress dominated by special interests and "inherently incapable of leadership." It was predictable that this misconception of his influence would foretell trouble for the eventual president and provoke congressional opposition.

Ninth, Carter's discourse in the three debates betrayed similar misconceptions regarding the rationality of the process of governing and the extent to which the success of a president involves the cooperation of others. He consistently called for "comprehensive" and "systematic" approaches to policy development, as well as for the "competence" and "good management" needed to ensure success—as if the "rational" approach, by means of comprehensive programs and competent management, would necessarily be successful. With regularity he repeated such phrases as "simple, efficient, purposeful, and manageable government," and "tough, competent management" of government. He claimed that the economic successes of Kennedy and Johnson were due to good management, and he blamed the Nixon and Ford budget deficits on Republican mismanagement. He often stressed the need for comprehensive policies, and charged that the Ford administration lacked comprehensive policies in such areas as energy, unemployment, nuclear proliferation, urban development, tax reform, and welfare. The message seemed clear: under a Carter presidency, there would be well-formulated plans to solve the nation's problems. Crisis management would give way to rational, comprehensive programs designed to resolve long-standing difficulties and avoid future crises.

But "comprehensive" policy development would almost certainly encounter political roadblocks. The legislative process depends, in part, on strategy, lobbying, political savvy; it is not simply a matter of the executive branch submitting rational and comprehensive policies. The legislative process is normally rather unhurried and moves in incremental steps. Congress could easily be overwhelmed if floods of comprehensive policies were sent down from the White House. In addition, the comprehensive policy or program approach, if insisted upon, might well delay enactment of widely agreed upon changes, while awaiting passage of the entire package. There is little doubt that a president should have comprehensive, long-range policy objectives in mind, but a strategy of progressive evolution toward those objectives would seem to be more politically sensible.

In addition, Carter's approach to comprehensive policy development seemed calculated to be non-ideological—perhaps because of an effort to avoid political conflict, or perhaps because of naiveté. He consistently called upon the nation to work together toward high goals: "I believe that if we are inspired, if we can achieve a degree of unity, if we can set our goals high enough and work toward recognized goals with industry and labor and agriculture, along with government at all levels, then we can achieve great things." Such expressed aspirations played down the ideological nature of many issues; in his effort to "achieve great things," Carter usually chose not to set forth a theoretical framework which would give consistency to his proposals. Several issues treated in the debates which later became prominent in the first two years of his presidency were inherently ideological: energy, taxes, welfare reform, urban policy, and the Panama Canal treaties, among others. These, surely, were not matters to be resolved simply through good management, comprehensive program development, and cooperation.

Tenth, the tendency toward hyperbole as well as the inflated conceptions of presidential power and of the rationality of comprehensive programs and good managment carry over into another observable factor—perhaps a danger. Hoping for so much, promising so much, trusting so much to good management, good will, and cooperation, Carter raised public expectations to dangerously high levels. In the fashion of John Kennedy, he campaigned on the need to "get the country moving again," although with different slogans. The nation, said Carter, was aimless and without purpose under the Ford administration. Strong and new leadership would activate the resources of the nation and engage it in the search for greatness: "And I believe that there's no limit placed on what we can be in the future if we can harness the tremendous resources— militarily, economically—and the stature of our people—the meaning of our Constitution—in the future." And, "we might have to do it slowly. There are no magic answers to it. But, I believe, together we can make great progress. We can correct our difficult mistakes and answer those very tough questions. I believe in the greatness of our country, and I believe the American people are ready for a change in Washington." We have been drifting, dormant, discouraged; but we can overcome.

Carter's uplifting rhetoric surely tapped the national mood; in the aftermath of "Vietnam, Cambodia, Chile, Pakistan, Angola, Watergate, CIA," the national audience needed assurance of the nation's essential goodness, and Carter sought to inspire and restore self-confidence. The inherent danger in this approach, of course, is that it produced great expectations for his presidency. Restoring "a government as good as its people" is a difficult task, whatever the precise meaning of that phrase. A presidential candidate who speaks of "a world of peace, with the threat of atomic weapons eliminated, with full trade, with our people at work, inflation controlled, openness in government, our people proud once again—Congress, citizens, president, secretary of state working in harmony and unity toward a common future; a world where people have enough to eat and a world where we care about those who don't" will surely be judged by demanding standards. And even if such a president actually accomplishes more than most of his predecessors, this may not be the public perception: the common view more likely will be that the idealist-leader has experienced failure after failure. Hence, one thing we should have learned from the debates is that Carter's expectations and aspirations, worthy and noble though they may be, reached out beyond the realm of the probable. And this, coupled with our sense of reality, should have led us to anticipate many failures in his presidency.

We are little tempted to add up these observations and offer a final evaluation of presidential potential. Who knows the exact weight to assign to these several merits and defects? There is too much of "perhaps" and "somewhat" to allow sure judgment. There lurks also the possibility that what we observe in the debates is by and large part of "the art of getting elected," which may differ significantly from "the art of governing." Besides, the outcome is fixed in history, whatever the assessment: the people judged on some grounds that Carter should govern.

The questions which beckon are related to the future rather than the past. What was wrong with the format of the 1976 debates, and can we design formats likely to eliminate past faults and succeed in promoting genuine debate? The next chapter assesses the 1976 format and provides reasons why a different format should be used in 1980. And our final chapter sketches four alternative formats for future presidential debates.

6. The Defective Debate Format

The physical setting for the debates was a semicircular set, painted blue and white, and provided with two waist-high podiums about eight feet apart. Behind each podium was a swivel chair of bar-stool height on which one candidate could be seated while the other was speaking. The three panelists and the moderator sat at a table in front of the debaters. The audience inside the theatre, a well-behaved "tickets only" audience, was essentially a stage prop; the real audience of millions was linked to this physical setting by television and radio. The speakers were almost as stiff and formal as the setting, each speaking always from behind his podium as if strapped in place. Although Carter sometimes sat while Ford was speaking, the president stood during Carter's speeches, perhaps to better portray presidential stature. Both remained erect and practically motionless during most of the twenty-eight-minute audio interruption in the first debate and, strangely, exchanged no remarks in the entire time.[1]

Each debate commenced with a recitation of the ground rules. The panel members then asked questions and the candidates responded. In the first and second debates, the speaker to whom a question was addressed had three minutes in which to respond; in the third debate, response time was two and one-half minutes. If the panelist chose to ask a follow-up question "for further clarification," the speaker had up to two minutes to reply to the follow-up. The other candidate then responded in a two-minute rejoinder speech. The order of speaking alternated: in one round, the original and follow-up questions went to one speaker; in the next round, to the other. Prepared notes were not permitted, although each speaker could make notes and refer to them during debate. There were no opening statements by the candidates, but each was given three or four minutes for a peroration or closing statement. The first debate focused on domestic issues and economic policy; the second, on foreign policy and national defense; and any matter was fair game in the third. The debate between the vice-presidential candidates involved minor but significant changes in format.[2]

The debate format was satisfactory to very few commentators. In fact, critics complained of numerous format defects. *Time* questioned the role of the panelists, the length of the broadcasts, the candidates' tendency to present campaign speeches, and the "dehumanizing" formality and stiffness of the debates.[3] The *New York Times* objected to the "show business nature" of the debates—"grooming by professional image-makers," and subordination of substance to appearance. Joseph Lelyveld lamented, "It may simply be beyond human ingenuity to conceive of a format for a Presidential debate that would not be instantly subverted and turned into a contest of image-making."[4] Several *New York Times* editorials pointed out other problems: the format invited "scoring," not debate; the use of the press panel hindered direct debate between the candidates; important issues were "barely touched"; the candidates served up "too many prepared positions to which to retreat under challenge."[5] The *Washington Post* said the format "is neither a press conference nor a debate, but rather a little of each. The candidates do not really engage each other under the rules as now formulated. They do not meet. They do not argue. They are at once granted unfair opportunities (to slam back at an opponent without his being able to return the shot) and spared the obligation of answering questions raised by their own answers."[6] Eric Sevareid remarked that the candidates did not have enough time for their rejoinder speeches, and so the quality of debate suffered: "Very brief segments tighten the nerves and force such compression of language that oversimplification is inevitable. A simple debating point is all that can be made." Further, said Sevareid, "True debate can reveal truth through the adversary procedure, by wearing away the obvious, the superficial, and the demogoguery; but that takes time. The classic Lincoln-Douglas debates revealed to many the true dimensions of the slavery-extension question. But this could never have happened if those two masters of premise, evidence, and conclusion had been obliged to speak in two- and three-minute snippets of monitored time." Sevareid thought that the debates ought to have opened with the presentation of "philosophical opening statements" and not with questions from the panel. Let the candidates, "not the interrogators, set the tone of the proceedings."[7] Critics noted repeatedly that the format was a hybrid, with the outcomes hardly deserving to be called debates. James M. Naughton's column after the first debate described the affair as the "simultaneous appearance of opposing candidates . . . [and] not a debate at all. It was, rather, a mutual news conference."[8] A *New York Times* editorial claimed that the format promoted "a gigantic TV show of 'Meet the People.' "[9] Columnist Tom Wicker sounded a common theme among critics—that the debates, far from throwing light on issues, promoted discourse of low quality: ". . . the most serious criticism of the debates goes to the reason usually given for holding them—that they would lift the level of Presidential campaigning by focusing attention on the issues. On the contrary, in what is widely conceded to be the most trivial and vituperative campaign in memory, the televised debates afforded the two candidates opportunity to make more misrepresentations, false claims, calculated appeals and empty promises than probably ever were offered so directly to a long-suffering electorate." Wicker added that the emphasis was not on thoughtful and enlightened responses but on "visual impact, confident mannerisms, slick debating points, exaggerated positions and facile use of evidence."[10] Haynes Johnson, immediately after the second debate, complained of "the same dreary format, the same stiff setting, the same long-winded questions and often long-winded responses. It showed even more how disappointingly sterile these press conferences in the guise of 'debates' have been." Johnson noted that the press seemed "more intrusive" in the debate: "Few questions were short, simple and direct. . . . For the most part, the questions were rambling and discursive. They were usually of the two- or three- or four-part variety. . . . At times the members of the press seemed to [be] making speeches of their own. . . ." Mused Johnson, "The problem was, maybe we heard too much from the press and not enough from the prospective President."[11]

Most of these judgments were made in connection with the first and second debates. Critics were more generous in their commentaries on the third. Indeed, William Greider declared, "At last, it worked. Their rough edges were gone, the nervous fluffs were inconsequential. The third and final televised presidential debate did exactly what it was supposed to do— provide a sharp portrait of the choice." In this debate, he continued, "substance triumphed over stylistic bumbles," and the panelists' questions "were much tougher, more accusatory than in the previous debates" and this tough questioning "improved the quality of the show."[12] UPI writer Arnold Sawislak said that "the final debate was what all three were supposed to be: a discussion of issues that illuminated the differences between the two men. . . ."[13] David Broder and Edward Walsh judged that the final debate "featured a serious discussion of a wide variety of substantive issues. . . ."[14] The *New York Times* and the *Washington Post* praised the debate. The *Post* informed the reader that "the third debate reached, at last, a level worthy of the office at stake"; and the debate was conducted with dignity and skill, and differences between candidates were illuminated. The *Times* judged that "the level of discourse was markedly higher and more coherent than in their first two debates"; also, the *Times* observed that the panelists' questions "were tougher than they have been," and that the tough questions were particularly damaging to Ford.[15] These critics judged correctly that the third debate was more informative and higher in quality than the previous ones, but their suggestion that the "tough questioning" by the panelists made the difference was mistaken. It was not the "toughness" of the panel that contributed to improved debate. The key factor was that the panelists succeeded more often than their predecessors in placing debatable propositions, rather than questions, before the speakers.

Most of the preceding comments on the debates were essentially correct, although they did not go far enough in identifying critical flaws. In this chapter, defects in the format are grouped into two major categories for purposes of discussion. The most serious flaw was created by the competing demands *to answer* and *to debate*. This produced a basic dilemma for the candidates, because both demands could not be satisfied concurrently or well: the candidates actually debated very little, and they rarely provided complete answers to questions. The format was not suited to either debating or answering; and its shortcomings made adequate debate practically impossible. Secondly, certain defects in the rules and design of the format reduced the extent to which issues could be explained and debated, denied equal opportunity to the contestants, and almost certainly assured discourse of mediocre quality. One of these defects, the inclusion of panelists in the format, not only contributed to the low quality of the debates but also introduced forceful third-party contestants.

THE BASIC DILEMMA: ANSWERING VS DEBATING

The fundamental flaw in the Ford-Carter debates lay at the very core of the format design: candidates were expected to answer questions put to them by panelists and at the same time to debate each other. Under the circumstances, it was to the candidates' credit that they sometimes managed both tasks—whatever the quality of their responses. Their frequent failure to answer and debate skillfully was more a signal of defects in the format than in their competence or effort.

DID THE CANDIDATES RESPOND TO THE QUESTIONS?

Sticking to the Subject. Their six perorations aside, Ford and Carter together presented 103 speeches—originals, follow-ups, and rejoinders. Each of these was analyzed to determine how much of its content was relevant to the question asked by the panelist. This analysis indicates that 32 of Carter's speeches and 34 of Ford's speeches were highly relevant.[16] This is 65 percent of their combined total of speeches—a surprising percentage in view of the many constraints upon the speakers. This does not tell us whether the candidates answered questions completely or well but only that a certain number of their speeches were "in the ballpark"—that is, within the range of subject matter implied by the question. For example, Carter's first speech in the first debate may be judged by critics to be a poor or inadequate answer, but it was highly relevant to Reynolds' question regarding the steps needed to reduce unemployment: there was no peripheral matter, no attack on Ford policies, and no digression.

A breakdown of the above total indicates some striking differences, particularly between original speeches and rejoinders. The content in a very large number of original speeches—36 out of a total of 40—was highly relevant to the subject of the panelists' questions. In addition, 13 out of 23 follow-up speeches were highly relevant to the corresponding questions. Thus, out of 63 original and follow-up speeches, 78 percent ranked high in relevance. A different pattern appears in the rejoinder speeches: 17 of the 40 rejoinders were highly relevant, 10 were moderately so, and 13 had little relevance to the questions. A comparison of rejoinders with original speeches shows that the content in 90 percent of original speeches was highly relevant, but in only 43 percent of the rejoinders was this true. Two facts help to explain this difference: first, the speaker in the original speech position was not burdened by criticism from his opponent—at least not within the round; and second, because both the original and the follow-up speeches occurred right after the panelist's question, there was a natural tendency for speakers to be constrained by the question.

If the rejoinder speaker spent less of his time in responding to the panelist's question than did the original speaker, where or to what was the content of his speech directed? The factor operating most consistently was the intervening speech or speeches of the previous speaker. The content in more than half of the rejoinders (22 out of 40) was closely related to the immediately preceding speech or speeches of the opponent. Eight were moderately relevant and 9 showed little relevance to the preceding speech.[17] This indicates clearly that a main function of the rejoinder was to refute or respond to the speeches of the opponent. Ideally, given the format rationale, the rejoinder would be highly responsive both to the questions posed by the panelist and to the preceding speech or speeches by the opponent. The natural dynamics of the debates worked in opposition to this ideal.

Answering the Question. In addition to its degree of relevance, each speech was analyzed to determine the extent to which it actually answered the question. Four categories were used to classify the 103 speeches. (1) The speech, in whole or in some part, answered the question *completely.* For example, in the first debate, Reynolds' opening question to Carter asked what his first steps to reduce unemployment would be, and Carter's speech answered completely [1]. (2) The speech *partially* answered the question. Ford was asked why his rationale for the pardon of former President Nixon did not apply to Vietnam draft evaders. He answered in a partial way by explaining his policy on draft evaders and resisters and by stating his reasons for the Nixon pardon; but he did not directly explain why his rationale for the Nixon pardon did not extend to draft evaders [I:10]. (3) The speech answered *in part;* that is, it answered one or more parts, but not all, of a multiple question of two, three, or four parts. For example, Elizabeth Drew asked Carter a follow-up question which had two parts, one subordinate to the other: first, how would Carter save enough money through tax reforms to provide tax relief? And second, would Carter "do away with all business deductions, and what other kinds of preferences'' would he eliminate? Carter's speech answered the second question but not the first [I:26]. (4) Finally, the speech *did not answer* the question at all. Robert Maynard, noting that Carter once enjoyed a ''20-point lead or better in the polls,'' asked specifically, ''Can you tell us what caused the evaporation of that lead, in your opinion?'' Carter first provided a correction of Maynard's description of the polls, and then discussed some aspects of his campaign; but his speech did not answer the question [III:33].

Forty-one of the 103 speeches *completely answered* the corresponding questions (Ford, 20; Carter, 21). Twenty-three of the speeches *partially answered* questions (Ford, 16; Carter, 7). Multiple questions were answered *in part* in 21 speeches (Ford, 9; Carter, 12). Eighteen of the speeches *did not answer* the questions (Ford, 8; Carter, 10). Thus, 62 speeches were defective in the sense that they failed to answer the questions completely.

Why did so many speeches fail to provide complete answers to questions? In a few cases, the candidates apparently chose not to face up to a difficult question, either because no answer came readily to mind, or because a forthright answer was politically risky. At one point, Ford skirted a complete answer to questions by Nelson, who asked him to say whether or not he would open the books on an early Watergate investigation—one which Nelson implied had been squelched with Ford's help [III:6,7]. Similarly, in the third debate, Carter did not answer the question squarely when Kraft called upon him and Ford to specify the sacrifices they expected of the public if their proposals were enacted [III:3].

Secondly, some questions were global, vague, hostile, repetitious, or contained implied criticisms of the candidate addressed. As a consequence, some speeches ignored the question, answered incompletely, or answered the implied charge rather than the stated question. For example, Valeriani's tripartite and global question in the second debate contained the implied charge that Carter's ''outsider'' status required him to make special revelations. Carter could not possibly have answered this question within his time limits. Instead of trying to do so, he chose to answer the implied charge [II:5]. A question by Maynard clearly asserted that Carter's campaign was floundering and asked him to explain why. Obviously, Carter was not inclined to admit that his campaign was in trouble; instead, he "corrected" the questioner's interpretation of the polls and delivered a commonplace on the nature of his campaign [III:33].

A third reason, and perhaps the most important one, for the inability of candidates to answer questions completely must be attributed to the format, which permitted panelists to ask multiple questions (their number and variety were discussed in chapter 3). The completeness of the candidates' responses to single and multiple questions in their original and follow-up speeches reveals the problem clearly. Single questions were answered completely 59 percent of the time. Multiple questions were answered completely only 16 percent of the time. A total of nineteen multiple questions were asked, and only three were answered completely.[18] One was not answered at all, eleven were answered in part, and four were answered partially.

Two additional factors, discussed earlier in detail, decreased the candidates' responsiveness to panel questions and were involved in the failure of many speeches to answer questions completely. Each candidate frequently took time to try to answer charges and arguments made previously by his opponent. And both Ford and Carter used numerous speeches for the purpose of issue-building, departing deliberately from the sphere of influence of the questions in order to introduce new agenda items.

Out of the forty rejoinder speeches, fourteen did not answer the questions at all. Candidates clearly found it easier to answer completely when the questions were single: eight of the thirteen rejoinders delivered in response to single questions answered the questions completely; but only four of the twenty-seven rejoinders responding to multiple questions answered completely. Almost three-fourths of the rejoinders (twenty-eight out of forty) either gave incomplete answers or failed totally to answer the questions introduced by panelists in the respective rounds. As the summary indicates, Ford and Carter performed about equally in this respect.

Completeness of Answers in Rejoinder Speeches

	Answered Completely		Answered Partially		Answered in Part		Not Answered	
	Ford	Carter	Ford	Carter	Ford	Carter	Ford	Carter
Single questions	6	2	1	0	0	0	3	1
Multiple questions	1	3	2	1	4	6	3	7
Totals	7	5	3	1	4	6	6	8

What accounts for the very low responsiveness of rejoinder speeches? In the first place, there was temporal and psychological distance between the panelist's original question and the rejoinder. This caused a "drift" of attention in which the original question lost much of its saliency. Secondly, the attacks, criticisms, charges, and arguments made by the speaker who had just given the original speech (or the original and follow-up speeches) also contributed to low responsiveness. Intervening between the original question and the rejoinder, these naturally drew the attention of the rejoinder speaker to matters close at hand and further reinforced the drift from the original question.

A third factor was the "piling up" of panel questions on the rejoinder speaker, leaving him far fewer chances to handle single questions. The rejoinder speaker received single questions in only thirteen instances, whereas the speaker in the original position had twenty-six opportunities to respond to single questions. This happened because two separate questions—an original and a follow-up—had already been asked of the other candidate in many instances before the rejoinder speaker had a chance to respond. As a result, he often faced two questions, one or both of which might even have multiple parts.[19] The need to respond to two questions instead of one made it much more difficult to answer any question completely. And when the accumulated questions included one or more multiple questions, the rejoinder speaker had almost no chance to give complete answers.

In rounds without follow-up questions and speeches, the panelist's question initiated a response by one candidate which was followed immediately by the rejoinder of the other candidate. The probability was not only much greater in these rounds that the original speaker and the rejoinder speaker would address the same question, but also that the speaker in the rejoinder position would answer the question completely. In all three debates, there were seventeen rounds with no follow-up questions: the rejoinder speaker answered the original questions completely in 53 percent, or nine, of these rounds. (Two were answered partially; two answered in part; and four not answered.) But in twenty-two rounds where follow-up questions and speeches intervened between the original questions and the rejoinders, only 9 percent, or two, or the rejoinder speeches answered the questions completely. (One was answered partially; ten answered in part; and nine not answered.)

Another important reason for low responsiveness of rejoinder speeches can be traced to the one-sided questioning allowed by the format and practiced by the panelists. It was shown earlier that thirty-seven of the sixty-three questions were tailored to the candidate in the original speech position. Questions directed pointedly at the original speaker were often inappropriate for the rejoinder speaker. Many of the questions were so one-sided that the rejoinder speaker had no burden to respond—in fact, could not *answer* in any meaningful sense.

There are correctives for such obvious format defects. Multiple questions were asked: the remedy is to ask single questions. One-sided and hostile questions were used in the debates: the remedy is to use questions free of hostility and equally applicable to both speakers, thereby placing on each an equal burden of response. Global, vague, and repetitious questions caused unnecessary problems: replace them with well-conceived, planned questions that are sharply focused and phrased without ambiguity and needless repetition. The format invited attention "drift" between the question and the rejoinder speaker's reply: this fault is easily remedied if the moderator restates the question prior to the rejoinder speech. Follow-up questions often introduced material unrelated to the original questions and, in general, increased the chances that rejoinders would miss contact with original questions: the remedy is to eliminate follow-up questions and speeches, which as a class had minimal value anyway. Finally, in a period of two minutes the rejoinder speaker sometimes had to answer original and follow-up questions of a multiple nature, plus arguments and charges set forth by his opponent in five minutes of speaking time. Eliminating follow-up questions, insisting that panelists pose single questions, and providing more time for rejoinders are changes that would make the rejoinder speaker's task more manageable.

Most of all, the format needs drastic overhaul because its basic flaw is fatal to the idea and practice of debate. Ford and Carter were required by the format to answer, but they were expected to debate. They did engage in some debate, but usually only by rebelling against the system—leaving a question inadequately answered in order to engage each other. The only remedy for this is radical alteration through shifting either to a clear version of a "question and answer" format that permits no combat or to a clear "debate" format that frees candidates from the obligation to answer questions.

DID THEY DEBATE?

If debate is understood to be discourse involving two or more speakers who display competing positions and aims, then Ford and Carter (and sometimes the panelists) engaged in debate. But this definition is loose, and a debate format built on it seldom leads to the clash of arguments and ideas that ordinarily marks genuine debate. Genuine debate is relative to an issue, and an issue is formed when speakers differ with respect to a recognized proposition. Clear and sharp debate occurs when speakers affirm and deny a proposition in some or all aspects, and when each speaker provides supporting argumentation for his affirmation or denial. In this sense, genuine debate took place in a little more than half of the forty rounds—in twenty-two, to be exact. When debate did occur, often only parts of the speeches in a round argued relative to a proposition in contention. It is also true that debate between Ford and Carter most often centered on matters introduced by them, not by the panelists.

Furthermore, because debate rounds typically began with a question instead of a proposition, there was no evident issue or proposition guiding the speakers' discourse; thus even when genuine debate did occur, one could hardly know what was at issue until the rejoinder speaker had his say.

Before identifying the rounds in which the candidates did debate, as well as those in which they did not, we shall examine the opening round of the first debate to illustrate one important reason why debate did not occur more often—namely, the failure of panelists to place *propositions* before the speakers. In this round, as in the majority of all rounds, the panelists asked questions, most of which were one-sided and not suited to elicit debate. Frank Reynolds' opening question is a case in point:

REYNOLDS: Mr. President, Governor Carter. Governor, in an interview with the Associated Press last week, you said you believed these debates would alleviate a lot of concerns some voters have about you. Well, one of those concerns, not an uncommon one about candidates in any year, is that many voters say they don't really know where you stand. Now, you have made jobs your number one priority, and you have said you are committed to a drastic reduction in unemployment. Can you say now, Governor, in specific terms, what your first step would be next January, if you are elected, to achieve that?

The question is flawed in three ways. First, it introduces a side issue—that voters are concerned about Carter and don't know where he stands. Second, and more important, the question is one-sided in asking what *Carter* would do to reduce unemployment. Third, there is no proposition which can be debated except the one related to a side issue. Reynolds' question provided a proposition in this instance, but on the wrong topic. (When Richard Valeriani asked a question containing a side issue in the second debate, Carter responded to it rather than to the question [II:C].)

Reynolds' question asked Carter what specific first step he would take to reduce unemployment, if elected. Carter replied that he would seek the cooperation of business, labor, industry, and government; channel research and development funds into areas likely to generate jobs; induce the private sector to cooperate in such areas as housing, where jobs might be created;

devise programs for the reduction of unemployment in the central city; and increase production in all possible ways. He thus answered the question, but not in relation to any perceivable issue or proposition. Reynolds then asked a follow-up question not closely related to the first: Was Carter willing to consider wage and price controls? Again there was no proposition or issue announced. Carter answered, in essence, that he saw no need for wage and price controls. The first round concluded with Ford's rejoinder, which began by attacking Carter for lack of specificity and for failing to talk about the Humphrey-Hawkins bill. Then, in about half of his rejoinder, Ford gave a position statement on unemployment: expand the private sector, reduce federal taxes, give tax incentives to business, and institute work programs for young people.

In this first round, then, there were two brief position statements drifting onto the airwaves, but no clash of ideas and arguments. There was no point at issue, and no proposition to affirm or deny. The candidates needed debatable propositions, rather than the questions asked by Reynolds. He could have stated, for example: Governor Carter, you have identified unemployment as our number one economic problem. Would you please address this proposition: *That unemployment can be significantly reduced without increased budget deficits and a continuing inflationary spiral.* With such a proposition announced at the beginning and both candidates aware that they were expected to address it, the likelihood of debate would have been sharply increased. A debate proposition obviously must be one on which the candidates may be expected to differ; otherwise it is an idle proposition.

The defective questioning and lack of debate in the first round were evident time and again in other rounds. The second round of the first debate commenced with Gannon's question, tailored to Ford: "How is it possible to promise further tax cuts and to reach your goal of balancing the budget?" Position statements instead of debate occurred in this round. A proposition was needed; for example, *It is not possible to balance the budget and at the same time provide significant tax reductions.* The fourth round began with Reynolds' one-sided question to Ford about his pardon of Richard Nixon and his intentions regarding Vietnam draft evaders. Again, position statements were given, but there was no debate. Panelists failed to set forth propositions in round after round, leaving the speakers free to serve up position statements which often floated lazily side by side, making little or no contact.

The candidates developed argumentative support for affirmation and denial of *the same proposition* in only twenty-two debate rounds. An examination of the rounds shows that propositions of debate were established more often by the candidates than by the panelists. Neither the candidates nor the debate audience usually knew exactly what proposition was at issue until the rejoinder speaker offered his response. It is absolutely clear, moreover, that the format offered a miserable vehicle for serious and sustained debate. In the following summary, the rounds are identified by the letter indicating the question which initiated each round, and the propositions are paraphrased.

I:E. There will be a 60-billion-dollar surplus in fiscal year 1981 with which to fund new programs. The first instance of genuine debate occurred in the third round when Carter initiated this proposition in response to Drew's challenge that there would not be enough money to pay for new programs and balance the budget. Her "question" came close to stating a proposition related to Carter's. The issue between the candidates, however, was on the proposition announced by Carter and argued by him in two speeches [7,8]. Ford's rejoinder argued that the surplus probably was a fiction, but if it was real, then it ought to be returned to taxpayers [9]. The failure of panelists to set forth clear and debatable propositions when initiating a round caused two defects which marred this and numerous other rounds. First, with no initial proposition stated at the beginning of the round, neither Carter (while speaking) nor the debate audience could know what was at issue; both had to await Ford's rejoinder speech before they could know what proposition was in contention. Secondly, the rejoinder speaker obtained significant advantages because he was privileged to make an issue or not, as he wished; moreover, because his was the final speech in the round, he had the last word on the subject.

I:I. Carter's reorganization of the Georgia state government was successful and *Under Nixon and Ford the White House staff expanded greatly.* Both propositions were initiated and argued by Carter in his original and follow-up speeches [13,14] and disputed by Ford in his rejoinder [15].

I:K The Ford administration has turned the economy around and *The Ford administration will provide a balanced budget.* Both propositions were initiated and argued affirmatively by Ford [16,17] and argued negatively by Carter [18].

I:M. The country has no national energy policy. A question by Reynolds invited the candidates to clash on the use of nuclear energy and also perhaps on the safety of nuclear power plants. Instead, they disputed the proposition initiated by Carter in his answer to Reynolds [19]. In this round and in the two rounds summarized above [I:I,K], the original speaker and the audience did not know what propositions would be "in debate" until the rejoinder speaker had his say.

I:O. Ford administration policies have led to increased employment and *Ford's vetoes have saved over 9 billion dollars in federal expenditures.* In this round, we note again the distance between the propositions actually debated and the question specifically posed. Gannon asked Ford, "Why do you think it is better to pay out unemployment compensation to idle people than to put them to work in public service jobs?" Converted into a proposition, the question becomes *Ford prefers to pay unemployment compensation to idle people rather than employ them in public service jobs.* Ford did not speak to the implied proposition, which was hostile to him phrased as either a question or a proposition. The point to note here is that the candidates clashed not on Gannon's proposition (question) but on those initiated by Ford.

I:Q. Present tax policies are "a disgrace" because they favor the rich and penalize the non-rich. Carter argued this proposition when Drew asked him to explain how he would achieve savings by reforming tax policies. Although he mentioned several approaches [25,26] in answer to Drew's questions, neither the questions nor his proposed reforms were the subject of clash in this unit. Indeed, there was no way to know what was at issue between the candidates until Ford's rejoinder. In this speech, Ford cited the Associated Press interview in which Carter supposedly advocated increased taxes for the middle-income taxpayer; in addition, he argued that Carter was deriding tax policies written by the Democratic Congress [27].

I:S. A Republican president is needed to check the high-spending Democratic Congress. This proposition had virtually no relationship to Reynolds' questions [S,T], both of which were significantly weak. Ford articulated the proposition and argued it affirmatively in his follow-up speech [29], and Carter attacked it in his rejoinder [30].

I:U. The president of the United States and the chairman of the Federal Reserve Board should serve coterminous terms and *Federal Reserve Board Chairman Arthur Burns' policies have been defective.* Carter initiated both propositions in response to Gannon's questions, and Ford offered refutation in his rejoinder. The clash in this unit was less pronounced than in those noted earlier, in part because both candidates had been requested to keep their speeches short.

II:B. The United States has enjoyed many recent successes in foreign policy and *Carter looks with sympathy to a Communist government in NATO.* Ford argued the first of these propositions more fully than the second [3], but Carter responded sharply to both in his rejoinder [4]. Trewhitt had asserted that American foreign policy suffered several setbacks in recent years—in Vietnam, Angola, and elsewhere. Ford's propositions directly countered the implications in Trewhitt's remarks.

II:C. The Ford administration has conducted foreign policy in secrecy and excluded the American people from processes of decision-making. Carter argued this proposition in response to Valeriani's tripartite question, although the matter was remote from the question. In his follow-up, Valeriani asked Carter how he would involve the public in decision-making. Ford's rejoinder sought to refute Carter's arguments [7].

II:E. The Russians have been getting the better of us in foreign affairs and *There is no Soviet domination of Eastern Europe.* In his original speech, Ford argued against the first proposition, which was implicit in Frankel's question. Near the end of this speech, Ford asserted that "there is no Soviet domination of Eastern Europe and there never will be under a Ford administration" [8]. When Frankel in his follow-up question asked for an explanation of this statement, Ford argued in support of it [9]. Carter's rejoinder took issue with Ford's Eastern Europe claim briefly, renewed the charge of secrecy in the Ford administration's conduct of foreign policy, and then rebutted Ford's arguments that his policies had been successful [10].

II:G. The Ford administration has not maintained the U.S. commitment to Israel. In his original and follow-up speeches, Carter offered arguments related to three propositions: the United States has become the arms merchant of the world, the Ford administration has not maintained our commitment to Israel, and the absence of a national energy policy at home hurts the U.S. abroad. None of these three propositions had been solicited by Trewhitt's questions. Taking issue with one of the three in his rejoinder, Ford defended his administration's aid to Israel as well as arms sales to Iran [13].

II:M. Progress in SALT talks has slowed—perhaps because of domestic politics. After Trewhitt's question initiated this proposition, Ford's speech provided an account of the talks and affirmed his determination to see that negotiations move forward successfully [20,21]. Part of Carter's rejoinder clashed directly with Ford's arguments [22].

II:O. American foreign policy has not been conducted on high principle and with clear purpose. Carter initiated and devoted his whole speech to this proposition [23]. Most of Ford's rejoinder argued directly in opposition to it [24].

II:S. Ford did not act responsibly in the Mayaguez *affair.* This proposition was strongly implied in Valeriani's question to Ford, who defended his handling of the matter [30]. Carter rebutted Ford rather delicately, criticizing him chiefly for not informing the public immediately of the circumstances [31].

II:T. The Ford administration should be blamed for the Arab boycott of American businesses. This proposition was initiated by Carter, who argued it vehemently [32]. Ford denied it in his rejoinder, but at the same time proposed remedies [33].

III:F. Carter erred in making public his position regarding a possible future Soviet attack on Yugoslavia. Joseph Kraft's question initiated this proposition. Carter argued against it in his original speech [9], whereas Ford argued in his rejoinder that it was correct [11]. This was one of only a few rounds in which the entire speeches of both candidates were directed to a proposition set forth in a panelist's question.

III:I. Carter's choice of Mondale as his vice-presidential running mate was based on sound criteria and represented a better choice than Ford's selection of Dole. Carter argued for the proposition in more than 50 percent of the speech in which he initiated it [14], and Ford's entire rejoinder was refutative [15]. The question by Nelson which had introduced the round included no suggestion of this proposition.

III:J. The Ford administration's record on environmental problems is "hopeless." When Kraft stated the proposition at the close of a long question, Ford used his full time to refute it [16]. Carter then sought to refute Ford and affirm the proposition in his entire rejoinder [17]. This debate round furnished one of the most interesting and informative exchanges in the three debates. The candidates debated sharply and systematically, and apparently genuine differences in views were revealed. One reason for the clarity and sharpness of debate was the fact that Kraft introduced the round by stating the proposition, which was clear to both speakers at the very beginning. But it should be noted that three parties engaged in debate: Kraft, who initiated charges against Ford and set forth the proposition; Ford, who responded defensively to Kraft; Carter, who refuted Ford and affirmed that Kraft was right.

III:K. The Ford administration has no urban policy. Asked by Maynard what his own urban policy would be, Carter stated the proposition and attacked his opponent [18]. Ford's entire rejoinder was refutative, arguing that his administration had taken important steps toward revitalizing the American city [19].

III:L. The Ford administration has made little progress in areas of civil rights. This proposition was declared, and accompanied by supporting evidence, in a question posed by Nelson. Ford's entire speech argued (in rebuttal to Nelson) that his civil rights record was very good [20]. Carter's rejoinder argued almost entirely against the same proposition [21]. In this round, as in the round on environmental problems, the panelist issued the charge against Ford, who suffered the blows of both Nelson and Carter. Some commentaries on the last debate found this round to be most informative. For example, the *New York Times* judged that the third debate was more informative than previous ones, and praised the round on civil rights: "The substance of the debate illustrated more clearly than the others the difference in the leadership styles of the two candidates, Mr. Ford's passive, Mr. Carter's active. The difference was evident, for example, in the answers to a question about what the president would do for blacks. Mr. Ford's emphasized that his administration was enforcing existing law 'to the letter' and that existing agencies that help blacks have functioned effectively. Mr. Carter, in contrast, argued that the problem requires not merely 'minimum enforcement of the law, it requires an aggressive searching out and reaching out to help people who especially need it.' "[20]

III:R. The Ford administration's economic record is a "rotten" one. The panelist—in this case, Kraft—again set forth charges leading up to a proposition at the conclusion of his question to Ford, "Isn't that really a rotten record, and doesn't your administration bear most of the blame for it?" Ford argued against the proposition [30,31] and Carter argued for it [32].

Certain observations can be made in regard to the twenty-two rounds which contained sustained argumentation by both speakers in relation to a proposition.

First, the speakers were responsible more often than the panelists for initiating propositions which led to genuine debate. Ford and Carter initiated the debated propositions in fifteen rounds; the panelists did so in seven rounds. This is clear evidence that the panelists often failed in their responsibility to set forth well-designed questions or propositions for debate.

Second, although the speakers debated in each of these twenty-two rounds, they devoted entire speeches to the contended propositions in only a few rounds. In most instances, only a part of each speech argued the propositions.

Third, the proposition at issue was usually unknown until the candidate in the rejoinder position made his speech. In many of the rounds in which debate took place, neither the original speaker nor the debate audience knew what was at issue until the rejoinder was presented.

Fourth, the rounds in which debated propositions were initiated by panelists had several features in common. The propositions were either explicitly stated or strongly implied in the questions in every case, and frequently were set forth at the beginning of debate rounds. This is a necessary condition for debate. Unfortunately, the questions containing the explicit or implied propositions were also hostile and sharply tailored to the candidate addressed, which is not a necessary condition for debate. In six of the seven rounds, this one-sidedness placed a double burden on Ford: he was forced to set forth his position in response to a one-sided and hostile question, and he was then attacked in Carter's rejoinder with no opportunity for refutation within the round. The panelists could have functioned more ably in these rounds had they kept their remarks free of hostility and converted each question into a proposition which afforded equal opportunity and fairness to both speakers.

If Ford and Carter engaged in genuine debate on a proposition in only twenty-two of the forty rounds of "mini-debate," what happened in the other eighteen rounds? In six of the remaining rounds, the candidates simply did not differ significantly on the issue or question before them. For example, they basically agreed in answering a question on normalization of relations with mainland China, although Carter chided Ford for lack of effort [II:14,15,16]. Similarly, their positions expressed little clash and no significant contrast in response to a question about the Panama Canal [II:28,29]. Trewhitt's question about restoration of relations with Vietnam was answered approximately the same way by both candidates, although Carter tongue-lashed Ford for allegedly failing to pursue efforts to obtain an accounting of servicemen missing in action [II:34,35]. Maynard's question to Carter about the "low level of the campaign" drew apologies and pledges from both Carter and Ford [III:4,5].[21] Nelson's question regarding the candidates' criteria and philosophy on Supreme Court appointments elicited no clash or contrasting positions [III:27,28,29]. And in the round begun by Nelson's questions and charges to Ford on Watergate, Carter chose not to give a rejoinder [III:6,7]. (The absence of clash or contrasting positions on the issues or questions placed before them does not mean that the candidates' speeches were without argumentation, charges, and countercharges.)

The candidates' speeches in two rounds simply missed connection because they were addressed to different propositions. Even though highly argumentative, the speeches essentially "fired past each other." One clear example of this occurred in the first round of the second debate when Carter's original speech launched a broadside attack on Ford's foreign policy, going to the conclusion that the policy had failed. Ford's rejoinder did not argue against the proposition initiated by Carter, but rather to the claim that Carter had advocated inconsistent and undesirable reductions in defense spending [1,2]. The other round came at the end of the third debate. Asking Carter to account for his drop in the public opinion polls, Maynard implied strongly that something must be wrong with Carter or his campaign to account for loss of a 20-point lead. Maynard thus submitted two propositions: Carter once enjoyed a 20-point lead; and he lost the lead due to some fault of his own. Carter's speech argued in response to the first proposition, denying that a lead of such magnitude ever existed [33]. Ford addressed the second proposition—that Carter lost the lead because of his own inconsistencies and distortions [34]. This set of speeches clearly shows the possible outcome of a panelist's failure to pose a single proposition.

The remainder of the rounds contained speeches which included contrasting positions but no clash on propositions by means of sustained argument. In the first debate, for example, Ford and Carter presented contrasting positions in regard to reducing unemployment, but did not clash on a proposition [A]. The same thing occurred on the topics of tax reduction and spending [C], pardon of Vietnam draft evaders [G], and proper control of intelligence agencies [V]. In the second debate, they presented contrasting positions in answer to Frankel's question about the role of morality in foreign policy [P] and in response to Frankel's challenge: How bad do things have to get before the budget for defense is decreased in order to allow spending for other purposes? [K] Four units in the third debate exhibited contrasting positions, but no clash on propositions by means of sustained argument [A,H,M,N].

The fault lay mainly in the nature and phrasing of panel questions in practically all of the rounds which resulted in basic agreement, "firing past each other," or contrasting but undebated positions. Panelists usually asked questions that were not easily converted into propositions, or they stated or implied propositions on which the candidates were not likely to clash.

Many of the questions placed heavy pressure on the candidates to respond to the panelists—a factor which also sharply reduced the chances for debate. In twenty-three of the forty rounds, the questions included implicit or explicit challenges to one or the other candidate, who in turn was practically forced to direct explanation or argument to the questioner. Ford was the candidate most often drawn into controversy with the panelists and distracted from debate with his opponent. He was heavily pressured by the panel in fourteen rounds, while Carter was pressured in nine rounds. And because Ford was not adept in the art of turning a hostile and one-sided question to his advantage, the pressure exerted by the panels was especially harmful to him.

In one round of the first debate, Reynolds challenged Ford to justify his pardon of Richard Nixon and show why the rationale for that pardon did not extend to Vietnam draft evaders [G]; Ford's original speech, directed solely to the panelist, was dominated by this challenge. Valeriani's questions on the *Mayaguez* affair [S] in the second debate practically compelled Ford to defend himself with justifications to

Valeriani. This type of pressure occurred six times in both the first debate [C,E,G,K,O,Q] and the second debate [A,B,C,E,O,S]. But the third debate was the most domineering of all: in eleven rounds, panelists employed questions containing challenges, propositions, or claims (almost always hostile) which forced the candidates to respond with explanations or arguments to the panel.[22] Ford had to defend himself in numerous original speeches against hostile propositions which included charges and implications: for example, his economic policies were defective [A,R] and his stand on handgun control confused [N]; he was involved in an early effort to cover up the Watergate affair [D]; he should have fired General Brown [H]; his record on environmental issues and civil rights was bad [J,L]. Carter was challenged four times by similar panel charges: his conduct of the campaign was faltering [C,T]; his statement on Yugoslavia had not been "cleared" [F]; his experience and the quality of his advisers were deficient, and thus his ability to make future key appointments was questionable [I].

Because debate requires that a proposition be affirmed and denied by means of sustained argumentation, there can be little genuine debate without a proposition. Yet the panelists rarely set propositions before the speakers. Moreover, even when doing so, the panelist frequently tailored the proposition so narrowly that the candidate addressed was not only drawn into dispute with the panelist but became more vulnerable to attack in his opponent's rejoinder speech. The rejoinder speaker already enjoyed a natural advantage in format position because he always had the last word in each round. In addition, he often had the privilege of defining what was at issue and of closing debate on that issue with his own choice of arguments. These problems could be minimized by providing for a proposition statement at the beginning of each round, by furnishing guidelines to aid panelists in framing propositions that are fair and likely to generate debate between the candidates, and by permitting the original speaker to respond to the rejoinder. Nevertheless, the hybrid format—part debate and part press conference—would remain flawed at its core.

Three formats designed to encourage genuine debate are recommended in the next chapter, plus one designed to encourage informative answers to questions. Before describing new formats, however, we should identify other major defects in the Ford-Carter debates.

OTHER DEFECTS IN THE RULES AND FORMAT

Extended debate was impossible. The design of the debates allowed the candidates to engage each other, if at all, only in short segments or rounds initiated by panelists' questions. The rounds—ranging in time from about three minutes to eight and one-half minutes—included at least one speaker's original speech and the other's rejoinder, and in several rounds a follow-up question and speech as well. The first debate contained twelve rounds and the second and third debates each contained fourteen rounds. All of the rounds together comprised the forty "mini-debates" within the three encounters. Argumentation seldom crossed the boundaries of these short rounds; that is, a candidate only rarely used his time in one round to refute or comment on a point made by his adversary in an earlier round.[23] Some subjects were treated in more than one round, of course (unemployment, taxes, budget-balancing, etc.), but genuine debate was limited almost totally to the short bursts within each round.

A radically different format would have been required in order for Ford and Carter to debate after the fashion of Lincoln and Douglas: no panels, no rounds, no "questions"—only a proposition in contention, necessary time in which to develop positions, and artistry. When Lincoln and Douglas criss-crossed Illinois in a series of debates, they knew that the issue was slavery and its extension. And they had time to prepare their speeches in advance of each debate. Both conditions seem elementary and eminently reasonable. How irrational that Ford and Carter employed a format which forced them to debate highly important matters without any knowledge of the propositions to be placed before them and in the absence of time for reflection, research, and preparation! Such conditions invite shallow thought, little genuine debate, poor argumentation, routine campaign commonplaces, and not least important, nonsense and error. Not only were they unable to know the propositions to be debated, but they were also prevented from using prepared notes—a rule that made little sense when one considers that presidential debates are not memorization tests.

Many commentators, before the first debate, recalled the problems afflicting the 1960 Kennedy-Nixon format and cited the Lincoln-Douglas debates as a more appropriate model. Nevertheless the Ford-Carter format repeated the essential features of the Kennedy-Nixon model. As a result, there was hardly any chance in 1976 for the kind of debate James Reston called for in a column written before the first debate: "We need to know, not what the President and the Governor think about the past, but about what visions and policies they have for the last years of the Seventies." The debates should point toward the future: "This is what we'd like to hear from Messrs. Ford and Carter in the debates: a serious, even if troubled, inquiry about the coming years rather than debating points about the mistakes of the past."[24] Reston's aspirations, shared by many, might have been met through a format suited to those ends—a format permitting thoughtful preparation and time for rigorous and extended discourse in relation to known propositions.

Slicing the debates into forty rounds and authorizing the panelists to establish an agenda by means of their original and follow-up questions led to several striking defects. In the first place, too many items were placed on the agenda: panelists asked sixty-three "questions" in the three debates, but there were actually about ninety questions because some were multiple. When twenty-five to thirty questions, agenda items, or propositions are included in one ninety-minute presentation, there is no possibility for focused debate or adequate answers. Secondly, too much was left to the discretion of the panels, who performed poorly as agenda setters. The questions with which they chose to establish the agenda were sometimes low-priority, repetitious, one-sided, and hostile questions; sometimes "press conference" questions; and sometimes vague, multiple, and argumentative questions. Third, the principals in the presidential debates had no formal part in establishing the agendas, although in retrospect we know that Ford and Carter set forth more debated issues than the panelists. It seems peculiar that no formal mechanism was provided through which the debaters themselves could help choose the issues to be debated. Fourth, there was no continuity of ideas, no unifying theme—indeed, not even a slender thread—linking one round to the next round in any of the debates. At the very least, the format should have provided for three- or four-minute opening statements in which each speaker could make a broad and principled statement of political philosophy and preview his approach to the issues slated for discussion. Fifth, the forty rounds in a press conference format invited the candidates to use well-rehearsed commonplaces rather than providing thoughtful answers to important questions or rigorous argument on disputed propositions.

Original speeches were limited to three minutes in the first and second debates and to two and one-half minutes in the third. Follow-up speeches and rejoinders were limited to two minutes. If the intention was to obtain informative answers as well as debate between the speakers, such time limitations were absurdly short. In fact, even without debate, an adequate answer for some of the questions in the brief span of two or three minutes was an unreasonable expectation. In the second debate, for example, Richard Valeriani posed a triple question to be answered in three minutes [II:C]. Just *one part* of the three-part question asked Carter to present his concept of the national interest! Or consider the question asked by Joseph Kraft: "As you look ahead in the next four years, what sacrifices are you going to call on the American people to make, what price are you going to ask them to pay to realize your objectives?" [III:A] This was an excellent question that deserved to be fully and carefully answered, but both candidates evaded it. The simple truth is that a three-minute response could only have touched its surface, even with hours to prepare an answer. Careful reflection, mustering of information and argument, and provision of subtle qualifications and perspectives would have been required in order for Ford and Carter to answer the question squarely without committing political suicide. The question deserved to be the focus of a sixty- or ninety-minute debate, but evasion was the sole recourse in a three-minute reply.

The lack of adequate time was felt most keenly when the speakers presented their rejoinders: as noted earlier, they pressed to their time limits and beyond, struggling to answer questions and criticisms, provide rebuttal, and set out contrasting positions. At the very least, rejoinder speeches should have been three minutes in length. However, extending the rejoinder time by one minute would not eliminate the problem of time inequality. Without follow-up questions, speaking time would have been equal if each candidate had three minutes in a round. But the introduction of the follow-up question gave the original speaker in a round a total of five minutes. In the three debates, twenty-three rounds contained follow-up speeches: Ford gave an original plus a follow-up speech in thirteen rounds, and Carter in ten. In each case, the speaker in the original speech position could use four and one-half to five minutes of speaking time, while his opponent was limited to two minutes. This allowed the original speaker not only to answer the questions to some degree, but also to pile up so many charges and criticisms that the rejoinder speaker could not answer the original and follow-up questions and still respond adequately to his opponent's charges. This problem of unequal time was further compounded by the fact that the original speaker had been the rejoinder speaker moments earlier at the conclusion of the previous round and consequently delivered three speeches in succession for a total of nearly seven minutes. Carter's skill in using such opportunities to pile up charges and criticisms against Ford was described in chapter 4. Ford's meager two-minute rejoinder provided little defense when this occurred.

The time imbalance and sequence of speeches in the rounds created potential strategic advantages, especially if a speaker had speed and quick wit. Speaker A, who received the original and sometimes the follow-up question, had three important advantages over Speaker B, the rejoinder speaker. First, when the questions put to him by the panel were "plums"—non-hostile questions that he could answer with ease—he could be genially persuasive for up to five minutes. Carter received easy questions on government reorganization, energy policy, and unemployment, for example; similarly, Ford received easy questions on China policy, SALT talks, and the anti-Washington attitude. Second, Speaker A had more opportunity to initiate new agenda items, especially when he received non-hostile questions. Carter seized this opportunity far more often than Ford. The rejoinder speaker was forced to defend himself in most rounds, and had little time to add items to the agenda. Third, as noted previously, Speaker A could pile up charges, criticisms, and arguments against his opponent and, if he was quick enough, could even use three consecutive speeches for a total of seven minutes for this purpose. These advantages, natural to the format, invited strategies of attack instead of information and debate from Speaker A. He could score best not by faithfully answering the question but by initiating charges—jabbing and striking to throw his opponent on the defensive and deny him the opportunity of a strong and persuasive rejoinder.

At the same time, Speaker A's position had several serious disadvantages. He had to speak immediately after the question, with no time for reflection. As the primary target of the panel, he frequently received one-sided and hostile questions. During his original speech, the panel was a potential threat because he had no way of anticipating the substance or tone of a possible follow-up question. He was also under the gun of the rejoinder speaker, but seldom knew where the point of attack would be located until after his own speech was finished. Because the panelists only rarely set forth a proposition at the beginning of the round, Speaker A often spoke before knowing what was at issue and thus could hardly engage in debate. Finally, he had no opportunity—unless he took valuable time from a future round—to rebut his opponent's rejoinder.

Speaker B, the rejoinder speaker, enjoyed several important advantages and one major disadvantage. In the first place, he had more freedom: he could ignore the panel questions or deal with them in part, as suited his purpose; he could focus on the speeches of his opponent; or he could introduce new issues or criticisms. Unlike his opponent, Speaker B was not burdened by the original or follow-up questions, and his rejoinder was not subject to panel questioning. The original and follow-up questions ordinarily lost saliency in the flow of speeches; the public was not likely to notice if Speaker B failed to respond to the questions. He had not only more options but also more material to choose from: he could select for rebuttal whatever he wished from his opponent's speeches. Furthermore, when one-sided and hostile questions were addressed to Speaker A, the rejoinder speaker was left with nearly absolute freedom to score, unburdened by either panel questions or by A's speeches. He usually had the privilege of defining what was at issue between himself and his opponent; and because he had the last speech in a debate round, he could also close debate on the contended issue—a striking advantage. Finally, Speaker B had the opportunity to take notes and outline a coherent response during his opponent's speeches. The one major disadvantage which marked the rejoinder was too little time to answer questions, respond to charges, set forth position statements, and debate. On balance, however, the rejoinder was by far the stronger speech position.

Chapter 3 identified the many defects arising from the presence of the panels. Here we focus on the chief flaws of the panels, the most significant of which was their active presence in the debates as a third party—a force to be reckoned with. The panels were the formal agenda builders, empowered to determine what should be debated; and in performing this role, they used thirty-two minutes of valuable debate time. They went beyond asking questions: they challenged, argued, accused; they sometimes forced candidates into submissive response, and sometimes debated. They pressured both candidates with one-sided and hostile questions, but Ford, especially, suffered under their questioning. One panel took upon itself the authority to change the debate format.[25] Why should any panel exercise such power? It is clear that debate can take place without questioners: nothing is needed except propositions for debate, the two candidates, and perhaps a moderator. A panel might be used well in the preparation of propositions to be debated, but it need not (and, we think, should not) be a participant. The fact that all of the panelists chosen for the Ford-Carter debates were journalists proved to be a matter of consequence. Following their traditions, they treated the debates as joint news conferences. Many of their questions were the transitory news conference variety. They often appeared unaware of the need to convert even important topics or issues into debatable propositions. They brought to the debates an adversarial attitude common in their profession and, in some instances, seemed eager to confront and (in Kraft's words) to "unmask" the candidates. They may have considered themselves to be the public's defenders or advocates, although it is not clear that they merited the role more than persons with other backgrounds or professions. It is possible that journalists—to a greater extent than others—may be attracted more to the hoopla of a campaign than to its substance, more to the immediate event than to the distant goal, and more to the hot and spicy story than to the complex issue. Study of the presidential campaign reveals the extent to which the press was party to many of the inane topics which captured national attention. After all, it was the press that played up major "non-issues" in the campaign—Carter's *Playboy* interview, accusations that Ford was being investigated for possible illegal acceptance of gifts, Agriculture Secretary Earl Butz's vulgar ethnic joke, to cite only a few. Many of the debate questions posed by the journalists touched upon short-term, hot, "newsworthy now," but minor topics.

In a column written before the debates commenced, James Reston wondered why reporters should participate in the debates and warned that they "will tend to question on the past and present conflicts," whereas other questioners might "concentrate on the future."[26] After the first debate, Charles B. Seib of the *Washington Post* came down hard on his colleagues: "Drop the panel of reporters. News people had no business on that Philadelphia stage. Taking a direct part in a political event went beyond the journalistic function. And, to be brutal about it, the reporters made no real contribution."[27] Seib's final judgment was probably hyperbolic, but the issue he raised must be faced. In the future, participation of journalists should not be taken for granted.

The debate format used by Ford and Carter was a reality which influenced their rhetoric. The rules and conditions under which they spoke limited what they could say, how well the issues could be treated, and how extensively they could debate each other; in short, their rhetoric was sharply limited by the reality of the format. Critics who complained of the debate rhetoric should recognize that their complaints apply equally to the format. If there is aspiration to improve the quality of presidential debates in the future, then surely there must be aspiration to improve the quality of the format. The best-designed format will not lead inevitably to political discourse of high quality, since we cannot specify the abilities and motives of those who debate: if they are utterly incapable of rich political discourse, the best format may be of little benefit. It is certain, however, that if the candidates are talented and have their eyes upon truth as well as victory, a good debate format will be one necessary condition for any presidential debate that contributes richly to our political life.

Without the creation and use of new formats, there will be a tendency to repeat what is recent and familiar—the format used by Nixon and Kennedy and by Ford and Carter. It should not be used again without major changes. Chapter 7 provides a modification of the Ford-Carter format and three other formats designed to meet the needs of the candidates and the public.

7.
The Design of
Future Presidential Debates

Political debates are desirable public policy as a means to inform
the electorate, elevate the quality of political discourse, and give
opponents equal and adequate opportunity to discuss their views
on public issues. Ideally, debates should be welcomed by
contenders as an avenue of effective campaigning and a means
of enriching public dialogue. However, common sense dictates
that debates do not serve the public interest when they cloud
issues and spread misinformation, or when they encourage
candidates to merely "score" against each other rather than
actually debate. Political candidates certainly will not think
debates are in their interest if the format repeatedly forces them
into high risk situations where a slip of the tongue or an error
could bring them public ridicule, endanger national security,
and possibly demean the office they seek to win.

No single debate format is ideal. What may be acceptable as
the best possible design will be relative to several factors, one of
which is the verbal skill of the candidates: if one is a demon-
strably skilled debater and the other is not, then a design
somehow accommodating both will be right for them. Another
factor is the status of the candidates: the incumbent may wish to
avoid debate in the Ford-Carter format, which gives advantage

to a challenger who has rehearsed his answers during months of campaigning and which makes the incumbent a large target for the panelists' questions and the challenger's attacks. A third factor is the character of the campaign: if it is keyed to three or four vital issues on which the candidates differ, probably the public interest will be served by a series of debates focusing squarely on those issues; but if candidates take approximately identical positions on key issues, debates calculated chiefly to inform the public about the character and abilities of the candidates might be most valuable. Other factors come easily to mind: the attractiveness of the candidates, their articulateness, how comfortable they feel in one format or another, whether they read well from manuscript or perform best in extemporaneous speaking, their standing in the public opinion polls, who has greater campaign momentum, etc. Although political considerations clearly will enter into the selection of a suitable debate format, one may hope that the ideal of sound political discourse will serve as a regulative principle forceful enough to lead candidates and sponsors to select a format which serves truth and the public interest, as well as the political ends of the candidates. Several formats can be sketched out, but no one of them is perfect for all situations. All admit of variations, and at least one ought to meet the contingencies of any specific campaign. Presidential debates in one season obviously might use two or more different formats.

Several criteria have guided us in devising four formats. In the first place, as a set the formats ought to be non-refusable; that is, whatever the contingencies of a particular presidential campaign, the candidates ought to be able to agree on one of the four, or on some combination. Second, no format should repeat the critical flaw of the Ford-Carter debates—the competing demands to answer and to debate; formats should encourage either genuine debate or thoughtful answers. Third, any format should provide candidates equal and adequate time in which to think and speak. Fourth, candidates ought to know in advance of their meeting what matters are to be discussed and what propositions to be debated. The public also should have this information in advance to be better prepared as listeners. Fifth, there should be a mechanism by which the candidates or their representatives participate in establishing the debate agenda. Sixth, it is desirable that candidates share the same stage and speak alternately in order to assure that the audience listens to both. This does not mean necessarily that the speakers must literally share the same stage; indeed, using the "policy address format" they might debate from different locations, and their speeches might be prepared on film before broadcast time. But ideally they should appear within the same time slot and share the same television screen, which is after all the principal "stage" on which political campaigning is conducted. Finally, the format should not place unreasonable demands and risks on the candidates: they should not have to set aside two or three days before each debate in order to memorize details related to a multitude of subjects; they should not be forced to answer important and hazardous questions that have not been analyzed with care; they should not be subjected to hostile and "off the wall" questions; in short, they should not have to undergo extraordinary risks. Anthony Lewis, observing the troubled Gerald Ford campaigning in California the day after his second-debate blunder, justly lamented the undue risks we ask our candidates to run: "Watching Gerald Ford that day, one thought again: What a strange way America has to elect its Presidents, how subject to accidents, how cruel to the participants. One unfortunate remark in an interview, one slip, one perceived failure of command, and the audience in the arena gives a terrible signal of rejection."[1] Any format should minimize risks and unreasonable demands. This criterion in conjunction with the others should help ensure that debates will be attractive to candidates and valuable to the public. Given options among several workable formats, candidates who refuse to debate in any format or to come to agreement on a reasonable compromise open themselves to public chastisement.

NEWS INTERVIEW FORMAT

This is not a debate structure, but a format of answers to questions posed by a single interviewer or by a panel. The objective is informative dialogue assisted by skillful questioning. It resembles, but doesn't duplicate, such familiar television programs as "Face the Nation," "Meet the Press," "Issues and Answers," "Bill Moyers' Journal," and "The MacNeil/Lehrer Report." What are the essential features?

The candidates appear together for a session of sixty or ninety minutes and discuss one or two principal issues—for example, health and welfare. Five or six sessions are scheduled, perhaps one each week. The setting and atmosphere is informal, with candidates and interviewers seated in a physical arrangement that is non-adversarial. Both the setting and the nature of the interview should invite *inquiry* into the causes and possible solutions of problems. Harassing questions which drive candidates to defensive positions or force them to take adversarial roles should be avoided. The objectives are *inquiry, discussion,* and *problem solving.*

The format features flexibility as well as informality. If a line of thought is more fruitful and rich than anticipated, let the interviewer and candidates pursue it; after all, the desired result is in-depth discussion of important issues. In keeping with informality and flexibility, there are no rigid structures and time limits governing the remarks by candidates, although the moderator must exercise good judgment to assure general observance of the principles of equal and adequate time.

Because this is a non-confrontational format, debate and sharp exchanges between candidates are not allowed. Yet a candidate who sees a chance for an easy score may be tempted to take it. He should understand that he risks being cut off by the interviewer and reprimanded with no chance for immediate response.

To help assure the goal of inquiry and to avoid debate, there is no formal opportunity for one candidate to comment on the answers given by the other, as in the Ford-Carter debates. Instead, both candidates answer the question posed by the interviewer; and the flow of messages is always from interviewer to candidate A to interviewer to candidate B to interviewer, etc. This is not to suggest that a candidate should be kept from promoting an idea or policy that competes with that of his opponent. This can be done properly through the artful guidance of the interviewer.

The interviewer or panel members and the candidates or their representatives meet well in advance of each session and plan what should be the major issues and leading questions. In the planning stage, candidates are asked to contribute topics and issues. For example, if the first session is to treat subjects of national health and welfare, the candidates indicate to the panel members what they believe to be the problems and issues needing discussion. The panel should be committed to incorporating some of the candidates' suggestions.

Each session should begin and close with statements by both candidates—at the beginning a three- or four-minute reflective statement relating to the issues to be discussed, and at the close a two- or three-minute summary.

The interviewer's demeanor and style is as important to success as that of the candidates. The interviewer or panelists must not consider themselves adversaries, unmaskers, public advocates or defenders, challengers, debaters, or "tough questioners." The role of the interviewer is that of a gentle Socrates practicing the art of midwife—coaxing from the candidates their best thought through skillful questions and suggestions. This format cannot tolerate a Joseph Kraft charging that Ford has a rotten record on the economy; rather, it calls for a Bill Moyers pointing out that the central cities are in trouble and, with good questions, drawing from each candidate his views and solutions. Since the character and skill of the interviewers are critical factors, it is proper that the candidates select those with whom they will converse.

There are several advantages of this format. First, being non-combative by design, it is less risky to candidates than other formats. It is not altogether without risk, of course, but if discussion goes by the rules and if the format succeeds in fostering informal discussion in an easy atmosphere, candidates should have few fears. They will not face attacks by questioners or by each other; they will not be pressed by one-sided and hostile questions; and they will not be placed in an adversarial relationship with each other or with the questioner. Second, since the element of combat is minimized and the format is designed to foster reflective discussion and inquiry rather than debate, two important consequences should follow: the press probably will not bill these sessions as the critical campaign events, which was done in 1976; and the press and others will not find it so easy to "score" the discussions in an effort to determine winner and loser, as they did in 1976. In other words, this format reduces pressure. Instead of rushing to judgment with accounts of who won or lost, press attention could focus on the quality of ideas, the analysis of problems, and the proposed solutions. Third, if the format is successful, it is very likely that the public will hear thoughtful and reasoned discussion of important issues by candidates, without the jabs, ad hominem arguments, and numerous other defects which marred the Ford-Carter debates. Finally, because this format is relatively safe for the candidates, it may be the only format on which they might agree, particularly if one or both refuse to engage in face-to-face debate.

A major disadvantage of this format is that it does not foster debate, indeed is designed to eliminate it; consequently, some audience members and commentators will be disappointed that there is no vigorous competition of ideas and positions. After announcement in 1976 that the Ford-Carter debates would not permit "head-to-head exchanges" between the candidates, an editorial in the *Los Angeles Times* complained that "they will be kept apart by a panel of three reporters. . . . They will never once confront each other directly during the three 90-minute appearances."[2] These and similar criticisms may be expected of the "discussions" in the news interview format. Another disadvantage is that these sessions possibly would generate less public interest and attract a smaller national audience than debates, because the elements of competition and high drama are significantly reduced. This disadvantage rests in part on a general assumption that the best format is one which attracts and holds the largest audience—an assumption not supported by fact, so far as we know. Indeed, it can be argued that the quality of debate or discussion may be expected to improve if the audience, though smaller, is more demanding. A third disadvantage is that candidates may repeat their campaign commonplaces in answering questions rather than providing more thoughtful analyses and solutions. We do not believe this to be a serious disadvantage; most members of the audience, not having heard those answers previously, will become better informed. (Reporters who have followed the campaign may be dissatisfied.) The speakers, aware in advance of the matters to be discussed, also will have opportunity to formulate fresh thought and material. Moreover, a skillful questioner can succeed in moving discussion beyond the range of commonplace answers.

Do any dangers or hazards attend the news interview format? The success of discussion in this format clearly depends not only on the abilities of the candidates, but on the skill of the interviewers as discussion facilitators; if interviewers are inept, the events will be dull and uninformative. The candidates also must depend on the interviewers to be fair and maintain the proper atmosphere; if the Socratic interviewer becomes accuser or inquisitor, the format's aims will not be met. Finally, each candidate entering this format must place considerable trust in the good intentions of the other—trust that the opponent will not use tactics inappropriate to the format and will follow the plan in good faith. One must expect that the element of competition will be present, however; thus candidate A may well criticize B's position while answering a question, and candidate B will seek to rebut A in his reply. Although the tendency to debate can be dampened by rules and good faith and by the interviewer's firm hand, it cannot be eliminated. If discussion slips into debate, there will be hazard to one or both candidates, because the format does not provide a suitable structure for debate; speakers are not assured of rebuttal time, for example.

MODIFIED FORD-CARTER FORMAT

In this format, candidates engage in face-to-face debate using a prescribed speaking order within rounds—similar to the design of the Ford-Carter debates. The format, however, eliminates or greatly reduces the main flaws evident in the 1976 debates.

There are three or four ninety-minute debates scheduled at appropriate intervals. Each debate is devoted to a topical area; for example, the economy in the first debate, foreign policy in the second, defense and national security in the third, and social welfare in the fourth.

A panel of experts, citizens, and candidates' representatives determine the particular propositions for the rounds of debate in each session. After propositions have been selected they are announced to the public a few days in advance of the debate. This not only provides candidates time to prepare, but gives the press an opportunity to educate the public on the background of issues to be debated. This pre-announcement of propositions somewhat reduces the element of spontaneity, but enhances the likelihood that candidates will debate knowledgeably before a public better prepared to hear and judge.

A moderator introduces the debates, announces the propositions for the rounds, enforces rules, and makes the transitions from speaker to speaker. If a panel is used to introduce propositions and perhaps to ask a question of each candidate within the rounds, panel members must be informed of their proper role.

Each debate begins with opening statements by the candidates and concludes with three- or four-minute closing statements. Candidates should not use their closing statements to attack or otherwise take unfair advantage of each other, since there is no further opportunity for rebuttal. They should link their closing statements closely to the issues in the just-concluded rounds of debate. In the Ford-Carter debates, this usually did not occur.

The number of rounds in a ninety-minute debate should not exceed five or six. Each round begins with statement of the proposition, accompanied perhaps with a brief statement of its importance.

OPTION A

Under one option, which excludes panelists' questions, the schedule of speeches is the following:

Statement of the proposition
Original speech by A: 4 minutes
Original speech by B: 4 minutes
Rebuttal speech by A: 3 minutes
Rebuttal speech by B: 3 minutes

This round of debate requires about fifteen minutes. In a ninety-minute debate, five rounds can be scheduled, leaving time for opening and closing statements.

OPTION B

If the format includes an opportunity for a panel to question each candidate, the questions should come between the original and rebuttal speeches. The time required for questions and answers means either that the speeches must be reduced in length or that the time allowed for each round must be increased. In no case should original speeches and rebuttals be reduced to less than three minutes each. If panel questions are part of the format, then a round of debate would consist of:

Statement of the proposition
Original speech by A: 3 minutes
Original speech by B: 3 minutes
Panelist's question to A: 15 seconds
Answer by A: 1 minute
Panelist's question to B: 15 seconds
Answer by B: 1 minute
Rebuttal speech by A: 3 minutes
Rebuttal speech by B: 3 minutes

Variations are possible for this and the former option. For example, candidates may prefer more time for their original or rebuttal speeches or both. They may prefer two sets of rebuttal speeches within each round. If the option in which panelists ask questions is the chosen format, candidates may wish to give panelists a somewhat larger role. Or instead of questions by panelists, the candidates might question each other within some or all rounds.

The propositions to be debated must be suitable and fair to both candidates, in the sense that they are equally debatable by each with advantage given to neither. The propositions must also be of such scope—neither too broad nor too narrow—that they can be debated in the available time. Candidates may speak from notes or manuscript as they wish. Since propositions are pre-announced and the candidates have prepared to speak to them, there is no point in a rule that forbids use of prepared material.

If the format works properly and the propositions are well designed to generate debate, the audience should witness in each round a pair of three- or four-minute original speeches which set out competing positions on the proposition, with supporting argument for each position; it is very likely that these original speeches also will contain challenges and charges addressed to the opponent. If no panelists' questions intervene between original speeches and rebuttals, then candidates can be expected to use their rebuttal speeches to refute, answer, and firm up their positions. The evident virtues of this modified format over the 1976 debate design are that the speakers know at the outset what should be at issue between them, they have equal time, and consequently the result should be well-focused debate throughout the round. It is possible to provide for panel questioning within each round, although this may interrupt the debate and perhaps divert it. On the other hand, skillful questioning sometimes can be used to clarify issues, probe candidates' positions in valuable ways, and bring a digressing speaker back to the proposition.

Several advantages recommend this format. First, it promotes face-to-face debate, which the news interview format prohibits. Second, it eliminates the major flaws of the 1976 debates: propositions are determined fairly and known in advance, speakers have more time and speeches within each round, and panels, if used, play a minimal role. Third, it calls for fast-paced debate covering four or five issues in each session; the pace and the competitive element should ensure audience interest. Fourth, this format provides for debate on the largest number of issues: fifteen to twenty "mini-debates" within four debates, surely enough to inform the electorate, but not so many as to trivialize the debates with shallow treatment of an unmanageable number of issues. Fifth, this format provides considerable control and predictability for candidates: they cannot be forced to dwell on an issue beyond a fixed time; they know the propositions they will debate and can anticipate to some extent the positions and arguments likely to be made by the opponent; they have an opportunity to answer each other's charges and arguments within the debate; and they can ably prepare for the relatively short speeches available to them, avoiding both wasted time and the unpredictable elements introduced by panelists in the 1976 debates.

The following are possible disadvantages. Although this format provides about fifteen minutes for debate on an issue and helps to assure that the time is used efficiently, it may be argued that important matters cannot be debated adequately when each speaker has only six or seven minutes within a round. There is truth in this argument, but there are also remedies: first, the propositions and issues for debate can be adjusted to the available time; and second, it is possible to lengthen the time for a round on an issue requiring fuller debate, if candidates agree. One of the advantages of the modified Ford-Carter format is that it alone of the four formats provides for rather quick movement from one round to another, but the Lincoln-Douglas format may be more appropriate for thorough and lengthy debate on a critical issue.

A second disadvantage of the modified Ford-Carter format is that it favors the candidate more skilled in debate. Even though the debate format provides equity in all areas where it can be guaranteed, the great unknown factor nevertheless is the verbal skill, cleverness, memory, and speed of the debaters. If there is evident inequality of skill between them, the one of lesser skill would not ordinarily prefer this format.

A third possible disadvantage is that one or more propositions set for debate may force candidates to take positions they would not wish to take in the heat of a campaign, or to engage in discussions they believe (rightly, perhaps) to run counter to the public interest. It seems clear that candidates should not be permitted to evade discussion of tough issues, but it seems equally clear that others ought not to have authority to compel them to debate just any matter. Candidates' representatives should have a strong voice, but not authority to veto a worthy issue or dictate any issue. Cooperative discussion and evaluation should prevail in the pre-debate meetings when propositions are determined.

Fourth, it is conceivable that candidates might overprepare and, in effect, present "canned" speeches. Because the propositions are known in advance, it is possible to prepare and memorize the original speeches for each round ahead of time. In addition, the candidates might rehearse units of argument to be employed in rebuttal speeches. In the worst conceivable scenario, both speakers come to the debate prepared with memorized original and rebuttal speeches and serve them up. The result would be position statements but no debate. This is highly improbable, however. Candidates surely would look foolish using recognizably "canned" speeches. Although they probably would prepare original speeches carefully, speakers could not prepare rebuttals in the same way. Each could (and would, in all likelihood) try to anticipate the opponent's positions and arguments and prepare arguments to be used in rebuttals, but this is not objectionable at all. We may expect this format to produce debate showing less spontaneity than the 1976 Ford-Carter debates. On the other hand, it should generate more and better debate.

Fifth, the speaking positions in a round probably will prove to be of unequal value. Speaker A, who presents the opening original speech, can seize the initiative by staking out a position which may surprise his opponent and throw him on the defensive. In addition, he may so define his own position as to embrace the position of his opponent, thus deflating Speaker B. However, Speaker B delivers the concluding rebuttal and has the last word in a round of debate. He actually has the opportunity for two rebuttal speeches, because his original speech as well as his rebuttal can be used to refute his opponent. On balance, Speaker A has a modest advantage; but the advantage is shared equally by both speakers, who alternate positions from round to round.

Finally, there is a hazard to either candidate if the other candidate prepares and drops a "bombshell"—an exceptionally hostile charge, a surprise announcement by an incumbent which robs the challenger of his position, etc. This is a potential hazard in any debate format, but is more likely to happen in a format in which all of the propositions to be debated are known in advance. A rule of conduct can provide partial protection against this. But the rule will be ineffective unless participants are committed to high-minded debate.

LINCOLN-DOUGLAS FORMAT

In 1858 Lincoln and Douglas, competing for a seat in the U.S. Senate, agreed to engage in a series of debates as they crisscrossed Illinois. In a letter to Douglas, Lincoln inquired, "Will it be agreeable to you to make an arrangement for you and myself to divide time, and address the same audiences during the present canvass?" Douglas accepted. The format worked out between them was expressed crisply in a Douglas letter to Lincoln: "I agree to your suggestion that we shall alternately open and close the discussion. I will speak at Ottawa one hour, you can reply, occupying an hour and a half, and I will then follow for half an hour. We will alternate in like manner in each successive place." They debated at Ottawa on August 21, 1858, and concluded the series with the seventh debate at Alton on October 5. There was no panel to determine propositions or pose questions.

The contemporary audience is probably unprepared to hear presidential candidates present such long speeches, even from Lincoln and Douglas. It perhaps would tolerate debates in the Lincoln-Douglas format if the speeches were reduced by half. This is roughly what the *New York Times* advised in a post-election editorial: "Debates should be encounters between contenders, not between contenders and a panel of questioners from the media or anywhere else. Much more could have been learned if the League of Women Voters had, by agreement with the nominees, picked four or five broad subjects for discussion and then left the participants to dispose of them. On foreign policy, for example, the contenders might have spoken freely for, say, thirty minutes each, choosing their own priorities, and then been allowed to dissect and rake over each other's presentation for another fifteen minutes apiece, with short rebuttals and summaries to follow."[3] While calling for debates in the fashion of Lincoln and Douglas, the *Times* suggested a structure not likely to assure success. The danger of simply turning candidates loose with blocks of time and broad discussion topics is that their position statements may go to different matters and their rebuttals make little contact on issues.

The chief features of the Lincoln-Douglas format can be maintained in a series of four or more debates, each one sixty to ninety minutes long, in which candidates engage each other face-to-face without third-party intervention. A moderator, if used, should present only a brief introduction and conclusion, keep time, and provide transitions between one speech and the next. It is essential that there be time for extended speeches, including position statements as well as rebuttals in order to probe the issues thoroughly and allow each candidate the necessary time to challenge the positions and arguments of his opponent. With the debate issues or propositions announced in advance and the candidates allowed ample opportunity to speak, we can rightfully expect speeches to show excellence of thought and style. All debates in the series might center upon a single issue, but more probably each would focus on a separate issue, for example one debate on the energy problem, another on the control of inflation, a third on a critical issue in foreign affairs, etc. The debate issues must be determined by the candidates, either with or without the assistance of an impartial panel, since it is essential that they are satisfied that the chosen issues involve clear propositions which they are able to debate.

This format has several advantages. More than any other, it encourages extended face-to-face debate, with adequate time for candidates to develop well-argued positions and engage each other with questions, challenges, and refutations. Second, this format provides conditions in which equally talented debaters may be expected to make their very best efforts. Not pressured by a panel of questioners, hurried from one proposition and round to the next, or forced to treat numerous unrelated issues, each can prepare with care what he wishes to say and can anticipate to some extent the arguments likely to be made by his opponent. Furthermore, the candidates have the opportunities of presenting well-prepared and polished position statements (manuscript speeches, if desired) as well as taking advantage of their extemporaneous speaking talents in the give and take of rebuttals. Finally, the focus on a few critical issues may elevate the tone and substance of the campaign. By selecting this format, candidates commit themselves to debate a handful of substantive issues on which they differ, which should have the effect of highlighting those issues.

One principal disadvantage of this format is that many issues will be passed by if debates deal with only a small number of critical issues. For example, candidates using the modified Ford-Carter format debate fifteen to twenty issues; using the Lincoln-Douglas format they debate only four or five. It may be argued that the format permitting debate on a larger number of issues is preferable because greater public education takes place. A second disadvantage is that the candidates, given time for lengthy speeches focused on one critical issue, may enter into minute detail and subtlety which escape audience comprehension. This is avoidable, but might occur. For example, in a debate on the problem of inflation, candidates might flood the audience with unintelligible statistics and dispute at length on complex interpretations of economic forces. Third, this format favors the verbally skillful candidate to a greater extent than does the modified Ford-Carter format. If a candidate is speedy, clever, and skilled in techniques of debate, with the ability to speak at length extemporaneously, he has a decided advantage. Extemporaneous speech was limited to three minutes in the 1976 debates; but a speaker may be required to speak for as long as ten minutes without use of prepared text in the Lincoln-Douglas format.

Finally, even with candidates evenly matched and other factors equal, this is still a high-risk debate format. A candidate who is thrown on the defensive, commits an error, or suffers some other embarrassment early in a debate may find himself suffering throughout most of the ninety-minute session: for there is no change of topic, movement to another round, or time to conceive a new strategy—in effect, no rescue. Also, if candidates elect the Lincoln-Douglas format, they may expect the press and the public to regard the debates as critical campaign events, as the major test between them, and as especially important because of novelty. This weight they might prefer to avoid, or at least reduce.

There are many ways to organize speeches within a Lincoln-Douglas format—both the order and length of speeches. If the organization of speeches used by Lincoln and Douglas were adapted to a ninety-minute period, the format would include a thirty-minute speech by A; a forty-five-minute speech by B; and a concluding fifteen-minute speech by A. This structure gives no assurance that there will be genuine debate; in fact, the candidates might simply present two independent position statements in the longer speeches, with the fifteen-minute rebuttal giving an advantage to A. Moreover, such long speeches might weary the present-day audience.

For modern Lincoln-Douglas encounters, there must be a format likely to generate debate, hold audience interest, and yet meet the ideal of speeches long enough to permit the contenders to deal thoughtfully and ably with important issues. Two possibilities are sketched here.

OPTION A

Under the first option, one speaker presents a position statement on the issue, and for a period of time this position statement becomes the object of debate. The other speaker subsequently presents his position statement on the same issue, which is also debated. Final rejoinders as well as closing statements conclude the debate.

Unit 1
- A's position statement on the issue: 20 minutes
- B's rebuttal: 10 minutes
- A's rejoinder: 5 minutes

Unit 2
- B's position statement on the issue: 20 minutes
- A's rebuttal: 10 minutes
- B's rejoinder: 5 minutes

Unit 3
- A's closing rejoinder: 5 minutes
- B's closing rejoinder: 5 minutes

Unit 4
- A's summary statement: 5 minutes
- B's summary statement: 5 minutes

This option enables each candidate to present a prepared twenty-minute position statement, with the speeches so ordered that A's position statement receives attention and debate prior to B's—an arrangement which allows debate to be focused sharply on both position statements. Moreover, alternating the speakers and mixing longer and shorter speeches should serve to hold audience interest.

OPTION B

Under the second option, the candidates present twenty-minute position statements after making brief opening remarks. One position statement immediately follows the other, after which the candidates present several rebuttal speeches. The function of the brief opening statements is to enable each to preview his position and outline anticipated points of dispute.

Unit 1
⎡ A's opening preview: 3 minutes
⎣ B's opening preview: 3 minutes

Unit 2
⎡ A's position statement on the issue: 20 minutes
⎣ B's position statement on the issue: 20 minutes

Unit 3
⎡ A's rebuttal: 5 minutes
  B's rebuttal: 5 minutes
  A's rebuttal: 5 minutes
  B's rebuttal: 5 minutes
  A's rebuttal: 5 minutes
⎣ B's rebuttal: 5 minutes

Unit 4
⎡ A's closing summary: 5 minutes
⎣ B's closing summary: 5 minutes

The provision for sharp debate in the numerous alternating rebuttal speeches is the major virtue of this option. However, a disadvantage is that the twenty-minute position statement of one candidate possibly may be overshadowed or otherwise lost in the battle. Indeed, it is also possible that the rebuttal speeches could drift to issues unrelated or only vaguely related to the major issue addressed in the position statements.

Both options may be modified by altering the length and number of speeches, but we believe that position statements of less than fifteen minutes would work in opposition to the major objective of the Lincoln-Douglas format. Because this format also requires numerous opportunities to engage in rebuttal and refutation, the number of rebuttals and rejoinders should not be significantly reduced either. Finally, it would be contrary to the objective of the format for candidates to discuss two or more different issues in one debate; if they wish to cover a wider territory, the modified Ford-Carter design is far more appropriate.

POLICY ADDRESS FORMAT

Debate does not have to occur in face-to-face encounter on a single platform and within a single time frame. Indeed, it is possible that the best debate may occur only when speakers have time between speeches for reflection on issues already raised, consultation with advisers, and preparation and presentation of speeches without the pressures and risks inherent in both the Ford-Carter and the Lincoln-Douglas formats. After all, the great and historic debates in Congress, science, and other fields are conducted over varying time spans and not compressed within a ninety-minute period. It should be noted also that newspaper columnists sometimes engage in advocacy and rebuttal; and when doing so, they ordinarily enjoy reflective leisure, opportunity for consultation with colleagues, and time to hone the script before going public. It seems reasonable that one possible format for presidential debate might allow candidates the same conditions.

The policy address format provides for debate by means of speeches prepared in advance of presentation. Candidates do not meet in face-to-face encounters, although their speeches may be scheduled in immediate sequence—for example one at 8:00 P.M. and the other at 8:30 on a given day. The speeches not only will be fashioned in advance of presentation but probably also with the assistance of advisers. To assure that genuine debate occurs, speakers clearly must agree upon the issues on which their policy addresses will focus; they must be certain that debatable propositions are associated with those issues; and they must agree to ground rules that require them to engage the issues and not simply present routine campaign speeches. Furthermore, to promote genuine debate, the policy addresses must be followed by a set of rebuttal speeches.

If the policy address format is selected, a minimum of four speeches will comprise an individual debate occurring not in one ninety-minute period but at intervals during a week. Four or more debates should be scheduled. Let us suppose that the first debate centers on an issue or set of closely related issues on foreign policy. Both candidates prepare thirty-minute or forty-five-minute policy addresses on the issue and present them either back-to-back or with a one-day interval. For example, A speaks on Sunday evening and B on Monday evening; A presents a thirty-minute rebuttal on Wednesday, and B provides a rebuttal on Thursday. In this manner, the speeches comprising one debate are spread throughout the week. If this pattern were repeated during four or five weeks of the campaign, the public could hear sixteen to twenty major policy addresses—possibly one of the most informative campaign events in recent history.

OPTION A

One option for this format places the policy addresses side by side within a sixty- or ninety-minute time frame. Early in the week, both candidates present a thirty- or forty-five-minute policy address on a predetermined issue or set of related issues. Later in the same week, they present side-by-side rebuttals not necessarily originating from the same location.

Monday Night
        Candidate A: policy address, 30 or 45 minutes
        Candidate B: policy address, 30 or 45 minutes
Wednesday Night
        Candidate A: rebuttal, 30 minutes
        Candidate B: rebuttal, 30 minutes

The major virtue of this option compared to the next one is that the audience, hearing both candidates in one evening, can better understand and compare positions and personal characteristics.

OPTION B

The second option differs only in one respect—that the speeches occur on different days.

Sunday: A's policy address, 30 or 45 minutes
Monday: B's policy address, 30 or 45 minutes
Wednesday: A's rebuttal, 30 minutes
Thursday: B's rebuttal, 30 minutes

The interval between speeches increases the probability of thoughtful debate. B's policy address is likely to take issue with the address presented by A on the previous day; A's rebuttal will be responsive to B's policy address and refutations; and finally, B's speech on the last day can respond to A's rebuttal. B gains two advantages with this arrangement: he has two opportunities for refutative speeches—his policy address and rebuttal—whereas A has only one; and B has the last word because his final rebuttal closes debate. Three other factors may cause candidates to view this option as less desirable than the first one. Since the speeches are separated in time, listeners may choose to tune in only the candidate already preferred. Or they may lose interest in the speeches and tune out. Finally, the interval of time between speeches may tempt candidates and others to issue public attacks and denunciations which influence and corrupt the context of discourse even though they are not part of the formal debate.

What virtues recommend the policy address format? First, all speeches, profiting from advance preparation, should be uniformly excellent in form and substance. The format virtually eliminates the possibility that debates will be marred by gross errors, slips of the tongue, shallow argumentation, and similar defects. Second, the candidates have maximum control over their debate performances: because their speeches can be perfected before delivery, they speak in an environment largely free of uncertainties and the kinds of risks inherent in other formats. Third, this format gives nearly equal opportunity to candidates possessing unequal debate skills. If A is clearly superior to B in debate skills, A will have a significant advantage in all formats except this one, where he has no occasion to use skills in extemporaneous debate. For this reason, the policy address format may be the right choice for candidates of disproportionate debate skills. Finally, it may be the only acceptable format to a candidate who is far ahead in public opinion polls and refuses face-to-face encounters on the assumption that he has much to lose and his opponent much to gain.

Absence of spontaneity is a major disadvantage of this format. With candidates presenting speeches prepared in advance, the debates will lack the extemporaneous give and take that often reveals important qualities of thought and character. We should remember, however, that candidates also engage in other campaign events, many of which reveal those qualities—in press conferences and news interview programs, for example. Another disadvantage is that debates in this format may be less competitive than one would expect in either the modified Ford-Carter or the Lincoln-Douglas formats. On the other hand, they may prove to be richer in content. Finally, the delay between the policy addresses and subsequent rebuttals opens the way for hazards. If candidate A severely attacks or unfairly characterizes B in a policy address, B must wait a day or two for his rebuttal opportunity and cannot respond immediately. Or again, A might upstage B by making a dramatic announcement or staking out a position in his policy address that grabs headlines; in such an instance, the lag between policy address and rebuttal could put B at a disadvantage. Such hazards can be avoided or minimized greatly if candidates adhere to ground rules. Finally, third parties—the press and other political speakers—might "corrupt" the debate with confusing, disruptive, and competitive messages during the intervals between policy addresses and rebuttals. Although this risk to some extent must be endured, the press and others can play an important constructive role at just this point—by helping to educate the public about the positions announced in policy addresses.

These format options exhaust the desirable possibilities. The candidates either engage in discussion and inquiry or they debate. The news interview format provides for discussion and inquiry. If they debate, they either do so face-to-face or at a distance. The policy address format provides for the latter. If they debate face-to-face, they cover either many issues or a few critical issues. The modified Ford-Carter format meets the first option; and the Lincoln-Douglas format meets the second. The conditions of genuine debate are built into each debate format: speakers have equal and adequate time; they know the issues and propositions to be debated; they need not expose themselves to extraordinary risks; and their debate is not likely to be significantly interrupted or colored by the discourse of third parties. Their method of engaging each other is structured by format and guided by ground rules that allow each candidate an opportunity to present excellent political discourse and advance his own cause.

The press-conference model used by Kennedy and Nixon in 1960 and by Ford and Carter in 1976 is unacceptable and should not be repeated. We agree completely with critics who contend that tough questioning of candidates by the press has great value. In the normal campaign season, however, candidates face the press frequently in rigorous encounters. The incumbent candidate is likely to have faced the press with regularity for years. Columnist George Will noted in a television commentary that "we have enough press conferences during campaigns." What we need, said Will, are genuine debates in which candidates "argue back and forth, with only minimal control."[4] Tough questioning by journalists in press conference settings is a valuable fixture of campaigns, but attempts to use the press conference pattern as a format for genuine presidential debates are doomed to failure.

The recommended formats are also suitable for debate between vice-presidential candidates, who ought to debate once or twice during the campaign. Given the precedent established in 1976 and the realities of campaigns, it is likely that only one debate would be scheduled between the vice-presidential candidates. If so, the modified Ford-Carter format probably would prove most valuable to the public, who, hearing the candidates debate five or six issues, would receive a broader view of their positions and characters than from debate in other formats.

How many debates should be scheduled? And should

debates stand as the centerpiece in a campaign? From the viewpoint of educational value to the public, there should be several debates rather than one or two. From the standpoint of political strategy, candidates should understand that the press and the public will probably attach importance to the debates in inverse proportion to their number, other things being equal. If only one debate is scheduled, that debate is likely to be regarded as critical; but if six or seven occur, no single one will bear extraordinary weight, and the series as a whole may be no more important psychologically than one debate. Furthermore, the debates will be reduced in psychological importance if other significant campaign events, such as independent major addresses, are also scheduled. Candidates who are reluctant to have critical importance attached to debates would be wise to schedule more rather than fewer debates. In addition, they would be wise to make several independent addresses to the national audience.

Presidential debates of high quality should serve the interests of the candidates. For one thing, candidates may be relieved somewhat of the strain, fatigue, and sheer monotony of stumping day after day, week after week, if several debates become a focal point of the campaign. And if a series of debates were scheduled in the five weeks preceding election day, perhaps the active campaign could be limited to that period. The result would be a significant reduction in the length of presidential campaigns—which actually happened in 1976 in the case of President Ford. In financial terms, a series of debates broadcast nationwide provides the contenders with the largest and most attentive audience at the least expense. Finally, if debates succeed in focusing attention on substantive issues, candidates may be freed to some extent from press coverage of campaign trivia, verbal slips, and the usual array of campaign non-issue topics. It is possible that a presidential campaign featuring substantive debates will stimulate more serious, in-depth press coverage than was seen in 1976.

Two considerations not under the control of candidates and sponsors could affect the prospects of future presidential debates. Congressional action may be needed to modify section

315 of the Federal Communications Act of 1934, which provides for "equal time" for all presidential candidates, to permit the two major party candidates to gain easier access to prime-time coverage. But if televised coverage of debates were prohibited by law, the major party candidates ought to debate, even in the absence of live broadcast coverage, simply in the interest of enriching national politics.

The second consideration is this: the institutionalizing of debates may further increase the power of candidates' images and personalities and decrease the power of political parties and ideologies. It is probable that debates will focus attention on *individuals,* who may or may not be linked securely to their parties. David Broder warns of this observable tendency: "As it happens, our presidential campaigns are already getting to look too much like nonpartisan popularity contests. They are already seen by too many people as a competition between individuals operating at a lofty level, far removed from the crass partisan battles of Congress or the state house." Broder does not argue against presidential debates, but urges that each candidate should be more closely linked to his party and its history: "What we need to do is tie these free-floating presidential characters down to the reality of their party's history, interests and philosophy, and not let them promise policies that will be quickly repudiated in office." The debates, Broder concludes, should be "as direct, uninhibited, lusty and . . . partisan as possible."⁵ Broder's prescription, if heeded by candidates and insisted upon by party leaders, might reduce the extent to which presidential debates feature individuals at the expense of parties. The tendency of presidential debates, however, is to focus attention on the candidates, detached from parties.

The sponsorship of presidential debates is also a matter of concern to Broder in the column just mentioned. Reacting to a Twentieth Century Fund task force recommendation that the League of Women Voters should again sponsor presidential debates in 1980, Broder argues that debates ought to be partisan affairs handled by the candidates and by the parties: "The sponsorship of presidential campaign debates is the province of the political parties. They pick the candidates, and logically, they ought to have the responsibility for presenting them to the public." Partisan battles imply partisan sponsorship. Broder's argument is plausible, but it is possible that everything he asks for can be accomplished if the debates are well designed, if questions or propositions clearly invite "partisan" debate, and if candidates ably debate and represent their parties. Whether debates are arranged by the candidates, the parties, or a non-partisan organization is not a critical choice. The value of the debates *is* critical.

The prospects for presidential debates of quality in 1980 and subsequent election years depend on three major factors. One can be easily provided—namely, format options structured to enable candidates to debate competently. The second would be a constructive contribution by the press, the major intermediary between candidates and public. The press, if it will, can prod a campaign toward high-minded discourse by its muscle and its example. Or the press can trivialize a campaign through dwelling on strategy, faux pas, irrelevancies, public opinion polls, and other such matters as were often dramatized by the press in 1976. The press, like the political contenders, has its favorite topics and plays its special games. One of its 1976 games was rushing to declare a winner and a loser after each debate, as Joseph Lelyveld pointed out: "The result was an unseemly, even grotesque rush to declare a 'winner' after each round of the competition. And on each occasion, subsequent polls showed that this process of scorekeeping seemed to induce millions of voters to reject their own impressions because the pollsters had not validated them."[6] This complaint was just, but the behavior of the press need not be unseemly. The press can observe principles which raise the level of political dialogue. But if—in its reporting and commentary—the press badly represents or colors a political campaign, it will be difficult to mount serious and excellent political debate.

Finally, establishing a tradition of presidential debate requires commitments from the candidates—first, a commitment to debate, and second, a commitment to debate well.

At the time of the Kennedy-Nixon debates, some observers thought that a tradition was in the making. Quincy Howe, moderator of the final Kennedy-Nixon debate, concluded by praising the candidates for their courage and for setting a high standard: "Surely they have set a new precedent. Perhaps they have established a new tradition." Of course, they did not: no presidential debates occurred in the election years between 1960 and 1976. Republican candidate Barry Goldwater did not press for debates in 1964; and the debate challenges offered by Democratic candidates Hubert Humphrey and George McGovern were spurned by Richard Nixon in 1968 and 1972. How can candidates be persuaded to debate, if not motivated by self-interest or public service? Steady prodding by the public, journalists, and public interest groups well in advance of the campaign may get agreements from candidates to debate if nominated. If commitment is sought after nomination, it is more likely that one or both may prefer to decline debates because of political expediency. One incentive to debate might be provided through distributing public campaign financing funds to only those candidates who agreed to debate if nominated.

But even if candidates agree to debate and agree upon a good format, there can be *great debate* only if both candidates go beyond the observance of elementary ground rules. There are regulative principles to be observed—to speak the truth as they know it, to deal with issues squarely, to face up to problems honestly, to debate in good faith and fairness, to place the public interest in the highest position—as Plato said, to do one's best to speak so as to please the gods, if not men. Steady commitment to these principles is a necessary condition for establishing a tradition of truly great debates.

National dialogue guided by these principles, involving candidates and other voices, incorporating rigorous inquiry and effective communication, and pressing always toward political and moral truth is at the core of the rhetoric of democracy. And the rhetoric of democracy is to be distinguished from the selling of candidates and ideas, which has for too long served as the principal mode of national politics.

Part 2

☆ ☆ ☆ ☆ ☆ ☆ ☆ ☆ ☆ ☆ ☆ ☆ ☆ ☆ ☆ ☆ ☆ ☆ ☆

First Debate

September 23, 1976 Philadelphia

NEWMAN: Good evening. I'm Edwin Newman, moderator of this first debate of the 1976 campaign between Gerald R. Ford of Michigan, Republican candidate for president, and Jimmy Carter of Georgia, Democratic candidate for president. We thank you, President Ford, and we thank you, Governor Carter, for being with us tonight.

There are to be three debates between the presidential candidates and one between the vice-presidential candidates. All are being arranged by the League of Women Voters Education Fund. Tonight's debate, the first between presidential candidates in sixteen years, and the first ever in which an incumbent president has participated, is taking place before an audience in the Walnut Street Theatre in Philadelphia, just three blocks from Independence Hall. The television audience may reach one hundred million in the United States and many millions overseas.

Tonight's debate focuses on domestic issues and economic policy. Questions will be put by Frank Reynolds of ABC News, James Gannon of the *Wall Street Journal,* and Elizabeth Drew of the *New Yorker* magazine.

Under the agreed rules, the first question will go to Governor

Carter. That was decided by the toss of a coin. He will have up to three minutes to answer. One follow-up question will be permitted with up to two minutes to reply. President Ford will then have two minutes to respond. The next question will go to President Ford with the same time arrangements, and questions will continue to be alternated between the candidates. Each man will make a three-minute statement at the end, Governor Carter to go first. President Ford and Governor Carter do not have any notes or prepared remarks with them this evening. Mr. Reynolds, your question for Governor Carter:

A   REYNOLDS: Mr. President, Governor Carter. Governor, in an interview with the Associated Press last week, you said you believed these debates would alleviate a lot of concerns some voters have about you. Well, one of those concerns, not an uncommon one about candidates in any year, is that many voters say they don't really know where you stand. Now, you have made jobs your number one priority, and you have said you are committed to a drastic reduction in unemployment. Can you say now, Governor, in specific terms, what your first step would be next January, if you are elected, to achieve that?

1   CARTER: Yes. First of all, is to recognize the tremendous economic strength of this country, and to set the putting back to work of our people as a top priority. This is an effort that ought to be done primarily by strong leadership in the White House, the inspiration of our people, the tapping of business, agriculture, industry, labor, and government at all levels to work on this project. We'll never have an end to the inflationary spiral, and we'll never have a balanced budget, until we get our people back to work.

There are several things that can be done specifically that are not now being done. First of all, to channel research and development funds into areas that will provide large numbers of jobs. Secondly, we need to have a commitment in the private sector to cooperate with government in matters like housing. Here a very small investment of taxpayers' money in the housing field can bring large numbers of extra jobs and the guarantee of mortgage loans and the putting forward of "202" programs[1] for housing for older people and so forth to cut down the roughly 20 percent unemployment that now exists in the construction industry.

Another thing is to deal with our needs in the central cities, where the unemployment rate is extremely high. Sometimes among minority groups, or those who don't speak English, or who are black, or young people, are 40 percent unemployment. Here a CCC-type program[2] would be appropriate to channel money into the sharing with private sector and also local and state governments to employ young people who are now out of work. Another very important aspect of our economy would be to increase production in every way possible—to hold down taxes on individuals and to shift the tax burdens onto those who have avoided paying taxes in the past. These kinds of specific things, none of which are being done now, would be a great help in reducing unemployment.

There is an additional factor that needs to be done and covered very succinctly, and that is to make sure that we have a good relationship between management—business—on the one hand, and labor on the other. In a lot of places where unemployment is very high, we might channel specific targeted job opportunities by paying part of the salary of unemployed people and also sharing with local governments the payment of salaries, which would let us cut down the unemployment rate much lower before we hit the inflationary level. But I believe that by the end of the first four years of the next term, we could have the unemployment rate down to 3 percent adult unemployment, which is about 4 to 4½ percent overall, control the inflation rate, and have a balance of growth of about 4 to 6 percent, around 5 percent, which would give us a balanced budget.

REYNOLDS: Governor, in the event you are successful and you do achieve a drastic drop in unemployment, that is likely to create additional pressure on prices. How willing are you to consider an incomes policy? In other words, wage and price controls?   B

CARTER: Well, we now have such a low utilization of our productive capacity, about 73 percent—I think it's about the lowest since the Great Depression years—and such a high unemployment rate now, 7.9 percent, that we have a long way to go in getting people to work before we have the inflationary   2 pressures. And I think this would be easy to accomplish, to get jobs down without having the strong inflationary pressures that would be necessary. I would not favor the payment of a given fixed income to people unless they are not able to work. But with tax incentives for the low-income groups, we could build up their income levels above the poverty level and not make welfare more profitable than work.

NEWMAN: Mr. President, your response.

3   FORD: I don't believe that Mr. Carter has been any more specific in this case then he has been on many other instances. I notice particularly that he didn't endorse the Humphrey-Hawkins bill,[3] which he has on occasions, and which is included as a part of the Democratic platform. That legislation allegedly would help our unemployment, but we all know that it would have controlled our economy; it would have added 10 to 30 billion dollars each year in additional expenditures by the federal government; it would have called for export controls on agricultural products.

In my judgment, the best way to get jobs is to expand the private sector, where five out of six jobs today exist in our economy. We can do that by reducing federal taxes, as I proposed about a year ago when I called for a tax reduction of 28 billion dollars: three-quarters of it to go to private taxpayers, and one-quarter to the business sector. We could add to jobs in the major metropolitan areas by a proposal that I recommended that would give tax incentives to business to move into the inner city, and to expand or to build new plants so that they would take a plant or expand a plant where people are and people are currently unemployed. We could also help our youth with some of the proposals that would give to young people an opportunity to work and learn at the same time, just like we give money to young people who are going to college. Those are the kind of specifics that I think we have to discuss on these debates, and these are the kind of programs that I'll talk about on my time.

NEWMAN: Mr. Gannon, your question to President Ford.

C   GANNON: Mr. President, I would like to continue for a moment on this question of taxes which you have just raised. You have said that you favor more tax cuts for middle-income Americans, even those earning up to thirty thousand dollars a year. That presumably would cost the treasury quite a bit of money in lost revenue. In view of the very large budget deficits that you have accumulated and that are still in prospect, how is it possible to promise futher tax cuts and to reach your goal of balancing the budget?

FORD: At the time, Mr. Gannon, that I made the recom- 4 mendation for a 28-billion-dollar tax cut, three-quarters of it to go to individual taxpayers and 25 percent to American business, I said at the same time that we had to hold the lid on federal spending, that for every dollar of a tax reduction we had to have an equal reduction in federal expenditures: a one-for-one proposition—and I recommended that to the Congress, with a budget ceiling of 395 billion dollars; and that would have permitted us to have a 28-billion-dollar tax reduction. In my tax reduction program for middle-income taxpayers, I recommended that the Congress increase personal exemptions from 750 dollars per person to 1,000 dollars per person. That would mean, of course, that for a family of four, that that family would have a thousand dollars more personal exemption—money that they could spend for their own purposes, money that the government wouldn't have to spend.

But if we keep the lid on federal spending, which I think we can, with the help of the Congress, we can justify fully a 28-billion-dollar tax reduction. In the budget that I submitted to the Congress in January of this year, I recommended a 50-percent cutback in the rate of growth of federal spending. For the last ten years the budget of the United States has grown from— about 11 percent per year. We can't afford that kind of growth in federal spending. And in the budget that I recommended, we cut it in half—a growth rate of 5 to 5½ percent. With that kind of limitation on federal spending, we can fully justify the tax reductions that I have proposed. And it seems to me, with the stimulant of more money in the hands of the taxpayer, and with more money in the hands of business to expand, to modernize, to provide more jobs, our economy will be stimulated so that we'll get more revenue and we'll have a more prosperous economy.

D   GANNON: Mr. President, to follow up a moment, the Congress
has passed a tax bill which is before you now, which did not
meet exactly the sort of outline that you requested. What is your
intention on that bill since it doesn't meet your requirements?
Do you plan to sign that bill?

5   FORD: That tax bill does not entirely meet the criteria that I
established. I think the Congress should have added another 10-
billion-dollar reduction in personal income taxes, including the
increase of personal exemptions from 750 to 1,000 dollars, and
Congress could have done that if the budget committees of the
Congress and the Congress as a whole had not increased the
spending that I recommended in the budget. I'm sure you know
that in the resolutions passed by the Congress, they have added
about 17 billion dollars in more spending by the Congress over
the budget that I recommended. So I would prefer in that tax bill
to have an additional tax cut and a further limitation on federal
spending.

Now, this tax bill that hasn't reached the White House yet,
but is expected in a day or two, it's about 1,500 pages. It has
some good provisions in it. It has left out some that I have
recommended, unfortunately. On the other hand, when you
have a bill of that magnitude, with those many provisions, a
president has to sit and decide if there's more good than bad;
and from the analysis that I've made so far, it seems to me that
that tax bill does justify my signature and my approval.

NEWMAN: Governor Carter, your response.

6   CARTER: Well, Mr. Ford is changing considerably his previous
philosophy. The present tax structure is a disgrace to this
country. It's just a welfare program for the rich. As a matter of
fact, 25 percent of the total tax deductions go for only 1 percent
of the richest people in this country. And over 50 percent of the
tax credits go for the 14 percent of the richest people in this
country. When Mr. Ford first became president in August of
1974, the first thing he did in October was to ask for a 4.7-
billion-dollar increase in taxes on our people in the midst of the
heaviest recession since the Great Depression of the 1940s. In
January of 1975, he asked for a tax change—a 5.6-billion-dollar

increase on low- and middle-income private individuals, a 6½-billion-dollar decrease on the corporations and the special interests. In December of 1975, he vetoed the roughly 18- to 20-billion-dollar tax reduction bill that had been passed by the Congress. And then he came back later on in January of this year and he did advocate a 10-billion-dollar tax reduction, but it would be offset by a 6-billion-dollar increase this coming January in deductions for Social Security payments and for unemployment compensation.

The whole philosophy of the Republican party, including my opponent, has been to pile on taxes on low-income people, to take them off on the corporations. As a matter of fact, since the late sixties when Mr. Nixon took office, we've had a reduction in the percentage of taxes paid by corporations from 30 percent down to about 20 percent. We've had an increase in taxes paid by individuals—payroll taxes—from 14 percent up to 20 percent, and this is what the Republicans have done to us. And this is why tax reform is so important.

NEWMAN: Mrs. Drew, your question to Governor Carter.

DREW: Governor Carter, you've proposed a number of new or E
enlarged programs including jobs, health, welfare reform, child care, aid to education, aid to cities, changes in Social Security, and housing subsidies. You've also said that you want to balance the budget by the end of your first term. Now you haven't put a price tag on those programs, but even if we priced them conservatively and we count for full employment by the end of your first term and we count for the economic growth that would occur during that period, there still isn't enough money to pay for those programs and balance the budget, by any estimates that I've been able to see. So, in that case, what would give?

CARTER: Well, as a matter of fact there is. If we assume a rate of `7
growth of our economy equivalent to what it was during President Johnson, President Kennedy, even before the Vietnamese war, and if we assume that at the end of the four-year period we can cut our unemployment rate down to 4 to 4½ percent; under those circumstances, even assuming no elimination of unnecessary programs and assuming an increase

in the allotment of money to finance programs, increasing as the inflation rate does, my economic projections, I think confirmed by the House and the Senate committees, have been with a 60-billion-dollar extra amount of money that can be spent in fiscal year '81, which would be the last year of this next term.

Within that 60-billion-dollars increase, there would be fit the programs that I have promised the American people. I might say, too, that if we see that these goals cannot be reached—and I believe they are reasonable goals—then I would cut back on the rate of implementation of new programs in order to accommodate a balanced budget by fiscal year '81, which is the last year of the next term. I believe that we ought to have a balanced budget during normal economic circumstances, and these projections have been very carefully made. I stand behind them. And if they should be in error slightly on the down side, then I'll phase in the programs that we've advocated more slowly.

F   DREW: Governor, according to the budget committees of the Congress that you've referred to, if we get to full employment, what they project at a 4-percent unemployment, and, as you say, even allowing for the inflation in the programs, there would not be anything more than a surplus of 5 billion dollars by the end of—by 1981. And conservative estimates of your programs would be that they'd be about 85 to 100 billion dollars. So how do you say that you're going to be able to do these things and balance the budget?

8   CARTER: Well, the assumption that you have described as different is in the rate of growth of our economy.

DREW: No, they took that into account in those figures.

8   CARTER: I believe that it's accurate to say that the committees to whom you refer, with the employment rate that you state, and with the 5- to 5½-percent growth rate in our economy, that the projections would be a 60-billion-dollar increase in the amount of money that we have to spend in 1981 compared to now, and in that framework would be fit any improvements in the programs.

Now this does not include any extra control over unnecessary spending, the weeding out of obsolete or obsolescent programs. We'll have a safety version built in with complete reorganization of the executive branch of government which I am pledged to do. The present bureaucratic structure of the federal government is a mess. And if I'm elected president, that's going to be a top priority of mine—to completely revise the structure of the federal government to make it economical, efficient, purposeful, and manageable for a change. And also I'm going to institute zero-based budgeting, which I used four years in Georgia, which assesses every program every year and eliminates those programs that are obsolete or obsolescent.

But with these projections, we will have a balanced budget by fiscal year 1981 if I'm elected president—keep my promises to the American people. And it's just predicated on very modest but, I think, accurate projections of employment increases and a growth in our national economy equal to what was experienced under Kennedy and Johnson before the Vietnam War.

NEWMAN: President Ford.

FORD: If it is true that there will be a 60-billion-dollar surplus   9
by fiscal year 1981, rather than spend that money for all the new programs that Governor Carter recommends and endorses and which are included in the Democratic platform, I think the American taxpayer ought to get an additional tax break, a tax reduction of that magnitude. I feel that the taxpayers are the ones that need the relief. I don't think we should add additional programs of the magnitude that Governor Carter talks about. It seems to me that our tax structure today has rates that are too high.

But I am very glad to point out that since 1969, during a Republican administration, we have had 10 million people taken off of the tax rolls at the lower end of the taxpayer area, and at the same time, assuming that I sign the tax bill that was mentioned by Mr. Gannon, we will, in the last two tax bills, have increased the minimum tax on all wealthy taxpayers. And I believe that by eliminating 10 million taxpayers in the last eight years and by putting a heavier tax burden on those in the higher tax brackets, plus the other actions that have been taken, we can give taxpayers adequate tax relief.

Now, it seems to me that as we look at the recommendations of the budget committees and our own projections, there isn't going to be any 60-billion-dollar dividend. I've heard of those dividends in the past. It always happens. We expected one at the time of the Vietnam War, but it was used up before we ever ended the war and taxpayers never got the adequate relief they deserved.

NEWMAN: Mr. Reynolds.

G   REYNOLDS: Mr. President, when you came into office, you spoke very eloquently of the need for a time for healing, and very early in your administration you went out to Chicago and you announced, you proposed, a program of case-by-case pardons for draft resisters to restore them to full citizenship. Some 14,000 young men took advantage of your offer, but another 90,000 did not. In granting the pardon to former President Nixon, sir, part of your rationale was to put Watergate behind us—to, if I may quote you again, "truly end our long national nightmare." Why does not the same rationale apply now, today, in our bicentennial year, to the young men who resisted in Vietnam, and many of them still in exile abroad?

10   FORD: The amnesty program that I recommended in Chicago in September of 1974 would give to all draft evaders and military deserters the opportunity to earn their good record back. About 14,000 to 15,000 did take advantage of that program. We gave them ample time. I am against an across-the-board pardon of draft evaders or military deserters.

Now, in the case of Mr. Nixon, the reason the pardon was given was that when I took office, this country was in a very, very divided condition. There was hatred, there was divisiveness, people had lost faith in their government in many, many respects. Mr. Nixon resigned, and I became president. It seemed to me that if I was to adequately and effectively handle the problems of high inflation, a growing recession, the involvement of the United States still in Vietnam, that I had to give a hundred percent of my time to those two major problems. Mr. Nixon resigned. That is disgrace—the first president out of thirty-eight that ever resigned from public office under pressure.

So when you look at the penalty that he paid and when you analyze the requirements that I had—to spend all of my time working on the economy, which was in trouble, that I inherited, working on our problems in Southeast Asia, which were still plaguing us—it seemed to me that Mr. Nixon had been penalized enough by his resignation in disgrace, and the need and necessity for me to concentrate on the problems of the country fully justified the action that I took.

REYNOLDS: I take it, then, sir, that you do not believe that you   H are going to reconsider and think about those 90,000 who are still abroad. Have they not been penalized enough? Many of them have been there for years.

FORD: Well, Mr. Carter has indicated that he would give a   11 blanket pardon to all draft evaders. I do not agree with that point of view. I gave, in September of 1974, an opportunity for all draft evaders, all deserters, to come in, voluntarily, clear their records by earning an opportunity to restore their good citizenship. I think we gave them a good opportunity—I don't think we should go any further.

NEWMAN: Governor Carter.

CARTER: Well, I think it's very difficult for President Ford to   12 explain the difference between the pardon of President Nixon and his attitude toward those who violated the draft laws.

As a matter of fact, I don't advocate amnesty; I advocate pardon. There's a difference, in my opinion, and in accordance with the ruling of the Supreme Court and according to the definition in the dictionary. Amnesty means that what you did was right; pardon means that what you did, whether it's right or wrong, you're forgiven for it. And I do advocate a pardon for draft evaders. I think it's accurate to say that two years ago when Mr. Ford put in this amnesty, that three times as many deserters were excused as were the ones who evaded the draft. But I think that now is the time to heal our country after the Vietnam War.

And I think that what the people are concerned about is not the pardon or the amnesty of those who evaded the draft, but whether or not our crime system is fair. We've got a sharp distinction drawn between white-collar crime: the big shots who are rich, who are influential, very seldom go to jail; those who are poor and who have no influence quite often are the ones who are punished. And the whole subject of crime is one that concerns our people very much. And I believe that the fairness of it is what is a major problem that addresses our leader, and this is something that hasn't been addressed adequately by this administration. But I hope to have a complete responsibility on my shoulders to help bring about a fair criminal justice system and also to bring about an end to the divisiveness that has occurred in our country as a result of the Vietnam War.

NEWMAN: Mr. Gannon.

I   GANNON: Governor Carter, you have promised a sweeping overhaul of the federal government, including a reduction in the number of government agencies you say would go down to about 200 from some 1,900. That sounds, indeed, like a very deep cut in the federal government, but isn't it a fact that you're not really talking about fewer federal employees or less government spending, but rather that you are talking about reshaping the federal government, not making it smaller?

13   CARTER: Well, I've been through this before, Mr. Gannon, as the governor of Georgia. When I took over, we had a bureaucratic mess like we have in Washington now. And we had 300 agencies, departments, bureaus, commissions, some fully budgeted, some not, but all having responsibility to carry out that was in conflict. And we cut those 300 agencies and so forth down substantially. We eliminated 278 of them. We set up a simple structure of government that could be administered fairly, and it was a tremendous success. It hasn't been undone since I was there. It resulted also in an ability to reshape our court system, our prison system, our education system, our mental health programs, and a clear assignment of responsibility and authority, and also to have our people once again understand and control our government.

I intend to do the same thing if I'm elected president. When I get to Washington, coming in as an outsider, one of the major responsibilities that I will have on my shoulder is the complete reorganization of the executive branch of government. We now have a greatly expanded White House staff. When Mr. Nixon went in office, for instance, we had 3½ million dollars spent on the White House and its staff. That has escalated now to 16½ million dollars in the last Republican administration. This needs to be changed. We need to put the responsibilities back on the cabinet members.

We also need to have a great reduction in agencies and programs. For instance, we now have in the health area 302 different programs administered by eleven major departments and agencies, sixty other advisory commissions responsible for this. Medicaid's in one agency; Medicare's in a different one; the check on the quality of health care's in a different one. None of them are responsible for health care itself. This makes it almost impossible for us to have a good health program.

We have just advocated this past week a consolidation of the responsibilities for energy. Our country now has no comprehensive energy program or policy. We have twenty different agencies in the federal government responsible for the production, the regulation, the information about energy, the conservation of energy, spread all over government. This is a gross waste of money. So tough, competent management of government, giving us a simple, efficient, purposeful, and manageable government would be a great step forward. And if I'm elected, and I intend to be, then it's going to be done.

GANNON: Well, I'd like to press my question on the number of federal employees—whether you would really plan to reduce the overall number or merely put them in different departments and relabel them. In your energy plan, you consolidate a number of agencies into one, or you would, but does that really change the overall?

CARTER: I can't say for sure that we would have fewer federal employees when I go out of office than when I come in. It took me about three years to completely reorganize the Georgia government. The last year I was in office, our budget was actually less than it was a year before, which showed a great improvement. Also we had a 2-percent increase in the number of

employees the last year. But there was a tremendous shift from
administrative jobs into the delivery of services. For instance, we
completely revised our prison system. We established eighty-
four new mental health treatment centers. And we shifted people
out of administrative jobs into the field to deliver better services.
The same thing would be done at the federal government level. I
accomplished this with substantial reductions in employees in
some departments. For instance, in the Transportation
Department, we cut back about 25 percent the total number of
employees. In giving our people better mental health care, we
increased the number of employees. But the efficiency of it, the
simplicity of it, the ability of people to understand their own
government and control it was the substantial benefit derived
from complete reorganization.

We have got to do this at the federal government level. If we
don't, the bureaucratic mess is going to continue. There's no
way for our people now to understand what their government is;
there's no way to get the answer to a question. When you come
to Washington, as a governor, to try to begin a new program for
your people, like the treatment of drug addicts, I found there
were thirteen different federal agencies that I had to go to to
manage the drug treatment program. In the Georgia government, we only had one agency responsible for drug treatment.
This is the kind of change that would be made. And it would be
of tremendous benefit in long-range planning, in tight
budgeting, saving the taxpayers' money, making the government
more efficient, cutting down on bureaucratic waste, having a
clear delineation of authority and responsibility of employees,
and giving our people a better chance to understand and control
their government.

NEWMAN: President Ford.

15   FORD: I think the record should show, Mr. Newman, that the
Bureau of Census—we checked it just yesterday—indicates that
in the four years that Governor Carter was governor of the state
of Georgia, expenditures by the government went up over 50
percent. Employees of the government in Georgia during his
term of office went up over 25 percent. And the figures also

show that the bonded indebtedness of the state of Georgia during his governorship went up over 20 percent. And there was some very interesting testimony given by Governor Carter's successor, Governor Busbee, before a Senate committee a few months ago on how he found the Medicaid program when he came into office following Governor Carter. He testified, and these are his words, the present Governor of Georgia—he says he found the Medicaid program in Georgia "in shambles."

Now, let me talk about what we've done in the White House as far as federal employees are concerned. The first order that I issued after I became president was to cut, or eliminate, the prospective 40,000 increase in federal employees that had been scheduled by my predecessor. And in the term that I've been president, some two years, we have reduced federal employment by 11,000. In the White House staff itself, when I became president, we had roughly 540 employees. We now have about 485 employees. So we've made a rather significant reduction in the number of employees in the White House staff working for the president. So I think our record of cutting back employees, plus the failure on the part of the governor's program to actually save employment in Georgia, shows which is the better plan.

NEWMAN: Mrs. Drew.

DREW: Mr. President, at Vail, after the Republican convention,   K
you announced that you would now emphasize five new areas. Among those were jobs and housing and health and improved recreational facilities for Americans, and you also added crime. You also mentioned education. For two years you've been telling us that we couldn't do very much in these areas because we couldn't afford it. And in fact we do have a 50-billion-dollar deficit now. In rebuttal to Governor Carter, a little bit earlier, you said that if there were to be any surplus in the next few years, you thought it should be turned back to the people in the form of tax relief. So, how are you going to pay for any new initiatives in these areas you announced at Vail you were going to now stress?

FORD: Well, in the last two years, as I indicated before, we had a   16
very tough time. We were faced with heavy inflation, over 12

percent; we were faced with substantial unemployment. But in the last twenty-four months, we've turned the economy around, and we've brought inflation down to under 6 percent; and we have reduced the—well we have added employment of about 4 million in the last seventeen months to the point where we have 88 million people working in America today, the most in the history of the country. The net result is, we are going to have some improvement in our receipts, and I think we'll have some decrease in our disbursements. We expect to have a lower deficit in fiscal year 1978.

We feel that with this improvement in the economy, we feel with more receipts and fewer disbursements, we can in a moderate way increase, as I recommended, over the next ten years, a new parks program that would cost a billion and a half dollars, doubling our national park system. We have recommended that in the housing program we can reduce down payments and moderate monthly payments. But that doesn't cost any more as far as the federal treasury is concerned. We believe that we can do a better job in the area of crime. But that requires tougher sentencing—mandatory, certain prison sentences for those who violate our criminal laws. We believe that you can revise the federal criminal code, which has not been revised in a good many years; that doesn't cost any more money. We believe that you can do something more effectively, with a moderate increase in money, in the drug-abuse program. We feel that in education we can have a slight increase, not a major increase. It's my understanding that Governor Carter has indicated that he approves of a 30-billion-dollar expenditure by the federal government as far as education is concerned. At the present time we're spending roughly 3 billion 500 million dollars. I don't know where that money would come from. But as we look at the quality-of-life programs—jobs, health, education, crime, recreation—we feel that as we move forward with a healthier economy, we can absorb the small necessary costs that will be required.

L   DREW: Sir, in the next few years would you try to reduce the deficit, would you spend money for these programs that you have just outlined, or would you, as you said earlier, return whatever surplus you got to the people in the form of tax relief?

FORD: We feel that with the programs that I have recommended,   17
the additional 10-billion-dollar tax cut, with the moderate increases in the quality-of-life area, we can still have a balanced budget which I will submit to the Congress in January of 1978. We won't wait one year or two years longer, as Governor Carter indicates. As the economy improves—and it is improving—our gross national product this year will average about 6-percent increase over last year; we will have a lower rate of inflation for the calendar year this year of something slightly under 6 percent; employment will be up; revenues will be up—we'll keep the lid on some of these programs that we can hold down as we have a little extra money to spend for those quality-of-life programs which I think are needed and necessary.

Now, I cannot and would not endorse the kind of programs that Governor Carter recommends. He endorses the Democratic platform, which, as I read it, calls for approximately sixty additional programs. We estimate that those programs would add 100 billion dollars minimum and probably 200 billion dollars maximum each year to the federal budget. Those programs you cannot afford and give tax relief. We feel that you can hold the line and restrain federal spending, give a tax reduction, and still have a balanced budget by 1978.

NEWMAN: Governor Carter.

CARTER: Mr. Ford takes the same attitude that the Republicans   18
always take. In the last three months before an election, they're always for the programs that they fight the other three and a half years. I remember when Herbert Hoover was against jobs for people. I remember when Alf Landon was against Social Security. And later President Nixon, sixteen years ago, was telling the public that John Kennedy's proposals would bankrupt the country and would double the cost.

The best thing to do is look at the record of Mr. Ford's administration and Mr. Nixon's before his. We had last year a 65-billion-dollar deficit, the largest deficit in the history of our country, more of a deficit spending than we had in the entire eight-year period under President Johnson and President Kennedy. We've got 500,000 more Americans out of jobs today than were out of work three months ago. And since Mr. Ford's been in office, in two years, we've had a 50-percent increase in unemployment—from 5 million people out of work to 2½ million more people out of work, and a total of 7½ million. We've also got a comparison between himself and Mr. Nixon. He's got four times the size of the deficits that Mr. Nixon even had himself.

This talking about more people at work is distorted, because with a 14-percent increase in the cost of living in the last two years, it means that women and young people have had to go to work when they didn't want to because their fathers couldn't make enough to pay the increased cost of food and housing and clothing.

We have, in this last two years alone, 120 billion dollars total deficits under President Ford, and at the same time we've had, in the last eight years, a doubling in the number of bankruptcies for small business; we've had a negative growth in our national economy, measured in real dollars; the take-home pay of a worker in this country is actually less now than it was in 1968, measured in real dollars. This is the kind of record that's there, and talk about the future and a drastic change or conversion on the part of Mr. Ford at this last minute is one that just doesn't go.

NEWMAN: Mr. Reynolds.

M   REYNOLDS: Governor Carter, I'd like to turn to what we used to call the energy crisis. Yesterday, a British government commission on air pollution, but one headed by a nuclear physicist, recommended that any further expansion of nuclear energy be delayed in Britain as long as possible. Now this is a subject that is quite controversial among our own people and there seems to be a clear difference between you and the president on the use of nuclear power plants, which you say you would use as a last priority. Why, sir? Are they unsafe?

19   CARTER: Well, among my other experiences in the past, I've been a nuclear engineer and did graduate work in this field. I

think I know the capabilities and limitations of atomic power. But the energy policy of our nation is one that has not yet been established under this administration. I think almost every other developed nation in the word has an energy policy except us.

We have seen the Federal Energy Agency established, for instance. In the crisis of 1973 it was supposed to be a temporary agency. Now it's permanent. It's enormous. It's growing every day. And I think the *Wall Street Journal* reported not too long ago, they have 112 public relations experts working for the Federal Energy Agency to try to justify to the American people its own existence.

We've got to have a firm way to handle the energy question. The reorganization proposal that I put forward is one first step. In addition to that, we need to have a realization that we've got about thirty-five-years-worth of oil left in the whole world. We're going to run out of oil. When Mr. Nixon made his famous speech on Operation Independence,[4] we were importing about 35 percent of our oil. Now we've increased that amount 25 percent. We now import about 44 percent of our oil. We need to shift from oil to coal. We need to concentrate our research and development effort on coal burning and extraction that's safe for miners, that also is clean burning. We need to shift very strongly toward solar energy and have strict conservation measures; and then, as a last resort only, continue to use atomic power.

I would certainly not cut out atomic power altogether. We can't afford to give up that opportunity until later. But to the extent that we continue to use atomic power, I would be responsible as president to make sure that the safety precautions were initiated and maintained. For instance, some that have been forgotten: we need to have the reactor core below ground level; the entire power plant, that uses atomic power, tightly sealed and a heavy vacuum maintained; there ought to be a standardized design; there ought to be a full-time atomic energy specialist, independent of the power company, in the control room full-time, twenty-four hours a day, to shut down the plant if an abnormality develops.

These kinds of procedures, along with evacuation procedures, adequate insurance, ought to be initiated. So, shift from oil to coal; emphasize research and development on coal use and also on solar power; strict conservation measures; not yield every time that the special interest groups put pressure on the president, like this administration has done; and use atomic energy only as a last resort with the strictest possible safety precautions. That's the best overall energy policy in the brief time we have to discuss it.

N   REYNOLDS: Well, Governor, on that same subject, would you require mandatory conservation efforts to try to conserve fuel?

20   CARTER: Yes, I would. Some of the things that can be done about this is a change in the rate structure of electric power companies. We now encourage people to waste electricity by giving the lowest rates to the biggest users. We don't do anything to cut down on peak load requirements. We don't have an adequate requirement for the insulation of homes, for the efficiency of automobiles. And whenever the automobile manufacturers come forward and say they can't meet the limits that the Congress has put forward, this Republican administration has delayed the implementation dates. In addition to that, we ought to have a shift to the use of coal, particularly in the Appalachian regions where the coal is located; a lot of very high-quality, low-carbon coal—I mean low-sulphur coal—is there. It's where our employment is needed. This would help a great deal.

So, mandatory conservation measures, yes. Encouragement by the president for people to voluntarily conserve, yes. And also the private sector ought to be encouraged to bring forward to the public the benefits from efficiency. One bank in Washington, for instance, gives lower interest loans for people who adequately insulate their homes or who buy efficient automobiles. And some major manufacturing companies, like Dow Chemical, have—through very effective efficiency mechanisms—cut down the use of energy by as much as 40 percent with the same outproduct. These kinds of things ought to be done. They ought to be encouraged and supported, and even required by the government, yes.

NEWMAN: President Ford.

FORD: Governor Carter skims over a very serious and a very   21
broad subject. In January of 1975 I submitted to the Congress
and to the American people the first comprehensive energy
program recommended by any president. It called for an increase in the production of energy in the United States. It called
for conservation measures so that we would save the energy that
we have. If you're going to increase domestic oil and gas
production, and we have to, you have to give to those producers
an opportunity to develop their land or their wells. I recommended to the Congress that we should increase coal production
in this country from 600 million tons a year to a billion 200
million tons by 1985. In order to do that, we have to improve
our extraction of coal from the ground. We have to improve our
utilization of coal: make it more efficient; make it cleaner. In
addition, we have to expand our research and development.

In my program for energy independence, we have increased,
for example, solar energy research from about 84 million dollars
a year to about 120 million dollars a year. We're going as fast as
the experts say we should. In nuclear power we have increased
the research and development, under the Energy Research and
Development Agency, very substantially to insure that our
nuclear power plants are safer, they they are more efficient, and
that we have adequate safeguards. I think you have to have
greater oil and gas production, more coal production, more
nuclear production. And in addition you have to have energy
conservation.

NEWMAN: Mr. Gannon.

GANNON: Mr. President, I'd like to return for a moment to this   O
problem of unemployment. You have vetoed or threatened to
veto a number of jobs bills passed or in development in the
Democratic Congress—the Democratic-controlled Congress.
Yet at the same time the government is paying out, I think it is,
17 billion, perhaps 20 billion dollars a year in unemployment
compensation caused by the high unemployment. Why do you
think it is better to pay out unemployment compensation to idle
people than to put them to work in public service jobs?

22 FORD: The bills that I've vetoed, the one for an additional 6 billion dollars, was not a bill that would have solved our unemployment problems. Even the proponents of it admitted that no more than 400,000 jobs would be made available. Our analysis indicates that something in the magnitude of about 150,000 to 200,000 jobs would be made available. Each one of those jobs would have cost the taxpayer 25,000 dollars. In addition, the jobs would not be available right now. They would not have materialized for about nine to eighteen months.

The immediate problem we have is to stimulate our economy now, so that we can get rid of unemployment. What we have done is to hold the lid on spending in an effort to reduce the rate of inflation. And we have proven, I think very conclusively, that you can reduce the rate of inflation and increase jobs. For example, as I have said, we have added some 4 million jobs in the last seventeen months. We have now employed 88 million people in America, the largest number in the history of the United States. We've added 500,000 jobs in the last two months. Inflation is the quickest way to destroy jobs, and by holding the lid on federal spending we have been able to do a good job, an affirmative job, in inflation, and as a result have added to the jobs in this country.

I think it's also appropriate to point out that through our tax policies we have stimulated added employment throughout the country: the investment tax credit, the tax incentives for expansion and modernization of our industrial capacity. It's my opinion that the private sector, where five out of the six jobs are, where you have permanent jobs, with the opportunity for advancement, is a better place than make-work jobs under the program recommended by the Congress.

P GANNON: Just to follow up, Mr. President. The Congress has just passed a 3.7-billion-dollar appropriation bill which would provide money for the public works jobs program that you earlier tried to kill by your veto of the authorization legislation. In light of the fact that unemployment again is rising, or has in the past three months, I wonder if you have rethought that question at all, whether you would consider allowing this program to be funded, or will you veto that money bill?

FORD: Well, that bill has not yet come down to the Oval Office,   23
so I am not in the position to make any judgment on it tonight.
But that is an extra 4 billion dollars that would add to the deficit,
which would add to the inflationary pressures, which would help
to destroy jobs in the private sector, not make jobs where the
jobs really are. These make-work, temporary jobs, dead end as
they are, are not the kind of jobs that we want for our people.

I think it's interesting to point out that in the two years that
I've been president, I've vetoed fifty-six bills. Congress has
sustained forty-two vetoes. As a result, we have saved over 9
billion dollars in federal expenditures. And the Congress, by
overriding the bills that I did veto, the Congress has added some
13 billion dollars to the federal expenditures and to the federal
deficit. Now, Governor Carter complains about the deficits that
this administration has had, and yet he condemns the vetoes that
I have made that have saved the taxpayer 9 billion dollars and
could have saved an additional 13 billion dollars. Now he can't
have it both ways. And, therefore, it seems to me that we should
hold the lid, as we have to the best of our ability, so we can
stimulate the private economy and get the jobs where the jobs
are—five out of six in this economy.

NEWMAN: Governor Carter.

CARTER: Well, Mr. Ford doesn't seem to put into perspective the   24
fact that when 500,000 more people are out of work than there
were three months ago or we have 2½ million more people out
of work than were when he took office, that this touches human
beings. I was in a city in Pennsylvania not too long ago near
here, and there were about four or five thousand people in the
audience—it was on the train trip; and I said, how many adults
here are out of work? About a thousand raised their hands.

Mr. Ford actually has fewer people now in the private sector
in nonfarm jobs than when he took office, and still he talks
about a success. Seven-point-nine percent unemployment is a
terrible tragedy in this country. He says he's learned how to
match unemployment with inflation. That's right. We've got the
highest inflation we've had in twenty-five years right now,
except under this administration, and that was fifty years ago.
And we've got the highest unemployment we've had, under Mr.

Ford's administration, since the Great Depression. This affects human beings, and his insensitivity in providing those people a chance to work has made this a welfare administration and not a work administration.

He hasn't saved 9 billion dollars with his vetoes. There's only been a net saving of 4 billion dollars, and the cost in unemployment compensation, welfare compensation, and lost revenues has increased 23 billion dollars in the last two years. This is a typical attitude that really causes havoc in people's lives, and then it's covered over by saying that our country has naturally got a 6-percent unemployment rate or a 7-percent unemployment rate and a 6-percent inflation. It's a travesty; it shows a lack of leadership. And we've never had a president since the War Between the States that vetoed more bills. Mr. Ford has vetoed four times as many bills as Mr. Nixon, per year, and eleven of them have been overridden. One of his bills that was overridden, he only got one vote in the Senate and seven votes in the House from Republicans. So this shows a breakdown in leadership.

NEWMAN: Governor Carter, under the rules I must stop you there. Mrs. Drew.

Q   DREW: Governor Carter, I'd like to come back to the subject of taxes. You have said that you want to cut taxes for the middle- and lower-income groups. But unless you're willing to do such things as reduce the itemized deductions for charitable contributions or home mortgage payments or interest or taxes or capital gains, you can't really raise sufficient revenue to provide an overall tax cut of any size. So how are you going to provide that tax relief that you're talking about?

25   CARTER: Now we have such a grossly unbalanced tax system, as I said earlier, that it is a disgrace. Of all the tax benefits now, 25 percent of them go to the 1 percent of the richest people in this country. Over 50 percent, 53 to be exact, percent of the tax benefits go to the 14 percent richest people in this country. And we've had a 50-percent increase in payroll deductions since Mr. Nixon went in office eight years ago. Mr. Ford has advocated, since he's been in office, over 5 billion dollars in reductions for

corporations, special interest groups, and the very, very wealthy who derive their income not from labor but from investments. That's got to be changed.

A few things that can be done: we have now a deferral system so that the multinational corporations who invest overseas, if they make a million dollars in profits overseas, they don't have to pay any of their taxes unless they bring their money back into this country. When they don't pay their taxes, the average American pays their taxes for them. Not only that, but it robs this country of jobs, because instead of coming back with that million dollars and creating a shoe factory, say in New Hampshire or Vermont, if the company takes the money down to Italy and builds a shoe factory, they don't have to pay any taxes on the money.

Another thing is a system called DISC[5] which was originally designed, proposed by Mr. Nixon, to encourage exports. This permits a company to create a dummy corporation to export their products and then not to pay the full amount of taxes on them. This cost our government about 1.4 billion dollars a year; and when those rich corporations don't pay that tax, the average American taxpayer pays it for them. Another one that's very important is the business deductions: jet airplanes, first-class travel, the 50-dollar martini lunch. The average working person can't take advantage of that, but the wealthier people can.

Another system is where a dentist can invest money in, say, raising cattle, and can put in 100,000 dollars of his own money, borrow 900,000 dollars—that makes a million—and mark off a great amount of loss through that procedure. There was one example, for instance, where somebody produced pornographic movies. They put in 30,000 dollars of their own money and got 120,000 dollars in tax savings. Well, these special kinds of programs have robbed the average taxpayer and have benefited those who are powerful and who can employ lobbyists and who can have the CPAs and the lawyers to help them benefit from the roughly 8,000 pages of the tax code. The average American person can't do it. You can't hire a lobbyist out of unemployment compensation checks.

R DREW: Governor, to follow up on your answer. In order for any kind of tax relief to really be felt by the middle- and lower-income people, you need about, according to congressional committees on this, you need about 10 billion dollars. Now you listed some things. The deferral on foreign income is estimated—that would save about 500 million dollars. DISC, you said, was 1.4 billion. The estimate at the outside, if you eliminated all tax shelters, is 5 billion. So where else would you raise the revenue to provide this tax relief? Would you, in fact, do away with all business deductions, and what other kinds of preferences would you do away with?

26 CARTER: No, I wouldn't do away with all business deductions. I think that would be a very serious mistake. But if you could just do away with the ones that are unfair, you could lower taxes for everyone. I would never do anything that would increase the taxes for those who work for a living or who are presently required to list all their income. What I want to do is not to raise taxes but to eliminate loopholes, and this is the point of my first statistics that I gave you—that the present tax benefits that have been carved out over a long period of years—fifty years—by sharp tax lawyers and by lobbyists have benefited just the rich. These programs that I described to you earlier—the tax deferrals for overseas, the DISC, and the tax shelters—they only apply to people in the 50,000-dollar-a-year bracket or up. And I think this is the best way to approach it, is to make sure that everybody pays taxes on the income that they earn and make sure that you take whatever savings there is from the higher income levels and give it to the lower- and middle-income families.

NEWMAN: President Ford.

27 FORD: Governor Carter's answer tonight does not coincide with the answer that he gave in an interview to the Associated Press a week or so ago. In that interview, Governor Carter indicated that he would raise the taxes on those in the medium- or middle-income brackets or higher. Now if you take the medium- or middle-income taxpayer, that's about 14,000 dollars per person. Governor Carter has indicated publicly, in an interview, that he

would increase the taxes on about 50 percent of the working people of this country.

I think the way to get tax equity in this country is to give tax relief to the middle-income people, who have an income from roughly 8,000 dollars up to 25,000 or 30,000 dollars. They have been short-changed as we have taken 10 million taxpayers off the tax rolls in the last eight years, and as we have added to the minimum tax provision to make all people pay more taxes. I believe in tax equity for the middle-income taxpayer, increasing the personal exemption. Mr. Carter wants to increase taxes for roughly half of the taxpayers of this country.

Now, the governor has also played a little fast and loose with the facts about vetoes. The records show that President Roosevelt vetoed on an average of fifty-five bills a year. President Truman vetoed on the average, while he was president, about thirty-eight bills a year. I understand that Governor Carter, when he was governor of Georgia, vetoed between thirty-five and forty bills a year. My average in two years is twenty-six, but in the process of that we have saved 9 billion dollars.

And one final comment. Governor Carter talks about the tax bills and all of the inequities that exist in the present law. I must remind him: the Democrats have controlled the Congress for the last twenty-two years, and they wrote all the tax bills.

NEWMAN: Mr. Reynolds.

REYNOLDS: I suspect that we could continue on this tax argument   S
for some time, but I'd like to move on to another area. Mr. President, everybody seems to be running against Washington this year. And I'd like to raise two coincidental events and ask you whether you think perhaps this may have a bearing on the attitude throughout the country. The House Ethics Committee has just now ended its investigation of Daniel Schorr, after several months and many thousands of dollars, trying to find out how he obtained and caused to be published a report of the Congress that probably is the property of the American people. At the same time, the Senate Select Committee on Standards and Conduct has voted not really to begin an investigation of a

United States senator because of allegations against him, that he may have been receiving corporate funds illegally over a period of years.[6] Do you suppose, sir, that events like this contribute to the feeling in the country that maybe there's something wrong in Washington? And I don't mean just in the executive branch, but throughout the whole government.

28   FORD: There is a considerable anti-Washington feeling throughout the country, but I think the feeling is misplaced. In the last two years we have restored integrity in the White House and we've set high standards in the executive branch of the government. The anti-Washington feeling, in my opinion, ought to be focused on the Congress of the United States. For example, this Congress very shortly will spend a billion dollars a year for its housekeeping, its salaries, its expenses, and the like. The next Congress will probably be the first billion-dollar Congress in the history of the United States. I don't think the American people are getting their money's worth from the majority party that run this Congress.

We, in addition, see that in the last four years the number of employees hired by the Congress has gone up substantial [sic], much more than the gross national product, much more than any other increase throughout our society. Congress is hiring people by the droves, and the cost, as a result, has gone up. And I don't see any improvement in the performance of the Congress under the present leadership.

So it seems to me, instead of the anti-Washington feeling being aimed at everybody in Washington, it seems to me that the focus should be where the problem is, which is the Congress of the United States, and particularly the majority in the Congress. They spend too much money on themselves; they have too many employees; there's some question about their morality. It seems to me that in this election the focus should not be on the executive branch, but the correction should come as the voters vote for their members of the House of Representatives or for their United States senator. That's where the problem is, and I hope there'll be some corrective action taken, so we can get some new leadership in the Congress of the United States.

REYNOLDS: Mr. President, if I may follow up. I think you've   T
made it plain that you take a dim view of the majority in the
Congress. Isn't it quite likely, sir, that you will have a
Democratic Congress in the next session if you are elected
president, and hasn't the country a right to ask whether you can
get along with that Congress or whether we'll have continued
confrontation?

FORD: Well, it seems to me that we have a chance, the Re-   29
publicans, to get a majority in the House of Representatives.
We will make some gains in the United States Senate. So there
will be different ratios in the House as well as in the Senate, and
as president I will be able to work with that Congress.

But let me take the other side of the coin, if I might. Sup-
posing we had had a Democratic Congress for the last two
years and we had had Governor Carter as president. He has,
in effect, said that he would agree with all of—he would dis-
approve of the vetoes that I have made and would have added
significantly to expenditures and the deficit in the federal
government. I think it would be contrary to one of the basic
concepts in our system of government, a system of checks and
balances. We have a Democratic Congress today, and fortunately, we've had a Republican president to check their excesses with my vetoes. If we have a Democratic Congress next
year and a president who wants to spend an additional 100
billion dollars a year or maybe 200 billion dollars a year with
more programs, we will have, in my judgment, greater deficits
with more spending, more dangers of inflation. I think the
American people want a Republican president, to check on any
excesses that come out of the next Congress if it is a Democratic
Congress.

NEWMAN: Governor Carter.

CARTER: Well, it's not a matter of Republican and Democrat;   30
it's a matter of leadership or no leadership. President
Eisenhower worked with a Democratic Congress very well. Even
President Nixon, because he was a strong leader at least, worked
with a Democratic Congress very well. Mr. Ford has vetoed, as I
said earlier, four times as many bills per year as Mr. Nixon. Mr.

Ford quite often puts forward a program just as a public relations stunt and never tries to put it through the Congress by working with the Congress. I think under President Nixon and Eisenhower, they passed about 60 to 75 percent of their legislation. This year Mr. Ford will not pass more than 26 percent of all the legislative proposals he puts forward. This is government by stalemate, and we've seen almost a complete breakdown in the proper relationship between the president, who represents this country, and the Congress, who collectively also represent this country.

We've had Republican presidents before who've tried to run against a Democratic Congress, and I don't think it's the Congress that's Mr. Ford's opponent. But if he insists that I be responsible for the Democratic Congress, of which I have not been a part, then I think it's only fair that he be responsible for the Nixon administration in its entirety, of which he was a part. That, I think, is a good balance. But the point is that a president ought to lead this country. Mr. Ford, so far as I know, except for avoiding another Watergate, has not accomplished one single major program for this country, and there's been a constant squabbling between the president and the Congress, and that's not the way this country ought to be run.

I might go back to one other thing. Mr. Ford has misquoted an AP news story that was in error to begin with. That story reported several times that I would lower taxes for lower- and middle-income families, and that correction was delivered to the White House, and I'm sure that the president knows about this correction, but he still insists on repeating an erroneous statement.

NEWMAN: President Ford, Governor Carter, we no longer have enough time for two complete sequences of questions. We have only about six minutes left for questions and answers. For that reason we will drop the follow-up questions at this point, but each candidate will still be able to respond to the other's answers. To the extent that you can, gentlemen, please keep your remarks brief. Mr. Gannon.

U   GANNON: Governor Carter, one important part of the government's economic policy apparatus that we haven't talked about is the Federal Reserve Board. I'd like to ask you something about what you've said, and that is that you believe that a president ought to have a chairman of the Federal Reserve Board whose views are compatible with his own. Based on the record of the last few years, would you say that your views are compatible with those of Chairman Arthur Burns, and if not, would you seek his resignation if you are elected?

CARTER: What I have said is that the president ought to have a   31
chance to appoint the chairman of the Federal Reserve Board to have a coterminous term—in other words, both of them serve the same four years. The Congress can modify the supply of money by modifying the income tax laws. The president can modify the economic structure of our country by public statements and general attitudes and the budget that he proposes. The Federal Reserve has an independent status that ought to be preserved.

I think that Mr. Burns did take a typical erroneous Republican attitude in the 1973 year when inflation was so high. He assumed that the inflation rate was because of excessive demand and therefore put into effect tight constraint on the economy; very high interest rates—which is typical also of a Republican administration; tried to increase the tax payments by individuals, cut the tax payments by corporations. I would have done it opposite. I think the problem should have been addressed by increasing productivity, by having put people back to work so they could purchase more goods, lower income taxes on individuals, perhaps raise them if necessary on corporations in comparison. But Mr. Burns in that respect made a very serious mistake.

I would not want to destroy the independence of the Federal Reserve Board, but I do think we ought to have a cohesive economic policy, with at least the chairman of the Federal Reserve Board and the president's terms being the same, and letting the Congress, of course, be the third entity with independence subject only to the president's veto.

NEWMAN: President Ford, your response.

FORD: The chairman of the Federal Reserve Board should be   32
independent. Fortunately he has been, during Democratic as

well as Republican administrations. As a result, in the last two years we have had a responsible monetary policy. The Federal Reserve Board indicated that the supply of money would be held between 4 to 4½ and 7 and 7½. They have done a good job in integrating the money supply with the fiscal policy of the executive and legislative branches of the government. It would be catastrophic if the chairman of the Federal Reserve Board became the tool of the political party that was in power. It's important for our future economic security that that job be non-political and separate from the executive and the legislative branches.

NEWMAN: Mrs. Drew.

V DREW: Mr. President, the real problem with the FBI and in fact all of the intelligence agencies is there are no real laws governing them. Such laws as there are tend to be vague and open-ended. Now you have issued some executive orders. But we've learned that leaving these agencies to executive discretion and direction can get them and in fact the country in a great deal of trouble. One president may be a decent man; the next one might not be. So, what do you think about trying to write in some more protection by getting some laws governing these agencies?

33 FORD: You are familiar, of course, with the fact that I am the first president in thirty years who has reorganized the intelligence agencies in the federal government—the CIA,⁷ the Defense Intelligence Agency, the National Security Agency, and the others. We've done that by executive order; and I think we've tightened it up, we've straightened out their problems that developed over the last few years. It doesn't seem to me that it's needed or necessary to have legislation in this particular regard.

I have recommended to the Congress, however—I'm sure you're familiar with this—legislation that would make it very proper, in the right way, that the attorney general could go in and get the right for wiretapping under security cases. This was an effort that was made by the attorney general and myself working with the Congress, but even in this area, where I think new legislation would be justified, the Congress has not responded. So I feel in that case, as well as in the reorganization of the intelligence agencies, as I've done, we have to do it by executive order. And I'm glad that we have a good director in George Bush, we have good executive orders, and the CIA and the DIA, and NASA—or NSA—are now doing a good job under proper supervision.

NEWMAN: Governor Carter.

CARTER: Well, one of the very serious things that's happened in   34
our government in recent years and has continued up until now is the breakdown in the trust among our people and the . . . [At this point the debate was interrupted by equipment failure. After repairs, Newman explained:]

NEWMAN: We very much regret the technical failure that lost the sound as it was leaving this theatre. It occurred during Governor Carter's response to what would have been and what was the last question put to the candidates; that question went to President Ford. It dealt with the control of government intelligence agencies. Governor Carter was making his response and had very nearly finished it.[8] He will conclude that response now, after which President Ford and Governor Carter will make their closing statements. Governor.

CARTER: There has been too much government secrecy and not   34
enough respect for the personal privacy of American citizens.

NEWMAN: It is now time for the closing statements which are to be up to four minutes long. Governor Carter, by the same toss of the coin that directed the first question to you, you are to go first now.

CARTER: Well, tonight we've had a chance to talk a lot about the   35
past. But I think it's time to talk about the future. Our nation in the last eight years has been divided as never before. It's a time for unity. It's a time to draw ourselves together: to have a president and a Congress that can work together—with mutual respect, for a change; cooperating, for a change; in the open, for a change, so the people can understand their own government. It's time for government, industry, labor, manufacturing, agriculture, education, other entities in our society, to cooperate. And it's a time for government to understand and to cooperate with our people.

For a long time our American citizens have been excluded, sometimes misled, sometimes have been lied to. This is not compatable with the purpose of our nation. I believe in our country. It needs to be competent. The government needs to be well managed, efficient, economical. We need to have a government that's sensitive to our people's needs: to those who are poor; who don't have adequate health care; who have been cheated too long with our tax programs; who've been out of jobs; whose families have been torn apart. And we need to restore the faith and the trust of the American people in their own government.

In addition to that, we've suffered because we haven't had leadership in this administration. We've got a government of stalemate, and we've lost the vision of what our country can and ought to be. This is not the America that we've known in the past. It's not the America that we have to have in the future.

I don't claim to know all the answers, but I've got confidence in my country. Our economic strength is still there. Our system of government—in spite of Vietnam, Cambodia, CIA, Watergate[9]—is still the best system of government on earth. And the greatest resource of all are the 215 million Americans, who still have within us the strength, the character, the intelligence, the experience, the patriotism, the idealism, the compassion, the sense of brotherhood on which we can rely in the future to restore the greatness to our country.

We ought not to be excluded from our government any more. We need a president who can go in—who derives his strength from the people. I owe the special interests nothing. I owe everything to you, the people of this country. And I believe that we can bind our wounds. I believe that we can work together. And I believe that if we can tap the tremendous untapped reservoir of innate strength in this country, that we can once again have a government as good as our people, and let the world know what we still know and hope for—that we still live in the greatest, and the strongest, and the best country on earth.

NEWMAN: President Ford.

36   FORD: On November 2nd all of you will make a very, very important decision. One of the major issues in this campaign is

trust. A president should never promise more than he can deliver, and a president should always deliver everything that he's promised. A president can't be all things to all people. A president should be the same thing to all people.

Another issue in this campaign: Governor Carter has endorsed the Democratic platform, which calls for more spending, bigger deficits, more inflation, or more taxes. Governor Carter has embraced the record of the present Congress dominated by his political party. It calls for more of the same. Governor Carter in his Acceptance Speech called for more and more programs, which means more and more government. I think the real issue in this campaign, and that which you must decide on November 2nd, is whether you should vote for his promises or my performance in two years in the White House.

On the Fourth of July we had a wonderful two-hundredth birthday for our great country. It was a superb occasion. It was a glorious day. In the first century of our nation's history, our forefathers gave us the finest form of government in the history of mankind. In the second century of our nation's history, our forefathers developed the most productive industrial nation in the history of the globe. Our third century should be the century of individual freedom for all our 215 million Americans today and all that join us.

In the last few years government has gotten bigger and bigger. Industry has gotten larger and larger. Labor unions have gotten bigger and bigger. And our children have been the victims of mass education. We must make this next century the century of the individual. We should never forget that a government big enough to give us everything we want is a government big enough to take from us everything we have. The individual worker in the plants throughout the United States should not be a small cog in a big machine. The member of a labor union must have his rights strengthened and broadened. And our children in their education should have an opportunity to improve themselves based on their talents and their abilities.

My mother and father, during the Depression, worked very hard to give me an opportunity to do better in our great country. Your mothers and fathers did the same thing for you and others.

Betty and I have worked very hard to give our children a brighter future in the United States, our beloved country. You and others in this great country have worked hard and done a great deal to give your children and your grandchildren the blessings of a better America. I believe we can all work together to make the individuals in the future have more, and all of us working together can build a better America.

NEWMAN: Thank you, President Ford. Thank you, Governor Carter. Our thanks also to the questioners and to the audience in this theater.

We much regret the technical failure that caused a twenty-eight-minute delay in the broadcast of the debate. We believe, however, that everyone will agree that it did not detract from the effectiveness of the debate or from its fairness. The next presidential debate is to take place on Wednesday, October 6th, in San Francisco, at 9:30 P.M., Eastern Daylight Time. The topics are to be foreign and defense issues. As with all three debates between the presidential candidates and the one between the vice-presidential candidates, it is being arranged by the League of Women Voters Education Fund in the hope of promoting a wider and better-informed participation by the American people in the election in November. Now, from the Walnut Street Theatre in Philadelphia, good night.

The Second Debate

October 6, 1976   San Francisco

FREDERICK: Good evening. I'm Pauline Frederick of NPR,[1] moderator of this second of the historic debates of the 1976 campaign between Gerald R. Ford of Michigan, Republican candidate for president, and Jimmy Carter of Georgia, Democratic candidate for president. Thank you, President Ford, and thank you, Governor Carter, for being with us tonight.

This debate takes place before an audience in the Palace of Fine Arts Theatre in San Francisco. An estimated 100 million Americans are watching on television as well. San Francisco was the site of the signing of the United Nations Charter thirty-one years ago. Thus, it is an appropriate place to hold this debate, the subject of which is foreign and defense issues.

The questioners tonight are Max Frankel, associate editor of the *New York Times;* Henry L. Trewhitt, diplomatic correspondent of the *Baltimore Sun;* and Richard Valeriani, diplomatic correspondent of NBC News.

The ground rules tonight are basically the same as they were for the first debate two weeks ago. The questions will be alternated between candidates. By the toss of a coin, Governor Carter will take the first question. Each question sequence will be as follows: the question will be asked and the candidate will have up to three minutes to answer. His opponent will have up to two minutes to respond. And prior to the response, the questioner may ask a follow-up question to clarify the candidate's answer, when necessary, with up to two minutes to reply. Each candidate will have three minutes for a closing statement at the end. President Ford and Governor Carter do not have notes or prepared remarks with them this evening, but they may take notes during the debate and refer to them. Mr. Frankel, you have the first question for Governor Carter.

A FRANKEL: Governor, since the Democrats last ran our foreign policy, including many of the men who are advising you, the country's been relieved of the Vietnam agony and the military draft; we've started arms control negotiations with the Russians; we've opened relations with China; we've arranged the disengagement in the Middle East; we've regained influence with the Arabs without deserting Israel; now maybe we've even begun a process of peaceful change in Africa. Now, you've objected in this campaign to the style with which much of this was done, and you've mentioned some other things that you think ought to have been done. But do you really have a quarrel with this Republican record? Would you not have done any of those things?

1 CARTER: Well, I think this Republican administration's been almost all style and spectacular, and not substance. We've got a chance tonight to talk about, first of all, leadership, the character of our country, and a vision of the future. In every one of these instances, the Ford administration has failed, and I hope tonight that I and Mr. Ford will have a chance to discuss the reason for those failures.

Our country's not strong anymore. We're not respected anymore. We can only be strong overseas if we're strong at home, and when I become president we'll not only be strong in those areas but also in defense, a defense capability second to none.

We've lost in our foreign policy the character of the American people. We've ignored or excluded the American people and the Congress from participation in the shaping of our foreign policy. It's been one of secrecy and exclusion. In addition to that, we've had a chance to become now, contrary to our longstanding beliefs and principles, the arms merchant of the whole world. We've tried to buy success from our enemies, and, at the same time, we've excluded from the process the normal friendship of our allies.

In addition to that, we've become fearful to compete with the Soviet Union on an equal basis. We talk about detente. The Soviet Union knows what they want in detente and they've been getting it. We have not known what we've wanted, and we've been out-traded in almost every instance.

The other point I want to make is about our defense. We've got to be a nation blessed with a defense capability that's efficient, tough, capable, well-organized, narrowly focused fighting capability. The ability to fight if necessary is the best way to avoid the chance for, or the requirement to fight.

And the last point I want to make is this. Mr. Ford, Mr. Kissinger have continued on with the policies and failures of Richard Nixon. Even the Republican platform has criticized the lack of leadership in Mr. Ford and they've criticized the foreign policy of this administration. This is one instance where I agree with the Republican platform.

I might say this in closing, and that is, that as far as foreign policy goes, Mr. Kissinger has been the president of this country. Mr. Ford has shown an absence of leadership, and an absence of a grasp of what this country is and what it ought to be. That's got to be changed. And that is one of the major issues in this campaign of 1976.

FREDERICK: President Ford, would you like to respond?

FORD: Governor Carter again is talking in broad generalities. Let me take just one question that he raises: the military strength and capability of the United States. Governor Carter in November of 1975 indicated that he wanted to cut the defense budget by 15 billion dollars. A few months later he said he wanted to cut the defense budget by 8 or 9 billion dollars. And more recently he talks about cutting the defense budget by 5 to 7 billion dollars. There is no way you can be strong militarily and have those kind of reductions in our military appropriation.

Now let me just tell you a little story. About late October of 1975, I asked the then secretary of defense, Mr. Schlesinger, to tell me what had to be done if we were going to reduce the defense budget by 3 to 5 billion dollars. A few days later, Mr. Schlesinger came back and said, if we cut the defense budget by 3 to 5 billion dollars, we will have to cut military personnel by 250,000, civilian personnel by 100,000, jobs in America by 100,000. We would have to stretch out our aircraft procurement; we would have to reduce our naval construction program; we would have to reduce the research and development for the Army, the Navy, the Air Force, and Marines by 8 percent; we would have to close twenty military bases in the United States immediately. That's the kind of a defense program that Mr. Carter wants. Let me tell you this straight from the shoulder: you don't negotiate with Mr. Brezhnev from weakness, and the kind of a defense program that Mr. Carter wants will mean a weaker defense and a poorer negotiating position.

FREDERICK: Mr. Trewhitt, a question for President Ford.

B   TREWHITT: Mr. President, my question really is the other side of the coin from Mr. Frankel's. For a generation, the United States has had a foreign policy based on containment of Communism. Yet we have lost the first war in Vietnam; we lost a shoving match in Angola; Communists threaten to come to power by peaceful means in Italy; and relations generally have cooled with the Soviet Union in the last few months. So let me ask you, first, what do you do about such cases as Italy, and secondly, does this general drift mean that we're moving back toward something like an old cold war relationship with the Soviet Union?

3   FORD: I don't believe we should move to a cold war relationship. I think it's in the best interest of the United States, and the world as a whole, that the United States negotiate rather than go back to the cold war relationship with the Soviet Union.

I don't look at the picture as bleakly as you have indicated in your question, Mr. Trewhitt. I believe that the United States has had many successes in recent years and recent months as far as the Communist movement is concerned. We have been successful in Portugal, where a year ago it looked like there was a very great possibility that the Communists would take over in Portugal. It didn't happen. We have a democracy in Portugal today. A few months ago, or I should say maybe two years ago, the Soviet Union looked like they had continued strength in the Middle East. Today, according to Prime Minister Rabin, the Soviet Union is weaker in the Middle East than they have been in many, many years. The facts are, the Soviet Union relationship with Egypt is at a low level. The Soviet Union relationship with Syria is at a very low point. The United States today, according to Prime Minister Rabin of Israel, is at a peak in its influence and power in the Middle East.

But let's turn for a minute to the southern African operations that are now going on. The United States of America took the initiative in southern Africa. We wanted to end the bloodshed in southern Africa. We wanted to have the right of self-determination in southern Africa. We wanted to have majority rule with the full protection of the rights of the minority. We wanted to preserve human dignity in southern Africa. We have taken the initiative, and in southern Africa today the United States is trusted by the black front-line nations and black Africa; the United States is trusted by the other elements in southern Africa. The United States foreign policy, under this administration, has been one of progress and success. And I believe that instead of talking about Soviet progress, we can talk about American successes.

And may I make an observation on part of the question you asked, Mr. Trewhitt? I don't believe that it's in the best interest of the United States and the NATO nations to have a Communist government in NATO. Mr. Carter has indicated he would look with sympathy to a Communist government in NATO. I think that would destroy the integrity and the strength of NATO, and I am totally opposed to it.

CARTER: Now, Mr. Ford, unfortunately, has just made a statement that's not true. I have never advocated a Communist government for Italy; that would obviously be a ridiculous thing for anyone to do who wanted to be president of this country. I think that this is an instance of deliberate distortion, and this has occurred also in the question about defense. As a matter of fact, I've never advocated any cut of 15 billion dollars in our defense budget.

As a matter of fact, Mr. Ford has made a political football out of the defense budget. About a year ago he cut the Pentagon budget 6.8 billion dollars. After he fired James Schlesinger, the political heat got so great that he added back about 3 billion dollars. When Ronald Reagan won the Texas primary election, Mr. Ford added back another one and a half billion dollars. Immediately before the Kansas City convention,[2] he added back another 1.8 billion dollars in the defense budget. And his own Office of Management and Budget testified that he had a 3-billion-dollar cut insurance added to the defense budget under the pressure from the Pentagon. Obviously this is another indication of trying to use the defense budget for political purposes, which he's trying to do tonight.

Now, we went into south Africa late, after Great Britain, Rhodesia, the black nations had been trying to solve this problem for many, many years. We didn't go in until right before the election, similar to what was taking place in 1972, when Mr. Kissinger announced "peace is at hand," just before the election at that time.[3] And we have weakened our position in NATO because the other countries in Europe supported the democratic forces in Portugal long before we did. We stuck to the Portugal dictatorships much longer than other democracies did in this world.

FREDERICK: Mr. Valeriani, a question for Governor Carter.

C   VALERIANI: Governor Carter, much of what the United States does abroad is done in the name of the national interest. What is your concept of the national interest? What should the role of the United States in the world be? And in that connection, considering your limited experience in foreign affairs, and the fact that you take some pride in being a Washington outsider, don't you think it would be appropriate for you to tell the American voters, before the election, the people that you would like to have in key positions, such as secretary of state, secretary of defense, national security affairs adviser at the White House?

CARTER: Well, I'm not going to name my cabinet before I get 5 elected. I've got a little ways to go before I start doing that.

But I have an adequate background, I believe. I am a graduate of the U.S. Naval Academy, the first military graduate since Eisenhower. I've served as governor of Georgia and have traveled extensively in foreign countries and South America, Central America, Europe, the Middle East, and in Japan.

I've traveled the last twenty-one months among the people of this country. I've talked to them and I've listened. And I've seen at first hand, in a very vivid way, the deep hurt that's come to this country in the aftermath of Vietnam and Cambodia and Chile and Pakistan and Angola and Watergate, CIA revelations.[4] What we were formerly so proud of—the strength of our country, its moral integrity, the representation in foreign affairs of what our people are, what our Constitution stands for—has been gone. And in the secrecy that has surrounded our foreign policy in the last few years, the American people, the Congress, have been excluded.

I believe I know what this country ought to be. I've been one who's loved my nation as many Americans do. And I believe that there's no limit placed on what we can be in the future if we can harness the tremendous resources—militarily, economically—and the stature of our people—the meaning of our Constitution—in the future.

Every time we've made a serious mistake in foreign affairs, it's been because the American people have been excluded from the process. If we can just tap the intelligence and ability, the sound common sense, and the good judgment of the American people, we can once again have a foreign policy to make us proud instead of ashamed. And I'm not going to exclude the American people from that process in the future as Mr. Ford and Kissinger have done.

This is what it takes to have a sound foreign policy: strong at home, strong defense, permanent commitments, not betray the principles of our country, and involve the American people and the Congress in the shaping of our foreign policy. Every time Mr. Ford speaks from a position of secrecy in negotiations, in secret treaties that have been pursued and achieved, in sup-

porting dictatorships, in ignoring human rights, we are weak
and the rest of the world knows it.

So these are the ways that we can restore the strength of our
country. And they don't require a long experience in foreign
policy. Nobody has that except a president who served a long
time or a secretary of state. But my background, my experience,
my knowledge of the people of this country, my commitment to
our principles that don't change—those are the best bases to
correct the horrible mistakes of this administration and restore
our own country to a position of leadership in the world.

D   VALERIANI: How, specifically, Governor, are you going to bring
the American people into the decision-making process in foreign
policy? What does that mean?

6   CARTER: First of all, I would quit conducting the decision-
making process in secret, as has been a characteristic of Mr.
Kissinger and Mr. Ford. In many instances we've made
agreements, like in Vietnam, that have been revealed later on to
our embarrassment. Recently Ian Smith, the president of
Rhodesia, announced that he had unequivocal commitments
from Mr. Kissinger that he could not reveal. The American
people don't know what those commitments are. We have seen
in the past a destruction of elected governments like in Chile,
and the strong support of military dictatorship there. These
kinds of things have hurt us very much.

I would restore the concept of the fireside chat, which was an
integral part of the administration of Franklin Roosevelt. And I
would also restore the involvement of the Congress. When
Harry Truman was president, he was not afraid to have a strong
secretary of defense. Dean Acheson, George Marshall were
strong secretaries of state (excuse me, state). But he also made
sure that there was a bipartisan support. The members of
Congress—Arthur Vandenberg, Walter George[5]—were part of
the process. And before our nation made a secret agreement, or
before we made a bluffing statement, we were sure that we had
the backing not only of the president and the secretary of state,
but also of the Congress and the people. This is a responsibility
of the president. And I think it's very damaging to our country
for Mr. Ford to have turned over this responsibility to the
secretary of state.

FREDERICK: President Ford, do you have a response?

FORD: Governor Carter again contradicts himself. He complains 7
about secrecy and yet he is quoted as saying that in the attempt
to find a solution in the Middle East that he would hold unpublicized meetings with the Soviet Union, I presume for the
purpose of imposing a settlement on Israel and the Arab
nations.

But let me talk just a minute about what we've done to avoid
secrecy in the Ford administration. After the United States took
the initiative in working with Israel and with Egypt and
achieving the Sinai II agreement[6]—and I'm proud to say that not
a single Egyptian or Israeli soldier has lost his life since the
signing of the Sinai agreement—but at the time that I submitted
the Sinai agreement to the Congress of the United States, I
submitted every single document that was applicable to the Sinai
II agreement. It was the most complete documentation by any
president of any agreement signed by a president on behalf of
the United States.

Now as far as meeting with the Congress is concerned:
during the twenty-four months that I've been the president of
the United States, I have averaged better than one meeting a
month with responsible groups or committees of the Congress—
both House and Senate. The secretary of state has appeared, in
the several years that he's been the secretary, before eighty
different committee hearings in the House and in the Senate.
The secretary of state has made better than fifty speeches all
over the United States explaining American foreign policy. I
have made myself at least ten speeches in various parts of the
country where I have discussed with the American people
defense and foreign policy.

FREDERICK: Mr. Frankel, a question for President Ford.

FRANKEL: Mr. President, I'd like to explore a little more deeply   E
our relationship with the Russians. They used to brag back in
Khruschev's day that because of their greater patience and
because of our greed for business deals that they would sooner
or later get the better of us. Is it possible that, despite some
setbacks in the Middle East, they've proved their point?
Our allies in France and Italy are now flirting with Com-

munism; we've recognized a permanent Communist regime in East Germany; we've virtually signed in Helsinki an agreement that the Russians have dominance in Eastern Europe; we've bailed out Soviet agriculture with our huge grain sales; we've given them large loans, access to our best technology; and if the Senate hadn't interfered with the Jackson amendment,[7] maybe you would have given them even larger loans. Is that what you call a two-way street of traffic in Europe?

8   FORD: I believe that we have negotiated with the Soviet Union since I've been president from a position of strength. And let me cite several examples. Shortly after I became president, in December of 1974 I met with General Secretary Brezhnev in Vladivostok and we agreed to a mutual cap[8] on the ballistic missile launchers at a ceiling of 2,400, which means that the Soviet Union, if that becomes a permanent agreement, will have to make a reduction in their launchers that they now have or plan to have. I negotiated at Vladivostok with Mr. Brezhnev a limitation on the MIRVing[9] of their ballistic missiles at a figure of 1,320, which is the first time that any president has achieved a cap, either on launchers or on MIRVs.

It seems to me that we can go from there to the grain sales.[10] The grain sales have been a benefit to American agriculture. We have achieved a five-and-three-quarter-year sale of a minimum of 6 million metric tons, which means that they have already bought about 4 million metric tons this year and are bound to buy another 2 million metric tons to take the grain and corn and wheat that the American farmers have produced in order to have full production. And these grain sales to the Soviet Union have helped us tremendously in meeting the costs of the additional oil—the oil that we have bought from overseas.

If we turn to Helsinki—I'm glad you raised it, Mr. Frankel. In the case of Helsinki, thirty-five nations signed an agreement, including the secretary of state for the Vatican. I can't under any circumstances believe that His Holiness the Pope would agree by signing that agreement that the thirty-five nations have turned over to the Warsaw Pact nations the domination of Eastern Europe. It just isn't true. And if Mr. Carter alleges that His Holiness by signing that has done it, he is totally inaccurate. Now, what has been accomplished by the Helsinki agreement?

Number one, we have an agreement where they notify us and we notify them of any military maneuvers that are to be undertaken. They have done it in both cases where they've done so. There is no Soviet domination of Eastern Europe and there never will be under a Ford administration.

FREDERICK: Governor Carter.

FRANKEL: I'm sorry, could I just follow? Did I understand you   F to say, sir, that the Russians are not using Eastern Europe as their own sphere of influence and occupying most of the countries there and making sure with their troops that it's a Communist zone, whereas on our side of the line, the Italians and the French are still flirting with the possibility of Communism?

FORD: I don't believe, Mr. Frankel, that the Yugoslavians   9 consider themselves dominated by the Soviet Union. I don't believe that the Rumanians consider themselves dominated by the Soviet Union. I don't believe that the Poles consider themselves dominated by the Soviet Union. Each of those countries is independent, autonomous. It has its own territorial integrity. And the United States does not concede that those countries are under the domination of the Soviet Union. As a matter of fact, I visited Poland, Yugoslavia, and Rumania to make certain that the people of those countries understood that the president of the United States and the people of the United States are dedicated to their independence, their autonomy, and their freedom.

FREDERICK: Governor Carter, have you a response?

CARTER: Well, in the first place, I'm not criticizing His Holiness   10 the Pope. I was talking about Mr. Ford. The fact is that secrecy has surrounded the decisions made by the Ford administration. In the case of the Helsinki agreement, it may have been a good agreement, at the beginning. But we have failed to enforce the so-called Basket Three part, which insures the right of people to migrate, to join their families, to be free, to speak out. The Soviet Union is still jamming Radio Free Europe. Radio Free Europe is being jammed. We've also seen a very serious problem with the so-called Sonnenfeldt Document, which apparently Mr. Ford has just endorsed, which said that there's an organic linkage between the Eastern European countries and the Soviet Union, and I would like to see Mr. Ford convince the Polish-Americans and the Czech-Americans and the Hungarian-Americans in this country that those countries don't live under the domination and supervision of the Soviet Union behind the Iron Curtain.

We also have seen Mr. Ford exclude himself from access to the public. He hasn't had a tough, cross-examination-type press conference in over thirty days. One press conference he had without sound.

He's also shown a weakness in yielding to pressure. The Soviet Union, for instance, put pressure on Mr. Ford, and he refused to see a symbol of human freedom recognized around the world, Aleksandr Solzhenitsyn.[11] The Arabs have put pressure on Mr. Ford, and he's yielded, and has permitted a boycott, by the Arab countries, of American businesses who trade with Israel or who have American Jews owning or taking part in the management of American companies. His own secretary of commerce had to be subpoenaed by the Congress to reveal the names of businesses who were subject to this boycott. They didn't volunteer the information; he had to be subpoenaed.

And the last thing I'd like to say is this: this grain deal with the Soviet Union in '72 was terrible, and Mr. Ford made up for it with three embargoes, one against our own ally in Japan. That's not the way to run our foreign policy, including international trade.

FREDERICK: Mr. Trewhitt, a question for Governor Carter.

G   TREWHITT: Governor, I'd like to pick up on that point, actually, and on your appeal for a greater measure of American idealism in foreign affairs. Foreign affairs come home to the American public pretty much in such issues as oil embargoes and grain sales—that sort of thing. Would you be willing to risk an oil embargo in order to promote human rights in Iran and Saudi Arabia, withhold arms from Saudi Arabia for the same purpose, or as a matter of fact you've perhaps answered this final part, but would you withhold grain from the Soviet Union in order to promote civil rights in the Soviet Union?

CARTER: I would never single out food as a trade embargo item.   11
If I ever decided to impose an embargo, because of a crisis in
international relationships, it would include all shipments of all
equipment. For instance, if the Arab countries ever again
declare an embargo against our nation on oil, I would consider
that not a military but an economic declaration of war. And I
would respond instantly and in kind. I would not ship that Arab
country anything. No weapons, no spare parts for weapons, no
oil drilling rigs, no oil pipe, no nothing. I wouldn't single out
just food.

Another thing that I'd like to say is this: in our international
trade, as I said in my opening statement, we have become the
arms merchant of the world. When this Republican administration came into office, [12] we were shipping about 1 billion
dollars worth of arms overseas. Now—10 to 12 billion dollars
worth of arms overseas to countries that quite often use these
weapons to fight each other.

The shift in emphasis has been very disturbing to me,
speaking about the Middle East. Under the last Democratic
administration, 60 percent of all weapons that went into the
Middle East were for Israel. Seventy-five percent were for Israel
before. Now, 60 percent go to the Arab countries, and this does
not include Iran. If you include Iran—our present shipment of
weapons to the Middle East—only 20 percent goes to Israel. This
is a deviation from idealism; it's a deviation from a commitment
to our major ally in the Middle East, which is Israel; it's a
yielding to economic pressure on the part of the Arabs on the oil
issue; and it's also a tremendous indication that under the Ford
administration we have not addressed the energy policy
adequately.

We still have no comprehensive energy policy in this country.
And it's an overall sign of weakness. When we are weak at
home, economically—high unemployment, high inflation, a
confused government, a wasteful defense establishment—this
encourages the kind of pressure that's been put on us successfully. It would have been inconceivable ten, fifteen years
ago, for us to be brought to our knees with an Arab oil embargo,
but it was done three years ago, and they're still putting pressure

on us from the Arab countries—to our discredit around the world.

These are the weaknesses that I see. And I believe it's not just a matter of idealism. It's a matter of being tough. It's a matter of being strong. It's a matter of being consistent. Our priorities ought to be first of all to meet our own military needs; secondly, to meet the needs of our allies and friends; and only then should we ship military equipment to foreign countries. As a matter of fact, Iran is going to get eighty F14s before we even meet our own Air Force orders for F14s. And the shipment of Spruance-class destroyers to Iran are much more highly sophisticated than the Spruance-class destroyers that are presently being delivered to our own Navy. This is ridiculous and it ought to be changed.

H TREWHITT: Governor, let me pursue that if I may. If I understand you correctly you would in fact, to use my examples, withhold arms from Iran and Saudi Arabia, even if the risk was an oil embargo, and if they should be securing those arms from somewhere else, and then if the embargo came, then you would respond in kind. Do I have it correctly?

12 CARTER: Iran is not an Arab country, as you know; it is a Moslem country. But if Saudi Arabia should declare an oil embargo against us, then I would consider that an economic declaration of war. And I would make sure that the Saudis understood this ahead of time, so there would be no doubt in their mind. I think under those circumstances, they would refrain from pushing us to our knees, as they did in 1973 with their previous oil embargo.

FREDERICK: President Ford.

13 FORD: Governor Carter apparently doesn't realize that since I've been president we have sold to the Israelis over 4 billion dollars in military hardware. We have made available to the Israelis over 45 percent of the total economic and military aid since the establishment of Israel twenty-seven years ago. So the Ford administration has done a good job in helping our good ally, Israel, and we're dedicated to the survival and security of Israel.

I believe that Governor Carter doesn't realize the need and necessity for arms sales to Iran. He indicates he would not make those. Iran is bordered very extensively by the Soviet Union. Iran has Iraq as one of its neighbors. The Soviet Union and the Communist-dominated government of Iraq are neighbors of Iran, and Iran is an ally of the United States. It's my strong feeling that we ought to sell arms to Iran for its own national security and as an ally—a strong ally—of the United States. The history of our relationship with Iran goes back to the days of President Truman, when he decided that it was vitally necessary, for our own security as well as that of Iran, that we should help that country. And Iran has been a good ally. In 1973, when there was an oil embargo, Iran did not participate. Iran continued to sell oil to the United States. I believe that it's in our interest, and in the interest of Israel and Iran and Saudi Arabia, for the United States to sell arms to those countries. It's for their security as well as ours.

FREDERICK: Mr. Valeriani, a question for President Ford.

VALERIANI: Mr. President, the policy of your administration is   I
to normalize relations with mainland China. Now, that means establishing at some point full diplomatic relations and obviously doing something about the mutual defense treaty with Taiwan. If you are elected, will you move to establish full diplomatic relations with Peking, and will you abrogate the mutual defense treaty with Taiwan? And as a corollary, would you provide mainland China with military equipment if the Chinese were to ask for it?

FORD: Our relationship with the People's Republic of China is   14
based upon the Shanghai Communiqué of 1972. And that communiqué calls for the normalization of relations between the United States and the People's Republic. It doesn't set a time schedule. It doesn't make a determination as to how that relationship should be achieved in relationship to our current diplomatic recognition and obligations to the Taiwanese government. The Shanghai Communiqué does say that the differences between the People's Republic on the one hand and Taiwan on the other shall be settled by peaceful means.

The net result is, this administration, and during my time as the president for the next four years, we will continue to move for normalization of relations in the traditional sense, and we will insist that the disputes between Taiwan and the People's Republic be settled peacefully as was agreed in the Shanghai Communiqué of 1972.

The Ford administration will not let down, will not eliminate or forget our obligation to the people of Taiwan. We feel that there must be a continued obligation to the people, the some 19 or 20 million people, in Taiwan. And as we move during the next four years, those will be the policies of this administration.

J   VALERIANI: And, sir, the military equipment for the mainland Chinese?

15   FORD: There is no policy of this government to give to the People's Republic, or to sell to the People's Republic of China, military equipment. I do not believe that we, the United States, should sell, give, or otherwise transfer military hardware to the People's Republic of China, or any other Communist nation, such as the Soviet Union and the like.

FREDERICK: Governor Carter?

16   CARTER: Well, I'd like to go back just one moment to the previous question, where Mr. Ford, I think, confused the issue by trying to say that we're shipping Israel 40 percent of our aid. As a matter of fact, during this current year, we're shipping Iran, or have contracted to ship to Iran, about 7½ billion dollars worth of arms, and also to Saudi Arabia about 7½ billion dollars worth of arms.

Also in 1975, we almost brought Israel to their knees after the Yom Kippur war[13] by the so-called reassessment of our relationship to Israel. We, in effect, tried to make Israel the scapegoat for the problems in the Middle East. And this weakened our relationships with Israel a great deal and put a cloud on the total commitment that our people feel toward the Israelis. There ought to be a clear, unequivocal commitment, without change, to Israel.

In the Far East, I think we need to continue to be strong. And I would certainly pursue the normalization of relationships with the People's Republic of China. We opened up a great opportunity in 1972, which has pretty well been frittered away under Mr. Ford, that ought to be a constant inclination toward friendship. But I would never let that friendship with the People's Republic of China stand in the way of the preservation of the independence and freedom of the people on Taiwan.

FREDERICK: Mr. Frankel, a question for Governor Carter.

FRANKEL: Governor, we always seem in our elections, and K maybe in between too, to argue about who can be tougher in the world. Give or take a few billion dollars, give or take one weapon systems [sic], our leading politicians and I think you two gentlemen seem to settle roughly on the same strategy in the world, at roughly the same Pentagon budget cost. How bad do things have to get in our own economy, or how much backwardness and hunger would it take in the world to persuade you that our national security and our survival required very drastic cutbacks in arms spending and dramatic new efforts in other directions?

CARTER: Well, always in the past, we've had an ability to have a 17 strong defense and also to have a strong domestic economy, and also to be strong in our reputation and influence within the community of nations.

These characteristics of our country have been endangered under Mr. Ford. We are no longer respected. In a showdown vote in the United Nations or in any other international council we are lucky to get 20 percent of the other nations to vote with us. Our allies feel that we have neglected them. The so-called Nixon shocks against Japan have weakened our relationships there. Under this administration we've also had an inclination to keep separate the European countries, thinking that if they're separate, then we can dominate them and proceed with our secret, Lone Ranger–type diplomatic efforts.

I would also like to point out that we in this country have let our economy go down the drain: the worst inflation since the Great Depression; the highest unemployment of any developed nation of the world. We have a higher unemployment rate in this country than Great Britain, than West Germany. Our unemployment rate is twice as high as it is in Italy; it's three or four times as high as it is in Japan. And that terrible circumstance in this country is exported overseas. We comprise about 30 percent of the world's economic trade power influence. And when we're weak at home, weaker than all our allies, that weakness weakens the whole free world. So, strong economy is very important.

Another thing that we need to do is to reestablish the good relationships that we ought to have between the United States and our natural allies and friends. They have felt neglected. And using that base of strength and using the idealism, the honesty, the predictability, the commitment, the integrity of our own country—that's where our strength lies. And that would permit us to deal with the developing nations in a position of strength.

Under this administration we've had a continuation of the so-called balance of power politics, where everything is looked on as a struggle between us on the one side, the Soviet Union on the other. Our allies, the smaller countries, get trampled in the rush. What we need is to try to seek individualized bilateral relationships with countries regardless of their size and to establish world-order politics, which means that we want to preserve peace through strength.

We also want to revert back to the stature and the respect that our country had in previous administrations. Now, I can't say when this can come. But I can guarantee it will not come if Gerald Ford is reelected and this present policy is continued. It will come if I'm elected.

L   FRANKEL: If I hear you right, sir, you're saying, guns and butter both. But President Johnson also had trouble keeping up both Vietnam and his domestic programs. I was really asking: when do the needs of the cities and our own needs and those of other backward and even more needy countries and societies around the world take precedence over some of our military spending? Ever?

18   CARTER: Well, let me say very quickly that under President Johnson, in spite of the massive investment in the Vietnam War, he turned over a balanced budget to Mr. Nixon. The unemployment rate was less than 4 percent. The inflation rate under Kennedy and Johnson was about 2 percent—one-third what it is under this administration. So we did have at that time, with good management, the ability to do both. I don't think anybody can say that Johnson and Kennedy neglected the poor and the destitute people in this country or around the world.

But I can say this: the number one responsibility of any president, above all else, is to guarantee the security of our nation; an ability to be free of the threat of attack or blackmail; and to carry out our obligations to our allies and friends; and to carry out our legitimate foreign policy. They must go hand in hand. But the security of this nation has got to come first.

FREDERICK: President Ford.

FORD: Let me say very categorically: you cannot maintain the   19
security and the strength of the United States with the kind of defense budget cuts that Governor Carter has indicated. In 1975, he wanted to cut the budget 15 billion dollars. He's now down to a figure of 5 to 7 billion dollars. Reductions of that kind will not permit the United States to be strong enough to deter aggression and maintain the peace.

Governor Carter apparently doesn't know the facts. As soon as I became president, I initiated meetings with the NATO heads of state and met with them in Brussels to discuss how we could improve the defense relationship in Western Europe. In November of 1975, I met with the leaders of the five industrial nations in France for the purpose of seeing what we could do, acting together, to meet the problems of the coming recession. In Puerto Rico this year, I met with six of the leading industrial nations' heads of state to meet the problem of inflation so we would be able to solve it before it got out of hand. I have met with the heads of government bilaterally, as well as multi-laterally. Our relations with Japan have never been better. I was the first United States president to visit Japan, and we had the emperor of Japan here this past year, and the net result is, Japan and the United States are working more closely together now than at any time in the history of our relationship. You can go around the world, and let me take Israel for example. Just recently President Rabin said that our relations were never better.

FREDERICK: Mr. Trewhitt, a question for President Ford.

TREWHITT: Mr. President, you referred earlier to your meeting   M
with Mr. Brezhnev at Vladivostok in 1974. You agreed on that occasion to try to achieve another Strategic Arms Limitation—SALT—agreement within the year. Nothing happened in 1975,

or not very much publicly, at least, and those talks are still dragging, and things got quieter as the current season approached. Is there a bit of politics involved there, perhaps on both sides, or, perhaps more important, are interim weapons developments—and I'm thinking of such things as the cruise missile and the Soviet SS20, intermediate-range rocket—making SALT irrelevant, bypassing the SALT negotiations?

20 FORD: First we have to understand that SALT I expires October 3, 1977. Mr. Brezhnev and I met in Vladivostok in December of 1974 for the purpose of trying to take the initial step so we could have a SALT II agreement that would go to 1985. As I indicated earlier, we did agree on a 2,400 limitation on launchers of ballistic missiles. That would mean a cutback in the Soviet program; it would not interfere with our own program. At the same time we put a limitation of 1,320 on MIRVs. Our technicians have been working since that time, in Geneva, trying to put into technical language an agreement that can be verified by both parties.

In the meantime, there has developed the problem of the Soviet Backfire, their high-performance aircraft, which they say is not a long-range aircraft and which some of our people say is a [sic] intercontinental aircraft. In the interim, there has been the development, on our part primarily, the cruise missiles—cruise missiles that could be launched from land-based mobile installations, cruise missiles that could be launched from high-performance aircraft like the B52s or the B1s, which I hope we proceed with, cruise missiles which could be launched from either surface or submarine naval vessels.

Those gray-area weapons systems are creating some problems in the agreement for a SALT II negotiation. But, I can say that I am dedicated to proceeding, and I met just last week with the foreign minister of the Soviet Union, and he indicated to me that the Soviet Union was interested in narrowing the differences and making a realistic and a sound compromise. I hope and trust, in the best interest of both countries and in the best interest of all people throughout this globe, that the Soviet Union and the United States can make a mutually beneficial agreement, because if we do not—and SALT I expires on October 3, 1977—you will unleash again an all-out nuclear arms race with the potential of a nuclear holocaust of unbelievable dimensions. So it's the obligation of the president to do just that, and I intend to do so.

TREWHITT: Mr. President, let me follow that up by—I'll submit   N
that the cruise missile adds a whole new dimension to the arms competition, and then cite a statement by your office to the Arms Control Association a few days ago in which you said that the cruise missile might eventually be included in a comprehensive arms limitation agreement, but that in the meantime it was an essential part of the American strategic arsenal. Now, may I assume from that that you're tending to exclude the cruise missile from the next SALT agreement, or is it still negotiable in that context?

FORD: I believe that the cruise missiles which we are now   21
developing in research and development across the spectrum from air, from the sea or from the land, can be included within a SALT II agreement. They are a new weapons system that has a great potential, both conventional and nuclear armed. At the same time, we have to make certain that the Soviet Union's Backfire, which they claim is not an intercontinental aircraft and which some of our people contend is, must also be included if we are to get the kind of an agreement which is in the best interests of both countries. And I really believe that it's far better for us and for the Soviet Union and, more importantly, for the people around the world that these two superpowers find an answer for a SALT II agreement before October 3, 1977. I think good will on both parts, hard bargaining by both parties, and a reasonable compromise will be in the best interest of all parties.

FREDERICK: Governor Carter.

CARTER: Well, Mr. Ford acts like he's running for president for   22
the first time. He's been in office two years, and there has been absolutely no progress made toward a new SALT agreement. He has learned the date of the expiration of SALT I, apparently.

We've seen in this world a development of a tremendous threat to us. As a nuclear engineer myself, I know the limitations and capabilities of atomic power. I also know that as far as the human beings on this earth are concerned, that the non-proliferation of atomic weapons is number one. Only the last few days, with the election approaching, has Mr. Ford taken any interest in a nonproliferation movement. I advocated last May in a speech at the United Nations that we move immediately as a nation to declare a complete moratorium on the testing of all nuclear devices, both weapons and peaceful devices; that we not ship any more atomic fuel to a country that refuses to comply with strict controls over the waste which can be reprocessed into explosives. I've also advocated that we stop the sale by Germany and France of reprocessing plants to Pakistan and Brazil. Mr. Ford hasn't moved on this.

We also need to provide an adequate supply of enriched uranium. Mr. Ford, again, under pressure from the atomic energy lobby, has insisted that this reprocessing—or, rather, re-enrichment—be done by private industry and not by the existing government plants. This kind of confusion and absence of leadership has let us drift now for two years with a constantly increasing threat of atomic weapons throughout the world. We now have five nations that have atomic bombs, that we know about. If we continue under Mr. Ford's policy, by 1985 or '90, we'll have twenty nations that have the capability of exploding atomic weapons. This has got to be stopped. That is one of the major challenges and major undertakings that I will assume as the next president.

FREDERICK: Mr. Valeriani, a question for Governor Carter.

O   VALERIANI: Governor Carter, earlier tonight you said, "America is not strong anymore," "America is not respected anymore"; and I feel that I must ask you: do you really believe that the United States is not the strongest country in the world? Do you really believe that the United States is not the most respected country in the world? Or is that just campaign rhetoric?

23   CARTER: No, it's not just campaign rhetoric. I think that militarily we are as strong as any nation on earth. I think we've got to stay that way and continue to increase our capabilities to meet any potential threat. But as far as strength derived from commitment to principles; as far as strength derived from the unity within our country; as far as strength derived from the people, the Congress, the secretary of state, the president sharing in the evolution and carrying out of our foriegn policy;

as far as strength derived from the respect of our own allies and friends, their assurance that we will be staunch in our commitment, that we will not deviate, and that we'll give them adequate attention; as far as strength derived from doing what's right—caring for the poor, providing food, becoming the breadbasket of the world instead of the arms merchant of the world: in those respects, we're not strong.

Also, we'll never be strong again overseas unless we're strong at home. And with our economy in such terrible disarray and getting worse by the month—we've got 500,000 more Americans unemployed today than we had three months ago; we've got two and a half million more Americans out of work now than we had when Mr. Ford took office. This kind of deterioration in our economic strength is bound to weaken us around the world; and we not only have problems at home, but we export those problems overseas.

So, as far as the respect of our own people toward our own government; as far as participation in the shaping of concepts and commitments; as far as the trust of our country among the nations of the world; as far as dependence of our country in meeting the needs and obligations that we've expressed to our allies; as far as the respect of our country, even among our potential adversaries: we are weak. Potentially, we're strong. Under this administration, that strength has not been realized.

FREDERICK: President Ford.

FORD: Governor Carter brags about the unemployment during 24 Democratic administrations and condemns the unemployment at the present time. I must remind him that we're at peace, and during the period that he brags about unemployment being low, the United States was at war.

Now let me correct one other comment that Governor Carter has made. I have recommended to the Congress that we develop the uranium enrichment plant at Portsmouth, Ohio, which is a publicly owned U.S. government facility, and have indicated that the private program which would follow on in Alabama is one that may or may not be constructed. But I am committed to the one at Portsmouth, Ohio.

The governor also talks about morality in foreign policy. The foreign policy of the United States meets the highest standards of morality. What is more moral than peace? And the United States is at peace today. What is more moral in foreign policy than for the administration to take the lead in the World Food Conference in Rome in 1974 when the United States committed 6 million metric tons of food—over 60 percent of the food committed for the disadvantaged and underdeveloped nations of the world? The Ford administration wants to eradicate hunger and disease in our underdeveloped countries throughout the world. What is more moral than for the United States, under the Ford administration, to take the lead in southern Africa, in the Middle East? Those are initiatives in foreign policy which are of the highest moral standard, and that is indicative of the foreign policy of this country.

FREDERICK: Mr. Frankel, a question for President Ford.

P   FRANKEL: Mr. President, can we stick with morality? For a lot of people it seems to cover a bunch of sins. Mr. Nixon and Mr. Kissinger used to tell us that instead of morality we had to worry in the world about living with and letting live all kinds of governments that we really didn't like—North and South Korean dictators, Chilean fascists, Chinese Communists, Iranian emperors, and so on. They said the only way to get by in a wicked world was to treat others on the basis of how they treated us, and not how they treated their own people.

But more recently, we seem to have taken a different tack. We seem to have decided that it is part of our business to tell the Rhodesians, for instance, that the way they're treating their own black people is wrong, and they've got to change their government, and we put pressure on them. We were rather liberal in our advice to the Italians as to how to vote. Is this a new Ford foreign policy in the making? Can we expect that you are now going to turn to South Africa and force them to change their government, to intervene in similar ways to end the bloodshed, as you called it, say, in Chile or Chilean prisons, and to throw our weight around for the values that we hold dear in the world?

25   FORD: I believe that our foreign policy must express the highest standards of morality, and the initiatives that we took in southern Africa are the best examples of what this ad-

ministration is doing and will continue to do in the next four years. If the United States had not moved when we did in southern Africa, there's no doubt there would have been an acceleration of bloodshed in that tragic part of the world. If we had not taken our initiative, it's very, very possible that the government of Rhodesia would have been overrun and that the Soviet Union and the Cubans would have dominated southern Africa. So the United States, seeking to preserve the principle of self-determination, to eliminate the possibility of bloodshed, to protect the rights of the minority as we insisted upon the rights of the majority, I believe followed the good conscience of the American people in foreign policy.

And I believe that we have used our skill. Secretary of State Kissinger has done a superb job in working with the black African nations, the so-called frontline nations. He has done a superb job in getting the Prime Minister of South Africa, Mr. Vorster, to agree that the time had come for a solution to the problem of Rhodesia. Secretary Kissinger, in his meeting with Prime Minister Smith of Rhodesia, was able to convince him that it was in the best interests of whites as well as blacks in Rhodesia to find an answer for a transitional government and then a majority government.

This is a perfect example of the kind of leadership that the United States under this administration has taken. And I can assure you that this administration will follow that high moral principle in our future efforts in foreign policy, including our efforts in the Middle East, where it is vitally important, because the Middle East is the crossroads of the world. There have been more disputes, and it's an area where there's more volatility than any other place in the world. But because Arab nations and the Israelis trust the United States, we were able to take the lead in the Sinai II agreement. And I can assure you that the United States will have the leadership role in moving toward a comprehensive settlement of the Middle Eastern problems—I hope and trust as soon as possible—and we will do it with the highest moral principles.

FRANKEL: Mr. President, just clarify one point. There are lots of majorities in the world that feel they're being pushed around by minority governments. And are you saying they can now expect to look to us for not just good cheer, but throwing our weight on their side in South Africa, or on Taiwan or in Chile, to help change their governments as in Rhodesia?

26 FORD: I would hope that as we move to one area of the world from another—and the United States must not spread itself too thinly—that was one of the problems that helped to create the circumstances in Vietnam—but as we as a nation find that we are asked by the various parties, either one nation against another or individuals within a nation, that the United States will take the leadership and try to resolve the differences.

Let me take South Korea as an example. I have personally told President Pack[14] that the United States does not condone the kind of repressive measures that he has taken in that country. But I think, in all fairness and equity, we have to recognize the problem that South Korea has. On the north they have North Korea with 500,000 well-trained, well-equipped troops; they are supported by the People's Republic of China; they are supported by the Soviet Union. South Korea faces a very delicate situation. Now, the United States in this case, this administration, has recommended a year ago, and we have reiterated it again this year, that the United States, South Korea, North Korea, and the People's Republic of China sit down at a conference table to resolve the problems of the Korean peninsula. This is a leadership role that the United States under this administration is carrying out. And if we do it, and I think the opportunities and the possibilities are getting better, we will have solved many of the internal domestic problems that exist in South Korea at the present time.

FREDERICK: Governor Carter.

27 CARTER: I notice that Mr. Ford didn't comment on the prisons in Chile. This is a typical example, maybe of many others, where this administration overthrew an elected government and helped to establish a military dictatorship. This has not been an ancient-history story. Last year under Mr. Ford, of all the Food for Peace that went to South America, 85 percent went to the military dictatorship in Chile.

Another point I want to make is this: he says we have to

move from one area of the world to another. That's one of the problems with this administration's so-called shuttle diplomacy. While the secretary of state's in one country, there are almost 150 others that are wondering what we're going to do next. What will be the next secret agreement? We don't have a comprehensive, understandable foreign policy that deals with world problems, or even regional problems.

Another thing that concerned me was what Mr. Ford said about unemployment, insinuating that under Johnson and Kennedy that unemployment could only be held down when this country is at war. Karl Marx said that the free enterprise system in a democracy can only continue to exist when they are at war or preparing for war. Karl Marx was the grandfather of Communism. I don't agree with that statement. I hope Mr. Ford doesn't either.

He has put pressure on the Congress—and I don't believe Mr. Ford would even deny this—to hold up on nonproliferation legislation until the Congress agreed for an 8-billion-dollar program for private industry to start producing enriched uranium.

And the last thing I want to make is this: he talks about peace, and I'm thankful for peace. We were peaceful when Mr. Ford went into office. But he and Mr. Kissinger and others tried to start a new Vietnam in Angola, and it was only the outcry of the American people and the Congress, when this secret deal was discovered, that prevented our renewed involvement in that conflagration which was taking place there.

FREDERICK: Gentlemen, I'm sorry to say we do not have time enough for two complete sequences of questions. We now have only twelve minutes left. Therefore I would like to ask for shorter questions and shorter answers. And we also will drop the follow-up question. Each candidate may still respond, of course, to the other's answer. Mr. Trewhitt, a question for Governor Carter.

TREWHITT: Governor Carter, before this event, the most communications I received concerned Panama. Would you, as president, be prepared to sign a treaty which at a fixed date, yielded administrative and economic control over the Canal

R

Zone and shared defense, which, as I understand it, is the position the United States took in 1974?

28   CARTER: Well, here again, the Panamanian question is one that's been confused by Mr. Ford. He had directed his diplomatic representative to yield to the Panamanians full sovereignty over the Panama Canal Zone at the end of a certain period of time. When Mr. Reagan raised this question in Florida, Mr. Ford not only disavowed his instructions but he also even dropped, parenthetically, the use of the word *detente*.

I would never give up complete control or practical control of the Panama Canal Zone. But I would continue to negotiate with the Panamanians. When the original treaty was signed back in the early 1900s, when Theodore Roosevelt was president, Panama retained sovereignty over the Panama Canal Zone. We retained control, as though we had sovereignty.

Now, I would be willing to go ahead with negotiations. I believe that we could share more fully responsibilities for the Panama Canal Zone with Panama. I would be willing to continue to raise the payment for shipment of goods through the Panama Canal Zone. I might even be willing to reduce to some degree our military emplacements in the Panama Canal Zone. But I would not relinquish practical control of the Panama Canal Zone any time in the foreseeable future.

FREDERICK: President Ford.

29   FORD: The United States must and will maintain complete access to the Panama Canal. The United States must maintain a defense capability of the Panama Canal. And the United States will maintain our national security interest in the Panama Canal. The negotiations for the Panama Canal started under President Johnson and have continued up to the present time. I believe those negotiations should continue. But there are certain guidelines that must be followed, and I've just defined them.

Let me take just a minute to comment on something that Governor Carter said. On nonproliferation: in May of 1975, I called for a conference of nuclear suppliers. That conference has met six times. In May of this year, Governor Carter took the first initiative, approximately twelve months after I had taken my initiative a year ago.

FREDERICK: Mr. Valeriani, a question for President Ford.

VALERIANI: Mr. President, the Government Accounting Office   S
has just put out a report suggesting that you shot from the hip in
the *Mayaguez* rescue mission[15] and that you ignored diplomatic
messages saying that a peaceful solution was in prospect. Why
didn't you do more, diplomatically, at the time, and—a related
question—did the White House try to prevent the release of that
report?

FORD: The White House did not prevent the release of that   30
report. On July 12th of this year, we gave full permission for the
release of that report. I was very disappointed in the fact that the
GAO released that report, because I think it interjected political
partisan politics at the present time.

But let me comment on the report. Somebody who sits in
Washington, D. C. eighteen months after the *Mayaguez* incident
can be a very good grandstand quarterback. And let me make
another observation. This morning, I got a call from the skipper
of the *Mayaguez*. He was furious, because he told me that it was
the action of me, President Ford, that saved the lives of the crew
of the *Mayaguez*. And I can assure you that if we had not taken
the strong and forceful action that we did, we would have been
criticized very, very severely for sitting back and not moving.
Captain Miller is thankful. The crew is thankful. We did the
right thing. It seems to me that those who sit in Washington
eighteen months after the incident are not the best judges of the
decision-making process that had to be made by the National
Security Council and by myself at the time the incident was
developing in the Pacific.

Let me assure you that we made every possible overture to
the People's Republic of China and through them to the
Cambodian government. We made diplomatic protest to the
Cambodian government through the United Nations. Every
possible diplomatic means was utilized. But at the same time, I
had a responsibility—and so did the National Security Council—to meet the problem at hand, and we handled it responsibly,
and I think Captain Miller's testimony to that effect is the best
evidence.

FREDERICK: Governor Carter.

31   CARTER: Well, I'm reluctant to comment on the recent report. I haven't read it. I think the American people have only one requirement—that the facts about *Mayaguez* be given to them accurately and completely. Mr. Ford has been there for eighteen months. He had the facts that were released today immediately after the *Mayaguez* incident. I understand that the report today is accurate. Mr. Ford has said, I believe, that it was accurate and that the White House made no attempt to block the issuing of that report. I don't know if that's exactly accurate or not. I understand that both the Department of State and the Defense Department have approved the accuracy of today's report, or yesterday's report, and also the National Security Agency.

I don't know what was right or what was wrong or what was done. The only thing I believe is that whatever the knowledge was that Mr. Ford had, should have been given to the American people eighteen months ago, immediately after the *Mayaguez* incident occurred. This is what the American people want. When something happens that endangers our security, or when something happens that threatens our stature in the world, or when American people are endangered by the actions of a foreign country—just forty sailors on the *Mayaguez*—we obviously have to move aggressively and quickly to rescue them. But then, after the immediate action is taken, I believe the president has an obligation to tell the American people the truth and not wait eighteen months later for the report to be issued.

FREDERICK: Gentlemen, at this time we have time for only two very short questions. Mr. Frankel, a question for Governor Carter.

T   FRANKEL: Governor Carter, if the price of gaining influence among the Arabs is closing our eyes a little bit to their boycott against Israel, how would you handle that?

32   CARTER: I believe that the boycott of American businesses by the Arab countries because those businesses trade with Israel or because they have American Jews who are owners or directors in the company is an absolute disgrace. This is the first time that I remember, in the history of our country, when we've let a foreign country circumvent or change our Bill of Rights. I'll do

everything I can as president to stop the boycott of American businesses by the Arab countries. It's not a matter of diplomacy or trade with me; it's a matter of morality. And I don't believe that the Arab countries will pursue it when we have a strong president who will protect the integrity of our country, the commitment of our Constitution and Bill of Rights, and protect people in this country who happen to be Jews. It may later be Catholics, it may later be Baptists who are threatened by some foreign country. But we ought to stand staunch. And I think it's a disgrace that so far Mr. Ford's administration has blocked the passage of legislation that would have revealed by law every instance of the boycott, and it would have prevented the boycott from continuing.

FREDERICK: President Ford.

FORD: Again, Governor Carter is inaccurate. The Arab boycott   33
action was first taken in 1952, and in November of 1975 I was the first president to order the executive branch to take action, affirmative action through the Department of Commerce and other cabinet departments, to make certain that no American businessman or business organization should discriminate against Jews because of an Arab boycott.

And I might add that my administration, and I'm very proud of it, is the first administration that has taken an antitrust action against companies in this country that have allegedly cooperated with the Arab boycott. Just on Monday of this week I signed a tax bill that included an amendment that would prevent companies in the United States from taking a tax deduction if they have in any way whatsoever cooperated with the Arab boycott. And last week when we were trying to get the Export Administration Act through the Congress—necessary legislation— my administration went to Capitol Hill and tried to convince the House and the Senate that we should have an amendment on that legislation which would take strong and effective action against those who participate or cooperate with the Arab boycott.

One other point. Because the Congress failed to act, I am going to announce tomorrow that the Department of Commerce will disclose those companies that have participated in the Arab boycott. This is something that we can do. The Congress failed to do it, and we intend to do it.

FREDERICK: Mr. Trewhitt, a very brief question for President Ford.

U   TREWHITT: Mr. President, if you get the accounting of missing-in-action you want from North Vietnam—or from Vietnam, I'm sorry—now, would you then be prepared to reopen negotiations for restoration of relations with that country?

34   FORD: Let me restate our policy. As long as Vietnam—North Vietnam—does not give us a full and complete accounting of our missing-in-action, I will never go along with the admission of Vietnam to the United Nations. If they do give us a bona fide, complete accounting of the 800 MIAs, then I believe that the United States should begin negotiations for the admission of Vietnam to the United Nations, but not until they have given us the full accounting of our MIAs.

FREDERICK: Governor Carter.

35   CARTER: One of the most embarrassing failures of the Ford administration, and one that touches specifically on human rights, is his refusal to appoint a presidential commission to go to Vietnam, to go to Laos, to go to Cambodia, and try to trade for the release of information about those who are missing in action in those wars. This is what the families of MIAs want. So far, Mr. Ford has not done it. We've had several fragmentary efforts by members of the Congress and by private citizens. Several months ago the Vietnam government said we are ready to sit down and negotiate for release of information on MIAs. So far, Mr. Ford has not responded. I also would never normalize relationships with Vietnam, nor permit them to join the United Nations, until they've taken this action. But that's not enough. We need to have an active and aggressive action on the part of the president, the leader of this country, to seek out every possible way to get that information which has kept the MIA families in despair and doubt, and Mr. Ford has just not done it.

FREDERICK: Thank you, Governor Carter. That completes the questioning for this evening. Each candidate now has up to three

minutes for a closing statement. It was determined by the toss of
a coin that Governor Carter would take the first question, and
he now goes first with his closing remarks. Governor Carter.

CARTER: The purpose of this debate and the outcome of the   36
election will determine three basic things: leadership, upholding
the principles of our country, and proper priorities and commitments for the future.

This election will also determine what kind of world we leave
our children. Will it be a nightmare world, threatened with the
proliferation of atomic bombs, not just in five major countries
but dozens of smaller countries that have been permitted to
develop atomic weapons because of a failure of our top
leadership to stop proliferation? Will we have a world of hunger
and hatred? And will we be living in an armed camp, stripped of
our friendship and allies, hiding behind a tight defense that's
been drawn in around us because we're fearful of the outside
world? Will we have a government of secrecy that excludes the
American people from participation in making basic decisions
and therefore covers up mistakes and makes it possible for our
government—*our* government—to depart from the principles of
our Constitution and Bill of Rights?

Or will we have a world of peace, with the threat of atomic
weapons eliminated, with full trade, with our people at work,
inflation controlled, openness in government, our people proud
once again—Congress, citizens, president, secretary of state
working in harmony and unity toward a common future; a
world where people have enough to eat and a world where we
care about those who don't. Can we become a breadbasket of
the world instead of the arms merchant of the world? I believe
we can and we ought to.

Now, we've been hurt in recent years in this country, in the
aftermath of Vietnam, Cambodia, Chile, Pakistan, Angola,
Watergate, CIA. We've been hurt. Our people feel that we've
lost something precious. That's not necessary. I want to see our
nation returned to a posture and an image and a standard to
make us proud once again. I remember the world of NATO and
the world of Point Four and the world of the Marshall Plan and
the world of the Peace Corps.[16] Why can't we have that once

again? We ought to be a beacon for nations who search for peace and who search for freedom, who search for individual liberty, who search for basic human rights. We haven't been lately. We can be once again. We'll never have that world leadership until we are strong at home.

And we can have that strength if we return to the basic principles. It ought not to be a strength of bombast and threats. It ought to be a quiet strength, based on the integrity of our people, the vision of the Constitution, and an innate strong will and purpose that God's given us in the greatest nation on earth, the United States.

FREDERICK: President Ford.

37   FORD: As we have seen tonight, foreign policy and defense policy are difficult and complex issues. We can debate methods, we can debate one decision or another, but there are two things which cannot be debated: experience and results.

In the last two years, I have made policy decisions involving long-range difficulties and policies and made day-to-day judgments not only as president of the United States but as the leader of the free world.

What is the result of that leadership? America is strong. America is free. America is respected. Not a single young American today is fighting or dying on any foreign battlefield. America is at peace, with freedom. Thank you and good night.

FREDERICK: Thank you, President Ford. Thank you, Governor Carter. I also want to thank our questioners and the audience here this evening.

The third and final debate between President Ford and Governor Carter will take place on October the 22nd at 9:30 P.M. Eastern Daylight Time on the campus of the College of William and Mary in Williamsburg, Virginia. The subject matter will cover all issues.

These debates are sponsored by the League of Women Voters Education Fund to help voters become better informed on the issues and to generate greater voter turnout in the November election.

Now, from the Palace of Fine Arts Theatre in San Francisco, good night.

Third Debate

October 22, 1976   Williamsburg

WALTERS: Good evening. I'm Barbara Walters, moderator of the last of the debates of 1976 between Gerald R. Ford, Republican candidate for president, and Jimmy Carter, Democratic candidate for president. Welcome, President Ford. Welcome, Governor Carter. And thank you for joining us this evening.

This debate takes place before an audience in Phi Beta Kappa Memorial Hall on the campus of the College of William and Mary in historic Williamsburg, Virginia. It is particularly appropriate in this Bicentennial year that we meet on these grounds to hear this debate. Two hundred years ago, five William and Mary students met at nearby Raleigh Tavern to form Phi Beta Kappa, a fraternity designed, they wrote, to search out and dispel the clouds of falsehood by debating without reserve the issues of the day. In that spirit of debate, without reserve, to dispel the clouds of falsehood, gentlemen, let us proceed.

The subject matter of this debate is open, covering all issues and topics. Our questioners tonight are Joseph Kraft, syndicated columnist; Robert Maynard, editorial writer for the *Washington*

323

Post; and Jack Nelson, Washington bureau chief of the *Los Angeles Times.*

The ground rules tonight are as follows. Questioners will alternate questions between the candidates. A candidate has up to two and a half minutes to answer the question. The other candidate then has up to two minutes to respond. If necessary, a questioner may ask a follow-up question for further clarification, and in that case the candidate has up to two minutes to respond. As was initially agreed to by both candidates, the answers should be responsive to the particular questions.

Finally, each candidate has up to three minutes for a closing statement. President Ford and Governor Carter do not have prepared notes or comments with them this evening, but they may make notes and refer to them during the debate.

It has been determined that President Ford would take the first question in this last debate, and Mr. Kraft, do you have that first question for President Ford?

A KRAFT: Mr. President, I assume that the Americans all know that these are difficult times and that there's no pie in the sky and that they don't expect something for nothing. So, I'd like to ask you as a first question, as you look ahead in the next four years, what sacrifices are you going to call on the American people to make, what price are you going to ask them to pay to realize your objectives? Let me add, Governor Carter, that if you felt that it was appropriate to answer that question in your comments as to what price it would be appropriate for the American people to pay for a Carter administration, I think that would be proper, too. Mr. President?

1 FORD: Well, Mr. Kraft, I believe that the American people in the next four years under a Ford administration will be called upon to make those necessary sacrifices to preserve the peace which we have; which means of course that we will have to maintain an adequate military capability; which means of course that we will have to add, I think, a few billion dollars to our defense appropriations to make certain that we have adequate strategic forces, adequate conventional forces.

I think the American people will be called upon to be in the forefront in giving leadership to the solution of those problems that must be solved in the Middle East, in southern Africa, and any problems that might arise in the Pacific. The American people will be called upon to tighten their belts a bit in meeting some of the problems that we face domestically.

I don't think that America can go on a big spending spree with a whole lot of new programs that would add significantly to the federal budget. I believe that the American people, if given the leadership that I would expect to give, would be willing to give this thrust to preserve the peace and the necessary restraint at home to hold the lid on spending so that we could, I think, have a long overdue and totally justified tax decrease for the middle-income people, and then with the economy that would be generated from a restraint on spending and a tax reduction primarily for the middle-income people, then I think the American people would be willing to make those sacrifices for peace and prosperity in the next four years.

KRAFT: Could I be a little bit more specific, Mr. President? Doesn't your policy really imply that we're going to have to have a pretty high rate of unemployment over a fairly long time, that growth is going to be fairly slow, and that we're not going to be able to do very much in the next four or five years to meet the basic agenda of our national needs in the cities, in health, in transit, and a whole lot of other things like that?

FORD: Not at all.

KRAFT: Aren't those the real costs?

FORD: No, Mr. Kraft, we're spending very significant amounts of money now, some 200 billion dollars a year, almost 50 percent of our total federal expenditure by the federal government at the present time for human needs. Now we will probably have to increase that to some extent. But we don't have to have growth in spending that will blow the lid off and add to the problems of inflation.

I believe we can meet the problems within the cities of this country, and still give a tax reduction. I proposed, as you know, a reduction to increase the personal exemption from 750 to 1,000 dollars. With the fiscal program that I have, and if you look at the projections, it shows that we will reduce unemployment, that we will continue to win the battle against inflation, and at the same time give the kind of quality of life that I believe is possible in America: a job, a home for all those that'll work and save for it, safety in the streets, health care that is affordable. These things can be done if we have the right vision and the right restraint and the right leadership.

WALTERS: Thank you. Governor Carter, your response, please.

3   CARTER: Well, I might say first of all that I think in case of the Carter administration the sacrifices would be much less. Mr. Ford's own environmental agency has projected a 10-percent unemployment rate by 1978 if he's president. The American people are ready to make sacrifices if they are part of the process—if they know that they will be helping to make decisions and won't be excluded from being an involved party to the national purpose. The major effort that we must put forward is to put our people back to work.

And I think that this is one example where a lot of people have selfish, grasping ideas now. I remember 1973, in the depth of the energy crisis,[1] when President Nixon called on the American people to make a sacrifice, to cut down on the waste of gasoline, to cut down on the speed of automobiles. There was a tremendous surge of patriotism, that "I want to make a sacrifice for my country." I think we could call together, with strong leadership in the White House, business, industry, and labor and say, "Let's have voluntary price restraints. Let's lay down some guidelines so we don't have continuing inflation."

We can also have an end to the extremes. We now have one extreme, for instance, of some welfare recipients who, by taking advantage of the welfare laws, the housing laws, the Medicaid laws, and the food stamp laws, make over 10,000 dollars a year, and they don't have to pay any taxes on it. At the other extreme, just 1 percent of the richest people in our country derive 25 percent of all the tax benefits. So both those extremes grasp for advantage, and the person who has to pay that expense is the middle-income family who's still working for a living; and they have to pay for the rich who have privilege and for the poor who are not working.

But I think that a balanced approach, with everybody being part of it, and a striving for unselfishness, could help, as it did in 1973, to let people sacrifice for their own country. I know I'm ready for it. I think the American people are, too.

WALTERS: Thank you. Mr. Maynard, your question to Governor Carter.

MAYNARD: Governor, by all indications, the voters are so turned   C off by this election campaign so far that only half intend to vote. One major reason for this apathetic electorate appears to be the low level at which this campaign has been conducted. It has digressed frequently from important issues into allegations of blunder and brainwashing and fixations on lust and *Playboy*.[2] What responsibility do you accept for the low level of this campaign for the nation's highest office?

CARTER: I think the major reason for a decrease in participation   4 that we've experienced ever since 1960 has been the deep discouragement of the American people about the performance of public officials. When you've got 7½, 8 million people out of work and you've got three times as much inflation as you had during the last eight-year Democratic administration, when you have the highest deficits in history, when you have it becoming increasingly difficult for a family to put a child through college or to own a home, there's a natural inclination to be turned off. Also, in the aftermath of Vietnam and Cambodia and Watergate and the CIA revelations, people have felt that they've been betrayed by public officials.

I have to admit that in the heat of a campaign—I've been in thirty primaries during the springtime—I've been campaigning for twenty-two months—I've made some mistakes. And I think this is part of just being a human being. I have to say that my campaign has been an open one, and the *Playboy* thing has been of very great concern to me. I don't know how to deal with it exactly. I agreed to give the interview to *Playboy*. Other people have done it who are notable—Governor Jerry Brown, Walter Cronkite, Albert Schweitzer, Mr. Ford's own secretary of treasury, Mr. Simon, William Buckley, many other people. But they weren't running for president. And in retrospect, from hindsight, I would not have given that interview had I to do it over again. If I should ever decide in the future to discuss my deep Christian beliefs and condemnation and sinfulness, I'll use another forum besides *Playboy*.

But I can say this: now, I'm doing the best I can to get away from that; and during the next ten days, the American people will not see the Carter campaign running television advertisements and newspaper advertisements based on a personal attack on President Ford's character. I believe that the opposite is true with President Ford's campaign, and I hope that we can leave those issues in this next ten days about personalities and mistakes of the past—we've both made some mistakes—and talk about unemployment, inflation, housing, education, taxation, government organization, stripping away of secrecy, and the things that are crucial to the American people. I regret the things in my own long campaign that have been mistaken, but I'm trying to do away with those the last ten days.

WALTERS: Thank you, Governor Carter. President Ford, your response.

5   FORD: I believe that the American people have been turned off in this election, Mr. Maynard, for a variety of reasons. We have seen on Capitol Hill, in the Congress, a great many allegations of wrong-doing, of alleged immorality. Those are very disturbing to the American people. They wonder how an elected representative can serve them and participate in such activities serving in the Congress of the United States. Yes, and I'm certain many, many Americans were turned off by the revelations of Watergate—a very, very bad period of time in American political history. Yes, and thousands, maybe millions of Americans were turned off because of the problems that came out of our involvement in Vietnam. But, on the other hand, I found on July 4th of this year, a new spirit born in America. We were celebrating our Bicentennial. And I find that there is a movement as I travel around the country of greater interest in this campaign.

Now, like any hard-working person seeking public office, in the campaign inevitably sometimes you will use rather graphic language, and I'm guilty of that just like I think most others in the political arena. But I do make a pledge that in the next ten days when we're asking the American people to make one of the most important decisions in their lifetime—because I think this election is one of the most vital in the history of America—that we do together what we can to stimulate voter participation.

WALTERS: Thank you, President Ford. Mr. Nelson, your question to President Ford.

NELSON: Mr. President, you mentioned Watergate, and you   D became president because of Watergate. So don't you owe the American people a special obligation to explain in detail your role of limiting one of the original investigations of Watergate— that was the one by the House Banking Committee? And I know you've answered questions on this before, but there are questions that still remain and I think people want to know what your role was. Will you name the persons you talked to in connection with that investigation, and since you say you have no recollection of talking to anyone from the White House, would you be willing to open for examination the White House tapes of conversations during that period?

FORD: Mr. Nelson, I testified before two committees, House and   6 Senate, on precisely the questions that you have asked. And the testimony under oath was to the effect that I did not talk to Mr. Nixon, to Mr. Haldeman, to Mr. Ehrlichman or to any of the people at the White House. I said I had no recollection what- soever of talking with any of the White House legislative liaison people. I indicated under oath that the initiative that I took was at the request of the ranking members of the House Banking and Currency Committee on the Republican side, which was a legitimate request and a proper response by me.

Now that was gone into by two congressional committees; and following that investigation, both committees over- whelmingly approved me, and both the House and the Senate did likewise. Now, in the meantime, the special prosecutor, within the last few days, after an investigation himself, said there was no reason for him to get involved, because he found nothing that would justify it. And then, just a day or two ago, the attorney general of the United States made a further investigation and came to precisely the same conclusion.

Now, after all of those investigations by objective, responsible people, I think the matter is closed once and for all. But to add one other feature: I don't control any of the tapes. Those tapes are in the jurisdiction of the courts and I have no right to say yes or no. But all the committees, the attorney general, the special prosecutor, all of them have given me a clean bill of health. I think the matter is settled once and for all.

E   NELSON: Well, Mr. President, if I do say so, though, the question is that I think you still have not gone into details about what your role in it was. And I don't think there was any question about whether or not there was a criminal prosecution, but whether you have told the American people your entire involvement in it. And whether you would be willing—even though you don't control the tapes—whether you would be willing to ask that the tapes be released for examination.

7   FORD: That's for the proper authorities who have control over those tapes to make that decision. I have given every bit of evidence, answered every question that's been asked me by any senator or any member of the House. Plus the fact that the special prosecutor, on his own initiation, and the attorney general on his initiation—the highest law enforcement official in this country—all of them have given me a clean bill of health. And I've told everything I know about it. I think the matter is settled once and for all.

WALTERS: Governor Carter, your response.

8   CARTER: I don't have any response.

WALTERS: Thank you. Then we will have the next question from Mr. Kraft to Governor Carter.

F   KRAFT: Governor Carter, the next big crisis spot in the world may be Yugoslavia. President Tito is old and sick and there are divisions in his country. It's pretty certain that the Russians are going to do everything they possibly can after Tito dies to force

Yugoslavia back into the Soviet camp. But last Saturday you said, and this is a quote, "I would not go to war in Yugoslavia even if the Soviet Union sent in troops." Doesn't that statement practically invite the Russians to intervene in Yugoslavia? Doesn't it discourage Yugoslavs who might be tempted to resist? And wouldn't it have been wiser on your part to say nothing and to keep the Russians in the dark, as President Ford did, and as I think every president has done since President Truman?

CARTER: In the last two weeks, I've had a chance to talk to two men who have visited the Soviet Union, Yugoslavia, and China. One is Governor Averell Harriman, who visited the Soviet Union and Yugoslavia, and the other one is James Schlesinger, whom I think you accompanied to China. I got a complete report back from those countries from these two distinguished gentlemen.   9

Mr. Harriman talked to the leaders in Yugoslavia, and I think it's accurate to say that there is no prospect, in their opinion, of the Soviet Union invading Yugoslavia should Mr. Tito pass away. The present leadership there is fairly uniform in their purpose; I think it's a close-knit group; and I think it would be unwise for us to say that we will go to war in Yugoslavia if the Soviets should invade, which I think would be an extremely unlikely thing.

I have maintained from the very beginning of my campaign—and this was a standard answer that I made in response to the Yugoslavian question—that I would never go to war or become militarily involved in the internal affairs of another country unless our own security was directly threatened. And I don't believe that our security would be directly threatened if the Soviet Union went into Yugoslavia. I don't believe it will happen. I certainly hope it won't. I would take the strongest possible measures, short of actual military action there by our own troops, but I doubt that that would be an eventuality.

KRAFT: One quick follow-up: did you clear the response you made with Secretary Schlesinger and Governor Harriman?   G

CARTER: No, I did not.   10

WALTERS: President Ford, your response.

11   FORD: Well, I firmly believe, Mr. Kraft, that it's unwise for a president to signal in advance what options he might exercise if any international problem arose.

I think we all recall with some sadness that at the period of the late 1940s, early 1950s, there were some indications that the United States would not include South Korea in an area of defense. There are some who allege—I can't prove it true or untrue—that such a statement in effect invited the North Koreans to invade South Korea. It's a fact they did.

But no president of the United States, in my opinion, should signal in advance to a prospective enemy, what his decision might be or what option he might exercise. It's far better for a person sitting in the White House, who has a number of options, to make certain that the other side, so to speak, doesn't know precisely what you're going to do. And therefore, that was the reason that I would not identify any particular course of action when I responded to a question a week or so ago.

WALTERS: Thank you. Mr. Maynard, your question to President Ford, please.

H   MAYNARD: Sir, this question concerns your administrative performance as president. The other day, General George Brown, the chairman of the Joint Chiefs of Staff, delivered his views on several sensitive subjects, among them Great Britain, one of this country's oldest allies. He said, and I quote him now, "Great Britain, it's a pathetic thing. It just makes you cry. They are no longer a world power. All they have are generals, admirals, and bands." End quote. Since General Brown's comments have caused this country embarrassment in the past, why is he still this nation's leading military officer?

12   FORD: I have indicated to General Brown that the words that he used in that interview, in that particular case and in several others, were very ill advised. And General Brown has indicated his apology, his regrets, and I think that will, in this situation, settle the matter.

It is tragic that the full transcript of that interview was not released and that there were excerpts—some of the excerpts—

taken out of context. Not this one, however, that you bring up. General Brown has an exemplary record of military performance. He served this nation with great, great skill and courage and bravery for thirty-five years. And I think it's the consensus of the people who are knowledgeable in the military field that he is probably the outstanding military leader and strategist that we have in America today.

Now he did use ill-advised words, but I think in the fact that he apologized, that he was reprimanded, does permit him to stay on and continue that kind of leadership that we so badly need as we enter into negotiations under the SALT II agreement; or if we have operations that might be developing in the Middle East or in southern Africa or in the Pacific, we need a man with that experience, that knowledge, that know-how. And I think in light of the fact that he has apologized, would not have justified my asking for his resignation.

WALTERS: Thank you. Governor Carter, your response.

CARTER: Well, just briefly. I think this is the second time that   13 General Brown has made a statement for which he did have to apologize. And I know that everybody makes mistakes. I think the first one was related to the unwarranted influence of American Jews on the media and on the Congress. This one concerned Great Britain. I think he said that Israel was a military burden on us and that Iran hoped to reestablish the Persian empire. I'm not sure that I remembered earlier that President Ford had expressed his concern about the statement or apologized for it.

This is something, though, that I think is indicative of a need among the American people to know how the commander in chief, the president, feels; and I think the only criticism that I would have of Mr. Ford is that, immediately when the statement was revealed, perhaps a statement from the president would have been a clarifying and a very beneficial thing.

WALTERS: Mr. Nelson, your question now to Governor Carter.

NELSON: Governor, despite the fact that you've been running for   I president a long time now, many Americans still seem to be uneasy about you. They don't feel that they know you or the people around you. And one problem seems to be that you haven't reached out to bring people of broad background and national experience into your campaign or your presidential plans. Most of the people around you on a day-to-day basis are people you've known in Georgia. Many of them are young and relatively inexperienced in national affairs. And doesn't this raise a serious question as to whether you would bring into a Carter administration people with the necessary background to run the federal government?

14   CARTER: I don't believe it does. I began campaigning twenty-two months ago. At that time, nobody thought I had a chance to win. Very few people knew who I was. I came from a tiny town, as you know—Plains—and didn't hold public office, didn't have very much money. And my first organization was just four or five people plus my wife and my children—my three sons and their wives.

And we won the nomination by going out into the streets, barber shops, beauty parlors, restaurants, stores, in factory shift lines, also in farmers' markets and livestock sale barns—and we talked a lot and we listened a lot and we learned from the American people. And we built up an awareness among the voters of this country, particularly those in whose primaries I entered—thirty of them—nobody's ever done that before—about who I was and what I stood for.

Now we have a very, very wide ranging group of advisers who help me prepare for these debates and who teach me about international economics and foreign affairs, defense matters, health, education, welfare, government reorganization—I'd say several hundred of them, and they're very fine and very highly qualified.

The one major decision that I have made since acquiring the nomination, and I share this with President Ford, is the choice of the vice-president. I think this would be indicative of the kind of leaders that I would choose to help me if I am elected. I chose Senator Walter Mondale. And the only criterion that I ever put forward in my own mind was who among the several million people in this country would be the best person qualified to be president if something should happen to me, and to join me in being vice-president if I should serve out my term. And I'm convinced now, more than I was when I got the nomination, that Walter Mondale was the right choice.

And I believe this is a good indication of the kind of people I would choose in the future. Mr. Ford has had that same choice to make. I don't want to say anything critical of Senator Dole, but I've never heard Mr. Ford say that that was his primary consideration—who is the best person I could choose in this country to be president of the United States? I feel completely at ease knowing that someday Senator Mondale might very well be president. In the last five vice-presidential nominees—incumbents—three of them have become president. But I think this is indicative of what I would do.

WALTERS: President Ford, your response, please.

FORD: The governor may not have heard my established criteria   15
for the selection of a vice-president, but it was a well-established criteria [sic] that the person I selected would be fully qualified to be president of the United States. And Senator Bob Dole is so qualified: sixteen years in the House of Representatives and in the Senate, very high responsibilities on important committees.

I don't mean to be critical of Senator Mondale, but I was very, very surprised when I read that Senator Mondale made a very derogatory, very personal comment about General Brown after the news story that broke about General Brown. If my recollection is correct, he indicated that General Brown was not qualified to be a sewer commissioner. I don't think that's a proper way to describe a chairman of the Joint Chiefs of Staff who has fought for his country for thirty-five years, and I'm sure the governor would agree with me on that.

I think Senator Dole would show more good judgment and discretion than to so describe a heroic and brave and very outstanding leader of the military. So I think our selection of Bob Dole as vice-president is based on merit. And if he should ever become the president of the United States, with his vast experience as a member of the House and a member of the Senate, as well as a vice-president, I think he would do an outstanding job as president of the United States.

WALTERS: Mr. Kraft, your question to President Ford.

J   KRAFT: Mr. President, let me assure you, and maybe some of the viewing audience, that being on this panel hasn't been, as it may seem, all torture and agony. One of the heartening things is that I and my colleagues have received literally hundreds and maybe even thousands of suggested questions from ordinary citizens all across the country who want answers.

FORD: That's a tribute to their interest in this election.

KRAFT: I'll give you that. But, let me go on, because one main subject on the minds of all of them has been the environment. They're particularly curious about your record. People really want to know why you vetoed the strip-mining bill. They want to know why you worked against strong controls on auto emissions. They want to know why you aren't doing anything about pollution of the Atlantic Ocean. They want to know why a bipartisan organization such as the National League of Conservation Voters says that when it comes to environmental issues, you are—and I'm quoting—"hopeless."

16   FORD: First, let me set the record straight. I vetoed the strip-mining bill, Mr. Kraft, because it was the overwhelming consensus of knowledgeable people that that strip-mining bill would have meant the loss of literally thousands of jobs, something around 140,000 jobs. Number two, that strip-mining bill would have severely set back our need for more coal, and Governor Carter has said repeatedly that coal is the resource that we need to use more in the effort to become independent of the Arab oil supply. So, I vetoed it because of a loss of jobs and because it would have interfered with our energy independence program.

The auto emissions: it was agreed by Leonard Woodcock, the head of the UAW,[3] and by the heads of all of the automobile industry—we had labor and management together saying that those auto emissions standards had to be modified.

But let's talk about what the Ford administration has done in the field of environment. I have increased, as president, by over 60 percent, the funding for water treatment plants in the United States—the federal contribution.

I have fully funded the land and water conservation program—in fact, have recommended, and the Congress approved, a substantially increased land and water conservation program. I have added in the current-year budget the funds for the National Park Service. For example, we proposed about 12 million dollars to add between four and five hundred more employees for the National Park Service.

And a month or so ago, I did likewise say over the next ten years, we should expand—double—the national parks, the wilderness areas, the scenic river areas. And then, of course, the final thing is that I have signed and approved of more scenic rivers, more wilderness areas since I've been president than any other president in the history of the United States.

WALTERS: Governor Carter.

CARTER: Well, I might say that I think the League of Conservation Voters is absolutely right. This administration's record on environment is very bad.   17

I think it's accurate to say that the strip-mining law which was passed twice by the Congress—and only lacked two votes, I believe, of being overridden—would have been good for the country. The claim that it would have put 140,000 miners out of work is hard to believe, when at the time Mr. Ford vetoed it, the United Mine Workers was supporting the bill. And I don't think they would have supported the bill had they known that they would lose 140,000 jobs.

There's been a consistent policy on the part of this administration to lower or to delay enforcement of air pollution standards and water pollution standards. And under both President Nixon and Ford, monies have been impounded that would have gone to cities and others to control water pollution.

We have no energy policy. We, I think, are the only developed nation in the world that has no comprehensive energy policy to permit us to plan in an orderly way how to shift from increasingly scarce energy forms—oil—and have research and development concentrated on the increased use of coal, which I strongly favor—the research and development to be used primarily to make the coal burning be clean.

We need a heritage trust program, similar to the one we had in Georgia, to set aside additional lands that have geological and archeological importance, natural areas for enjoyment. The lands that Mr. Ford brags about having approved are in Alaska, and they are enormous in size, but as far as the accessibility of them by the American people, it's very far in the future.

We've taken no strong position in the control of pollution of our oceans. And I would say the worst threat to the environment of all is nuclear proliferation; and this administration, having been in office now for two years or more, has still not taken strong and bold action to stop the proliferation of nuclear waste around the world, particularly plutonium. Those are some brief remarks about the failures of this administration. I would do the opposite in every respect.

WALTERS: Mr. Maynard, to Governor Carter.

K   MAYNARD: Governor, federal policy in this country since World War II has tended to favor the development of suburbs at the great expense of central cities. Does not the federal government now have an affirmative obligation to revitalize the American city? We have heard little in this campaign suggesting that you have an urban reconstruction program. Could you please outline your urban intentions for us tonight?

18   CARTER: Yes, I'd be glad to. In the first place, as is the case with the environmental policy and energy policy that I just described, and the policy for nonproliferation of nuclear waste, this administration has no urban policy. It's impossible for mayors or governors to cooperate with the president, because they can't anticipate what's going to happen next. A mayor of a city like New York, for instance, needs to know eighteen months or two years ahead of time what responsibility the city will have in administration and in financing in things like housing, pollution control, crime control, education, welfare, and health.

This has not been done, unfortunately. I remember the headline in the *Daily News* that said, "Ford to New York: Drop Dead."[4] I think it's very important that our cities know that they have a partner in the federal government.

Quite often Congress has passed laws in the past, designed to help people with the ownership of homes and with the control of crime and with adequate health care and better education programs and so forth. Those programs were designed to help those who need it most. And quite often this has been in the very poor people and neighborhoods in the downtown urban centers. Because of the greatly advantaged persons who live in the suburbs—better education, better organization, more articulate, more aware of what the laws are—quite often this money has been channelled out of the downtown centers where it's needed.

Also I favor all revenue sharing money being used for local governments, and also to remove the prohibitions in the use of revenue sharing money so that it can be used to improve education and health care. We have now, for instance, only 7 percent of the total education cost being financed by the federal government. When the Nixon-Ford administration started, this was 10 percent. That's a 30-percent reduction in the portion that the federal government contributes to education in just eight years. And, as you know, the education costs have gone up tremendously.

The last point is that the major thrust has got to be to put people back to work. We've got an extraordinarily high unemployment rate among downtown urban ghetto areas, particularly among the very poor and particularly among minority groups, sometimes 50 or 60 percent. And the concentration of employment opportunities in those areas would help greatly not only to reestablish the tax base, but also to help reduce the extraordinary welfare cost.

One of the major responsibilities on the shoulders of New York City is to finance welfare. And I favor the shifting of the welfare cost away from the local governments altogether. And over a longer period of time, let the federal government begin to absorb part of it that's now paid by the state governments. Those things would help a great deal with the cities, but we still have a very serious problem there.

WALTERS: President Ford.

FORD: Let me speak out very strongly. The Ford administration does have a very comprehensive program to help our major metropolitan areas. I fought for, and the Congress finally went along with, a general revenue sharing program whereby cities and states—the cities two-thirds and the states one-third—get over 6 billion dollars a year in cash for which they can provide many, many services, whatever they really want. In addition, we in the federal government make available to cities about 3 billion, 300 million dollars in what we call community development.

In addition, as a result of my pressure on the Congress, we got a major mass transit program over a four-year period: 11 billion, 800 million dollars. We have a good housing program that will result in cutting the down payments by 50 percent and having mortgage payments lower at the beginning of any mortgage period. We're expanding our homestead housing program.

The net result is, we think under Carla Hills—who's the chairman of my Urban Development and Neighborhood Revitalization Program—we will really do a first-class job in helping the communities throughout the country. As a matter of fact, that committee under Secretary Hills released about a seventy-five-page report with specific recommendations so we can do a better job in the weeks ahead. And in addition, the tax program of the Ford administration, which provides an incentive for industry to move into our major metropolitan areas, into the inner cities, will bring jobs where people are and help to revitalize those cities as they can be.

WALTERS: Mr. Nelson, your question next to President Ford.

L   NELSON: Mr. President, your campaign has run ads in black newspapers saying that, quote, "for black Americans, President Ford is quietly getting the job done." Yet, study after study has shown little progress in desegregation and, in fact, actual increases in segregated schools and housing in the Northeast. Now, civil rights groups have complained repeatedly that there's been lack of progress and commitment to an integrated society during your administration. So how are you getting the job done for blacks and other minorities, and what programs do you have in mind for the next four years?

20   FORD: Let me say at the outset, I'm very proud of the record of this administration. In the cabinet I have one of the outstanding, I think, administrators as the Secretary of Transportation,

Bill Coleman. You're familiar, I'm sure, with the recognition given in the Air Force to General James, and there was just approved a three-star admiral, the first in the history of the United States Navy. So, we are giving full recognition to individuals of quality in the Ford administration in positions of great responsibility.

In addition, the Department of Justice is fully enforcing, and enforcing effectively, the Voting Rights Act, the legislation that involves jobs, housing for minorities, not only blacks but all others. The Department of HUD[5] is enforcing the new legislation that outlaws—that takes care of red-lining.

What we're doing is saying that there are opportunities—business opportunities, educational opportunities, responsibilities—where people with talent, black or any other minority, can fully qualify. The Office of Minority Business, in the Department of Commerce, has made available more money in trying to help black businessmen or other minority businessmen than any other administration since the office was established. The Office of Small Business, under Mr. Kobelinski, has a very massive program trying to help the black community. The individual who wants to start a business or expand his business as a black businessman is able to borrow, either directly or with guaranteed loans. I believe, on the record, that this administration has been responsive and we have carried out the law to the letter, and I'm proud of the record.

WALTERS: Governor Carter, your response, please.

CARTER: The description just made of this administration's record is hard to recognize. I think it's accurate to say that Mr. Ford voted against the Voting Rights Acts, and against the Civil Rights Acts in their debative stage. I think once it was assured they were going to pass, he finally voted for it.

This country changed drastically in 1969 when the terms of John Kennedy and Lyndon Johnson were over and Richard Nixon and Gerald Ford became the presidents. There was a time when there was hope for those who were poor and downtrodden and who were elderly or who were ill or who were in minority groups, but that time has been gone.

21

I think the greatest thing that ever happened to the South was the passage of the Civil Rights Acts and the opening up of opportunities to black people of the chance to vote, to hold a job, to buy a house, to go to school, and to participate in public affairs. It not only liberated our black people, but it also liberated the whites.

We've seen in many instances in recent years in minority affairs section of Small Loan Administration—Small Business Administration—lend a black entrepreneur just enough money to get started and then to go bankrupt. The bankruptcies have gone up in an extraordinary degree.

FHA,[6] which used to be a very responsible agency that everyone looked up to to help own a home, lost 600 million dollars last year. There have been over 1,300 indictments in HUD, over 800 convictions, relating just to home loans. And now the federal government has become the world's greatest slum landlord.

We've got a 30 percent or 40 percent unemployment rate among minority young people, and there's been no concerted effort given to the needs of those who are both poor and black, or poor and who speak a foreign language. And that's where there's been a great generation of despair and ill health and lack of education, lack of purposefulness, and the lack of hope for the future. But it doesn't take just a quiet, dormant, minimum enforcement of the law. It requires an aggressive searching out and reaching out to help people who especially need it. And that's been lacking in the last eight years.

WALTERS: Mr. Kraft, to Governor Carter.

M   KRAFT: Governor Carter, in the nearly two-hundred-year history of the Constitution, there've been only, I think it's twenty-five amendments, most of them on issues of the very broadest principle. Now we have proposed amendments in many highly specialized causes, like gun control, school busing, balanced budget, school prayer, abortion, things like that. Do you think it's appropriate to the dignity of the Constitution to tack on amendments in wholesale fashion? And which of the ones that I listed— that is, balanced budget, school busing, school prayer, abortion, gun control—which of those would you really work hard to support if you were president?

CARTER: I would not work hard to support any of those. We've   22
always had, I think, a lot of constitutional amendments proposed, but the passage of them has been fairly slow, and few and far between. In the two hundred year history, there's been a very cautious approach to this. But quite often we have a transient problem. I'm strongly against abortion. I think abortion's wrong. I don't think the government ought to do anything to encourage abortion. But I don't favor a constitutional amendment on the subject. But short of the constitutional amendment, and within the confines of the Supreme Court rulings, I'll do everything I can to minimize the need for abortions with better sex education, family planning, with better adoptive procedures. I personally don't believe that the federal government ought to finance abortions, but I draw the line and don't support the constitutional amendment. However, I honor the right of people who seek the constitutional amendments on school busing, on prayer in the schools, and on abortion. But among those you named, I won't actively work for the passage of any of them.

WALTERS: President Ford, your response, please.

FORD: I support the Republican platform, which calls for the   23
constitutional amendment that would outlaw abortions. I favor the particular constitutional amendment that would turn over to the states the individual right of the voters in those states the chance to make a decision by public referendum. I call that the people's amendment. I think if you really believe that the people of a state ought to make a decision on a matter of this kind, that we ought to have a federal constitutional amendment that would permit each one of the fifty states to make the choice. I think this is a responsible and a proper way to proceed.

I believe also that there is some merit to an amendment that Senator Everett Dirksen proposed very frequently, an amendment that would change the Court decision as far as voluntary prayer in public schools. It seems to me that there should be an opportunity, as long as it's voluntary, as long as there is no compulsion whatsoever, that an individual ought to have that right.

So in those two cases, I think such a constitutional amendment would be proper. And I really don't think in either case they're trivial matters. I think they're matters of very deep conviction as far as many, many people in this country believe. And therefore, they shouldn't be treated lightly. But they're matters that are important. And in those two cases, I would favor them.

WALTERS: Mr. Maynard, to President Ford.

N   MAYNARD: Mr. President, twice you have been the intended victim of would-be assassins using handguns. Yet, you remain a steadfast opponent of substantive handgun control. There are now some 40 million handguns in this country, going up at the rate of 2.5 million a year. And tragically, those handguns are frequently purchased for self-protection and wind up being used against a relative or a friend. In light of that, why do you remain so adamant in your opposition to substantive gun control in this country?

24   FORD: Mr. Maynard, the record of gun control, whether it's in one city or another or in some states, does not show that the registration of a gun—handgun—or the registration of the gun owner has in any way whatsoever decreased the crime rate or the use of that gun in the committing of a crime. The record just doesn't prove that such legislation, or action by a local city council, is effective.

What we have to do, and this is the crux of the matter, is to make it very, very difficult for a person who uses a gun in the commission of a crime to stay out of jail. If we make the use of a gun in the commission of a crime a serious criminal offense, and that person is prosecuted, then, in my opinion, we are going after the person who uses the gun for the wrong reason.

I don't believe in the registration of handguns or the registration of the handgun owner. That has not proven to be effective, and therefore I think the better way is to go after the criminal, the individual who commits a crime in the possession of a gun and uses that gun for a part of his criminal activity. Those are the people who ought to be in jail. And the only way to do it is to pass strong legislation so that once apprehended, indicted, convicted, they'll be in jail and off the streets and not using guns in the commission of a crime.

MAYNARD: But Mr. President, don't you think that the   O
proliferation of the availability of handguns contributes to the
possibility of those crimes being committed? And there's a second
part to my follow-up, very quickly. There are, as you know
and as you've said, jurisdictions around the country with strong
gun-control laws. The police officials in those cities contend that
if there were a national law, to prevent other jurisdictions from
providing the weapons that then come into places like New
York, that they might have a better handle on the problem.
Have you considered that in your analysis of the handgun proliferation
problem?

FORD: Yes, I have. And the individuals with whom I've   25
consulted have not convinced me that a national registration of
handguns or handgun owners will solve the problem you're talking
about. The person who wants to use a gun for an illegal purpose
can get it whether it's registered or outlawed. They will be
obtained. And they are the people who ought to go behind bars.
You should not in the process penalize the legitimate handgun
owner. And when you go through the process of registration,
you in effect are penalizing that individual who uses his gun for
a very legitimate purpose.

WALTERS: Governor Carter.

CARTER: I think it's accurate to say that Mr. Ford's position on   26
gun control has changed. Earlier, Mr. Levi, his attorney general,
put forward a gun control proposal—which Mr. Ford later, I believe,
espoused—that called for the prohibition against the sale
of the so-called Saturday Night Specials. And it would have put
very strict control over who owned a handgun. I have been a
hunter all my life and happen to own both shotguns, rifles, and a
handgun. And the only purpose that I would see in registering
handguns and not long guns of any kind would be to prohibit
the ownership of those guns by those who've used them in the
commission of a crime, or who have been proven to be mentally
incompetent to own a gun. I believe that limited approach to the
question would be advisable and, I think, adequate. But that's
as far as I would go with it.

WALTERS: Mr. Nelson, to Governor Carter.

P NELSON: Governor, you've said the Supreme Court of today is, as you put it, moving back in a proper direction in rulings that have limited the rights of criminal defendants. And you've compared the present Supreme Court under Chief Justice Burger very favorably with the more liberal Court that we had under Chief Justice Warren. So exactly what are you getting at, and can you elaborate on the kind of Court you think this country should have? And can you tell us the kind of qualifications and philosophy you would look for as president in making Supreme Court appointments?

27 CARTER: While I was governor of Georgia, although I'm not a lawyer, we had complete reform of the Georgia court system. We streamlined the structure of the court, put in administrative offices, put a unified court system in, required that all severe sentences be reviewed for uniformity; and, in addition to that, put forward a proposal that was adopted and used throughout my own term of office, of selection of, for all judges and district attorneys or prosecuting attorneys, on the basis of merit. Every time I had a vacancy on the Georgia Supreme Court—and I filled five of those vacancies out of seven total, and about half the court of appeals judges, about 35 percent of the trial judges—I was given from an objective panel the five most highly qualified persons in Georgia. And from those five, I always chose the first or second one. So merit selection of judges is the most important single criterion. And I would institute the same kind of procedure as president, not only in judicial appointments, but also in diplomatic appointments.

Secondly, I think that the Burger Court has fairly well confirmed the major and most far-reaching and most controversial decisions of the Warren Court. Civil rights has been confirmed by the Burger court, hasn't been reversed, and I don't think there's any inclination to reverse those basic decisions: the one-man, one-vote rule, which is a very important one that struck down the unwarranted influence in the legislature of sparsely population areas of the states; the right of indigent or very poor accused persons to legal counsel—I think the Burger Court has confirmed that basic and very controversial decision of the Warren Court; also, the protection of an arrested person against unwarranted persecution in trying to get a false confession.

But, now, I think there have been a couple of instances where the Burger Court[7] has made technical rulings, where an obviously guilty person was later found to be guilty. And I think that in that case, some of the more liberal members of the so-called Warren Court agreed with those decisions. But the only thing that I have pointed out was, what I've just said, and that there was a need to clarify the technicalities so that you couldn't be forced to release a person who was obviously guilty just because of a small technicality in the law. And that's a reversal of position by the Burger Court with which I do agree.

NELSON: Governor, I don't believe you answered my question, though, about the kinds of people you would be looking for the Court, the type of philosophy you would be looking for if you were making appointments to the Supreme Court as president.   Q

CARTER: Okay, I thought I answered it by saying that it would be on the basis of merit. Once the search and analysis procedure had been completed, and once I'm given a list of the five or seven or ten best qualified persons in the country, I would make a selection from among those persons. If the list was, in my opinion, fairly uniform, if there was no outstanding person, then I would undoubtedly choose someone who would most accurately reflect my own basic political philosophy as best I could determine it—which would be to continue the progress that has been made under the last two courts, the Warren Court and the Burger Court.   28

I would also like to completely revise our criminal justice system—to do some of the things at the federal level in court reform, that I've just described, as has been done in Georgia and other states. And then I would like to appoint people who would be interested in helping with that. I know that Chief Justice Burger is. He hasn't had help yet from the administration and from the Congress to carry this out.

The emphasis, I think, of the court system should be to interpret the Constitution and the laws equally between property protection and personal protection. But when there's a very narrow decision—which quite often there's one that reaches the Supreme Court—I think the choice should be with human rights. And that would be another factor that I would follow.

WALTERS: President Ford.

29   FORD: Well, I think the answer as to the kind of a person that I would select is obvious. I had one opportunity to nominate an individual to the Supreme Court and I selected the Circuit Court of Appeals judge from Illinois, John Paul Stevens. I selected him because of his outstanding record as a Circuit Court of Appeals judge, and I was very pleased that an overwhelmingly Democratic United States Senate, after going into his background, came to the conclusion that he was fit and should serve, and the vote in his behalf was overwhelming. So, I would say somebody in the format of Justice Stevens would be the kind of an individual that I would select in the future, as I did him in the past.

I believe, however, a comment ought to be made about the direction of the Burger Court vis-a-vis the Court that preceded it. It seems to me that the *Miranda* case[8] was a case that really made it very, very difficult for the police, the law enforcement people in this country, to do what they could to make certain that the victim of a crime was protected and that those that commit crimes were properly handled and sent to jail. The *Miranda* case the Burger Court is gradually changing; and I'm pleased to see that there are some steps being made by the Burger Court to modify the so-called *Miranda* decision.

I might make a correction of what Governor Carter said, speaking of gun control. Yes, it is true, I believe that the sale of Saturday Night Specials should be cut out, but he wants the registration of handguns.

WALTERS: Mr. Kraft.

R   KRAFT: Mr. President, the country is now in something that your advisers call an economic "pause." I think to most Americans that sounds like an antiseptic term for low growth, unemployment standstill at a high level, decline in take-home pay, lower factory earnings, more layoffs. Isn't that really a rotten record, and doesn't your administration bear most of the blame for it?

FORD: Well, Mr. Kraft, I violently disagree with your 30
assessment. And I don't think the record justifies the conclusion
that you come to.

Let me talk about the economic announcements that were
made just this past week. Yes, it was announced that the GNP
real growth in the third quarter was at 4 percent. But do you
realize that over the last ten years, that's a higher figure than the
average growth during that ten-year period? Now, it's lower
than the 9.2-percent growth in the first quarter and it's lower
than the 5-percent growth in the second quarter. But every
economist—liberal, conservative—that I'm familiar with
recognizes that in the fourth quarter of this year and in the
fifth—the first quarter of next year that we'll have an increase in
real GNP.

But now let's talk about the pluses that came out this week.
We had an 18-percent increase in housing starts. We had a
substantial increase in new permits for housing. As a matter of
fact, based on the announcement this week, there will be, at an
annual rate, a million, eight hundred, and some thousand new
houses built, which is a tremendous increase over last year and a
substantial increase over the earlier part of this year.

Now, in addition, we had some very good news in the
reduction in the rate of inflation. And inflation hits everybody,
those who are working and those who are on welfare. The rate
of inflation as announced just the other day is under 5 percent,
and the 4.4 percent that was indicated at the time of the 4-
percent GNP was less than the 5.4 percent. It means that the
American buyer is getting a better bargain today because inflation is less.

KRAFT: Mr. President, let me ask you this: there has been an S
increase in layoffs, and that's something that bothers everybody
because even people that have a job are afraid they're going to
be fired. Did you predict that increase in layoffs? Didn't that
take you by surprise? Hasn't your administration been surprised
by this pause? In fact, haven't you been so obsessed with saving
money that you didn't even push the government to spend funds
that were allocated?

31   FORD: Mr. Kraft, I think the record can be put in this way, which is the way that I think satisfies most Americans. Since the depths of the recession, we have added 4 million jobs. Most importantly, consumer confidence, as surveyed by the reputable organization at the University of Michigan, is at the highest since 1972.

In other words, there is a growing public confidence in the strength of this economy. And that means that there will be more industrial activity. It means that there will be a reduction in the unemployment. It means that there will be increased hires. It means that there will be increased employment.

Now, we've had this pause, but most economists, regardless of their political philosophy, indicate that this pause for a month or two was healthy, because we could not have honestly sustained a 9.2-percent rate of growth which we had in the first quarter of this year.

Now, I'd like to point out as well that the United States' economic recovery from the recession of a year ago is well ahead of the economic recovery of any major free industrial nation in the world today. We're ahead of all of the Western European countries. We're ahead of Japan. The United States is leading the free world out of the recession that was serious a year, year and a half ago. We're going to see unemployment going down, more jobs available, and the rate of inflation going down. And I think this is a record that the American people understand and will appreciate.

WALTERS: Governor Carter.

32   CARTER: Well, with all due respect to President Ford, I think he ought to be ashamed of making that statement, because we have the highest unemployment rate now that we had at any time between the Great Depression caused by Herbert Hoover and the time President Ford took office. We've got 7½ million people out of jobs. Since he's been in office, 2½ million more American people have lost their jobs. In the last four months alone, 500,000 Americans have gone on the unemployment rolls. In the last month, we've had a net loss of 163,000 jobs.

Anybody who says that the inflation rate is in good shape now ought to talk to the housewives. One of the overwhelming results that I've seen in polls is that people feel that you can't plan anymore. There's no way to make a prediction that my family might be able to own a home or to put my kid through college. Savings accounts are losing money instead of gaining money. Inflation is robbing us. Under the present administrations—Nixon's and Ford's—we've had three times the inflation rate that we experienced under President Johnson and President Kennedy.

The economic growth is less than half today what it was at the beginning of this year. And housing starts—he compares the housing starts with last year. I don't blame him, because in 1975 we had fewer housing starts in this country, fewer homes built, than any year since 1940. That's thirty-five years. And we've got a 35-percent unemployment rate in many areas of this country among construction workers. Now, Mr. Ford hasn't done anything about it. And I think this shows a callous indifference to the families that have suffered so much. He has vetoed bills passed by Congress within the congressional budget guidelines— job opportunities for 2 million Americans.

We'll never have a balanced budget, we'll never meet the needs of our people, we'll never control the inflationary spiral, as long as we have 7½ or 8 million people out of work, who are looking for jobs. And we've probably got 2½ more million people who are not looking for jobs anymore because they've given up hope. That is a very serious indictment of this administration. It's probably the worst one of all.

WALTERS: Mr. Maynard.

MAYNARD: Governor Carter, you entered this race against President Ford with a 20-point lead or better in the polls. And now it appears that this campaign is headed for a photo finish. You've said how difficult it is to run against a sitting president. But Mr. Ford was just as much an incumbent in July when you were 20 points ahead as he is now. Can you tell us what caused the evaporation of that lead, in your opinion?

CARTER: Well, that's not exactly an accurate description of what happened. When I was that far ahead, it was immediately following the Democratic convention, and before the Republican convention. At that time, 25 or 30 percent of the

Reagan supporters said that they would not support President Ford. But as occurred at the end of the Democratic convention, the Republican party unified itself. And I think immediately following the Republican convention, there was about a 10-point spread. I believe that, to be accurate, I had 49 percent, President Ford had 39 percent.

The polls are good indications of fluctuations, but they vary widely, one from another. And the only poll I've ever followed is the one that, you know, is taken on election day. I was in thirty primaries in the spring, and at first it was obvious that I didn't have any standing in the poll. As a matter of fact, I think when Gallup ran their first poll in December of 1975 they didn't even put my name on the list. They had thirty-five people on the list. My name wasn't even there. And at the beginning of the year I had about 2 percent. So the polls to me are interesting, but they don't determine, you know, my hopes or my despair.

I campaign among people. I've never depended on powerful political figures to put me in office. I have a direct relationship with hundreds of people around the—hundreds of thousands of people around the country who are actively campaigning for me. In Georgia alone, for instance, I got 84 percent of the vote, and I think there were fourteen people in addition to myself on the ballot, and Governor Wallace had been very strong in Georgia. That's an overwhelming support from my own people who know me best. And today, we have about 500 Georgians at their own expense—just working people who believe in me—spread around the country involved in the political campaign.

So, the polls are interesting, but I don't know how to explain the fluctuations. I think a lot of it depends on current events—sometimes foreign affairs, sometimes domestic affairs—but I think our hold of support among those who are crucial to the election has been fairly steady. And my success in the primary season was, I think, notable for a newcomer, from someone who's outside of Washington, who never has been a part of the Washington establishment. And I think that we'll have a good result on November the second for myself and, I hope, for the country.

WALTERS: President Ford, your response.

FORD: I think the increase in the prospects as far as I'm con-   34
cerned and the less favorable prospects for Governor Carter
reflect that Governor Carter is inconsistent in many of the
positions that he takes. He tends to distort on a number of
occasions.

Just a moment ago, for example, he was indicating that in
the 1950s, for example, unemployment was very low. He fails to
point out that in the 1950s, we were engaged in the war in
Vietnam—I mean in Korea. We had 3,500,000 young men in the
Army, Navy, Air Force, and Marines. That's not the way to end
unemployment or to reduce unemployment.

At the present time we're at peace. We have reduced the
number of people in the Army, Navy, Air Force, and Marines
from 3,500,000 to 2,100,000. We are not at war; we have
reduced the military manpower by 1,400,000. If we had that
many more people in the Army, the Navy, the Air Force, and
Marines, our unemployment figure would be considerably less.
But this administration doesn't believe the way to reduce
unemployment is to go to war, or to increase the number of
people in the military. So you cannot compare unemployment,
as you sought to, with the present time, with the 1950s, because
the then administration had people in the military, they were at
war, they were fighting overseas. And this administration has
reduced the size of the military by 1,400,000; they're in the
civilian labor market, and they're not fighting anywhere around
the world today.

WALTERS: Thank you, gentlemen. This will complete our
questioning for this debate. We don't have time for more
questions and full answers. So, now, each candidate will be
allowed up to four minutes for a closing statement. And at the
original coin toss in Philadelphia a month ago, it was determined that President Ford would make the first closing
statement tonight. President Ford.

FORD: For twenty-five years I served in the Congress under five   35
presidents. I saw them work. I saw them make very hard
decisions. I didn't always agree with their decisions, whether
they were Democratic or Republican presidents. For the last two
years, I've been the president, and I have found from experience

that it's much more difficult to make those decisions than it is to second-guess them.

I became president at the time that the United States was in a very troubled time. We had inflation of over 12 percent; we were on the brink of the worst recession in the last forty years; we were still deeply involved in the problems of Vietnam. The American people had lost faith and trust and confidence in the presidency itself. That situation called for me to first put the United States on a steady course and to keep our keel well balanced, because we had to face the difficult problems that had all of a sudden hit America. I think most people know that I did not seek the presidency. But I am asking for your help and assistance to be president for the next four years.

During this campaign we've seen a lot of television shows, a lot of bumper stickers, and a great many slogans of one kind or another. But those are not the things that count. What counts is, that the United States celebrated its two-hundredth birthday on July 4th. As a result of that wonderful experience all over the United States, there is a new spirit in America. The American people are healed, are working together. The American people are moving again, and moving in the right direction.

We have cut inflation by better than half. We have come out of the recession and we're well on the road to real prosperity in this country again. There has been a restoration of faith and confidence and trust in the presidency, because I've been open, candid, and forthright. I have never promised more than I could produce, and I have produced everything that I promised. We are at peace. Not a single young American is fighting or dying on any foreign soil tonight. We have peace with freedom.

I've been proud to be president of the United States during these very troubled times. I love America just as all of you love America. It would be the highest honor for me to have your support on November 2nd and for you to say, "Jerry Ford, you've done a good job, keep on doing it." Thank you, and good night.

WALTERS: Thank you, President Ford. Governor Carter.

36   CARTER: The major purpose of an election for president is to choose a leader: someone who can analyze the depths of feeling

in our country, to set a standard for our people to follow, to inspire our people to reach for greatness, to correct our defects, to answer difficult questions, to bind ourselves together in a spirit of unity. I don't believe the present administration has done that. We have been discouraged and we have been alienated; sometimes we've been embarrassed and sometimes we've been ashamed. Our people are out of work, and there's a sense of withdrawal. But our country is innately very strong.

Mr. Ford is a good and decent man, but he's been in office now more than eight hundred days, approaching almost as long as John Kennedy was in office. I'd like to ask the American people what—what's been accomplished? A lot remains to be done.

My own background is different from his. I was a school board member, and a library board member, I served on a hospital authority, and I was in the state senate, and I was governor, and I'm an engineer, a naval officer, a farmer, a businessman. And I believe we require someone who can work harmoniously with the Congress, who can work closely with the people of this country, and who can bring a new image and a new spirit to Washington.

Our tax structure is a disgrace; it needs to be reformed. I was governor of Georgia for four years. We never increased sales taxes or income tax or property tax. As a matter of fact, the year before I went out of office we gave a 50-million-dollar refund to the property-taxpayers of Georgia.

We spend 600 dollars per person in this country—every man, woman and child—for health care. We still rank fifteenth among all the nations of the world in infant mortality. And our cancer rate is higher than any country in the world. We don't have good health care. We could have it.

Employment ought to be restored to our people. We've become almost a welfare state. We spend now 700 percent more on unemployment compensation than we did eight years ago when the Republicans took over the White House. Our people want to go back to work.

Our education system can be improved.

Secrecy ought to be stripped away from government and a maximum of personal privacy ought to be maintained.

Our housing programs have gone bad. It used to be that the average family could own a house. But now less than a third of our people can afford to buy their own homes.

The budget was more grossly out of balance last year than ever before in the history of our country—65 billion dollars—primarily because our people are not at work.

Inflation is robbing us, as we've already discussed, and the government bureaucracy is just a horrible mess. This doesn't have to be.

Now, I don't know all the answers. Nobody could. But I do know that if the president of the United States and the Congress of the United States and the people of the United States said, "I believe our nation is greater than what we are now," I believe that if we are inspired, if we can achieve a degree of unity, if we can set our goals high enough and work toward recognized goals with industry and labor and agriculture, along with government at all levels, then we can achieve great things.

We might have to do it slowly. There are no magic answers to it. But, I believe, together we can make great progress. We can correct our difficult mistakes and answer those very tough questions. I believe in the greatness of our country, and I believe the American people are ready for a change in Washington.

We've been drifting too long. We've been dormant too long. We've been discouraged too long. And we have not set an example for our own people. But I believe that we can now establish in the White House a good relationship with Congress, a good relationship with our people, set very high goals for our country, and with inspiration and hard work we can achieve great things, and let the world know—that's very important—but, more importantly, let the people in our own country realize that we still live in the greatest nation on earth. Thank you very much.

WALTERS: Thank you, Governor Carter, and thank you, President Ford. I also would like to thank the audience and my three colleagues—Mr. Kraft, Mr. Maynard, and Mr. Nelson—who have been our questioners.

This debate has, of course, been seen by millions of Americans and, in addition, tonight is being broadcast to 113 nations throughout the world. This concludes the 1976 presidential debate, a truly remarkable exercise in democracy, for this is the first time in sixteen years that the presidential candidates have debated. It is the first time ever that an incumbent president has debated his challenger. And the debate included the first between the two vice-presidential candidates.

President Ford and Governor Carter, we not only want to thank you, but we commend you for agreeing to come together to discuss the issues before the Americn people.

And our special thanks to the League of Women Voters for making these events possible. In sponsoring these events, the League of Women Voters Education Fund has tried to provide you with the information that you will need to choose wisely. The election is now only eleven days off. The candidates have participated in presenting their views in three ninety-minute debate[s] and now it's up to the voters, now it is up to you, to participate. The League urges all registered voters to vote on November 2nd for the candidate of your choice.

And now, from Phi Beta Kappa Memorial Hall on the campus of the College of William and Mary, this is Barbara Walters wishing you all a good evening.

The Vice-Presidential Debate: Dole and Mondale

October 15, 1976   Houston

HOGE: Good evening, I'm James Hoge, editor of the *Chicago Sun-Times,* and moderator of this third of the historic debates of the 1976 campaign. Tonight we have the vice-presidential candidates: for the Democrats, Senator Walter Mondale of Minnesota; for the Republicans, Senator Robert Dole of Kansas. Thank you, Senator Mondale, and thank you, Senator Dole, for being with us this evening.

This debate is taking place before an audience in the Alley Theatre in Houston, Texas. It is also being broadcast by radio and television to an audience estimated at some 85 million persons in this nation and overseas. As far as we can tell, this is the first formal debate ever held between vice-presidential candidates. Their views are important not only because they seek the second-highest office in the land, but because as potential vice-presidents they must be judged on their capacities to serve as president of the United States. For example, of the last five vice-presidents, three have become president due to death or resignation by a chief executive.

We will begin this debate tonight with opening statements of up to two minutes by each candidate. By the toss of a coin, it was determined that Senator Dole would go first. Senator Dole, your opening statement.

DOLE: Thank you very much. First, I wish to thank the League of Women Voters, and this is a great privilege and honor for me. I also want to thank my many friends in Russell, Kansas, for that big, long telegram I received today.

I think tonight may be sort of a fun evening. It's a very important evening. It's a very historic evening. But I've known my counterpart for some time and we've been friends, and we'll be friends when this debate is over. And we'll be friends when the election is over and he'll still be in the Senate.

I think, first of all, I should make it very clear that I'm most proud to be on the ticket with President Ford. I've known President Ford for sixteen years. Sixteen years—it's a long time. He's known me for that long. I know him to be a man of compassion and competence. He has that confidence, and he projects that leadership that America needs and that you need right now.

But I don't know much about Governor Carter. I've tried to find out. I know he's very ambitious. I know he wants to be president—he's been running for three years. But I know he's said at least one thing—that he does agree with my opponent, my friend Walter Mondale, probably the most liberal senator in the United States Senate. And that's really what this debate's all about.

If, by some tragic circumstance, one of us should become president of the United States, where do we stand on the issues? I would just say, in a very summary way, that I have a great deal of faith in you, the American people. I'm concerned about farmers and housewives and young people and professional people, working men and women. I think we can find our solutions, working together. My opponent has a record of voting for every inflationary spending program, except in defense, where he votes for every cut, and we'll explore that as this debate goes on.

HOGE: Thank you, Senator Dole. Senator Mondale, your opening statement.

MONDALE: I believe that most Americans would agree on the problems that this country faces and which the next administration must solve. They include the need, once again, for an economy that works. The economy today is in very, very bad shape: the highest unemployment since the Great Depression— 50 percent higher than when Mr. Ford took office; raging inflation, with the latest wholesale price indexes once again raising the specter of double-digit inflation. The purchasing power of the average American has slipped so much that it is now the equivalent of the purchasing power in 1965. It is not getting better; it is getting worse. All the leading indicators now point downward, and stock investors are now losing confidence, and over 50 billion dollars of value has disappeared from the stock market in less than a month.

We need a government that works, and we need a government that cares. And once again we have to get back to work on education, on health, on housing, on the environment, on energy. And we need a foreign policy that once again reflects the values and the beliefs of the American people.

This will take leadership, and we need leadership too. The Republican administration, the Republican party, has had eight years to solve these problems. All of them have gotten worse. The Republican ticket does not offer new plans for their solution, but is engaged in a frantic effort to defend the past. This nation desperately needs new leadership. The Carter-Mondale ticket would offer a new generation of leadership dedicated to solving the problems which I have listed, and that is the basis of our appeal.

HOGE: Thank you, gentlemen. The subject matter of tonight's debate, like that of the first two presidential debates, covers domestic and economic policies and foreign and defense issues. The questioners tonight are: Hal Bruno, chief political correspondent of *Newsweek* magazine; Marilyn Berger, White House correspondent of NBC News; and Walter Mears, special correspondent for the Associated Press.

Questions will be alternated between the two candidates. After a question is asked, the candidate will have up to two and a half minutes to respond. His opponent will then have two and a half minutes to reply to that. The first candidate then may reply to those remarks for up to one minute. I should mention at this point that I will intervene if a candidate is not addressing the question which has been posed to him. At the conclusion of the questioning, each candidate will be allowed up to three minutes for a closing remark. Senator Mondale and Senator Dole do not have prepared notes or comments with them this evening. However, they may make notes and refer to them during the debate.

We now begin with questions on domestic and economic policies. The first question goes to Senator Dole, as was determined by the coin toss. Mr. Bruno, you have the first question.

BRUNO: Senator Dole, presidential candidates always promise that their vice-president will play an important role, but it seldom turns out that way, and they usually wind up as stand-by equipment, which is the way Vice-President Rockefeller once described the job. What's your view of this office that you're seeking? Has President Ford told you what your role might be? And what would you like it to be?

DOLE: Well, I've said, as I've traveled around the country, and mostly in jest, that as they say "Why are you running for vice-president?" I've said, "Well, it's indoor work and no heavy lifting." But I've also thought very seriously about it. President Ford has discussed it with me. It's a great opportunity. It's a great responsibility. I can't stand here tonight in Houston, Texas, and say that come January, when I'll be sworn in as vice-president, that I'm going to do anything in the first hundred days, or even the second hundred days. But I have discussed it with President Ford. He's indicated two responsibilities that he's going to designate. One will be having some role in increasing our agricultural exports, because we believe—we believe together—that the future of American agriculture lies in its exports.

Also, because of my long association with families who had their sons or husbands as missing-in-action and prisoners of war, he indicated to me last week that I would have a role as his representative to try to get some accounting for the missing-in-action in Southeast Asia.

But beyond that, of course, our constitutional duty is to preside over the Senate and vote in case of a tie. We also serve on the National Security Council, Domestic Council, and whatever other assignments we may have from time to time.

I think probably one important aspect that we ought to talk about, and that's our vision for America. I believe that people viewing tonight, people who are watching us tonight, may well determine the role I play as vice-president. I believe that we're going forward in America under the leadership of President Ford, and I believe there'll be more and more challenges—positive challenges—for those of us who hold high office to serve the American people. And that's really what it's all about, whether we're vice-president, on the city council, a member of the legislature, or whatever. Our obligation is to the people. We must have faith in the American people, and I have that faith—where, I think the opponents have more faith in bigger government, more controls, and more interference with their everyday lives.

HOGE: Senator Mondale, your response.

MONDALE: The problems that our country faces are so great that a very strong role is required of the vice-president, and of all federal officials. I've discussed this matter extensively with Governor Carter, and as vice-president, I would have such a substantial role in both domestic and foreign policy. I would work with the president, for example, in this long overdue effort to basically restructure and reorganize the federal government: today it's a mess; there's no one in charge; there's great waste, great duplication; and the time has come for a long overdue reorganization. That would be one of the first tasks that I would have working with the new president. There would be a whole range of duties that I would have working with the president on problems of economic growth—we've got to get people back to work; attacking inflation; and finally getting a policy to keep the dollar worth a dollar; and the other problems that we face here at home.

One of the specific suggestions that we are considering now is that I would head up a task force to deal with the federal aspects of crime in America. Today the federal function in law enforcement is in disarray. The Drug Enforcement Administration is totally demoralized. The FBI is also under great difficulty. We need to have a coordinated, effective, a national attack on organized and hard crime—those crimes prohibited by federal law. We need to finally get a national effort that really makes sense, that stops the importation of these death-dealing, imported, illegal drugs. We need to have a new look at official lawlessness at the federal level, because we've seen too many instances where people in high public office violate the law themselves. And one of the things that we're considering is establishing an interdepartmental agency under the chairmanship of the vice-president to finally, at long last, put some strength behind a national effort to deal with these terrible problems in American life.

And may I close by saying that one of the reasons that I believe I'm going to be the vice-president is one of the reasons that my opponent mentioned, and that is that the present president imposed an embargo on farm exports four times in three years. And they want a change.

HOGE: Senator Dole, do you have a further comment?

DOLE: Well, I would just say to my good friend: I'm happy that you are going to be responsible for reorganization. I hope you don't pattern it after Governor Carter's efforts in Georgia. They added more bureaucrats to the government in Georgia; the cost of government went up; his human resources committee, or whatever it's called, was called an organizational nightmare by Governor Busbee, his successor.

I understand from Bobby Smith, who's supposed to be the Ag expert in the Carter campaign, that you're going to do away with the Department of Agriculture—that's in essence what he says. You're going to put it together with a lot of other things, and I know the farmers who may be viewing will be pleased to know that. They should also be pleased to know that Senator Mondale sponsors export licensing proposals in the Congress, which would make it necessary for farmers to get an export license before they could ship their goods overseas. And under his proposal, which is still pending—thank goodness, it hasn't passed, or we'd all be in difficulty—you wouldn't be able to ship anything now.

HOGE: Miss Berger, your question to Senator Mondale.

BERGER: Senator Mondale, the polls indicate that less than half of those eligible will vote in this coming election, and although you and Senator Dole have both touched on the very important issues that are before the country, many Americans feel that they're being short-changed by a campaign that has descended into a name-calling contest. For example, Governor Carter has said that President Ford has been brain-washed; President Ford says that Carter is slandering America. If the tone of the campaign worries the electorate, does it worry you, Senator Mondale?

MONDALE: There are many things that I think have contributed to this phenomenon that I find very, very discouraging—and that is, the great numbers of Americans do not plan to participate in the electoral process which is so crucial to a sound and effective nation. We can't solve our problems unless everyone helps.

There have been so many things that have dispirited the American people—that have fed frustration and despair. We've gone through the worst war in American history, that divided this country perhaps as much as it's ever been divided. We then went through the worst political scandal in American history, with the highest officers in government being found guilty or at least charged with guilt in very serious crimes. We then saw evidence that even our own intelligence agencies and law enforcement agencies, charged to enforce the law, had themselves violated the law.

And then we've seen a government that is unable to deal with the real problems that the American people face. People need jobs. It's a tragedy every time an able-bodied American is denied the opportunity to work. There are now 8 million Americans who can't find work. It's a tragedy when Americans work and find the value of their dollar disappearing. It's a tragedy when children can't get educated, when health care wipes them out, when senior citizens find that the attention and the credit that they're entitled to, through Social Security and Medicaid, is being taken from them.

These things have all contributed to a growing feeling in America that government does not respond to solve people's problems, that government lives by one standard and expects Americans to live by another; and because of that we have this large feeling in America, reflected in those surveys that were suggested in your question, that has contributed to this feeling that involvement in politics does not count. And if there's one hope that Governor Carter and I have, if there's one objective that's central above all, is that we can restore the faith in the American people by simply telling the truth, obeying the law, seeing problems as they really are, attacking the real questions, the real problems that affect Americans; and then I think we will see the restoration of public trust.

HOGE: Senator Dole, your response.

DOLE: Well, I think it's a very good question. It goes back to the party institutions. Maybe it's an indictment, in that sense, of those of us who seek office. It goes back to my basic premise, and that's faith in the people. It just seems to me that some of those who lust for power[1] are not really concerned about the people. They say they're concerned about the people, and they talk about the people. They never give us their positions. And so I think many Americans are sort of turned off. And they were turned off by the war in Southeast Asia. They were turned off by Watergate—I'll say that word first—they were turned off by Watergate. But we're looking ahead. They were probably turned off by what they saw in the U.S. House of Representatives. They've been turned off by a lot of things they've seen in politics. But I think they've been turned off, too, by promises and promises, and bigger and bigger spending programs, and more and more inflation. They're looking for leadership, they yearn for leadership, and they've found that leadership in President Ford.

Governor Carter talks about tax reform, talks about taxing the rich, he talks about nearly everyone. He said former President Johnson lied and cheated and distorted the facts. I think that turns a lot of people off. He was quick to apologize to Mrs. Johnson. He insulted Governor Wallace, but he was quick to apologize to Governor Wallace. Someone in the family insulted Billy Graham, but they were quick to apologize to Billy Graham.

I think it's time we stop apologizing and talk—it's time we started talking to you, the American people. We need your help. We want to restore faith in this system, and I think we can. Let's not promise what we can't deliver. Let's be honest with you, the voter; with you, the taxpayer. It's fine to talk about education, more this, more that, and more that. But there are 88 million people working in America that are going to pay the taxes, the highest number ever working in America. Some 40 percent of the population, the highest in history, are working now in America. And we're concerned about the 7.8 percent unemployed. We'll be concerned until that's reduced to 4 percent or 3 percent or wherever. But we can't lose sight of the number-one enemy, and that number-one enemy is inflation. And I think the American people are coming around. They're beginning to understand that President Ford says what he means and does what he says.

HOGE: Senator Mondale.

MONDALE: Well, who really has faith in the people? A candidate like Governor Carter who campaigns for the people, is out every day meeting and talking with the people, holds news conferences and answers questions of the news media, as he has every day for twenty-four months? Or a president who is in the White House not through election but through appointment, who has held only two pre-announced news conferences since February? Who trusts the people more? Governor Carter and Senator Mondale, who have disclosed our income tax returns so the American people can look at our private financial affairs and determine how we've conducted our affairs? Or President Ford and Senator Dole, who refuse to let the American people see their tax returns? Who trusts the people? A candidate like Governor Carter who tells the truth? Or a president like Mr. Ford who last week told the American people that he had fought the Arab boycott and sought legislation and sanctions against it, when the whole record shows he's proceeded in just the opposite direction?

HOGE: Thank you. Mr. Mears, your question for Senator Dole.

MEARS: Senator Dole, prior to your current campaign you sometimes expressed concern about a negative image of the Republican party. You're quoted as having said last spring that "we're in the unfortunate position of having a president vetoing bills and getting on the wrong side of people issues. He's vetoed the education bill, the jobs bill—you name it." Are you still concerned about the risk that Republicans will be perceived as opposed to what you call "people issues"? And do you think that President Ford has exercised the veto too frequently?

DOLE: Well, I might say at the outset, I haven't always agreed with President Ford and I've voted to override on occasions, but not every time as my counterpart has. I think President Ford— and hindsight's very good, particularly when you're on the ticket—and my hindsight is that the president's been very courageous. And there is a difference: you know, we look at our states, and we look at the bills, and we decide to sustain or override. The president—and particularly this president, who has the courage—President Ford looks at the nation. He looks at all the American people, and he makes that judgment: should I sign, can I sign, or must I veto this bill? And so he's vetoed sixty-two bills. I think the sixty-second happened today. And I say that's a courageous act repeated sixty-two times, because much of that legislation sounded good; some of it was good; but some of it we just couldn't have unless we're going to fuel the fires of inflation.

I don't suggest that every veto I must agree with. But I also suggest that I'm a Republican. I'm proud to be a Republican. We're sometimes perceived, as I've said before, as the anti-people party because we're not for more spending, we're not for more government. We're for a strong defense. We're for peace in the world.

Those aren't very attractive to some people. They want to know how much we're going to spend for this, and how much we're going to spend for that. Well, Senator Mondale could tell them that, because he votes for every piece of spending legislation that comes down the pike—unless it's in the area of defense, and then he votes for every budget cut. I think he's voted to cut the budget, in addition to what it had already been cut in the Congress, some 16 billion dollars: against the B1 bomber, which means a lot of jobs; against the C5A; against the Trident submarine; and the list goes on and on and on and on.

I believe the American people want us to be responsible. We've got to make the tough decisions. It's one thing to be in the office of the president or senator of the United States and vote for every spending program, never concern ourselves with inflation or the total cost. But I would only close by saying that I hope the viewers remember: we have a Democratic Congress; we've had one for twenty-two straight years. And so when anyone stands up to debate this Republican senator and tries to dump all the responsibility on a Republican president by the name of Gerald Ford, I just ask that question: Where have you been for twenty-two years?

Hoge: Senator Mondale, your response.

Mondale: Perhaps the most pronounced difference that separates the Democratic and the Republican candidates is reflected in the question that was just asked. There is practically no difference between the two parties in terms of how much they would spend. The Senate Budget Committee estimated that the Republican platform cost 50 billion dollars; the Democratic platform cost 40 billion dollars. The difference between the Democratic congressional budget, which I supported, and the president's budget was only 3 billion dollars in deficit; and if you remove the gimmickry in the president's budget, it was exactly the same.

The difference is in how we spend those resources, and I am unashamed of my support for programs to put people back to work. I am unashamed of my support for programs to build housing, so the families of this country can live in decent housing. I am unashamed of supporting education programs that give our kids a decent education. I am unashamed of supporting health programs that give people who get ill a chance to have decent health without being totally wiped out. And I am unashamed of supporting programs such as Medicare. My opponent voted against Medicare. Can you imagine voting against [a] program, as did the president, that would provide help for senior citizens after they're past their earning years, so that they could have decent health care without being wiped out? Now, where do the Republicans want to spend their money? Well, I'll tell you. First of all, this year they're spending 55 billion dollars in the cost of the recession that they created. We didn't give them this recession. We had full employment when they took over. Mr. Ford, in just two years, has increased unemployment by two and a half million Americans. They haven't solved inflation. And instead of trying to deal with the problem of unemployment—instead of that, they propose a 20-billion-dollar tax cut for wealthy corporations, despite the fact that just yesterday a newspaper carried a story that ten major corporations made massive amounts of money and didn't owe a dime in federal taxes. Ford Motor Corporation earned 800 million dollars and didn't owe a dime to the federal government—in fact, got 180 million dollars back. So between those tax cuts, and between the massive costs of unemployment, they spend much more than we would. But what do they get for it? We want to see money spent to help problems that people really face in their lives.

HOGE: Senator Dole.

DOLE: Well, we're all for those programs, Fritz; we just won't believe in excesses. I think, in retrospect, the elder care program that I voted for instead of Medicare was probably a better program, because Medicare—everybody gets the benefits, whether you're in need or not, once you reach age sixty-five. Now, they're having a lot of problems with Medicare.

I'm glad you mentioned Ford Motor Company not paying taxes. Again, the Democrats control the committee; I'm on the committee; Senator Mondale is on the Finance Committee. Henry Ford happens to be supporting Governor Carter. Maybe that's why. Governor Carter did have a little meeting with him at the 21 Club, met some small businessmen there, said, "Don't worry about taxes, I won't do anything for at least a year." That's after he said the tax system was a disgrace.

We have peace in this country today. That's important to me, important to mothers who may be listening. They talk about their full employment when we took over; that's because they had a full-grown war going in Southeast Asia. That's not the way we try to end unemployment in the Republican party.

HOGE: Mr. Bruno, your question to Senator Mondale.

BRUNO: Senator Mondale, everyone seems to agree that solving the economic problems of inflation and unemployment has to be given top priority. You and Governor Carter have a whole shopping list of things that you want to do. After the economic problem, what do you see as the next most urgent and crucial domestic problems? In what order of importance would you go to work on such problems as the decay and bankruptcy of the cities, tax reform, health insurance, help for the poor and the elderly? In short, after the economy, what would be the very specific priorities of a Carter administration?

MONDALE: You have to work on several problems at once, because they all demand the attention of the American people. One of the key problems would be to try to finally get a health insurance program to deal with the health crisis in America. In just the past two years, health costs in America have risen in the cities by over 25 percent. We have to do something about that. There's no hope under the Republican administration. Mr. Ford said he would veto any legislation if we sent it.

We have to do something about housing. We're in a housing depression. Today, nearly 20 percent of the building tradesmen in America are unemployed. We need to put them back to work to build housing that Americans need. We need to continue to build support, as the budget permits, for education. We need to get back to work on the problems of senior citizens.

Now, all of this has to be done prudently, within a budget, and within the constraints that our resources permit. But once we put people back to work, once we end this recession, which we will do, even the president's own estimates indicates that we will have somewhere between 60 and 70 billion dollars of increased revenues on existing tax rates just from economic growth, which we can use to work on these program[s]. Then we'll have tax reform, and I want to deal with this problem just a moment.

Mr. Dole has probably the worst record in favor of loopholes of any senator in the United States Senate. Mr. Ford has one of the worst records in favor of tax loopholes in the history of the House of Representatives. I have one of the best records of tax reform in the United States Senate. And I find it very peculiar to find two people who spent their congressional careers trying to block tax reform, that permits very wealthy Americans to avoid most of their taxes, to suddenly complain when the Congress hadn't passed the kind of legislation that we're talking about. What we're basically talking about is presidential leadership. We need leadership in the presidency to help support those of us in the Congress that have been pushing for tax reform. And then we will have it. It is now possible for people of great wealth, by using complete tax fictions, to avoid all or most their taxes. But most Americans listening to me tonight could hire the best tax lawyer in America and you couldn't save a dime. There are no loopholes for you.

HOGE: Senator Dole, your response.

DOLE: Well, I think Senator Mondale is a little nervous. But every time I think of loophole, I think of Governor Carter. I don't know why it comes to me, but I remember his '75 tax return—you've probably seen it, since it's public. His tax liability was 58,000 dollars. Not many Americans—I don't imagine many of you in the viewing audience had to worry about a 58,000-dollar tax bill. I didn't. But Governor Carter did, until he took off 41,000 dollars. That's called the investment tax credit. He bought some peanut machinery—going to use it next year. So he took 41,000 dollars off his tax and sent the government a check for 17,000 dollars. So how much did he pay on his income? Well, he paid about 12.8 percent. This is that same man, the same Governor Carter who runs around the country talking about tax reform, loopholes, and the rich.

I don't know who rates Senator Mondale on the Finance Committee. I don't know how they rated him on the Honeywell Amendment he offered, and the IDS Amendment he offered.[2] They never passed. They never got out of the Senate. They're both special interests amendments. That's all right, because those were his amendments. I don't know where Governor Carter's corporate returns are, and partnership returns—I haven't seen those published anywhere. But I know about his tax reform.

But I want to get back to the question, if that's all right. We're talking about the economy. What are we going to do after the economy is taken care of? Well, I don't know. It's occurred to me, and I'm certain it hasn't occurred to my counterpart, that we might—it's not illegal—to take some of that surplus and apply it to the national debt. We've never done it, but we wouldn't be put in jail if Congress voted to try to retire some of that debt, to take some of the pressure off the American working man, and the American working woman.

I get a little tired of Governor Carter's anti-business attitude. I know they get great support, monetary support from George Meany. In fact, I've been suggesting that George Meany was probably Senator Mondale's makeup man. He may or may not have been. They did a good job. But I think it's time the American people understand that this is a very serious election. And we've got a tough choice to make. Governor Carter talks about raising everyone's taxes above the median income. He didn't know what the median income was, of course. It's 14,000 dollars per American family. That's what it is. So I'd say, take a look, and you'll vote for Ford.

HOGE: Senator Mondale.

MONDALE: The question was, what would we do to deal with the human problems in America? The first thing we would do is to put people back to work. The most atrocious result of the Republican policy is massive unemployment. It cost us 50 billion dollars this year. Secondly, we will fight inflation. Today, inflation is three times worse than it was under the Democrats. And the latest indexes indicate that it's back on its way up. No effort to fight this at all.

We will have tax reform. There's no question about our commitment to tax reform; my record proves it; Governor Carter's positions prove that; we are fully committed to tax reform. And when the Republicans are raising money around the country, they say, "Give us some money to defeat Governor Carter because if he gets elected there'll be tax reform." And they are right when they say that, because we'll have tax reform and bring relief to the average income earner in this country. They know what Governor Carter is talking about. He's talking about the loopholes that favor Americans usually earning above 50,000 dollars a year.

HOGE: Thank you, Senator Mondale. We now turn to questions on foreign and defense issues. Miss Berger, you have the first question in the subject area, and it is for Senator Dole.

BERGER: Senator Dole, President Ford said in an interview this week that if he's elected he would like to see Henry Kissinger stay on as secretary of state. This hardly seems to square with the Republican platform, which appears to repudiate much of Kissinger's foreign policy. Which way do you go, Senator Dole: with President Ford or with the Republican platform?

DOLE: I go with both, and stay with Henry. You know, if we look back over history, President Washington had Thomas Jefferson for his secretary of state, Harry Truman had Dean Acheson for his secretary of state—both very strong men, both very active men, both very powerful men. Henry Kissinger's a powerful man. And I haven't always agreed with Henry Kissinger. But when I start disagreeing with Henry, I start looking at what he's done for America—about what he's done for the free world: I think about the breakthrough in China; I think about our increased responsive relations with the Soviet Union; I think about winding down the war that we inherited from another Democrat administration in Southeast Asia; I think most recently about his efforts in South Africa, where he's trying to protect the rights of the majority and the rights of the minority.

We sort of thought that Henry might have had a role to play in grain embargoes, so we weren't totally happy at that time.[3] We're not happy with embargoes—there'll not be any more embargoes, except in extreme circumstances, under a Ford-Dole administration. So I agree with the president. Secretary Kissinger has performed yeoman service. Anywhere you look you find Henry's tracks, and they're tracks that are right for America; they're tracks that are right for the free world.

And I wonder how many mothers, and how many fathers, and how many young men and young women who may be viewing tonight have really stopped to think about what this Republican administration has done. No one's being drafted, no one's going off to war, no one's being shot at, no one's being hospitalized, no one's being buried in America, not a single shot being fired in anger. And this is a Republican administration, this is a Republican policy, and this policy by and large has been spearheaded by one Henry Kissinger. And we can have our differences. And I looked at the platform; I was on the platform committee; I don't see any contradiction in that platform. I've read the morality section; I think it sustains President Ford and sustains Secretary Kissinger.

HOGE: Senator Mondale, your response.

MONDALE: The real question of the foreign policy of the next administration is the responsibility of the president of the United States. He is the person elected to discharge the responsibility of foreign policy. He is the person that must conduct it and lead this nation's efforts. And that's where, I think, the key difference between the two parties lie. We want a change; we want new leadership; and above all, we want a change of philosophy and direction. America's greatest strength is to be found in its values and its beliefs. And every time in our pursuit of foreign policy that we disregard those basic values of freedom, of democracy, of national independence, we pursue a policy that is not credible, is not sustainable, either overseas or at home. And let me say what I mean.

For example, in Africa: for seven and a half years it was the policy of this administration to support the colonial control of black Africa, and support white minority rule in majority black states. That was our explicit policy. And after that failed, and on the eve of this election, suddenly we've turned around and wanted to be believed as we pursued the policy that we should have pursued in the first place. Failure to follow our beliefs in the first instance is causing us great trouble in Africa.

Look at Greece. During the whole period that the military junta controlled Greek government, this administration cozied up to that military dictatorship, befriended them, did everything they could to support them. But once Greeks restored their own democracy, we've turned our back on them and have not assisted them in seeking a just and final settlement on the island of Cyprus.

Take the issue of the Middle East. This government of ours is pursuing a policy of permitting the vicious Arab boycott to continue in this country. They have not sought any reform. They are pursuing an arms-peddling policy in this world, in which we sell more arms by double of all the rest of the world put together. And last year alone or this year, we're selling and contracting for seven and a half billion dollars of arms for Saudi Arabia and only a billion four for Israel. We've lost our way, we need a new sense of values, and we intend to restore them.

HOGE: Senator Dole.

DOLE: Well, I noticed in all that discussion you never once criticized Secretary Kissinger. I don't recall Senator Mondale ever criticizing Secretary Kissinger.

As I think back, the Democrat policies, and their secret agreements at Yalta and Potsdam, and how this had the effect of enslaving Eastern Europe, and as I think of the leadership of President Roosevelt—and I think about that every day, because of a personal experience in World War II—I'm kind of thankful we have somebody who's concerned about peace. And whether Senator Mondale likes it or not, or whether Governor Carter likes it or not, and Governor Carter won't tell us who he's going to put in the cabinet—he probably doesn't know—I think it's kind of nice to be at peace in the world, to be respected in the world. We've had more respect than we've ever had. Prime Minister Rabin said our relations with Israel are at a peak, the highest they've been. The same is true of France and West Germany. We have a balanced peace in the Mideast because of our leadership.

HOGE: Mr. Mears, your question to Senator Mondale.

MEARS: Senator Mondale, you and Governor Carter have made an issue of President Ford's statement that there is no Soviet domination of Eastern Europe, a statement the president now says was in error.[4] I'd like to know whether there's any real difference between the two tickets on Eastern Europe, or whether this is simply an effort by the Democrats to attract voters of Eastern European backgrounds. What would a Democratic administration do that the Republicans are not doing to foster freedom in Eastern Europe? And what would a new administration do on the question that the president declined to answer yesterday: if an Eastern European nation attempted to overthrow Soviet domination, should the United States help?

MONDALE: Well, there are several things that we would do. The first thing we would do is to make clear, consistently, what the facts are in Eastern Europe. The comment that the president made, that Eastern Europe was independent and autonomous from Soviet control, is probably one of the most outrageous statements made by a president in recent political history. It's caused great confusion in Europe. Communist newspapers in Poland are praising the president because the statement helped give credibility to Soviet control. I'm glad the president finally apologized for that remark, but it's surprising that it took six days and several attempts before we finally received that apology.

What we think is needed in our policies with Eastern Europe, is not to deal with Eastern Europe as a bloc, as does this administration, but to deal with each country individually, on its own status directly, and not through the Soviet Union; to continue to identify with their aspirations for national independence, not because we are under any illusions about how easy it would be for them to become independent, but because it's important for us to identify—as the nation which above all stands for freedom and independence—with the aspirations of all people around the world for those same objectives.

Secondly, we would push that part of the Helsinki Accords known as Basket Three, which requires much opening up—

much more opening up—in people-to-people contacts, in informational contacts. This administration signed the Helsinki Accords, but has done practically nothing to push those agreements which would open up communications between our nation and our peoples and the peoples of Eastern Europe and the Soviet Union. As a matter of fact, it was just the other day, after several week's delay, before they even finally appointed representatives of the administration to the commission looking into the enforcement of that provision.

And finally, I think it's important that we honor people from Eastern Europe who stand as symbols of the human spirit's ability to stand up to police oppression. And I will never understand why this president of the United States refused to even receive and honor Mr. Solzhenitsyn who, perhaps above all people in the human race, stands as a symbol for the ability and the strength of spirit against police oppression.

HOGE: Senator Dole, your response.

DOLE: Well, I'm glad you mentioned Solzhenitsyn. I checked today with his interpreter, and I understand you've never met Mr. Solzhenitsyn and neither has Mr. Carter. Now, I've had the privilege of meeting Mr. Solzhenitsyn. Maybe you shook his hand somewhere.

But I want to move into the Eastern Europe sector. I'm reminded of how the Berlin Wall went up and who was in power when it went up. I think if we take a hard look at President Ford's record, rather than all the rhetoric that followed a mistake in the last debate about Poland, we'd know very clearly where President Ford not only stands but has stood for twenty-some years.

I think one way to let the people in Eastern Europe know of our concern is by trade. As President Ford said, they've never really given up hope. Their government may be dominated, their leaders of that government may be dominated by Soviet Russia, but the hearts and the minds of the Polish people or the Yugoslavs or the Rumanians or the Czechs or whoever have never been dominated. And they're good customers. You know, we have a favorable balance of trade with Eastern Europe. I think last year they exported almost a half billion dollars worth of goods and material, and we sent in about a billion dollars worth.

I just wish Governor Carter had a foreign policy. He doesn't have any; doesn't have any experience. He made some statement about Italy that bothers me because I was in World War II in Italy. My whole life changed because of my experience in Italy. I know the Italian people. I know they're God-fearing, freedom-loving people.

I couldn't quite understand what Governor Carter meant in *Playboy* magazine—I couldn't understand, frankly, why he was in *Playboy* magazine. But he was, and we'll give him the bunny vote. But I couldn't understand what he meant when he said that we ought to extend a hand of friendship to the Communists in Portugal and the governments of France and Italy, because by doing that, he simply invites difficulty from Communist leaders in those countries.[5] So I say, oh we're strong, we're firm, President Ford understands. We're still at peace. We still have those same hopes and aspirations of the Eastern Europeans. And that's what it's all about: freedom, peace, no bloodshed.

HOGE: Senator Mondale.

MONDALE: Well, I regret that Mr. Dole made that statement about Mr. Solzhenitsyn, because it's false. I have repeatedly spoken out in admiration of him. I served on the host committee receiving Mr. Solzhenitsyn in the United States Senate. He's a man that deserved to be honored, and it was a shame to me that the president of the United States, because we are fearful of offending the Soviet Union, failed to accord that high honor to Mr. Solzhenitsyn.

I'm also sorry that he's tried to misrepresent Governor Carter's position on the government that should control Portugal and Italy. The governor made it very clear that he hoped the non-Communists would continue to control those countries.

The biggest thing that we're doing today that is undermining those forces of democracy is the disarray of our economy here at home. With our tremendous unemployment, with our tremendous inflation, and the dominance of our economy on the economies of Western Europe, of Japan, and Canada, we have contributed to such conditions that it has strengthened the radical forces in those countries, and that's what we need to do to best help the democratic forces of those nations.

HOGE: Thank you, Senators. We have reserved time this evening for questions on general subjects. The first question in this area is from Mr. Bruno, and it is for Senator Dole.

BRUNO: Senator Dole, out there on the campaign trail you've been saying that a Carter-Mondale administration would take its orders from George Meany and the AFL-CIO. Yet Mr. Meany was among those who influenced President Ford on the grain embargo which you personally opposed. Now, how do you know that Mr. Meany will influence Governor Carter any more than he already has influenced President Ford, and what, if anything, is wrong with labor or business or farmers making their views known in the White House, as long as it's done openly and honestly?

DOLE: Oh, I don't have any quarrel, first of all, with anybody making their views known. I wish more businessmen would participate in active politics. In fact, I've held up labor as an example for others to follow, because they are very active. I just don't believe that labor leaders, whether it's Leonard Woodcock or George Meany or Jerry Wurf,[6] whoever, ought to make a decision for thousands and millions of working men and women who are concerned about spending. They're concerned about taxes; they're concerned about the gun control that Mondale and Carter favor; they're concerned about abortion; they're concerned about a lot of things. And their labor leader makes the decision that we're going to support the Carter-Mondale ticket.

Now, George Meany did exercise some influence on the first embargo. I don't know how much, because I wasn't privy to those meetings. He said he did it in the name of the consumer. Well, he really did it in the name of organized labor—to increase the shipping subsidy at the taxpayers' expense. Working with Mr. Gleason and the Longshoremen's Union, they refused to load the ships. And it really put the president in a very difficult spot. As I think back of all the Democrat senators who are now talking about embargoes, I can only recall one who spoke out at the time. That was Senator George McGovern. He had no allegiance and owed nothing to Mr. Meany because, as you know, Meany didn't support him in 1972. But all of a sudden the embargoes have cropped up as a great big issue.

I know how much strength labor leaders have. I know how much they're out there pushing voter registration. I know how much control they have in the Democratic party, and that's their right to have influence, but not to take over the party. They have great influence on Senator Mondale—always have had. He's got a 95 percent labor rating, or higher—the most liberal senator in the United States Senate, and that's his right. He wants to be liberal and spend your money, and tax and tax, and spend and spend—that's his right. First he was appointed as attorney general, and then appointed to the Senate.[7] Some of us had to run for what we have. But when you have things given to you, you like to give something else to someone else. You give away your tax money back to the taxpayers. And I just think that George Meany has every right to have influence, but not domination of a great party like the Democratic party.

HOGE: Senator Mondale.

MONDALE: Well, there are many things that could be said about that. I might begin first with voting records. There are many organizations that prepare voting records. I am pleased to have a very high rating in small business groups, among farmer groups—a much higher rating than my opponent, the senator from Kansas. Good ratings, high ratings, in housing and health and education, good ratings from organizations dealing with economic management. And I'm pleased by that. But perhaps one that's most appropriate tonight is an independent, dispassionate organization that represents the views of all Americans—conservative, liberal, moderate, and so on—called the League of Women Voters.

For five years, the League has prepared the list of the most crucial issues that they believe affects governmental effectiveness, that affects governmental honesty, that affects dealing with America's real problems. And I'm proud of the fact that in each of those five years the League of Women Voters has rated me 100 percent in favor of every one of those issues that they, on an independent and a bipartisan basis, have believed to be the most important to this country. And I note in that same record that my opponent was wrong half the time. He only was there 50 percent of the time, and I noted that the president of the United States, Mr. Ford, when he was in the Congress, was right only 35 percent of the time. And I think that says something about balance. We are in the mainstream of public life. We want to get along with business. We want to get along with farmers. We want to get along with labor. We think a president has to lead everyone. And that's the only way that a president can lead.

This president and his running mate think they can get elected by whipping labor on the back. Well, labor's got a right to participate in the public life of this country, as well as anyone else. Just take the embargo, for example. I was opposed, and said so at the time, of all the embargoes: the four imposed by the Republicans and the short one imposed by members of the labor movement. I thought it was wrong in both instances. This particular ticket here selects out Mr. Meany as the scapegoat. Well, you can't run this country trying to scapegoat Americans. You have to bring everybody together and have a united country, working together to solve our real problems. And that's another reason why we need Governor Carter.

HOGE: Senator Dole, any further response?

DOLE: Well, I would say as far as the League of Women Voters are concerned, you can look at that two ways: either I was wrong half the time or they were wrong half the time. And, I think, knowing the League of Women Voters, I think I'll take my interpretation. But with reference to—because they're very fine, but they tend to be a little bit liberal.

Now, George Meany: he wants the right-to-work law repealed in Texas and my state. Senator Mondale is for the repeal of the right-to-work laws; he wants to force you to join a labor union. Seventy-five percent of America's working men and women don't belong to labor unions, but they will if George

Meany and Governor Carter and Senator Mondale have their way.

They've also got some big Proposition 14 out in California, where organizers come on your property three hours a day and organize farmers, unionize farmers. Governor Carter's for that; I assume Senator Mondale is for that; certainly, Cesar Chavez is, and other labor leaders. I just say they ought to have influence; they shouldn't have domination.

What about your national security voting record where you get a zero every year? You talk about our defense.

HOGE: Thank you. Miss Berger, your question to Senator Mondale.

BERGER: Senator Mondale, you've criticized Mr. Ford for having defended Richard Nixon—that is, while Mr. Ford was vice-president. And you did see in your own political career that Hubert Humphrey suffered a great deal politically by standing with Lyndon Johnson almost to the end on Vietnam. And now you've acknowledged that you have differences with Governor Carter. You've said that an important mark of national leadership is the ability to put loyalty to principle above loyalty to party or even to the president of the United States. If push came to shove, would you put principle above loyalty to your running mate and possibly to the president of the United States? And what issues are important enough to do that?

MONDALE: The answer is, yes, I would. But I would not have accepted a place as the running mate of Governor Carter if I thought that was a real possibility. We had a long talk about the problem of independence between the two—the president and the vice-president. And I made it clear to him that I was not interested in serving in a role that was ceremonial, or serving in a role where if I really felt deeply about something, I was prevented from saying so. I did not want to go through that. I did not want to give up my position in the Senate where I have that right. We agreed that that would be the relationship. And during this campaign, on three separate occasions where I have disagreed with Mr. Carter, I've said so in the course of this campaign. And I think the whole issue of public trust and public faith is bound up very closely with that question.

We have had so much politics as usual, so much political trimming, that Americans have lost faith in public leadership. For example, in Watergate: when this nation's whole system of liberty was at stake, and the Ervin Committee was established to investigate wrongdoing by the president of the United States, my opponent introduced a resolution to slam the door shut on the Ervin Committee[8] so the people could not see and hear what was going on.

In the night of the Saturday Night Massacre,[9] perhaps the most treacherous moment in the history of American liberty, when the high officers, Richardson and Ruckelshaus, were fired for enforcing the law, fired by the president of the United States, both Mr. Ford and Mr. Dole stood up and defended Mr. Nixon. And if Mr. Nixon had gotten away with that massacre that night, he would probably still be president of the United States, and we would not have taught that crucial lesson that not even the highest officials in government can violate the law.

Never again can we permit that kind of politics-above-all to dominate this country. Even today, this administration is fighting all the Watergate reforms, opposed the appointment of a special prosecutor, opposed the reforms that were cried out for adoption following the revelations of the abuse of the CIA and the FBI. And with a record like that, and with all of the abuse of public faith and trust that we've been through, surely that, too, is another reason for a new generation of leadership.

HOGE: Senator Dole.

DOLE: Well, Watergate is a Republican problem, and I voted for the Watergate investigation. My opponent was absent. We're all absent sometimes, but he's absent more than others.

I think, also, it's well to point up that I did introduce a resolution to shut off the public hearings and to get down to business and get Watergate behind us. Democrats didn't want to do that. They were having great fun on TV every day. It looked for a while they didn't want to find a solution. But I remember

Senator Ervin's report, the chairman of the Watergate Committee, and he said in that report—and I was chairman of the Republican party during the Watergate years and I'm very proud to have been chairman—I've always said that the night Watergate happened was my night off, so you can't hook me for that. But Senator Ervin said, "Had Senator Dole been in charge, there wouldn't have been a Watergate."

So I don't want any rub off from Senator Mondale's statements to want any of you people to believe that he might be suggesting that somehow President Ford or Senator Dole was any way involved in Watergate. We were not. He brings it up all the time. He brings up the pardon all the time. He doesn't bring up the fact that we tried to extend the investigation of Watergate back into other areas, that they were voted down along straight party lines. That's their right. They control the Senate.

He doesn't bring up the fact that when the problem's in the House Democrats this year, the Speaker appointed three Democrats to investigate the Democrats. Can you imagine the hue and cry in America had the Republicans done that? Why, Mondale would have dropped dead. And that's the way it's been. That's the way it's been. But Watergate's our burden. We're going forward. It's behind us. And Governor Carter can talk about it, and Senator Mondale can talk about it.

But beyond that, I think we must say, as Senator Mondale has—and I don't quarrel with him—that if there comes a time when I'm the vice-president, I can't agree with the president, then I must say so. I think that's fundamental. I think we're both honorable men. I think we'd both make that judgment. The only mystery to me is how do you know what Governor Carter stands for. I've been trying to find out for six weeks. He has three positions on everything. That's why they're having three TV debates. So, I just suggest that maybe in the time remaining, Senator Mondale can tell us what his running mate stands for. The American people would like to know.

HOGE: Senator Mondale.

MONDALE: My candidate stands for jobs for all Americans. He stands for a government that fights inflation. He stands for tax reform, and to take those revenues and reduce taxes for the average American. He stands for a program at long last to solve the health crisis in America. He stands for at long last to get the housing industry back on its feet. He will support programs to give senior citizens a decent break. He will not try, as Mr. Ford did, to put a cap on Social Security so senior citizens were robbed of their inflationary adjustments. He will not destroy the housing programs for senior citizens as this Republican administration has done. Governor Carter stands for leadership. He's going to take charge. We need someone to lead this country. We haven't had it. Governor Carter will provide that leadership. And Governor Carter will restore to this nation a foreign policy that operates in the public and on the basis of the beliefs of the American people.

HOGE: Gentlemen, we have about five minutes left for short questions and short answers. Each sequence from now on will consist only of the question, the answer, and the other candidate's response. We'll drop the further response. The first question is from Mr. Mears to Senator Dole.

MEARS: Senator Dole, ten days ago when Senator Mondale raised the issues of Watergate and the Nixon pardon, you called it the start of the campaign mudslinging. Two years ago, when you were running for the Senate, you said that the pardon was prematurely granted and that it was a mistake. You were quoted by the *Kansas City Times* as saying, "you can't ignore our tradition of equal application of the law." Did you approve of the Nixon pardon when President Ford granted it? Do you approve of it now? And if the issue was fair game in your 1974 campaign in Kansas, why is it not an appropriate topic now?

DOLE: It is an appropriate topic, I guess. But it's not a very good issue, any more than the war in Vietnam would be, or World War II, or World War I, or the war in Korea—all Democrat wars, all in this century. I figured up the other day: if we added up the killed and wounded in Democrat wars in this century, it'd be about 1.6 million Americans, enough to fill the city of Detroit. Now, if we want to go back and rake that over and over and over, we can do that. I assume Senator Mondale doesn't want to do that. But it seems to me that the pardon of Richard Nixon is behind us. Watergate's behind us. If we have this vision for America, and if we're really concerned about those people out there and their problems—yes and their education and their jobs—we ought to be talking about that.

Now, I know it strikes a responsive chord for some to kick Richard Nixon around. I don't know how long you can keep that up. How much mileage is there in someone who's been kicked, whose wife suffered a serious stroke, who's been disgraced in office and stepped down from that office? And I think, after two years and some months, that it's probably a dead issue. But let them play that game. That's the only game they know.

HOGE: Senator Mondale.

MONDALE: I think Senator Dole has richly earned his reputation as a hatchet man tonight, by implying and stating that World War II and the Korean War were Democratic wars. Does he really mean to suggest to the American people that there was a partisan difference over our involvement in the war to fight Nazi Germany? I don't think any reasonable American would accept that. Does he really mean to suggest that it was only partisanship that got us into the war in Korea? Does he really mean to forget that part of the record where Mr. Nixon and the Republican party wanted us to get involved earlier in the war in Vietnam? And long after Mr. Nixon and the Republican party promised to finish the war in Vietnam, they kept urging us forward, and that in fact it was the Democratic Congress that passed the law ending the war in Vietnam and preventing a new war in Angola.

Now on Watergate: we're not charging, and he knows it, his involvement in Watergate. What we're saying is that they defended Mr. Nixon up to the last.

HOGE: Mr. Bruno, your question to Senator Mondale.

BRUNO: Senator Mondale, you cited the priorities of a Carter administration. At the same time, Governor Carter has promised to balance the federal budget within four years. Now, can we take just one of those items that you gave very high priority to that would be very costly: national health insurance.

Now, realistically, what are the chances of getting this program in a Carter-Mondale administration, or would it have to be postponed until the budget is balanced? Which comes first?

MONDALE: Well, I think both the presidential budget and our estimates agree that if we move back to full employment, as we intend to do, and achieve a 5½ percent real growth rate, as we did under Truman and as we did under Kennedy and Johnson, that within four years the revenues generated by that growth, without increasing taxes, will pay for the costs of the programs now in place, such as Social Security, pensions, and the rest— the ongoing programs that are essential in America, the defense program and the rest—and that we will have a full employment yield of somewhere between 70 and 80 billions of dollars.

Some of that can be used for tax relief, and it should be. Some of it should be, however, used for programs that at long last start dealing with the real problems that America faces, such as health care. Now, there are many different versions of health care. But we would work closely with Senator Kennedy, with Paul Rogers, and others, to develop a health program. Now, there's no question about the difference in spending. The Republicans would spend more than we do during that same period. But they would spend it, first, by 20 billion dollars in tax relief for wealthy businessmen, or wealthy corporations, and secondly, by the continuation of these economic policies that are costing us over 50 billion dollars a year. So the question is not spending. The question is the priorities.

HOGE: Senator Dole.

DOLE: Well, I would remind those who may be still tuned in that the Democrats still control the Congress. They did when we started this debate an hour and twenty minutes ago. They still do, by two-to-one margins almost. And they're responsible for legislation. I know Senator Long, who's chairman of our Finance Committee, would be very pleased to learn what Senator Mondale is going to do now with Governor Carter. Now, if they're talking about full employment, they're talking about the Humphrey-Hawkins bill, which they support. We don't know what it costs—20 billion dollars, 40 billion dollars, or more? Another government employment program. I'd like to add up the number of jobs Senator Mondale has cost this country in defense plants, defense jobs, in all his anti-defense votes. It would be hundreds and hundreds of thousands, and he knows it. He wants bigger welfare programs, bigger giveaway programs. We want to take care of those out of work. We want to take care of those in need. Let's not wreck our business system, let's not wreck our free enterprise system, just to prove a point.

HOGE: Thank you, Senators. That concludes the questioning for this evening. Each candidate now has up to three minutes for a closing statement. By the coin toss, it was determined that Senator Dole would make the first opening statement and take the first question. He now also goes first with his closing statement. Senator Dole.

DOLE: Well, first I wish to thank the panel for their indulgence and, of course, all those in the viewing audience who may still be with us.

I really hope—and I hadn't prepared any final statement in advance—I really hope you were listening and we were able to tell you who's concerned about the American people, which party has faith in the American people, which party and which candidates want bigger and bigger and bigger government, which candidates want more and more spending, more and more interference.

We added up five of the programs that Governor Carter and Mondale talk about—only five. They really want sixty-some new programs in their platform, or expanded programs. They want to create twenty-two new agencies or expand that many existing agencies. We only added up five programs, and the cost was 103 billion dollars—103 billion. That would cost every taxpayer in America several hundred dollars.

They don't care about inflation, the cruelest tax of all. And if you're in your living room watching tonight, and you're making 6,000 dollars a year on fixed income and there's a 6-percent inflation, that's 360 dollars a year; that's 30 dollars a month. That affects everybody in America. And add up your inflation if you let Carter and Mondale have their way. One spending program after another.

We're concerned about the poor. We're concerned about the sick. We're concerned about the disabled. We're concerned about those on Social Security. And we have programs for that. We're concerned about housing. Carla Hills announced one today to reduce the interest payments from 8½ to 8 percent for FHA and VA[10] homes. Governor Carter wants to preclude you from taking off your interest, your mortgage interest, as a tax deduction. He says nobody wants their taxes lowered. Well maybe not, if they were getting a 41,000-dollar tax credit, as he is.

I just say in my final minute: it's a great honor and a privilege to even be standing here. Whatever happens November 2nd, it's an honor and a privilege. It's an honor and a privilege to have known President Ford for sixteen years—sixteen years, as I said at the outset. He's a man of unparalleled decency and honesty and courage. He's a man we can be proud of. He's going to give us that leadership that America needs—all Americans, white, black, Spanish-speaking, rich, poor.

Don't be fooled by the words. Don't be fooled by the rhetoric. Don't be fooled by the promises, because somebody has to pay for those promises. Just take a look at the leadership. Take a look at President Ford, and thank President Ford for the fact that we live in peace and freedom, and your sons and your husbands and your relatives are home and they're safe. It could only happen in America. Thank you.

HOGE: Senator Mondale.

MONDALE: Americans are not interested in partisan debating points. They're not interested in how many debate points are scored. That means little to the lives of Americans. What really counts is whether this country can begin to solve those problems that are overwhelming so many Americans: record unemployment, the highest since the Great Depression, and getting worse; runaway inflation, three times worse than that under the Democratic party; deficits that are unbelievable. Just last year, under this administration, we had a deficit larger than all of the deficits created in the eight years of the Democratic administration; and under this Republican party, higher deficits than in the previous 192 years of this government's history.

Now, we recognize that you have to be prudent, that you have to live within a budget, that you have to deal with the resources that are at hand. There's no dispute on that. The question is how will those resources be used? And we believe that we need a government that works, that's efficient; but we also think we need a government that cares. We've cared too little for people in this country that have gotten sick and can't afford decent health care. We've cared too little for the thousands and thousands of American families that cannot get or afford decent housing. This administration has fought, time and time again, to cut back support for our senior citizens. They have no energy policy. They have no environmental policy. Those things must change.

We believe in a strong defense. We're not going to let this nation's defenses drop. But there's a big difference between waste and strength. And what we've been attacking is waste, because waste does not contribute to strength—it contributes to weakness. There are many problems in the Defense Department that require better management in order to get that increased strength.

We need leadership in this country to do all of those things. For eight years now, the Republicans have controlled government. For eight years, they've controlled the White House. And every one of those problems has gotten worse. They are not now proposing new policies and new directions. Tonight, you heard what they are doing: they are defending the past—"Everything is all right"; "The problems are not as bad as the statistics or the people believe, and therefore they might go away." That is not enough. This country cries out for new leadership. We need a fresh start, and the Carter-Mondale ticket promises that start. Not because we know all the answers—we know better. Not because we can do everything at once—because we know better than that. But because a good nation requires that we begin the effort.

HOGE: Thank you, Senator Mondale, and thank you, Senator Dole. I want to thank, as well, the audience here tonight and my colleagues who were our questioners.

The final debate in this series will be between the presidential candidates, Gerald Ford, and his challenger, Jimmy Carter. It will be held on October 22nd, at 9:30 P.M. Eastern Daylight Time on the campus of William and Mary College in Williamsburg, Virginia. The subject matter will cover all issues.

The sponsors of these debates is the League of Women Voters Education Fund, whose purpose is to promote greater participation by a better-informed electorate in the election on November 2nd. Now, from the Alley Theatre in Houston, Texas, good night.

Notes and Index

☆ ☆ ☆ ☆ ☆ ☆ ☆ ☆ ☆ ☆ ☆ ☆ ☆ ☆ ☆ ☆ ☆ ☆ ☆ ☆

Notes

CHAPTER 1

1 Walter Lippmann, *Essays in the Public Philosophy* (Boston: Little, Brown and Company, 1955), chap. 9, sec. 3.

2 Austin Ranney, *The Past and Future of Presidential Debates,* ed. Austin Ranney (Washington, D.C.: American Enterprise Institute for Public Policy Research, 1979), editor's preface.

3 J. Jeffery Auer, "The Counterfeit Debates," pp. 142–50 in *The Great Debates: Background—Perspective—Effects,* ed. Sidney Kraus (Bloomington: Indiana University Press, 1962). See pp. 147–48.

CHAPTER 2

1 Both presented election-eve thirty-minute broadcasts on all three commercial networks, but neither presented "addresses." On September 7, CBS Television aired a paid thirty-minute Ford speech entitled "The President Speaks," but this was an edited version of his acceptance speech presented at the Republican National Convention.

2 "The Debates," *Newsweek,* Sept. 27, 1976, p. 24.

3 Saul Friedman, *Detroit Free Press,* Aug. 25, 1976, p. A1.

4   "Contrasting Campaign Symbols," *New York Times,* Sept. 7, 1976, sec. 1, pp. 1, 22.

5   "Weighing the Effects of the Debates," *Washington Post,* Sept. 5, 1976, p. B7.

6   "The Election Outcome: One Week Later, The Politicians Tell How It Happened," *New York Times,* Nov. 10, 1976, p. A22.

7   Reported by Charles Mohr, "Carter Hopes for a 'Tie' in TV Debate and Gears for Tight-Budget Campaign," *New York Times,* Sept. 6, 1976, p. 16.

8   "American Journal: The Second Big Gamble of Jerry Ford's Political Life," *New York,* Sept. 6, 1976, p. 88.

9   Associated Press wire story (*Wisconsin State Journal,* Sept. 19, 1976).

10   "Aides Narrow Risk in Debate," *New York Times,* Sept. 20, 1976, pp. 1, 22.

11   Washington Post News Service (*Wisconsin State Journal,* Aug. 20, 1976).

12   Ron Nessen made the remark in New York on October 18, 1978, while publicizing his new book, *It Sure Looks Different from the Inside.*

13   "Will Ford Really Do?" *New York Times,* Oct. 10, 1976, sec. 4, p. 15.

14   "The Real Jerry Ford," *Washington Post,* Oct. 9, 1976, p. A17.

15   For example, just before the Michigan presidential primary election, opponent Morris Udall charged that Carter was fuzzy on the issues, saying, "You never know where he stands on any issue," and "Nobody could be less specific than Jimmy Carter." (Associated Press wire story, *Wisconsin State Journal,* May 17, 1976.)

16   Early in the campaign, Carter predicted that the Republicans would use "vicious personal attacks" against the Democratic ticket; the opposition, he said, is desperate (United Press wire story, Aug. 4, 1976). The attacks came in speeches by Dole and others, sometimes Ford; in radio and television commercials; and in mailings. The commercials were the "man-on-the-street" negative spots. Typically the camera would catch several persons one by one at their work or on the street, ordinary persons sharing one characteristic: they distrusted Carter, thought he had done nothing to speak of, thought he lacked experience, believed him to be an unknown quantity. Robert Teeter, Ford pollster, thought

these ads very effective, with Carter's inability to counter them almost costing him the election (David Broder, "Carter Rejected Advice to Hit Pardon," *Washington Post,* Nov. 6, 1976, pp. A1, 4).

The most widespread and objectionable of the anti-Carter campaign literature was a four-page "newspaper" entitled *Heartland,* dated October, 1976, and published by the President Ford Committee. It was a scandal sheet—on the one hand playing up Carter's *Playboy* interview, and on the other hand portraying Ford as a moral and religious leader. A column by William Safire appeared on the fourth page. In late October, Carter complained that Ford had authorized distribution of *Heartland* across the country, and denounced the publication in an interview on CBS TV Morning News, Oct. 26, 1976.

17   "Carter's Talks Have Conservative Ring," *Los Angeles Times,* Sept. 14, 1976, pt. 1, p. 5.

18   Associated Press wire story (*Wisconsin State Journal,* Sept. 19, 1976).

19   "The Computer-Driven Candidate," *Washington Post,* Sept. 12, 1976, p. C7.

20   Ford defended himself in the early days of September for not going on the campaign trail, saying on September 14 that he needed to stay in Washington while Congress was in session in order to keep it from going "off the deep end."

21   "*Playboy* Interview: Jimmy Carter," *Playboy,* Nov. 1976, p. 86. The interview, about nine pages in length, was the work of writer Robert Sheer, who interviewed Carter in many sessions, and of *Playboy* editor G. Barry Golson, who participated in the final interviewing session.

22   Carter said, "God says, Judge not, that ye be not judged. And I made the point that as President, I would certainly not condemn those who were different from me, but the one example that I used was about adultery, and it was possibly not a very fortunate choice. But, as you know, in the Sermon on the Mount, it says that if you even look with lust on a woman, you have in your own heart committed adultery. Therefore, don't condemn people who may have done even worse. And that was the illustration that I used, and it perhaps was an unfortunate illustration. But I don't have any apology to make for it. I thought it was a good way to let the American public, particularly the *Playboy* readers, know about

my religious beliefs. I think it was perhaps typical of my campaign. I might say this: I would rather run that kind of campaign, and even make a mistake every now and then, and let the American people have contact with me, than to hide in the Rose Garden for eight weeks and ignore the real needs of this campaign and to isolate myself from the American people. I made the right choice.''

23   On September 24, the day after the first debate, CBS Television "Evening News" commenced not with coverage of the debate but with this lead: "CBS News has learned that the Special Watergate Prosecutor is investigating whether contributions to President Ford, as a congressman, were laundered. Fred Graham has the details. . . .''

24   "I'll tell you what coloreds want. It's three things: first, a tight pussy; second, loose shoes; and third, a warm place to shit. That's all!" Quoted in John Dean, "Rituals of the Herd," *Rolling Stone,* Oct. 7, 1976, p. 57. The *Capital Times* of Madison, Wisconsin, was one of only a few dailies to print the punch line with no paraphrasing (Oct. 4, 1976, p. 1).

25   William Raspberry suggested that Ford seemed insensitive to the simple crudeness of the matter. "The way Mr. Ford actually handled the situation suggests that he had no interest in the matter beyond its effect on his election campaign." ("Earl Butz: Low Attitudes in High Places," *Washington Post,* Oct. 6, 1976, p. A15.)

26   Carter purposefully shunned the pardon issue, even though it could have been used to counter the Ford commercials which attacked Carter's record and image. According to David Broder, Pat Caddell remarked that Carter thought it "could have blown the election wide open if he had used it in mid-October. But he also knew it was a terribly divisive issue for the country . . . and he didn't want blood all over the floor." (David Broder, "Carter Rejected Advice to Hit Pardon," *Washington Post,* Nov. 6, 1976, pp. A1, 4.)

27   Les Brown, "Faulty 25-Cent Part Silenced the Debate," *New York Times,* Sept. 25, 1976, p. 1.

28   Ed Bradley reported, "Carter's strategists would like to see changes in the formats of the debates that would enable each candidate to follow up his opponent's rebuttal. They feel under the present format President Ford was able to make charges their

man never had a chance to answer." (CBS Television News, Sept. 26, 1976.)

29 R. W. Apple's column on September 27 in the *New York Times* opened with the poll results: "In the prevailing view of the American electorate, President Ford won his crucial first debate with Jimmy Carter on Thursday night, a poll by the New York Times and CBS News indicates. . . . Of the 1,167 respondents in the survey, 37 percent thought the President had the better of things, 24 thought Mr. Carter had won, 35 percent called it a draw and 4 percent were unwilling to express any opinion." Apple opined that Ford's "benefits from the debate . . . appeared to parallel those of John F. Kennedy after his debate against Richard M. Nixon in 1960." ("Voter Poll Finds Debate Aided Ford and Cut Carter Lead," pp. 1, 36.)

30 "Round Two to Carter," *Newsweek,* Oct. 18, 1976, p. 21.

31 "The Kissinger Round," *New York Times,* Sept. 26, 1976, sec. 4, p. 15.

32 "Ford's Toughest Week," *Time,* Oct. 18, 1976, p. 10.

33 Spencer's view of the Ford strategy and campaign came in an interview after the election. For example, see Larry Stammer, "E. Europe Error Was Crucial for Ford," *Los Angeles Times,* Dec. 8, 1976, pt. 1, pp. 1, 35.

34 "Carter Seemed More Confident," *Washington Post,* Oct. 7, 1976, pp. A1, 9.

35 "Carter Attacks Ford, Defends US Foreign Stance in 2d Debate," *New York Times,* Oct. 7, 1976, sec. 1, p. 1.

36 Bailey, Deardourff, and Eyre was the firm responsible for Ford's television commercials. Bailey's remarks were made in a speech at the Speech Communication Association convention, Dec. 2, 1977, in Washington, D.C.

37 *Milwaukee Journal,* Oct. 25, 1976, p. 37.

38 NBC "Today Show," Oct. 22, 1976.

CHAPTER 3

1 Walter R. Mears, "The Debates—A View from the Inside," *Columbia Journalism Review,* Jan./Feb., 1977, pp. 24-25.

2 Quoted in Jim Karayn, "After Carter's First 100 Days— Questions the Experts Would Like to Ask the President," *Parade,* May 1, 1977, pp. 5-6.

3   Congress of the United States, Congressional Budget Office, *Five-Year Budget Projections, Fiscal Years 1977–81* (Washington, D.C., Jan. 26, 1976), p. 8.

4   U.S. Bureau of the Census, *Statistical Abstract of the United States: 1976,* 97th ed. (Washington, D.C., 1976), p. 467, table 748: "Participation in Elections for President and U.S. Representatives: 1930–1974." The percentages of voting-age population voting in the presidential elections: 1932: 52.4; 1936: 56.9; 1940: 58.9; 1944: 56.0; 1948: 51.1; 1952: 61.6; 1956: 59.3; 1960: 62.8; 1964: 61.9; 1968: 60.9; and 1972: 55.5. The voter turnout in 1976 was higher than the forecast cited by Maynard: "The final turnout among voting-age population was 53.3 percent, two percentage points lower than the Nixon landslide of 1972 (55.4 percent), and nearly ten percentage points below 1960. This, despite the fact that roughly 80 million people voted, up two million and 3.3 percent over 1972. The percentage of turnout declined because the voting-age population meanwhile had grown by more than nine million people." Jay Rosenstein, "The Turnout—What Became of the 'Heavy Vote'?" *Columbia Journalism Review,* Jan./Feb., 1977, p. 38.

5   Questions which could have been asked of either candidate: I: B, D, M, N, S, and V; II: B, I, J, K, L, R, T, and U; III: A, K, M, and Q. Tailored questions which, if slightly rephrased, could have been asked of either candidate: I: A, G, and P; II: E, M, P, and Q; III: P. Of the remaining thirty-seven significantly one-sided questions, eighteen were addressed to Carter and nineteen to Ford. Ten of those addressed to Ford came in the third debate.

6   This fact represents a significant finding from applying a typology to all questions. The results of the coding, indicating the candidate to whom the questions were directed, are:

Questions asking the candidate to outline policies:
     Ford (12): I:D,L,P,V; II:B,I,J,M,N,Q,U; III:A
     Carter (14): I:A,B,M,N,U; II:C,D,G,K,R,T; III:K,M,Q
Questions asking candidate to defend policy intentions:
     Ford (3): I:C,H,K
     Carter (7): I:E,F,I,J,Q,R; II:L
Questions asking candidate to defend the record:
     Ford (15): I:G,O; II:E,P,S; III:B,D,E,H,J,L,N,O,R,S
     Carter (0)
Questions asking candidate to defend past statements:
     Ford (1): II:F
     Carter (4): II:O; III:F,G,P

Questions inviting one candidate to attack positions of the other:
Ford (0)
Carter (1): II:A
Other Questions:
Ford (2): I:S ("What is your opinion?"); I:T ("Defend future attitudes")
Carter (4): I:G ("Clarify past statement"); III:C ("Defend your campaign"); III:I ("Defend your qualifications and those of your advisers"); III:T ("Defend your campaign")

7 Douglass Cater, "Notes from Backstage," pp. 127–31, in Sidney Kraus, ed., *The Great Debates* (Bloomington: Indiana University Press, 1962), p. 128.

8 "The Foreign Policy 'Debate,' " *New York Times,* Oct. 8, 1976, p. A28.

9 Stanley Hoffman, " 'Instead of Which Both Candidates . . . ,' " *New York Times,* Oct. 10, 1976, sec. 4, p. 15.

10 Two-part questions: I: R, T, U; II: B, I, M, S; III: E, K, L, M, O, R. Three-part questions: II: C; III: D, P, S. Four-part questions: II: G; III: J.

11 After Carter's first one hundred days as president, the nine panelists in the Ford-Carter debates and the three in the Dole-Mondale debate were asked, "If you knew then what you know now about Carter, his policies, and his performance, what would you have asked him?" Answers were published in a *Parade* article, which reported that Richard Valeriani complained about the fact that Carter failed to delineate his concept of the "national interest" in the second debate: "At the debate I asked Carter what his concept of the 'national interest' was, and he really did not answer. I would ask him to define the term, which is the basis for so much of what the United States does abroad." Even after six months for reflection, Valeriani still seemed unaware of two things: (1) if a direct answer to a question is desired, the question itself ought to be singular and direct; and (2) the answer ought to be within the range of the possible. (Jim Karayn, "After Carter's First 100 Days," p. 5.)

12 Jack Nelson, "Debate Questions—Asked and Unasked—Leave Many Unhappy," *Los Angeles Times,* Oct. 25, 1976, pt. 1, p. 17.

13 Questions lacking focus and clarity: I:G,H,M,S,V; II:B,C,M,N; III:A,L,P.

14 Refutative questions: I:B,F,H,J,R,T; II:L; III:B,E,O,Q,S.

15 The attitude of omniscience is most pronounced in: I:E,F,K,L,Q,R,V; II:L; III:D,E,F,N,S,T. Omniscience is less

pronounced but detectable in: I:B,C,T; II:C,E,K,P; III:A,B,C,H,M.

16   Entrapment: I:E,F,K,L,Q,R; II:L; III:B,D,F,N.

17   Dilemma questions: I:B,C,E,F,G,K,L,Q,R; II:G,K,L; III:E,F.

18   Strongly hostile to Ford: I:K,L; II:S; III:B,D,E,H,J,L,N,O,R,S. Strongly hostile to Carter: I:E,F,Q,R; II:O; III:C,F,I,T. Slightly hostile to Ford: I:G,H,O,P,T; II:E,M,P; III:A. Slightly hostile to Carter: I:A,I,J; II:C,D,K,L; III:G,P,Q.

19   Bill Shipp, "The Real Winner of Great Debate III," *Atlanta Constitution*, Oct. 25, 1976, p. 4.

20   Drew made *Saturday Review*'s "Honor Role" for 1977—"A celebration of men and women who by the example of their lives have improved the quality of ours." Drew's citation (in part): "... because during the Ford-Carter debates she asked intelligent, substantial questions that helped to raise the discussions above the usual hoopla of campaign events. . . ." *Saturday Review*, Dec. 10, 1977, p. 10.

21   Shipp, "The Real Winner."

22   " 'The Medium Rebelled against the Message,' " *Washington Post*, Sept. 26, 1976, sec. C, p. 7. This article is an excerpt of a conversation with Marshall McLuhan on NBC's "Today Show" of September 24, 1976.

23   Quoted in Elizabeth Drew, "A Reporter in Washington, D.C.: Autumn Notes—I," *New Yorker*, Jan. 10, 1977, p. 55.

24   "How to Improve the Debates," *Time*, Oct. 4, 1976, p. 21.

25   William Greider, "Last Debate: Substance Over Bumbles," *Washington Post*, Oct. 23, 1976, p. A7.

26   Nelson, "Debate Questions."

27   Shipp, "The Real Winner."

28   Nelson, "Debate Questions."

29   Joseph Kraft, "A No-Win Debate," *Washington Post*, Sept. 26, 1976, p. C7.

30   Joseph Kraft, "The Last Debate," *Washington Post*, Oct. 24, 1976, p. B7.

CHAPTER 4

1   *Newsweek*'s "On to the Great Debates" provided this assessment of Ford in its September 6 issue: "Even without doing his homework, Ford brings many assets to a debate. He does not lose his composure under fire, he has a flair for handling facts and

figures . . . , and after 25 years in politics, he knows the issues and intricacies of government. But the President also has some serious drawbacks as a debater. He does not think particularly fast on his feet. He is a plodding, sometimes embarrassingly inarticulate extemporaneous speaker" (p. 13). Lou Cannon thought the debate format well suited to Ford—it "plays more to Ford's strengths than to his weaknesses," and according to Ford's aides and friends, he is "an inept platform speaker who talks in a monotone, and usually fails to inspire an audience. But there also is common agreement that the President is effective in question and answer situations because he conveys factual information in a sincere and believable manner." The debate format "is in fact a modified press conference, the forum where Ford performs at his best" (*Milwaukee Journal,* Sept. 19, 1976, pt. 5, p. 1). *Washington Star* writer Jack Germond wrote that "Jimmy Carter uses the language with far more skill and precision than most politicians, and he is controlled enough so that he rarely says things by accident" (*Wisconsin State Journal,* Sept. 13, 1976). Said Helen Dewar, "Carter is disciplined, quick footed, self-confident and articulate in parrying questions from reporters, which is what he and Ford will be doing in the so-called 'debates,' which will actually be more like joint press conferences tailored for television" (*Milwaukee Journal,* Sept. 19, 1976, pt. 5, p. 1). David Broder's column of Sept. 5, 1976, profiled both candidates: "Ford is verbally awkward, a man with a penchant for the fractured phrase. Carter is fluid, nimble, and uses words with rare appreciation for the shading of meanings." Ford's experience in the House in off-the-cuff debating has "prepared him for that kind of two-minute volley of views." Broder remarked that "this reporter has never seen Ford as awkward in a press conference situation when being hard-pressed as Carter sometimes was during the primary months. On the other hand, I have never heard from Carter sentences that made you wince, as Ford can easily deliver." ("Weighing the Effects of the Debates," *Washington Post,* Sept. 5, 1976, p. B7.)

2 I:13,14,19,25; II:1,5,11,17,23,28,32; III:14,18,27.

3 Carter: III:3,26. Ford: I:32; II:29; III:5,23,29.

4 Ford's aggressive rejoinders: I:3,9,15,27; II:2; III:34. Carter's: I:6,18,24,30; II:4,10,16,22,27,31,35; III:13,17,21,26,32.

5 Ford's defensive original and follow-up speeches in the third debate: 2,6,7,12,16,20,24,25,30,31. Carter's: 4,9,33.

6 David Broder's column just before the first debate correctly

predicted the strategies Ford would employ: Ford "can attempt to put Carter on the defensive by charging that the Democrat 'flip-flops' on the issues"; Ford can also "portray Carter as a classic, big-spending liberal Democrat"; and he can try to link Carter to the Democratic Congress. ("The Debates: Anticipating the Strategies," *Washington Post,* Sept. 15, 1976, p. A21.)

7   Especially tough questions were put to Carter in the first debate by Drew: E,F,Q,R. Gannon also posed questions concerning spending, but they were milder: I,J.

8   This result was contrary to the conventional wisdom offered by many commentators before the debates. Almost uniformly, they said that Ford would do best in the foreign policy debate and probably would be hard pressed to make a good showing in the first debate, which featured domestic issues playing to the strengths of the Democratic candidate.

9   A post-election analysis by Ford's pollster Robert Teeter, widely reported by the press, estimated that Ford's blunder came at a time when the Ford campaign was ahead of its timetable for overtaking Carter; but the blunder slowed Ford for ten days. (David Broder, "Carter Rejected Advice to Hit Pardon," *Washington Post,* Nov. 6, 1976, pp. A1, 22.) Tom Wicker called Ford's Eastern Europe statement "probably the most important political blunder since the Eagleton affair of 1972." ("Blunders, Mud and Similarity," *New York Times,* Oct. 12, 1976, p. 37.) R. W. Apple judged that Ford "may well have fatally damaged himself." ("The Ethnic Vote in the States That Really Count," *New York Times,* Oct. 10, 1976, sec. 4, p. 1.) Many writers noted that Ford struck a severe blow to his own image and credibility. Said Broder, Ford's "inability to show himself more knowledgeable and confident than Carter . . . cost the President much of the advantage of incumbency." (" 'Now the Burden Is on Ford,' " *Washington Post,* Oct. 10, 1976, p. C7.) *Time* said, "Ford's grasp of foreign policy and even his mere competence were called into question." ("Ford's Toughest Week," Oct. 18, 1976, p. 10.) Tom Wicker commented that Ford's gaffe "undercut two of Mr. Ford's strategic goals—to appear 'Presidential,' and to lay to rest any questions about his intelligence." ("A Run for the Finish," *New York Times,* Oct. 8, 1976, p. A29.)

10   The next day numerous press reports indicated that Busbee's remarks had been misinterpreted by Ford. In addition, Ford's figures were inaccurate: Georgia expenditures under Carter went up about 40 percent, not "over 50 percent," as Ford said.

11 An article by Kenneth Reich in the *Los Angeles Times* on March
21, 1975 (sec. 2, p. 4), attributed to Carter the view that 15 billion
dollars could be cut from the Ford defense budget for the year
without sacrificing national security. Columnist George Will,
reacting to Carter's denial in the second debate, wrote that the
candidate "lied about not having suggested a $15-billion defense
cut." (" 'Tiresome Little Men Clawing for Lincoln's Chair,' "
Washington Post, Oct. 14, 1976, p. A19.)

12 *Time* noted, "The day after the debate Ford went back on the
promise to release the list and lamely ordered publication only of
the names of firms that go along with the boycott 'in the future.' "
("The Battle, Blow By Blow," Oct. 18, 1976, p. 17.)

13 Units of Argument, by Type of Speech and Target

	Original Speeches		Follow-up Speeches		Rejoinders		Perorations	
	To Panelist	To Opponent	To Panelist	To Opponent	To Panelist	To Opponent	To Panelist	To Opponent
Debate I								
Carter	12	1	7	0	2	15	4	0
Ford	10	0	4	3	4	9	1	1
Subtotal	*22*	*1*	*11*	*3*	*6*	*24*	*5*	*1*
Debate II								
Carter	7	14	1	2	0	19	1	0
Ford	9	2	2	0	1	13	1	0
Subtotal	*16*	*16*	*3*	*2*	*1*	*32*	*2*	*0*
Debate III								
Carter	14	3	1	0	5	17	2	2
Ford	11	0	5	0	6	5	2	0
Subtotal	*25*	*3*	*6*	*0*	*11*	*22*	*4*	*2*
All Debates								
Carter	33	18	9	2	7	51	7	2
Ford	30	2	11	3	11	27	4	1
Total	*63*	*20*	*20*	*5*	*18*	*78*	*11*	*3*

14 Only a handful of the forty rejoinders concluded with more than
fifteen seconds remaining. Indeed, twenty-six rejoinders went over
the two-minute limit, and five came to a close with just seconds to
spare. By contrast, only ten of the forty original speeches went
overtime.

15 Speeches low in argumentation were usually short responses to
questions which asked for clarification, additional information,

or a position statement, rather than argument or justification. For example, one Carter speech in the first debate [I:26] simply clarified his previous answer to Drew's questions on tax relief. The follow-up question to which this speech was a response asked only for information, not justification. Similarly, a Trewhitt follow-up question asked whether he correctly understood Carter's position; in response, Carter clarified the position [II:12]. Valeriani's question to Ford about the possibility of providing arms to mainland China invited a position statement, not argument; in response, Ford provided his position [II:15]. Ford's two speeches on progress of SALT talks were essentially expository [II:20,21] in response to questions inviting information. Other speeches show low argumentation for these same reasons [II:26; II:29; III:28].

The remaining speeches that were low in argumentation occurred for a variety of reasons, some of which are discernible. In two speeches, Carter chose not to argue: following the questions to Ford on Watergate, he gave a "no comment" response [III:8]; and he gave a four-word answer to a question from Kraft [III:10]. Another Carter speech, shortened by equipment failure, also included no argumentation [I:34]. A Ford speech dealing with his position on Vietnam draft evaders was responsive to only one of two questions asked by Reynolds [I:11]; no doubt, a single, better-phrased question would have elicited the justification Reynolds apparently sought. In his opening speeches in the third debate, Ford outlined his views, but simply did not provide arguments or justifications probably sought by Kraft's question [III:1,2]. A Kraft question to Carter regarding constitutional amendments was diffuse, and thus allowed Carter to provide a position statement on abortion [III:22]. Carter's rejoinder after Ford defended his handling of the *Mayaguez* incident (the question was strikingly one-sided) was mildly critical of Ford and only about 25 percent argumentative [II:31].

16   Numerous commentators noted Carter's aggressiveness in the second debate. David Broder said that Carter brought to the debate "the coolness and toughness that had marked his assault on the Democratic nomination, but was so conspicuously lacking two weeks [before] during the first debate." And, "the critical change between the first and second debates was not in the subject matter but in the mood of the men. Carter had indeed 'taken the measure' of his opponent, as he said, while Ford had either misjudged his rival or overestimated his own capacities to con-

front him." (" 'Now the Burden Is on Ford,' " *Washington Post,* Oct. 10, 1976, p. C7.)

17 Carter usually referred to his opponent as "Mr. Ford," "President Ford," and "the president"; he often used the terms "his administration," or "this administration," and the "Ford administration." Ford usually referred to Carter as "Governor Carter," "the governor," or "Mr. Carter." The distribution of Carter's 173 references to Ford approximately matched his aggressiveness: in the first debate, he referred to Ford 49 times, in the second 81, and in the third 43. Ford's 83 references to Carter show a pattern of decline, as did his aggressiveness: he made 39 references to Carter in the first debate, 32 in the second, and only 12 in the third. In the second, "tough" debate, only two of Carter's speeches failed to make reference to Ford; on the other hand, ten of Ford's speeches failed to make reference to Carter.

The self-references by each candidate were counted, on the chance that something of interest would be signified. There was high incidence of personal pronouns and of such phrases as "I believe," "in my view," "my campaign." Ford made 411 such self-references, and Carter 434.

18 Carter directed only two out of fifteen units of argument to Ford, and Ford directed only one out of nineteen units to Carter.

19 In the first debate, rounds C,E,G,K,O,Q. In the second, rounds A,B,C,E,O,S.

20 Rounds A,C,D,F,H,I,J,L,N,R,T.

21 Ford was mainly defensive in response to hostile questions in: II:S; III:D,E,H,J,L,R. He was mainly aggressive in: I:K; III:B,S. In three rounds, he showed a mixture of aggressiveness and defensiveness: I:L; III:N,O. Carter was mainly defensive in: I:E,R. He was aggressive in: I:Q; III:C,I. He showed both aggressiveness and defensiveness in: I:F; III:F,T.

22 In rounds II:A,C,O; III:I.

23 I:1,6,8,12,13,14,18,19,20,25,35;   II:1,5,17,22,23,36; III:18,22,33,36.

24 I:13,14,19,25,35; II:5,17,36; III:36.

25 I:4,10.

26 I:9,17,29,36; II:37; III:23,24,35.

27 A column by Rowland Evans and Robert Novak after the second debate mentioned "Ford's own irremediable failings as a campaigner." One critical failure was "his inability to ad lib on the campaign stump without a carefully prepared and rehearsed

script." Moreover, "Ford's handlers had ignored a lesson cruelly imposed on them by defeats in last spring's primaries: While barely adequate reading a prepared speech, he is considerably less than adequate with an improvised stump speech delivered in a monotone shout." ("Ford's Uninspiring Counterattack," *Washington Post,* Oct. 16, 1976, p. A15.)

CHAPTER 5

1 I:12; II:10,16,22,27,35; III:17,21,32.
2 I:9,15,27,32.
3 I:6,12,18,24,30; II:4,10,16,22,27,31,35; III:17,32.
4 After the first debate, a *New York Times* editorial praised Carter's peroration as showing what the debates could be, in contrast to the numbing statistics of earlier speeches. "It was finally in his summation that Mr. Carter offered a glimpse of what many Americans had undoubtedly hoped the debates might offer." The editorial contrasted Ford's "banalities" with Carter's statements regarding "what our country can and ought to be." ("No Winner, but a Start," Sept. 26, 1976, sec. 4, p. 14.)
5 A number of commentators touched upon this difference between Carter and Ford. Anthony Lewis wrote that "the last debate was highly significant, but not in the sense of point-scoring. It was important because it focused attention on what should have been the critical issue in this campaign all along: the mind and record of Gerald Ford." Lewis underscored what he thought to be a major flaw—Ford's insensitivity, as evidenced in his third-debate speeches on unemployment, racial discrimination, the problems of the cities, and the environment. ("The Real Mr. Ford," *New York Times,* Oct. 25, 1976, p. 29.) A *Washington Post* editorial, written immediately after the last debate, said that Carter returned "to the style of candid realism and national vision that he seemed to have misplaced after the convention. A good many Democrats were beginning to have trouble recalling why they had nominated him. On Friday night he helped them remember. He offered a graceful apology for the *Playboy* affair. Instead of playing ping-pong with statistics, he talked about principles." The editorial concluded with a brief comparison of the two men, in which Carter emerged the favorite: "Carter thinks more carefully about the unused capacities of this nation" and follows "a broader sense of

American possibilities." ("The Final Debate," Oct. 24, 1976, p. B6.)

Columnist George F. Will said that only Carter in the 1976 campaign managed to produce "sparks of romance." Said Will, "All politics should be what Aneurin Bevan said socialism should be, 'the attempt to bring passion to the pursuit of qualified objectives.' It is significant that during the campaign only Carter consistently spoke the language of national 'greatness' and 'excellence.' Of course, Carter did not exactly sweep the land like a devouring flame. But in a relentlessly pedestrian political season Carter, by his rise from Dixie and obscurity, and by his occasional intimations of excellence, produced the only sparks of romance. Lesser politicians must learn and never forget what the finest politicians—like Disraeli and Churchill and de Gaulle and both Roosevelts—knew instinctively: Politics without romance is like meat without salt. The election was, in the end, a tentative endorsement of the candidate who displayed the broader emotional range and a deeper capacity for social sympathy. It was a vote for a little more spice in political life." ("The Contraction of the GOP," *Washington Post,* Nov. 4, 1976, p. A27.)

6   A few speeches, all by Carter, were judged to be superior: II:10, 23; III:4,13,14,17. The most feeble speeches were all by Ford: I:3,11,15,28; II:9,26; III:7,20,24,25,34.

7   This set of Ford and Carter speeches on civil rights was cited by the *New York Times* as evidence of the claim that the third debate was far more substantive and informative than earlier debates; the speeches told something of importance about the "leadership styles of the two candidates, Mr. Ford's passive, Mr. Carter's active." ("Practice Helps," Oct. 24, 1976, sec. 4, p. 1.)

8   For example, David E. Rosenbaum and Leslie H. Gelb of the *New York Times* wrote articles identifying specific errors. Many newspapers used wire service material to patch together stories identifying errors, as did the *Milwaukee Journal* with a long critique on Sept. 26 ("Sorting Out Debate Statistics," pp. 1, 13). Several columnists also pointed out defects. For the most part, however, the commentaries and news stories identified outright errors; they seldom noted defects in reasoning. David Rosenbaum concluded one article with this generous observation: "Of course, distortion and exaggeration are standard fare in political campaigns, a situation that is surely recognized by the

electorate. Presidential candidates Eisenhower, Kennedy, Johnson, and Nixon all made claims that, in retrospect, could not stand scrutiny. In this regard, Mr. Carter and Mr. Ford have been no worse than their predecessors, and they have been better than some" ("'Look at the Record' is an Invitation to a Fog," *New York Times,* Oct. 24, 1976, sec. 4, p. 4).

9 Jules Witcover, *Marathon, The Pursuit of the Presidency, 1972–1976* (New York: Signet, 1977), p. 634.

10 Ibid., p. 638. Other observers sought to explain the Ford blunder. George F. Will's column of October 14, 1976 said that Ford had known for a year that the Helsinki agreement would be a campaign issue, and for two months he had known he would be debating Carter. "He spent the days before the foreign policy debate being briefed about Helsinki and other matters. So when he spoke in the debate, and again after two days of pondering what he said in the debate, he probably was doing his best." Will also suggested that one might understand the President's remarks on Eastern Europe if Ford had been aroused from a deep slumber by someone shouting "Helsinki" (" 'Tiresome Little Men Clawing for Lincoln's Chair,' " *Washington Post,* p. A19).

Rowland Evans and Robert Novak gave a similar but more detailed interpretation of how the error occurred: "In a two-hour session with Secretary of State Henry Kissinger at the White House last Sunday, Mr. Ford was warned that Carter would be coming at him from the right rather than the left. He was told that Carter had attacked the Helsinki Treaty and a secret speech by State Department counselor Helmut Sonnenfeldt as ratifying Soviet hegemony over Eastern Europe. So, Mr. Ford entered the debate intent on refuting the 'Sonnenfeldt Doctrine' implying U.S. support of Soviet domination over Eastern Europe. The result was verbal overkill—absurdly claiming no such dominion exists, even in Poland. But that does not explain how Mr. Ford could so confuse reality to forget about four Soviet army divisions permanently stationed in Poland." Evans and Novak concluded by remarking that the core of Ford's problem was not to be traced to his advisers. The problem, they said, "is clearly Gerald Ford, who Wednesday night resurrected the old image of fumbler and stumbler he had very nearly shaken off" ("The Real Jerry Ford?" *Washington Post,* Oct. 9, 1976, p. A17).

11 During the campaign Carter consistently denied that he had advocated a budget cut of this magnitude. Ford's speech offered as solid fact what was actually conjectural.

12 Schlesinger's estimates were based on a cut of 10 billion dollars ("The Battle, Blow by Blow," *Time,* Oct. 18, 1976, p. 15).

CHAPTER 6

1 James Gannon wrote that the "most interesting aspect" of the 28-minute interruption "was the candidates' behavior toward each other. The two men didn't exchange a word, and they hardly even exchanged a glance. No small talk, no smiles, no recognition." Gannon's account of his preparation for and participation in the first debate, entitled "Our Man Survives the Great Debate, Is Glad It's All Over," appeared in the *Wall Street Journal,* Sept. 27, 1976, pp. 1, 19. Columnist George Will noted that the candidates "stood there like stumps . . . , not exchanging a word. Some people considered that silent stretch the intellectual high point of the campaign—for 27 minutes, neither man was misleading the nation" ("Viewpoint" commentary, NBC Television, March 27, 1979).

2 The Dole-Mondale debate format shows three changes. In the first place, the candidates made opening statements of two minutes duration before debate rounds, thus setting the tone and announcing principal themes that each would seek to emphasize. The second was elimination of follow-up questions. Third, the format provided for a one-minute answering speech, or rebuttal, by candidate A—the speaker to whom a question was originally put. Thus a round of debate consisted of: question by panelist; speech by candidate A; rejoinder speech by candidate B; then the one-minute rebuttal speech by A, which closed the round.

3 "How to Improve the Debates," *Time,* Oct. 4, 1976, p. 21.

4 "Lights—Camera—Candidates!" *New York Times,* Sept. 24, 1976, p. A24. Lelyveld's assessment of the format appeared in the *Times* Oct. 24, 1976, pt. 4, p. 1.

5 The *Times* editorial continued, "Messrs. Ford and Carter suffered from a severe case of overbriefing that filtered personal authenticity out of their responses. They came with too many pre-packaged answers. They had too many statistics to unleash, too many prepared positions to which to retreat under challenge" ("No Winner, but a Start," Sept. 26, 1976, sec. 4, p. 14). An October 10 *Times* editorial observed that "most of the basic issues of domestic policy (in the first) and of national defense and foreign policy (in the second) were barely touched or totally

ignored. Perhaps the two candidates will do better the third time around. . . ." ("Three Weeks to Go," sec. 4, p. 14). A *Washington Post* editorial on October 8 expressed concern about the premium placed upon "debating points. We're not certain this is the best way to let citizens judge the candidates' full qualities. We're still unhappy about the format, especially about the way the press panel, however acute its questioning may be, interferes with direct exchanges" ("Round Two," Oct. 8, 1976, p. A24).

6   "The Debates: A Remodeling Job," *Washington Post,* Sept. 26, 1976, p. C6.

7   Eric Sevareid commentary, CBS TV Evening News, Sept. 24, 1976.

8   "The Debates: A Marketplace In the Global Village," *New York Times,* Sept. 26, 1976, sec. 4, p. 1.

9   "Lights—Camera—Candidates," *New York Times,* Sept. 24, 1976, p. A24.

10   "Do We Really Need the Debates?" *New York Times,* Oct. 24, 1976, sec. 4, p. 15.

11   "Carter Seemed More Confident," *Washington Post,* Oct. 7, 1976, pp. A1, 9.

12   "Last Debate: Substance Over Bumbles," *Washington Post,* Oct. 23, 1976, p. A1.

13   United Press International wire story (*Wisconsin State Journal,* Oct. 23, 1976, sec. 1, p. 2).

14   "Third Debate Centers on Ford Record," *Washington Post,* Oct. 23, 1976, p. A1.

15   "The Final Debate," *Washington Post,* Oct. 24, 1976, p. B6; and "Practice Helps," *New York Times,* Oct. 24, 1976, sec. 4, p. 1.

16   The scale used for relevance of content was High, 70–100%; Moderate, 31–69%; and Low, 0–30%.

17   The Carter rejoinder that was practically lost in the first debate because of failure of audio equipment could not be assessed in terms of its responsiveness to Ford's preceding speech.

18   Only three original and follow-up speeches completely answered multiple questions: II:30; III:22,30.

19   The candidate in the rejoinder position on sixteen occasions faced a larger number of questions than his opponent in the preceding original or follow-up speech. As rejoinder speaker in the first debate, Ford faced double questions three times [3,9,21] and a triple question once [27]; in the same debate, Carter faced double

questions five times [6,12,18,24,30]. Fewer follow-up questions were asked in the second debate. Nevertheless, Ford received a four-part question in one of his rejoinders [7], while Carter had two double questions [10,27] and one triple question [22]. In the third debate Carter received a double question [3], a triple question [26], and a five-part question [32].

20   "Practice Helps," *New York Times,* Oct. 24, 1976, sec. 4, p. 1.

21   Carter did pledge to elevate the level of the campaign, and the press reported that Ford made a similar pledge; but in fact Ford's pledge was different, as the debate text indicates.

22   Rounds A,C,D,F,H,I,J,L,N,R,T.

23   In the first debate, Ford responded in only three rounds to a charge or argument offered earlier [17,27,29]; Carter did so in only one [30]. In the second debate, Ford twice responded to arguments or charges made against him in previous rounds [24,29], while Carter made three such responses [4,16,27]. In the final debate, Ford twice argued a matter initiated in a previous round [29,34].

24   "What Kind of Debates?" *New York Times,* Sept. 3, 1976, p. A19.

25   Before the debate, the third debate panelists planned to alter the format in the last minutes of the debate by asking the candidates to question each other (Jules Witcover, *Marathon,* p. 666).

26   "What Kind of Debates?" *New York Times,* Sept. 3, 1976, p. A19.

27   "Debates Without The Press," *Washington Post,* Oct. 1, 1976, p. A23.

CHAPTER 7

1   "Presidential Mystique," *New York Times,* Oct. 11, 1976, p. 29.

2   "Debates: Room for Improvement," *Los Angeles Times,* Sept. 3, 1976, pt. 2, p. 14.

3   "Campaigning by Debate," *New York Times,* Nov. 26, 1976, p. A22.

4   "Viewpoint," NBC Television, March 27, 1979.

5   "Yes, Aunt Agatha, Politics is Partisan," *Washington Post,* April 11, 1979, p. A27.

6   "Are the Debates Worth It?" *New York Times,* Oct. 24, 1976, sec. 4, p. 1.

THE FIRST DEBATE

1 The "202" programs, administered by the Department of Housing and Urban Development, offer long-term loans to private non-profit groups which provide rental and cooperative housing to the elderly and the handicapped.

2 Carter's reference is to the Civilian Conservation Corps, a New Deal federal program which from 1933 to 1942 provided work programs, such as reforestation, flood control, and soil conservation, for seventeen- to twenty-five-year-old youths of needy families.

3 The Humphrey-Hawkins bill, as it was written in 1976, would establish the goal of 3 percent adult unemployment. To do this, the federal government would provide hundreds of thousands of public-service jobs, becoming the employer of last resort.

4 Carter refers to "Project Independence," an effort launched by President Nixon in 1973 to increase domestic oil and gas production and decrease U.S. reliance on foreign sources.

5 "DISC" is the Domestic International Sales Corporation. Carter explains this provision of the tax code in his speech.

6 Daniel Schorr, at the time a correspondent for CBS News, obtained the secret report of a House committee which had been investigating recent activities of the Central Intelligence Agency. Schorr released this document to the *Village Voice,* which published the report. Appearing under subpoena before the House committee, Schorr refused to reveal how or from whom he obtained the document; the committee decided not to cite him for contempt of Congress. Reynolds' other reference is to "a United States Senator" accused of receiving illegal corporate contributions. Evidently Reynolds was referring to Senator Robert Dole, the 1976 Republican vice-presidential candidate. It was alleged that Dole received contributions from a Gulf Oil lobbyist; Dole was later exonerated.

7 Central Intelligence Agency.

8 Moderator Newman apparently did not realize that the technical failure occurred early in Carter's speech. Carter did not receive his allotted two minutes.

9 Here Carter is referring to recent events in American political history: the Vietnam war, American bombing of Cambodia, covert operations by the Central Intelligence Agency in foreign nations, and the complex of abuses of presidential office that took its

name from the burglary of the Democratic National Committee's headquarters in the Watergate building in Washington, D.C. Investigation of the affair, with all of its ramifications, led to a formal bill of impeachment by the House Judiciary Committee, but impeachment proceedings were suspended after Nixon's resignation on August 9, 1974.

THE SECOND DEBATE

1 National Public Radio.

2 The "Kansas City convention" was the 1976 Republican National Convention.

3 Secretary of State Henry Kissinger declared "peace is at hand" in Vietnam a few days before the 1972 presidential election. A peace treaty was signed on January 23, 1973.

4 Vietnam, Cambodia, Watergate, and "CIA revelations" have been explained earlier. An additional reference, "Chile," refers to alleged CIA involvement in the overthrow of Chilean President Salvador Allende in 1975; another, "Pakistan," alludes to the 1973 war between India and Pakistan; and "Angola" refers to fighting between rival tribes in the African country of Angola in 1975. President Ford and Secretary of State Kissinger secretly proposed that the United States provide aid to one side; when this became known, Congress and the public expressed strong opposition, and the plan was dropped.

5 Senators Arthur Vandenberg and Walter George were considered strong supporters of bipartisan foreign policy. Vandenberg, a Republican from Michigan, served from 1928 to 1953; George, a Democrat from Georgia, served from 1922 to 1957.

6 The Sinai II agreement was negotiated by Secretary of State Kissinger and was signed in Geneva on September 4, 1975. The agreement declared that "the conflict between Egypt and Israel and in the Middle East shall not be resolved by military force but by peaceful means." The document went on to describe the agreement as "a first step" within the framework of the Geneva peace conference and United Nations Security Council Resolution 338. It was considered significant for being the first territorial withdrawal by Israel under diplomatic rather than direct military pressure.

7 The "Jackson amendment" was a 1975 amendment by Senator Henry Jackson to the 1972 Trade Reform Act which linked grant-

ing most-favored-nation status to the Soviet Union with freer emigration of Russian Jews.

8   "Mutual cap" refers to a mutual limitation.

9   "MIRVing" refers to constructing Multiple Intercontinental Reentry Vehicles from conventional, singular ballistic missiles.

10   The United States conducted a major grain sale with the Soviet Union in 1972.

11   Alexandr Solzhenitsyn, a Nobel laureate in literature, was expelled by the Soviet Union in February 1974. President Ford, under pressure from Secretary of State Kissinger, refused to see Solzhenitsyn at the White House when he visited in July 1975. Kissinger thought that the Soviet Union would take offense if Ford met with Solzhenitsyn.

12   Carter means to refer to both President Nixon and President Ford in saying "when this Republican administration came into office." The period is from January 1969 to October 1976.

13   Egypt and Syria attacked Israel on October 6, 1973, the day of Yom Kippur, the Day of Atonement in the Jewish calendar. All public services in Israel were suspended, making it unusually difficult for the Israelis to mobilize their troops readily to meet the emergency. The fighting lasted for three weeks. Despite heavy initial casualties, the Israelis held the military advantage at the end of the war. The Arabs, however, had achieved their political objectives by destroying the belief that Israel was militarily invincible. Egypt's President Anwar Sadat believed that the experience of the war put greater pressure on Israel to come to the bargaining table.

14   Mr. Ford meant to say President Park (Park Chung-hee).

15   The USS *Mayaguez* was captured by the Cambodians in April 1975. President Ford ordered that military action be taken to rescue the ship and its crew.

16   "Point Four" refers to United States appropriations for technical assistance, both with trained personnel and with production goods, to improve education, health, sanitation, agriculture, power resources, transportation, and manufacturing in underdeveloped countries. This was proposed by President Truman as the fourth point in his Inaugural Address on January 20, 1949, and was implemented by Congress beginning June 5, 1950. The Marshall Plan was an American effort to rebuild Europe after World War II. It was conceived by Secretary of State George Marshall.

The Peace Corps was an agency established in 1961 for the purpose of sending American volunteers to developing countries to teach skills and help improve living conditions.

THE THIRD DEBATE

1 The Arab oil embargo occurred in 1973.
2 Carter gave a controversial interview to *Playboy* magazine, which appeared in its November 1976 issue.
3 United Automobile Workers.
4 In the fall of 1975, New York City faced bankruptcy. The city appealed to the federal government for loan guarantees and other forms of aid. President Ford initially rejected this request, prompting the headline in the *New York Daily News* cited by Carter.
5 The Department of Housing and Urban Development.
6 The Federal Housing Authority.
7 Carter probably meant to say "Warren Court" and not "Burger Court," judging from the context of his remarks.
8 The *Miranda* decision requires policemen to advise suspected criminals of their constitutional rights.

THE DOLE-MONDALE DEBATE

1 Dole apparently refers to Carter and his "lust in my heart" statement in the *Playboy* interview.
2 Honeywell, Inc. and Investors Diversified Services (IDS) are Minneapolis corporations.
3 Presidents Nixon and Ford imposed three grain embargoes, including one against Japan.
4 In the second presidential debate, Ford said, "There is no Soviet domination of Eastern Europe and there never will be under a Ford administration."
5 In his *Playboy* interview (November, 1976), Carter said, "In my speeches, I've made it clear that as far as Communist leaders in such countries as Italy, France and Portugal are concerned, I would not want to close the doors of communication, consultation and friendship to them. That would be an almost automatic forcing of the Communist leaders into the Soviet sphere of influence. I also think we should keep open our opportunities for the east

European nations—even those that are completely Communist—to trade with us, understand us, have tourist exchange and give them an option from complete domination by the Soviet Union" (p. 77).

6 At the time, Leonard Woodcock was president of the United Automobile Workers, George Meany was president of the American Federation of Labor/Congress of Industrial Organizations, and Jerry Wurf was president of the American Federation of State, County, and Municipal Employees.

7 Mondale was appointed attorney general of Minnesota in 1960, and was elected in 1962. In 1964, he was appointed U.S. Senator to replace Hubert Humphrey, who had been elected vice-president. Mondale was elected to the Senate in 1966 and 1972.

8 The "Ervin Committee" was the Senate Select Committee on Presidential Campaign Practices, headed by North Carolina Senator Sam Ervin, which conducted a public investigation of the Watergate affair.

9 The "Saturday Night Massacre" occurred on October 20, 1973. President Nixon fired Attorney General Elliot Richardson and his successor, William Ruckelshaus, for their failure to fire the Watergate Special Prosecutor, Archibald Cox.

10 Federal Housing Authority and Veterans Administration.

Index

DESIGNED BY RON FENDEL
COMPOSED BY FOX VALLEY TYPESETTING, MENASHA, WISCONSIN
MANUFACTURED BY FAIRFIELD GRAPHICS, FAIRFIELD, PENNSYLVANIA
TEXT IS SET IN TIMES ROMAN, DISPLAY LINES IN SERIF GOTHIC

Library of Congress Cataloging in Publication Data
Bitzer, Lloyd F
Carter vs. Ford.
Includes text of the 3 Carter-Ford debates
and of the Dole-Mondale debate.
Includes bibliographical references and index.
1. Presidents—United States—Election—1976.
2. Campaign debates—United States.
I. Rueter, Theodore, joint author.
II. Carter, Jimmy, 1924–   III. Ford, Gerald R., 1913–
JK526 1976.B57   324.973'0925   80-5110
ISBN 0-299-08280-6
ISBN 0-299-08284-9 pbk.